CARING FOR
SCHOOL-AGE
CHILDREN

SIXTH EDITION

CARING FOR

SCHOOL-AGE

CHILDREN

SIXTH EDITION

Phyllis M. Click
Jennifer Parker

WADSWORTH
CENGAGE Learning™

Australia • Brazil • Japan • Korea • Mexico • Singapore • Spain • United Kingdom • United States

WADSWORTH
CENGAGE Learning™

**Caring for School-Age Children,
Sixth Edition**
Phyllis M. Click and Jennifer Parker

Publisher/Executive Editor:
Linda Schreiber-Ganster

Acquisitions Editor: Mark Kerr

Senior Development Editor: Lisa Mafrici

Editorial Assistant: Genevieve Allen

Marketing Manager: Kara Kindstrom
Parsons

Media Editor: Elizabeth Momb

Assistant Editor: Caitlin Cox

Content Project Management:
PreMediaGlobal

Art Director: Maria Epes

Manufacturing Buyer: Linda Hsu

Rights Acquisitions Specialist, Text:
Dean Dauphinais

Rights Acquisitions Specialist, Image:
Dean Dauphinais

Production House/Compositor:
PreMediaGlobal

Cover Image: © SuperStock

Cover Designer: Larry Didona

For product information and technology assistance, contact us at
Cengage Learning Customer & Sales Support, 1-800-354-9706

For permission to use material from this text or product,
submit all requests online at **www.cengage.com/permissions**
Further permissions questions can be e-mailed to
permissionrequest@cengage.com

Library of Congress Control Number: 2010933131

Student Edition:

ISBN-13: 978-1-111-29813-5

ISBN-10: 1-111-29813-0

Wadsworth Cengage Learning
20 Davis Drive
Belmont, CA 94002
USA

Cengage Learning is a leading provider of customized learning solutions with office locations around the globe, including Singapore, the United Kingdom, Australia, Mexico, Brazil, and Japan. Locate your local office at **www.cengage.com/global**.

Cengage Learning products are represented in Canada by
Nelson Education, Ltd.

To learn more about Wadsworth Cengage Learning, visit
www.cengage.com/wadsworth

Purchase any of our products at your local college store or at our preferred online store **www.cengagebrain.com**

Printed in the United States of America
1 2 3 4 5 6 7 14 13 12 11 10

CONTENTS

SECTION 3
THE BACKGROUND

CHAPTER 8   PROGRAM PLANNING   133

SECTION 4
THE CURRICULUM

CHAPTER 17   QUALITY AND STANDARDS   333

PREFACE

A popular website recently described the top twelve trends in child care. The article listed new drop-in centers in gyms, recreation centers, and churches that offer high-quality options for busy parents. Many established child care centers have installed the latest technologies, changing the connection between parent and caregiver. Parents can access a videostream of classroom activities throughout the day to see what their children are learning and how they are doing. Newspaper and magazine ads for vacation destinations and child-friendly hotels and resorts highlight offerings of child care and special activities for children. Most significantly, research has established the importance of quality after-school programs as having a tremendous impact on children's academic achievement, self-esteem, and overall happiness.

This sixth edition of *Caring for School-Age Children* is designed for those who are preparing for a career in school-age child care. It can be used as the basis for a college or university course or for a series of in-service training sessions sponsored by boards of education or community agencies. The book can also be used as a reference for those who are already employed as teachers, aides, caregivers, leaders, or recreation supervisors.

This book will also help those in administrative positions, such as directors, principals, managers, or coordinators. It can guide them as they plan, operate, and assess the programs under their jurisdiction. In addition, parents of school-age children will find useful information for understanding their youngsters and participating in the operation of their children's child-care center.

RATIONALE

At the time the first edition of this book was written, school-age child care facilities were just beginning to be established. There was little information for those interested in how these programs should be planned, what should be included, and what goals were to be achieved. This sixth edition of *Caring for School-Age Children* reflects an increasing national interest in providing quality programs for the large numbers of children who spend their out-of-school time in a group setting. The Harvard Family Research

Project and the latest Developmentally Appropriate Practice published by the NAEYC stress that dialogue about these concerns should include ideas for providing safe places for children, in addition to giving children opportunities to explore cultural and gender issues. The dialogue should also include discussions on how to help children improve their academic success, get homework assistance, acquire social competence skills, and develop meaningful relationships with their peers and adults. In addition children should have opportunities to pursue their own interests and learn to appreciate good nutrition and physical fitness.

ORGANIZATION

The order of the sections and chapters in this new edition remains the same as in the previous edition. Section I, "*The People in Child Care*," introduces the reader first to the caregivers, then to the children, and finally, to the families. The caregivers are portrayed in the first chapter because the reader either already is or may become a caregiver. We discuss the characteristics of an effective caregiver, the education and experience needed, and ways in which the adults affect children's development. New in this chapter is an additional explanation of how to use the NAEYC Code of Ethical Conduct. Chapter 2 presents an overview of the development of children ages 5 to 12, with an emphasis on how children develop relationships as well as a discussion of children in groups. We discuss bullying–including the latest version, "cyber-bullying," when children use the latest technologies to harass others. Chapter 3 focuses on families, their makeup, their culture, family configurations, and the ways in which these factors affect the children.

Section II, "*How Children Grow and Develop*," presents information about children's stages of growth and the factors that affect their development. Chapters 4, 5, and 6 contain extensive coverage of children's physical, cognitive, and psychosocial development. Chapter 4 includes a discussion of the increasing rates of obesity in children, the causes of obesity, and how caregivers can help obese children. Chapter 6 includes the major theories of children's psychosocial and moral development. Chapter 7, which is titled "Helping Children Develop Social Competence", includes strategies and activities to help children become more effective socially, resolve conflicts, bolster their self-image, and become more cooperative. This chapter also covers the specific behaviors or characteristics that create problems for children; it includes ways to effectively guide children toward accepting others as well as changing their own behaviors.

Section III, "*The Background*," includes chapters on program planning and creating an environment. In Chapter 8, "Program Planning," the reader receives more extensive information about the NAEYC Developmentally Appropriate Practice, the anti-bias curriculum, intentional planning, and how to use a project approach. Chapter 9 focuses on planning an environment that enhances children's development.

Section IV, "*The Curriculum*," covers the day-to-day activities of a child care program. Each chapter has a segment on how that part of the curriculum contributes to or supports the development of the children for whom it is designed. The activities each begin with a stated purpose and include a list of materials for caregivers to have available. Chapters 10 and 11 cover games and the arts. Chapter 12, "Science and Math," reflects the newest thinking about children as natural scientists and mathematicians. It illustrates how that approach can be used to plan exciting activities that engage children in constructing knowledge about the world. Chapter 13, "*Helping Children Develop Literacy Competency*," focuses on helping caregivers develop a basic understanding of the process of learning to read and write, and how to engage children in meaningful, enjoyable activities that support their literacy skill development. Chapter 14, "Preparing Children for Adult Roles," offers ideas to help children explore a variety of jobs and workplaces. Chapter 15, "Getting Fit, Staying Fit," rounds out this section with important information on activities and programs to promote health and fitness.

The final section, Section V, "*Resources and Regulations*," includes a chapter on using community resources (Chapter 16) and another that discusses quality and standards for child care programs (Chapter 17). This is an important section because few states require any educational background for those who work in after-school child care settings. Here the reader can learn about the ways child care professionals are trying to upgrade the quality of experiences children have in their out-of-school time. Accreditation, credentialing, and evaluation are discussed.

NEW TO THIS EDITION

As requested by reviewers, we have added new material to this edition based on the latest research and information pertinent to school-age child care.

- Chapter 1 expands the use of the **NAEYC Code of Ethical Conduct**, showing how to use it in real-life situations.
- Chapter 2 adds **cyber-bullying** to the discussion on **bullying**. With widespread use of technology, children have found new and anonymous ways to harass others.
- Chapter 3 offers new research on **the effect of children's household arrangements**. It examines the impact of one-parent families, two-parent families, and other family configurations.
- Chapter 4 has new information on the increasing number of **children who are obese**, the causes of obesity, and how caregivers can help these children.
- Chapter 8 includes many new ideas that affect school-age child care. These include:

    1. The **latest version of DAP**. There are two core considerations for caregivers: knowledge of children's development and learning, and the importance of having goals for children that are challenging and achievable.
    2. The importance of **cultural and linguistic diversity**. Children should be able to use their home language while learning English, and their home language and culture should be respected.

3. The latest version of **Anti-Bias Curriculum**. Four goals are identified: self-awareness and positive social identities; joy in human diversity and caring human connections; recognition of unfairness; and empowerment to act against prejudice and discriminatory actions.

4. The **project approach to planning**. Children pursue research on a topic posed by the children or teacher, sustaining their involvement and integrating multiple curriculum components

5. **Intentional planning and teaching**. Child care leaders plan and conduct learning activities with attention to the program's goals and the children's development. Goals should be challenging but achievable, with consideration given to the development of individual children as well as the group.

6. **Service learning projects**. Projects can encompass many areas of the curriculum as children pursue service work related to environmental issues or other concerns.

- Chapter 9 discusses **"green" playscapes**. Current concerns about the environment make it imperative that play areas for children are places in which they can experience nature safely without fear of snakes, insects, or dangerous plants, and where adults need not worry about exposure to toxic substances.
- Chapter 12 is more concise and accessible than in previous editions. We have added some of the activities and lesson plans from this chapter to Appendix B.
- Chapter 13 includes an expanded discussion of **ways to support English language learners**. Caregivers will see how to plan intentionally language-rich environments, and how to sustain conversations with children about their interests and their experiences in and out of school.
- Chapter 14 discusses the importance of teaching children how to use the latest **technology** in preparation for their roles as adults.

SPECIAL LEARNING FEATURE OF THE TEXT

Several student-oriented learning tools are offered in each chapter, including the following:

- **New Chapter Openings**—Instead of Objectives listed at the beginning of each chapter, the sixth edition presents **Learning Outcomes** that align with the flow of chapter content. Each statement alerts the reader to the contents of the chapter and what can be learned after reading it.
- **Key Terms**—Each key term is an important concept for the student to remember. The term is highlighted in bold in the text, defined in the adjacent margin of the chapter, listed with its definition at the end of each chapter, and included in a convenient **Glossary** at the end of the text.

- **Summary**—The summary is a shortened version of the chapter information and provides the student with a quick reference to the chapter content. The summary has been reformatted in a bulleted style with short, concise statements.
- **Review Questions**—These questions are designed as a quick reference students can use to assess their comprehension and memory for important ideas in the chapter. If necessary, students can go back to the chapter to check their own answers.
- **Case Study**—The case studies depict real-life situations that anyone in child care may encounter. The questions at the end of each vignette help students ponder how they might have reacted in the situation, and offer some alternatives should they encounter a similar experience in the future.
- **Student Activities**—This section provides students with one more way to integrate their learning from the chapter. There are suggestions for additional activities or questions to consider as a way to solidify their learning.
- **Suggested Readings and Web Resources**—These sections list additional sources of information for students who wish to expand their learning. Citations may cover the same materials contained in the chapter, but may also include related topics.
- **Appendices**—Appendix A contains a **list of Internet sites** where students can find additional information on any of the topics in this text. All of the URLs were active at the time that we prepared this text. Appendix B is an extensive **collection of lesson plans** for students to use when planning their own curriculum. Each plan lists the materials needed, the procedure, the role of the adult, and additional activities to extend the lesson.

ANCILLARIES

Book Companion Website

The book-specific website at **www.cengage.com/education/click** offers students a variety of study tools and useful resources such as web quizzing, interactive flashcards of glossary terms, website activities, case studies, and more.

Professional Enhancement Text

The *Caring for School-Age Children Professional Enhancement* handbook for students, which is part of Cengage Learning's Early Childhood Education Professional Enhancement series, focuses on key topics of interest for future early childhood directors, teachers, and caregivers. Becoming a teacher is a process of continuing to grow, learn, reflect, and discover through experience. The Professional Enhancement text helps tomorrow's teachers along their way. Students will keep this informational supplement and use it for years to come in their early childhood practices.

Instructor's Manual with Test Bank

The Instructor's Manual with Test Bank (IMTB) is a chapter-by-chapter plan for organizing a course using this textbook. Features include a brief statement of the focus of each chapter, a chapter outline, classroom activities to enhance student learning, additional case studies that can be used for discussion, assignments for further learning, and guidelines for answering the review questions in the textbook. In addition, there is a Test Bank containing multiple choice, true/false, short answer, and completion questions for each chapter.

PowerLecture

This one-stop digital library and presentation tool consolidates your media resources, including preassembled Microsoft® PowerPoint® lecture slides, an image library with graphics from the book, and TeachSource Video Cases. In addition to a full Instructor's Manual and Test Bank, PowerLecture™ also includes ExamView® testing software with all the test items from the Test Bank in electronic format, enabling you to create customized tests in print or online.

WebTutor Toolbox™

WebTutor™ Toolbox for WebCT™ or Blackboard® provides access to all the content of this text's rich Book Companion Website from within your course management system. Robust communication tools—such as course calendar, asynchronous discussion, real-time chat, a whiteboard, and an integrated e-mail system—make it easy for your students to stay connected to the course.

ABOUT THE AUTHORS

Phyllis Click obtained her bachelor's and master's degrees from the University of California at Berkeley in psychology and child development. Throughout a long career, her interest in providing the best possible environment for young children led her to work in a variety of settings, from preschools to summer camps for older children as well as in programs for children with special needs. For several years she developed and taught in a preschool for children diagnosed with autism. Later she began working with adults, teaching college students, administering grant programs, and designing a curriculum for a private college for prospective teachers.

Now retired, she has been a consultant, helping others start or administer programs, and has published extensively. Her publications include another textbook for administrators of child care programs, articles in professional journals, and ancillary materials for other authors' textbooks.

She has participated in research studies that are cited in anthologies. She belongs to the National Association for the Education of Young Children, the California School-Age Consortium, and the Association for Childhood Education International.

Jennifer Parker is currently a professor teaching child development classes at Ventura College and is an early childhood consultant. Her college classes include students with diverse backgrounds and experience, ranging from beginning, entry-level child care workers to those who are currently teaching in infant-toddler, preschool, and school-age programs. She is also responsible for placing and supervising students in their student teaching experiences. As a consultant, she presents workshops on early math and literacy in the community.

She received her master's degree from California State University, Northridge, and has had extensive experience working with children, families, and adults. She founded a support program for parents of infants and toddlers in a developmentally appropriate environment, and has been a lead kindergarten teacher in an on-campus demonstration school where she also ran a summer camp program. She is currently the chair of the local Early Quality Improvement System, and sits on a variety of county advisory boards. She is a consultant and collaborator with the county's state funded after-school programs. She is also a member of the National Association for the Education of Young children and the California School-Age consortium..

AKNOWLEDGMENTS

A special thanks to Lisa Mafrici for her suggested changes to this edition. Her knowledge of what is important for child care workers and her recommendations for ways to present our ideas have been extremely helpful. Our thanks also go to all the other Cengage Learning staff members who carried the project from one step to another until the final pages were put together.

Jennifer Parker has been an invaluable co-author on this project. Her knowledge, her experience, and her writing have greatly added to the currency of this text.

Our sincere thanks go to the following reviewers who offered many excellent suggestions for additions to previous editions and those who reviewed the draft version of the updated edition. We appreciate their thoughtful comments.

- Sandy Basler, Jefferson College
- JaneMarie Dewailly, Arkansas State University
- Bridget Ingram, Arkansas State University
- Jennifer Koel, Aurora University
- Mary Larue, J Sargeant Reynolds Community College
- Donna Satterlee, Old Dominion University

The authors hope that this new edition will help those who are concerned for the welfare of the millions of children who spend their out-of-school time in organized-care programs. Our children deserve the best.

The People in Child Care

1

Caregivers: Who Are They?

THE NEED FOR CHILD CARE

In 2007, there were approximately 13.6 million single parents in the United States who were responsible for raising 21.2 million children. Most single parents are mothers (84 percent), but 16 percent of custodial parents are fathers (Wolf, 2009). Many of their children spend their out-of-school time in child care, but others care for themselves or participate in sports, religious activities or an arts program. Sixteen percent of preschoolers spend their day in a child care setting. Forty-seven percent of children in kindergarten through third grade are in some kind of non-parental care. Twenty-two percent of children in fourth through eighth grade care for themselves after school. With the downturn in the economy at the end of the first decade of the 21st century, some families have had to remove their children from an organized child care setting or choose a poor quality setting because they cannot afford anything better (Holland, 2009). Still the need for child care is high because of the large number of working parents. The quality of that care is essential to the well-being of children; and caregivers are an important element in determining that quality.

How Important Are Caregivers?

If you are already working in school-age child care, you may occasionally question your choice of profession. Or if you are just considering child care as a career, you may wonder if this is the right place for you. Children can be tiring, frustrating, and demanding. They can also be humorous, marvelously exciting, and fun. This chapter should help you decide whether you are the right person for these children and for the job.

LEARNING OUTCOMES

After reading this chapter, you should be able to:

✔ Discuss the need for child care.

✔ Describe the characteristics of an effective caregiver/teacher.

✔ State the education and experience requirements of a caregiver/teacher.

✔ Understand the caregiver's role in children's development.

✔ Discuss ethical considerations and be familiar with the NAEYC Code of Ethical Conduct.

Children want to solve their own problems and to feel empowered, while knowing an adult's help is available when needed.

caregiver
name for an adult in child care when the emphasis is on the caring role

recreational supervisor
name for an adult in child care when the emphasis is on the recreational aspects

developmentalist
name for an adult in child care who is versed in the developmental aspects of the child

educare
a name for an adult in child care reflecting the multifaceted aspect of working with school-age children

First, try to answer the question "What do children need from caregivers?" What did you want from the adults in your life? Children need security—a feeling they can trust adults and be trusted. They want freedom to be independent, while at the same time they like clear limits that define what they can or cannot do. They like adults who are flexible and can respond to new situations and interests with enthusiasm. They need affection, caring, and acceptance of their individual differences. They want to solve their own problems and to feel empowered, but they also want to have an adult's help available when needed. They want to be challenged to use their skills and abilities. Probably, most of all, they want to feel competent and successful.

What Are the Adults Called?

Many different titles are used to designate the adults who spend time with children in after-school programs. There is still no universally accepted designation that satisfies the need to indicate the importance of this type of work. Some adults prefer to be called teachers because they certainly do teach. Others emphasize their caring role and therefore prefer to be called **caregiver** or guide. This term may be unacceptable to many children in after-school settings because they feel they do not need to be "cared for." Those who emphasize the recreational aspect of after-school programs use **recreational supervisor** or counselor. Still others use the title of leader, aide, assistant, or child-care worker. J. Daniel (1995) has suggested using **developmentalist**, while Betty Caldwell, past president of National Association for the Education of Young Children (NAEYC), has coined the term **educare**. Until a universally accepted word is coined reflecting the multifaceted aspects of working with school-age children, each of the preceding is acceptable.

Characteristics of the Effective Caregiver/Teacher

If you want to be a caregiver or teacher of school-age children, you need certain characteristics. Do not be discouraged if you do not have every single quality in the following list. You will acquire some of these attributes as you gain experience.

Someone Who Really Likes School-Age Children

Liking school-age children should certainly be the first important characteristic for a caregiver because few people relate well to children of all ages. "Liking" school-age children means many things. It means being interested in these children, enjoying conversations with them, and seeking out time with them. It means appreciating each child's unique qualities and accepting their differences.

Someone Who Encourages Children to Be Independent

School-age children are striving to be autonomous. They want to do things for themselves and to solve their own problems. Often adults want children to be compliant and obedient. They may feel threatened when children say, "I want to do it my way." Others feel frightened by what might happen when children are allowed to do what they want. It is important that children develop a sense that they can do things for themselves and that they be given the opportunity to grow in independence.

Someone Who Understands Child Development

You should have a good knowledge of how children develop during middle childhood. You need to know the characteristics of children at each stage of development throughout the elementary years. What are their physical abilities? What are they capable of learning? What do these children need? How do they form their identities and acquire moral values?

It is important to be aware of the causes of behavior to better understand why a particular child responds the way he or she does. Why does one child willingly go along with the group while another wants to be alone? Why are the six-year-olds in your group suddenly rebelling against your ideas or directions? Why are some children easy to get along with some days, but impossible on others? To understand the "whys" of behavior, you need to know the emotional stresses most children go through at various stages of childhood.

When you do understand child development, it is easier to realize that often just the passage of time will result in changed behavior. In other words, children may just be going through an expected phase in their development. Soon their behavior will change as they move into the next stage. Beyond that, what behaviors may create problems for children themselves? What are the things that make it difficult for them to have friends or to accomplish what they want to do? Then—and this is the hard part—how can you help each child change his or her behavior into more mature actions? Knowledge of child development will help you find the answers.

You need knowledge of child development to understand how to provide guidance in positive ways. How you help a toddler change his behavior is very different from how you treat a nine-year-old. Toddlers need clear, firm limits to protect them from harm. Nine-year-olds must feel empowered to manage their own behavior. Therefore, you allow as much freedom as possible while teaching them to set their own limits. It is a subtle guidance that respects the child's desire to be competent.

Understanding development is basic to planning any activities in school-age child care. You need to know what children are capable of doing or learning. With that knowledge you can plan age-appropriate activities at which children are likely to succeed. Sometimes the children themselves have ideas for projects that are way beyond their capabilities. You must guide them to choose things they can do while challenging them to progress to the next level of developmental abilities.

Someone Who Is a Good Role Model

Although parents still continue to be important, school-age children will be looking to you as a model. They watch what you do and listen to your words. They sometimes imitate you as they develop their own standards for behavior. Therefore, you should have the characteristics you want children to have. Honesty, dependability, fairness, and trustworthiness are some of the traits you might consider. You could add flexibility, caring, tolerance, and patience. You could also include a happy disposition and an optimistic outlook.

Whenever possible, child-care groups should have both male and female leaders. The majority of elementary school teachers are female. Boys spend a large part of their day without a male role model. When these children are being raised by single mothers, they may miss having a relationship with a caring male. A male leader in child care can help fill the gap. Girls, too, need male child care workers to help them develop their own identities in relation to males. Both girls and boys need time spent with members of both genders to help them learn to trust adults outside their homes.

Someone Who Has Lots of Interests

You should know a lot about many things. Your own curiosity and interests should lead you to seek out information you can share with children. They will be fascinated by what you know about stars, electricity, dinosaurs, or many other topics. Know also where to look for answers to their questions. Know how to find information in your local library, and have a sense of what is available in your community. You can also help children use the Internet for research on subjects that interest them. When you share children's excitement about learning, you encourage rather than discourage their desire to discover.

You should be able to do a lot of things. Virtually any skill you have can be shared. If you are adept at woodworking, you can teach children how to use tools. If you know how to knit or crochet, children can learn those skills as well. Learn how to do other things that could interest children. There are many "how-to" books that will help. You can also learn from someone who already has these skills.

You should be willing to learn from children. Often there is more than one way of doing things. A child may show you an approach you would not have thought of yourself. But you have to be willing to consider alternatives rather than assuming there is one absolute right way. Many children have information and skills they can share with the group. Be willing to listen to children and provide opportunities for others to listen as well.

Someone Who Allows Freedom While Setting Limits

School-age children are trying to move from dependence on adults to independence. Consequently, they need the freedom to make their own decisions and set their own rules. This freedom bolsters their self-esteem. You must be willing to give up or share control when it is appropriate. For instance, you may want to set rules that involve safety, but allow the children to write their own code of conduct in the group.

On the other hand, when limits are needed, you must be able to set them firmly and consistently. You have to be able to say "no" and mean it. That is not always as easy as it sounds. Children test how far they can go before you stop them, and they want to feel secure in the knowledge that you will not let them go too far. You should communicate clearly that it is not all right to run around the pool area, for example. Explain why the rule is necessary, then enforce it. You will gain their respect and trust.

Sometimes you have to balance individual freedoms with group rights. One child cannot be allowed to work at a noisy project alone when the rest of the group is listening to a story. If a group of children wants to play with blocks, one child cannot be allowed to take all the blocks. However, at other times individual rights must be considered. Some children need to have exclusive use of materials or space for a period of time. Others want to be able to choose another child as a partner for an activity. You need a great deal of sensitivity to children to decide when to meet individual or group needs.

Someone Who Has Good Communication Skills

Communication includes both the ability to convey messages and to listen. You should be able to do both well. When you give children directions, they should be stated clearly. There should be no ambiguity about your meaning. "You have five minutes to finish what you are doing before snack time" is a clear statement. "It will be snack time in a few minutes" leaves room for confusion. What is a few minutes? Five? Three? Ten? You should also be able to express your feelings honestly. "I don't like it when you call me names" lets a child know exactly how you feel. In addition, good communication skills involve the ability to write in an organized, concise manner. You may need to write out information for children, parents, or other staff members.

The other side of communication is the willingness to listen. Children often need to talk about school, their families, or their friends. You should be willing to listen and interested in what they have to say. Children are not the only ones who appreciate a good listener. Parents and other staff members occasionally need a "friendly ear." There is one last reminder about communication: It is important when you work with children not to talk down to them. Use language that is appropriate for their developmental level and ability to understand.

Someone Who Can Guide Children in Social Problem Solving

Children without social skills do not have friends, and that often leads to either aggressive or passive behaviors. These are the children who become bullies or who sit quietly in the background alone. They need help to change their behaviors so they can make and keep friends. A sensitive

What characteristics do men bring to after-school programs?

adult can help these children understand what is preventing them from achieving their goals or making friends. The most effective ways to help children learn techniques that allow them to have friends include discussing strategies in small groups and modeling friendships among adults. Individual children can be coached. You can review the behaviors that led to the child being excluded and suggest alternative behaviors. Encourage the child to practice the new behaviors, and then evaluate the results. Sometimes it even helps to set up a private signal system, such as a hand sign, word, or phrase. If aggressive behavior has prevented the child from being part of a group, signal her to remind her to try an alternate method. Conflict resolution is discussed further in Chapter 7.

Someone Who Enjoys Physical Activity

You should like to play active games and sports with children. Children who attend elementary school spend a large part of their day sitting down. When they come to child care, they need to be involved in activities that allow them to move around. They want to be able to play games outdoors, climb, run, jump, skate, or do whatever else is available. Both you and the children will get a great deal of pleasure doing some of these activities together. That requires a lot of energy and good health on your part.

Someone Who Cares About Families

All children you work with are part of a family. As described in Chapter 3, these families will have many distinct characteristics. They may be like your own family or very different. It is up to you to get to know the family members—especially parents. Find out what they are like and what they want for their children. Become familiar with their cultural values and the standards they set for their family, then be supportive and avoid criticizing them. Find ways to strengthen their role as parents. You should see child care as a family service, not just a place for children.

You should be the kind of person parents can talk to. What parents want most is an indication that you know their children and care about them. They want to hear what their children did during the day and how their children are getting along. Sometimes they may want to talk about their children's problems. Do not feel you must have solutions; just be willing to listen. Often it is enough just to listen to a parent talk about the difficulties of working and having time for children. Parents do not always want advice, just understanding.

Someone Who Understands the Role of a Caregiver

You are both a parent and a teacher when you work in an after-school program. Your job has aspects of both relationships. At times your role is to be a listener. When children arrive at child care, they may need someone to talk to about their day or to discuss problems. At other times you become a disciplinarian who sets limits or administers appropriate consequences when children overstep limits. You may have to see that they get their homework done. These are things a parent does. At other times you become an instructor. In the course of a day's activities, you will often teach them some of the same things they learn in school. They may need help with math concepts when they work on projects. They may need help reading a recipe while cooking a snack. You may encourage them to pursue their interest in astronomy, then praise their accomplishments. You explain instructions when they play a game. Your role, therefore, is a combination of teacher and parent; but your primary role is to see that children are well cared for while their parents are at work.

Someone Who Is Able to Work as Part of a Team

You should be able to get along with other adults as well as you do with children. Other staff members within your center depend on you or have to coordinate their activities with yours. Therefore, you must be willing to share responsibilities, space, and materials. Sometimes you have to be ready to do more than is expected of you. You should see working with children as a profession, not just a job. When you do, you will respect fellow workers and receive their respect in return.

Being part of a team may also mean working with elementary school personnel. This can be difficult because caregivers often seem to be invisible—not seen as part of the school. When your center is part of a school system, you are likely to be housed on the school grounds. You will have to work out the arrangements for sharing indoor and outdoor space. You may have to order materials through the school office. In order to foster a good working relationship, initiate ways to inform school personnel about your program. Let the principal know about any special activities. Offer to put up a display of children's artwork. Talk to parents at a PTA meeting. Get to know the teachers and inform them of the children's activities in child care. A healthy relationship with school personnel is worth the effort it takes to establish and maintain.

Education and Experience

Each child care center will have its own requirements for staff members. Criteria for employment are usually based on guidelines mandated by local or state licensing regulations, as well as by the funding sources that support the program. In addition, each situation will have demands based on the needs of the program or the children to be served. In general, two broad areas of education and experience are usually required in school-age child care.

Some center directors look for personnel who have strong backgrounds in early childhood education. Staff members must be knowledgeable in the development of young children. Directors also want people with expertise and experience in planning a curriculum for "school-agers." Many caregivers who fit these requirements have completed courses in early childhood education and worked in preschool programs. In addition, they may have had the opportunity to work with five- or six-year-olds. More and more colleges and universities are offering courses in school-age child care.

The finest caregivers enjoy positive relationships with parents.

Other directors seek personnel who have strong backgrounds in recreation. These staff members know a lot of games suitable for this age level. Staff members should be aware of activities that are safe for young children. Caregivers with this kind of background probably have taken courses in physical education and recreation. They may have had experience supervising playground situations or working in summer camps.

As you look at these two areas of background and experience, it probably occurs to you that a good caregiver needs both. You are absolutely right. It would certainly be ideal if that were so. In most child care situations, however, the problem is resolved by hiring staff with skills that complement one another. In each group, one person may have an early childhood education background while one may come from recreation programs.

To further achieve an ideal staff balance in a child-care program, it would be necessary to have a staff that is ethnically comparable with the surrounding community. It also helps to have people of different age levels. A staff member over the age of 30 will bring a different perspective to the care of children than a 20-year-old.

By now you should have a picture of the kind of person who will make a good teacher or caregiver of school-age children. Let us take one last look at the role of a caregiver in children's development.

THE CAREGIVER'S ROLE IN CHILDREN'S DEVELOPMENT

In general terms, your role as caregiver is to foster all aspects of children's development. The ways in which you do that have been implied by the description of characteristics needed for the job. However, look at it in another way. Children have specific needs; your job is to help fulfill them.

- Children need security; you provide a secure environment.
- Children need to trust themselves and others; you show you can be trusted and that you trust them.
- Children need to be independent; you allow freedom within limits.
- Children need to develop interests; you encourage and foster those interests.
- Children need a positive self-image; you appreciate their similarities and differences.
- Children need to feel competent; you provide opportunities for them to be successful.
- Children need to acquire values; you offer a positive role model for them to imitate.
- Children need to belong to a group; you include each child and encourage friendships.
- Children need to solve their own problems; you allow them to solve their problems, but provide help when needed.

As you can see, having a part in the development of young children is an awesome task. But should you choose this as a career, you will find it is

Children have specific needs; your job is to help fulfill them.

never boring, for you are constantly challenged. You will find that children force you to grow in order to keep up with their demands. It is certainly a job that will keep you learning for many years into the future.

ETHICAL CONSIDERATIONS

Whether you are experienced or just starting out, as an early childhood educator you will be faced with situations that call for difficult decisions. For example, you suspect that a child in your class is being exposed to sexually explicit experiences. Or a fellow teacher is taking home paper and paint to use with his own child. How do you decide on the right way to respond to either of these situations—or even whether to do anything at all? Your own personality or personal attributes will affect how you react to situations, how you think, and what you feel. Early childhood educators tend to be caring, empathetic people who try to be fair. Unfortunately, these qualities are not always enough to guide you when you are faced with ethical dilemmas.

values
the qualities we believe to be intrinsically desirable and that we strive to achieve in ourselves

morality
our perception of what is good or right

ethics
a study of right, wrong, duty, and obligation

Your values also play a part in helping to decide what to do. **Values** are the qualities people believe to be intrinsically desirable and strive to achieve in themselves. Personal values are the basis for professional values. However, not everyone has the same values, and others may not understand the choices you make. A good example is the dilemma you face when a parent asks you to discipline her child in a way that is counter to your values. You may truly believe yours is the right way, but the parent may have just as strong a conviction.

Your sense of morality also affects your decisions. **Morality** is the perception of what is good or right. Morality also includes beliefs about how people should behave and the kind of obligations they have to one another. During their early years, children are taught by their parents or their religion that it is wrong to lie or steal and that it is right to be truthful and treat others kindly. This becomes the core of their moral sense as adults.

However, as professionals, caregivers need another standard by which to decide how to resolve problems. They need a code of **ethics** that outlines responsibilities in ways that everyone can agree on. Ethics is the study of right, wrong, duty, and obligation. Ethics and morality are closely related and, in fact, are often used interchangeably; but ethics implies a conscious deliberation regarding moral choices.

NAEYC Code of Ethical Conduct

The National Association for the Education of Young Children (NAEYC) has developed a Code of Ethical Conduct that "offers guidelines for responsible behavior and sets forth a common basis for resolving the principal ethical dilemmas encountered in early childhood care and education" (Feeney & Freeman, 1999). The code focuses on the daily interactions with children from birth through age eight and their families in preschools, child-care centers, kindergartens, and primary classrooms. The code consists of four sections, each addressing a particular area of professional relationships. The sections are (1) children, (2) families, (3) colleagues, and (4) community and society. Each section addresses responsibilities, ideals, and principles. The intent is to portray exemplary professional practice and define practices that are required, prohibited, and permitted.

Ideals

I-l.1 To be familiar with the knowledge base of early childhood care and education and to keep current through continuing education and in-service training.

I-1.2 To base program practices upon current knowledge in the field of child development and related disciplines and upon particular knowledge of each child.

I-1.3 To recognize and respect the uniqueness and potential of each child.

I-1.4 To appreciate the special vulnerability of children.

I-1.5 To create and maintain safe and healthy settings that foster children's social, emotional, cognitive, and physical development, and that respect their dignity and their contributions.

The following extract from Section I, Ethical Responsibilities to Children, will give you a sense of the content of the code:

> Childhood is a unique and valuable stage in the life cycle. Our paramount responsibility is to provide safe, healthy, nurturing, and responsive settings for children. We are committed to supporting children's development, respecting individual differences, helping children learn to live and work cooperatively, and promoting health, self-awareness, competence, self-worth, and resiliency.

Every early childhood professional should read the full text of the Code of Ethical Conduct that can be found in *Ethics and the Early Childhood Educator* listed in the references at the end of this chapter or on the Internet at www.NAEYC.org.

A typical situation faced by many caregivers involves balancing the needs of an individual child against the needs of the group. For example, one child in the group is overly aggressive, terrorizing other children. If the adult focuses on helping that one child, attention may be diverted from others who need help or attention. Yet one child cannot be allowed to hurt others or make them afraid. Parents of the other children may also begin to complain that their children do not want to come to school because they are afraid or they are not getting the necessary attention. Caregivers faced with this situation may look to the code for guidance.

The second item, I-1.2 listed above, cautions the adult "to base program practices upon current knowledge and research in the field of early childhood education." This means acquiring a knowledge of children's behavior. What is typical behavior for a particular age level and what may be considered atypical? The adult dealing with an overly aggressive child must consider whether the behavior is a normal stage of development or an indication of more serious problems. The caregiver must also "create and maintain safe and healthy settings that foster children's social, emotional, cognitive, and physical development." After weighing all the information, the caregiver may decide that setting clearer and more consistent limits will help manage this child in the classroom. The caregiver may also decide that this child needs to be referred for further testing, and possibly to a different setting. The NAEYC Code provides clear guidelines for caregivers that make it easier for them to make decisions affecting every child, family, their colleagues, and their community.

SUMMARY

- School-age children have specific needs, including: to trust and be trusted, to be independent, to have challenges, to be accepted for who they are, and to be successful.

- Many different titles are used to designate the adults who spend time with children in after-school programs: teacher, caregiver, guide, recreational supervisor, counselor, leader, aide, assistant, and child-care worker. All these names are acceptable.

- Those who care for school-age children should be people who have a variety of qualities, beyond simply liking children.

- Child care programs may require personnel who have a background in either early childhood education or recreation.

- The role of a caregiver with school-age children is to foster all aspects of children's development.

- Caregivers sometimes have to make decisions that require them to consider their own values or sense of what is right or wrong.

- NAEYC has developed a Code of Ethical Conduct that offers guidelines for responsible behavior.

KEY TERMS

caregiver	ethics	recreational supervisor
developmentalist	morality	values
educare		

REVIEW QUESTIONS

1. List the reasons child care workers need a knowledge of child development.

2. Describe the qualities of a good role model for school-age children.

3. This chapter suggests a child care teacher should have a lot of interests. Explain the reasons for that statement.

4. Effective communication has two parts. What are they?

5. Describe ways to foster your relationship with parents.

6. Why is it important for caregivers to be able to work together as a team?

7. What kinds of education and experience should be required to qualify as a caregiver?

Case Study

Alberto is nine and speaks with a slight accent because his home language is Spanish. He is often the butt of teasing and does not seem to know how to make friends. He frequently sits by himself in the reading area or at the science table. The caregivers in the group tend to leave him alone because he isn't creating any problems, but they do intervene when other children tease him. They send the tormentors to a quiet place for a time-out. One caregiver really wants to help Alberto make at least one friend, but doesn't know how.

1. How could you help Alberto react in a way to stop the teasing?

2. What would be a more effective way to help the teasers change their behavior?

3. What are three things you could do to help Alberto make a friend?

STUDENT ACTIVITIES

1. Visit two different types of school-age programs. Choose, for instance, one that is operated by a city recreation department and one that is part of a corporation. In what ways are the children's activities the same or different in these two programs?

2. Observe several child care teachers interact with children. How do their styles differ? Describe the one you would use as your own model for interactions with children.

3. Interview the director of a school-age child care program. What are the qualities he or she looks for when hiring new staff members?

4. In class, do "Quick Writes." These are short statements in response to a question or completing a sentence. Be prepared to share these statements with classmates when finished. Spend one minute responding to "One teacher was my favorite because _____." Highlight three main characteristics and then prioritize them. Finally, state why the first priority item is the most important.

5. Write an advertisement for the perfect school-age caregiver.

SUGGESTED READINGS

Bender, J., Flatter, C. H., & Sorrentino, J. M. (2000). *Haifa childhood: Quality programs for out-of-school hours* (2nd ed.). Nashville: School-Age Notes.

California State Department of Education. (1994). *Kid's time, a school-age program guide*. Sacramento: Author.

Elicker, J., & Fortner-Wood, C. (1995). Adult-child relationships in early childhood programs. *Young Children*, 51(1), 69–78.

Gratz, R., & Boulton, P. (1996). Erikson and early childhood educators: Looking at ourselves and our profession developmentally. *Young Children*, 51(5), 74–78.

Kaiser, B., & Rasminsky, J. S. (2003). Opening the culture door. *Young Children*, 58(4), 53–56.

Musson, S. (1994). *School-age care, theory and practice*. Don Mills, Ont: Addison-Wesley.

Stapen, C. (1988). Caring for your child-care person. *Working Woman*, 13, 148.

Whitebook, M., Howes, C, Phillips, D., & Pemberton, C. (1989). Whocares? Child care teachers and the quality of care in America. *Young Children*, 45(1), 41–45.

WEB RESOURCES

http://www.ccw.org
Center for Child Care Workforce: Nonprofit, research, education, and advocacy organization committed to improving child care teachers.

http://www.wheelock.edu
Wheelock College: Provides programs in education and child and family studies.

http://www.naccp.org
National Association for Child Care Professionals: Goal is to improve and strengthen the credibility of those who lead the child care industry.

http://www.naeyc.org
National Association for the Education of Young Children: a professional organization that promotes excellence in early childhood education.

REFERENCES

Daniel, J. (1995). Advancing the care and education paradigm: A case for developmentalists. *Young Children*, 50(2), 2.

Feeney, S., & Freeman, N. K. (1999). *Ethics and the early childhood educator: Using the NAEYC Code*. Washington, DC: NAEYC.

Holland, S. (2009). Impact of the economy on child care, Parents and the price of child care. Retrieved from the Internet, www.earlychildhoodfocus.org.

Wolf, J. (2009). Single parent statistics. Retrieved from the Internet, About.com.

2

The Children

DEVELOPMENT OF SELF

Middle childhood, between ages five and twelve, is an important period when children develop a sense of who they are, what they can do, and how others perceive them. It is a time when the focus of their daily lives is on school and their self-esteem is closely tied to school success. Most children enter kindergarten eager to learn and are optimistic in their evaluation of self and their expectations for academic success (Stipek & MacIver, 1989). When they first begin reading and writing, they have little idea of how successful they will be and cannot accurately assess their own competency. Young children assume they are successful because either they put a lot of effort into their activities or they are just lucky. As they get older and more experienced, they become more realistic. They begin to compare and evaluate their own success with the success of their peers. They learn that different people have different abilities, enabling them to achieve at varying levels. They may find they are good at reading but not so capable at math (Halsey, 2004).

A second way children develop a sense of self is through their feelings of power. One source of power is their status with their peers. They measure and compare themselves to others. Are they liked and looked up to? Are they similar to their peers in appearance, dress, and abilities? If they answer in the affirmative, they feel more powerful. Another source of power is inner control over their own behavior—in other words, being able to behave in ways that their parents and society view favorably. They also develop good self-esteem if they are accomplishing their goals and expanding their skills.

LEARNING OUTCOMES

After reading this chapter, you should be able to:

✔ State the factors that are important to children's sense of self.

✔ Discuss bullying and ways to help the bully and the victim.

✔ Discuss the importance of having a friend, and how child care leaders can help children make friends.

✔ Understand the typical developmental characteristics of children during middle childhood.

Middle childhood is an important period when the focus is on school and self-esteem is closely tied to school success.

rough and tumble play
aggressive behavior, but the children usually have positive facial expressions or may be laughing

At times, aggressive behavior turns into "**rough and tumble play**" and is particularly prevalent in boys. To the outsider, the attacking, teasing, threatening, pushing, or wrestling looks the same as hostile aggression. Caregivers can observe signs that distinguish rough and tumble play from hostile aggression. Usually the children have positive facial expressions or may be laughing. They do not use their full force and do not hit hard; they push just hard enough to make an impact on the other child. They can be observed to alternate roles, each being on top or being the aggressor. At the end of the play, they happily continue to participate in other activities together.

A final standard by which school-age children evaluate themselves is in terms of good or bad behavior. In Chapter 6, Lawrence Kohlberg (1963) describes moral behavior in middle childhood as being nice to others, behaving in ways that others approve of, and obeying rules or laws. During this period children become increasingly aware of how others evaluate their behavior. When parents, teachers, or peers react positively to them or disapprove of their actions, they label themselves good/nice or bad/not nice. Reputations acquired during middle childhood may affect an individual's behavior into adolescence and adulthood.

Race may also play a part in how children perceive themselves and others. Holmes (1995) studied kindergarten children in several schools in southern California. She found that the content of children's self-concepts and the way children perceive themselves and convey information about themselves is linked to their cognitive maturation. At the kindergarten level, children concentrated on specific, observable characteristics: gender, skin color, eye color, and language. The children described themselves by saying, "I have brown skin" or "My eyes are brown." According to Holmes, older children at a higher cognitive level will portray themselves as having personal preferences or personality traits—"I'm pretty good at sports and have a lot of friends."

Holmes found that socialization experiences were important factors affecting children's subjective feelings about themselves. For example, children who experienced repeated negative interactions with others from a group different from their own may incorrectly assume that the negativism was due to their being African American or because they spoke Spanish rather than English.

In the same way, when children had limited interactions with others from a group different from their own and those interactions were negative, they tended to categorize all people from that group as being alike. They saw the group as homogeneous, even though they had only interacted with a few members. One negative encounter led to an erroneous conclusion about the group, thus giving rise to stereotyping and prejudice.

Bullying and Cyber-Bullying

At times school-age children test their power and their place in a group by bullying others. **Bullying** is unprovoked aggression intended to inflict injury or discomfort on the victim, and can be either direct or indirect. Boys more often use a direct form: hitting, teasing, threatening, humiliating, mobbing, or taunting. Girls tend to engage in indirect methods such as gossiping, spreading rumors, or enforcing social isolation. Students who engage in bullying behaviors often seem to care little for the feelings of their victims.

The latest method of bullying others is online bullying or **cyber-bullying**. According to a survey done by Amanda Lenhart (2009), 32 percent of children between the ages of 11 and 19 said they had been bullied by electronic means. Fifteen percent of teens reported having private material forwarded without permission; 13 percent received threatening messages; 13 percent said someone had spread rumors about them; and 6 percent had someone post an embarrassing picture of them online. The aggressor uses electronic devices such as e-mail, instant messaging, text messaging, blogs, mobile phones, pagers, and websites. This method is particularly destructive to the target, because the bullies can remain anonymous and make the information available to large numbers of people. A particularly destructive example of cyber-bullying is when girls take locker-room pictures and post them online. Another example is the online voting booth. Pictures and names of students are posted, and others are asked to vote for who is the "hottest, the ugliest, the biggest geek, the wimpiest fag." (Bowman [2001] Retrieved March 2007 from www.edweek.org). The bully can use temporary e-mail accounts, false names in chat rooms, and instant messaging programs to hide his identity. Thus, the harasser does not have to be bigger or stronger and needs less energy and courage to hurt her victim.

bullying
unprovoked aggression intended to inflict injury or discomfort on the victim

cyber-bullying
Use of electronic means to bully others

Children who are victims of bullying may be physically different from their peers in size, race, or in the way they dress, and may be called insensitive names such as "sissy" or "dork." They often feel helpless, anxious, insecure, cautious, and suffer from low self-esteem. They may also display sadness and isolate themselves. Loss of appetite may be accompanied by headaches and sleep deprivation. The effects of bullying carry over to these children's schoolwork where they may have trouble concentrating and show poor academic performance. Some of the victims of bullying become overly aggressive themselves.

Bullies themselves are also hurt by this behavior. They do not learn to manage their emotions or how to cope when difficulties arise. They fail to develop empathy for others and don't learn how to have real relationships with other people. Instead they continue to blame others for their problems and never take responsibility for their own behavior. They may display physical aggression and disruptive behavior. They ridicule others with constant teasing and encourage their peers to exclude others. These children often challenge authority and show disrespect.

The best way for children to deal with a bully is not to respond. The bully sees that the behavior is not getting the result intended. Victims of cyber-bullying can avoid chat rooms, change their e-mail address, use preferences or privacy tools to block the person, and use caller ID for their cell phones. If the victim is unable to stand up to the bully, adults need to intervene and stop the behavior, immediately following it with increased supervision to stop potential incidents before they begin.

Child care personnel certainly need to monitor computer usage and cell phone activity. They can adopt a policy of zero tolerance for bullying of any kind and manage it when it does occur. In addition they can ensure adequate supervision of children, inside and outside, so bullying activities can be stopped immediately. They can also add activities to the curriculum that promote individual competencies, self-confidence, and emotional management techniques. Some of the activities outlined in Chapter 7, such as "Fighting Fair," "Getting to Know You," and "Y'All Come Up," are a few of the examples. Chapter 7 also contains suggestions for helping children develop social competence in order to stand up to bullies. Caregivers should emphasize respecting others, and use their own behavior as a role model. Finally, collaboration with parents will help reinforce the anti-bullying message.

Implications for Child Care Staff Members

Children's feelings about themselves develop not in a vacuum, but rather within the context of their daily experiences and their contacts with others. Many factors influence the development of self-esteem and social competence. According to Katz and McClellan (1997), these factors are "the children's attachments to their primary caregivers within the family; the modeling, guidance, and support of parents and teachers; the opportunity to observe peers and interact with them; and children's relationships with non-family adults involved in their care and education and those involved in the neighborhood and community in which they spend a large proportion

If a child is unable to stand up to a bully, adults need to intervene and stop the behavior immediately followed by increased supervision to prevent incidents before they begin.

of their time" (p. 13). Caregivers can encourage children's positive feelings about themselves by:

- **Providing authentic feedback to children rather than empty praise.** Help them to evaluate their own skills realistically and to set feasible goals for themselves. "You were having a hard time learning to use the saw, but you figured out how to do it. Look how well you were able to cut a straight line for the side of your birdhouse."

- **Providing supportive intervention to children who have been rejected or are having difficulty gaining acceptance from their peers.** Offer help to upgrade skills that bring acceptance in the classroom or playground. Teach children how to be successful. "I can see that you were hurt you weren't chosen for their team. Suppose I help you practice so you will be able to play better." Or "Not everyone can be a good basketball player. Remember how great you are when we put on plays."

- **Accepting children's feelings rather than denying or belittling their importance.** Be a sensitive listener. "I can see you're pretty mad about something today. If you feel like talking about it, I'm ready to listen."

- **Providing positive encounters with persons from different racial or ethnic backgrounds.** Invite a Black, Asian, or Latino musician to visit the class and share their music with the children.

- **Scheduling adult visitors who can talk about their culture or experiences.** Ask an adult to present a craft or music activity representative of their culture.

"Mom, me, Dad, and Rascal, my dog." Carissa, age 6.

- **Encouraging multicultural groups to work together on activities that require cooperation and compromise.** Invite children from an ethnically different child care group to participate in an activity such as a swim meet, game, or picnic. Expect each group to work on planning for the activity.

PEER GROUPS: HOW CHILDREN DEVELOP FRIENDSHIPS

Beginning in the preschool period, when children first understand the meaning of the word "friend," the need to have friends becomes increasingly important. As children's cognitive abilities change, so do their concepts of friendship and its purpose. At first there is a mutual dependence on friends to share activities, carry on conversations, and provide support for attempts at independence from parents. Young school-age children choose friends who are the same gender, have similar interests, and share similar values. There is very little cross-gender fraternization and, in fact, even some antagonism toward members of the opposite sex. Girls pal around with girls, tell each other secrets, watch movies, and talk on the telephone. The leader of a group of girls is chosen for her managerial skills, for having new ideas, and for being thoughtful, friendly, and organized (Edwards, 1994). Boys get together to skateboard, play video games, share a hobby, or compete in organized sports.

Older school-age children rely on friends for intimate conversations about problems, dreams, and expectations. Friends are seen as people who will remain loyal and can be relied on when life is difficult. The circle of friends gradually becomes smaller as children become more selective about the qualities of a friend. Often, by age 10, both boys and girls have a single best friend, although this exclusivity tends to occur more frequently with girls.

School-age children choose friends who have the same interests.

By the end of middle childhood, many girls have only one best friend on whom they depend for all their social needs (Gilligan, Murphy, & Tappan, 1990). By age nine everyone knows who is best friends with whom, and no one would think of trying to disrupt the pair.

This closeness of friend relationships makes it difficult for children who have not found a companion. It is also heart wrenching when one of a pair of friends becomes more mature than the other and moves on to other alliances. The deserted partner experiences difficulty in finding a new companion.

Middle childhood is also a period when children form themselves into cliques, clubs, or gangs with the primary purpose of gaining independence from adults. Each group has its own vocabulary, dress code, rules, and activities (Opie & Opie, 1959). The group provides a mutual support system and a sense of solidarity as children learn to sharpen their social skills. Those who belong build self-esteem, but those who are excluded face difficulties socially and often academically as well.

Adler and Adler (1998) followed 200 elementary school-age children in their community. They found that children were keenly aware of the importance of **cliques**, which grant power to those who belong and the ability to exclude those children who are not welcome. Some of the influence is positive, as it helps children learn appropriate social behavior and the consequences of misbehavior. Clique members tend to have similar characteristics. During middle childhood they have similar interests or come from similar backgrounds. When the cliques continue into high school, they are identified as the jocks, the nerds, the druggies, the artists, or the intellectuals. Cliques provide children with a social identity and a sense of belonging.

cliques
groups of children who have similar characteristics and interests

Cliques can be extremely limiting, prescribing very specific ways of behaving, dressing, or associating with others outside the group (Adler and Adler,1998). Those outside the group can be derided for wearing the wrong clothes, being members of a different race or religion, or being too studious. Clique members may even carry on "negative campaigns" against chosen targets, heaping verbal abuse and humiliation on them. To stay in the group and be accepted, as well as to gain the resulting feelings of power, members go along with this behavior. The consequence is that bigotry and racism become part of children's value systems and increase their need to conform to standards that may conflict with values they have been taught at home.

In the case of **gangs**, the purpose may be even more negative. Not only do gangs operate outside the realm of adults; they may even be antisocial. Gangs sometimes prey upon others who have problems with their identity or self-confidence (Anthony, Julianne, 1996). Membership in a gang gives the participant a sense of belonging and a feeling of power as well as providing an outlet for his or her anger. The result is that gang members often engage in vandalism or criminal activities that put them in legal jeopardy.

The need to form groups may be observed in the child care setting as well as in the community. The number of individuals involved is usually smaller than in school or in the neighborhood, but the same dynamics

gangs
groups of children who gather together to be out of the realm of adults but also to be antisocial

Best friends.

are evident. Friendships form and break up. Groups congregate and then change. But the need to belong remains strong in all children, with those who are not included feeling left out and unhappy.

Some children seem to make friends easily and are sought out, while others find friendships extremely difficult. Certain social skills are necessary and may be in the formative stage during middle childhood. The first is the ability to understand that others may have views different from their own. Younger children are egocentric, believing that they are the center of the universe and that friends are there to satisfy them. "He's my friend because he plays with me" or "He's my friend because he shares his toys with me." Older children begin to realize that others have needs and feelings, too. In order to make and maintain a friendship, they must make compromises to accommodate the other's needs or feelings. They may have to negotiate whether they want to go to a party or just hang out at the mall if they want to be together.

A second essential skill for making friends is the ability to recognize that others have separate identities and feelings of their own. Although children tend to choose friends who are like themselves, each has a different characteristic and way of reacting. It is a difficult lesson to learn that sometimes a best friend can be upset and want to be alone.

Finally, children have to understand that each encounter with others is part of a relationship. They tend to isolate incidents and fail to see the broader importance of their behavior in specific situations. If they lash out at another child in anger, they do not immediately recognize that this behavior will have consequences for their ability to form a friendship with that person. They must learn that they must curb certain behaviors in order to have friends.

Implications for Child Care Staff Members

Teachers and caregivers in after-school programs can have a significant impact on children's ability to make friends and be part of a group.

- Allow children opportunities to spend time with a friend without the pressure of having to engage in an activity. Let them "just hang out" in a corner of the room or an outdoor area.
- Encourage children to take another's point of view. Ask "How do you think he feels when you call him that name?" Or, for a younger child, ask "How would you feel if someone called you that name?"
- Help children recognize their own psychological characteristics and see that others can accept those qualities. An adult who says "Thanks for helping me understand that sometimes you just want to be alone" does that.
- Nurture children's ability to examine the basis for friendship. Lead discussions about what makes a good friend and how to maintain friendships. Help individual children develop a plan to change behaviors that interfere with friendships.
- Discuss alternative ways of behaving, encourage the child to test the behavior, and then evaluate the results. Give honest appraisal and positive

"This is me." Sarah, age 6.

feedback for desired outcomes. "When you asked how you could help rather than just pushing into his activity, he made a place for you."

- Discourage attempts to exclude individual children from activities. Suggest ways each can contribute. "Evan has good ideas about how to build a ramp. He can show you how to get the cars to the upper level of your parking structure."

OVERVIEW OF DEVELOPMENTAL STAGES

The following summary of typical developmental characteristics of children during middle childhood should provide further help in understanding the children in your care. However, the list is merely a prediction of when these behaviors will occur. There will be wide variations from child to child, with some behaviors happening earlier in some children and later in others.

Five- to Seven-Year-Old Children

Family Relationships

- are more independent of parents, but still need rules
- need assurance of being loved
- have a sense of duty and take on family responsibilities
- develop a conscience

Peers

- begin to see others' points of view
- rely on their peer group for self-esteem
- criticize differences in others
- have two or three best friends
- exhibit little interaction between boys and girls
- can learn to share and take turns
- can participate in organized games

School

- want approval from teacher for achievement
- are eager to learn and succeed in school
- are influenced by a teacher's attitudes and values

Emotions

- begin to inhibit aggression and resolve problems with words
- use humor, often expressed in riddles, practical jokes, or nonsense
- learn to postpone immediate rewards for delayed gratification

- become sensitive to what others think
- become concerned with issues of right and wrong or fair and unfair

Thinking

- are usually clear about differences between fantasy and reality
- can sustain interest for long periods of time
- give more thought and judgment to decisions
- have a good memory for concrete ideas and can remember two things for short periods of time
- can understand and abide by rules
- have a natural curiosity and often ask "why" questions

Language

- learn that words and pictures represent real objects
- can remember and relate past and present events
- sometimes use language aggressively
- understand more language than they use in their communication
- may tease others whose language differs from their own

Physical Development

- develop at different rates, girls faster than boys
- have good small-muscle and eye-hand coordination
- are able to handle simple tools and materials
- have a high energy level

Eight- to Ten-Year-Old Children

Family Relationships

- need parental guidance and support for school achievements
- rely on parents for help in assuming personal and social responsibilities

Peers

- are overly concerned about conforming to peer-imposed rules
- are competitive
- become antagonistic toward the opposite gender, leading to quarrels or teasing
- develop interests specific to their gender
- form same-gender cliques
- spend a lot of energy in physical game playing

School

- are more competitive in school activities
- still need teacher approval and attention
- believe academic achievement is important

Emotions

- react to feelings of others and are sensitive to criticism
- look for friendly relationships with adults
- make value judgments about their own behavior and set standards for self
- are aware of the importance of belonging
- exhibit strong conformation to gender role
- are independent and self-sufficient
- begin to develop moral values

Thinking

- are capable of sustained interest; can make plans, then carry them out
- can begin to think logically about practical problems
- begin to understand cause and effect
- understand abstract concepts such as time and the value of money

Language

- exhibit widely varying abilities to use language or to read
- use language to communicate ideas, spend a lot of time in discussion
- can use more abstract words
- often resort to slang and profanity

Physical Development

- view physical skills as important in determining status and self-concept
- exhibit gender differences; girls are taller, stronger, and more skillful in small-muscle activities
- have a high energy level
- girls begin a growth spurt toward end of this period
- take responsibility for their own personal hygiene

Eleven- to Thirteen-Year-Old Children

Family Relationships

- ready to make their own decisions outside the family
- aware that parental influence is decreasing
- sometimes rebellious, but still need input on family values

Peers

- rely on peer group to model and set standards for behavior
- choose friends based on common interests
- seek information about appropriate gender roles from peers
- may conform rigidly to role assigned by peer group
- place greater importance on team games
- develop divergent interests based on gender

- may develop crushes and hero worship
- are often self-conscious and may become boisterous to cover anxiety
- are interested in the opposite gender; girls are more interested than boys
- face decisions regarding behavior: sex, drugs, and alcohol

School

- worry when entering a new school setting
- begin to question adult authority, particularly in school
- often focus on school for social experience
- are reluctant to attend child care; are bored or think they can care for themselves

Emotions

- may lack self-confidence, be shy or introspective
- worry about what others think, especially peers
- may be moody
- may experience great stress caused by physical changes heralding puberty
- develop own value systems, although influenced by peers
- seek self-identity; may result in rebellious behavior

Thinking

- can now move from dependence on concrete thinking to abstract concepts
- can apply logic and solve problems
- can consider more than one solution to problems
- enjoy problem-solving games and puzzles

Language

- have a good command of spoken and written language
- can use language to discuss feelings, thus bringing about self-understanding
- are often argumentative and contradict adults

Physical Development

- boys begin adolescent growth spurt
- adolescent growth peaks in girls, who experience changes in body proportions
- in girls, secondary gender characteristics develop: breasts, menstruation
- early maturing is related to positive self-image
- boys have improved motor development and coordination and can excel at sports
- girls and boys master physical skills necessary for playing games

SUMMARY

- Middle childhood is an important period when children develop a sense of who they are, what they can do, and how others perceive them. Children also develop a sense of self through feelings of power and the acceptance of their peers.

- School-age children can be aggressive as they test their own power and use bullying or teasing to assert their dominance.

- The final standard by which school-age children evaluate themselves is in terms of good or bad behavior. Beginning in the preschool period, when children first learn the meaning of the word "friend," the need to have a friend becomes increasingly important.

- Later, in middle childhood, children form cliques, clubs, or gangs with the main purpose of gaining independence from adults.

- A caregiver should understand the common developmental characteristics of middle childhood to be able to help the children in their care.

KEY TERMS

bullying   cyber-bullying   rough and tumble play
clique   gangs

REVIEW QUESTIONS

1. Describe the changes that take place in children's assessment of their school achievement.

2. This chapter stated that children derive some of their sense of self through feelings of power. What are the sources of that power?

3. Explain the importance of peers in determining children's sense of self.

4. Why is cyber-bullying so destructive to the child who is the target?

5. State three ways in which child care leaders can help children increase their self-esteem.

6. Compare the criteria for choosing friends among young school-age children with those of older children.

7. What is the primary purpose of groups, clubs, and gangs? Are there other purposes?

8. What are the positive aspects of belonging to a clique or group? What are the negatives?

9. List and explain the three skills children need in order to make friends.

10. What would you say to a child to achieve the following:

   a. encourage her to take another's point of view
   b. help him recognize his own psychological characteristics
   c. evaluate her attempts to change behaviors that interfere with friendships

Case Study

Justin is an eight-year-old Vietnamese boy who was adopted by his Caucasian parents when he was only three months old. His two older siblings had been born into the family before he was chosen. The siblings are both boys, much larger than Justin, and both involved in school sports. Justin wants to follow in their footsteps but finds it difficult to match their success. In his after-school program, Justin loves to paint and creates some beautiful watercolor paintings that his caregiver displays on the bulletin board. However, Justin still longs to join in when the other children are playing baseball. He is usually the last one to be chosen for a team and is booed or called names when he strikes out. When this happens, he goes back to the bench and appears to be struggling to keep from crying. He doesn't cry, but is reluctant to try again when it is his turn at bat.

1. What do you think are the causes of Justin's lack of confidence in his own abilities? What are some things his caregiver can do to help him feel better about himself?

2. Are there ways his family can help?

3. What group games could caregivers facilitate that would encourage teamwork and ultimately help Justin feel a valued part of the team?

STUDENT ACTIVITIES

1. Observe children on a school playground or in a park. Notice how they group themselves. Are there mixed-gender or single-gender groups? How many children are in each group? What are they playing? Write a short paper describing your observations, and relate what you saw to the information in this chapter. Compare your findings with those of your classmates.

2. In small groups, discuss your own perceptions of the following:
   a. an ethnic group different from your own
   b. people who do not speak English

3. Describe the experiences that have led you to your perceptions. Were some of your perceptions based on prejudices? What can you do to change your beliefs?

4. Ask the children in your child care group to draw a picture of themselves. Bring the pictures to class. Choose two to share with classmates. Show the pictures and tell what you think the pictures say about the children's self-esteem.

5. Write an article on bullying or cyber-bullying for your program's parent newsletter. Include information on the causes of bullying and advice on how to help both the bully and the victim.

WEB RESOURCES

http://www.hhs.gov
U.S. Department of Health and Human Services antibullying program. Click on Families and Children. In search slot, type Bullying.

http://www.pta.org
Click on Topics for a section on Parent Topics. Search for Child Safety, then to Bullying.

http://www.cyberbullying.org/
A good resource for examples, information, and what can be done to help prevent cyberbullying.

REFERENCES

Adler, P. A., & Adler, P. (1998). *Peer power: Preadolescent culture and identity.* Piscataway, NJ: Rutgers University Press.

Anthony, J. (1996). Gangs. Retrieved from the Internet at http://library.thinkquest.org. 2009.

Bowman, D. H. (2001). Survey of students documents the extent of bullying. *Education Week on the Web*, May 2, 2001.

Edwards, C. P. (1994). Leadership in groups of school-age girls. *Developmental Psychology*, 30(6), 920-927.

Gilligan, C., Murphy, J. M., & Tappan, M. B. (1990). Moral development beyond adolescence. In Charles N. Alexander & Ellen J. Langer (Eds.), *Higher stages of human development.* New York: Oxford University Press.

Halsey, P. (2004). Self-efficacy: One teachers' concern for reading improvement students. *Ohio Reading Teacher*, Fall 2003–Spring 2004.

Holmes, R. N. (1995). *How young children perceive race.* Thousand Oaks, CA: Sage.

Katz, L. G., & McClellan, D. E. (1997). *Fostering Children's Social Ccompetence.* Washington DC: NAEYC.

Kohlberg, L. (1963). Development of children's orientation towards a moral order (Part 1), Sequence in the development of moral thought. *Vita Numana*, 6, 11–36.

Lenhart, A. (2009). Cyberbullying: What research is telling us. Presented at the National Association of Attorneys General Year of the Child Conference, Philadelphia, PA.

Opie, I., & Opie, P. (1959). *The lore and language of children.* New York: Clarendon.

Stipek, D. J., & MacIver, D. (1989). Developmental change in children's assessment of intellectual competence. *Child Development*, 60, 521–538.

3

Families: Where Children Are Nurtured

THE CHANGING FAMILY

Historically, humans have always grouped themselves together in tribes, clans, networks, or families. In her book *Families*, J. Howard (1978) writes, "The trouble we take to arrange ourselves in some semblance of families is one of the imperishable habits of the human race." Although people continue to group together, as society changes, the definition of family changes. The meaning most widely used by scholars in the past signified parents and their biological children, whether dwelling together or not. Legal experts have also stressed the biological relationships, but broadened the definition to include any person related by blood. This definition is becoming less meaningful in today's surrogate parenting situations. Another definition would include a group of kin and others living together day by day. Some contemporary researchers broaden the definition even further. They state that a family is an *attitude*—an identification with and among a group of individuals who support and nurture one another. Kevin and Elizabeth, whose families are shown in the drawings that appear in this chapter, even included their pets as important members of their families. Families can also be defined by their function. A well-functioning family supports its members in developing their full potential. The family nurtures children in the following five ways (Berger, 2000):

- Meeting basic needs for food, clothes, and shelter.
- Encouraging learning through guidance and motivation.
- Developing self-esteem by helping children to feel competent.
- Nurturing friendships with peers.
- Creating an atmosphere of harmony and stability in the home.

LEARNING OUTCOMES

After reading this chapter, you should be able to:

✔ Describe the current family forms.

✔ Discuss the effects of home environment on children.

✔ Understand the role of caregivers in relation to helping children and their parents.

"My family." Tai, age 7.

nuclear (intact) family
mother, father, and children

extended family
members of nuclear family plus grandparents, cousins, aunts, and uncles

single-parent family
father or mother and children

reconstituted or blended family
families that include children from previous marriages plus those from the present union

multiracial family
marriage between two adults of different races

When most of us hear the word *family*, we still think first of the **nuclear (intact) family** or the **extended family**. The nuclear family is made up of mother, father, and children, if any. The extended family comprises these members plus grandparents, cousins, aunts, and uncles. The number of children who live in extended families has declined. According to the 2008 census, the average family size in the United States is 3.22 members.

The **single-parent family** is headed by either the father or the mother and is indicative of changes in family composition. In 2008, nearly 14.5 million children lived in a single-parent household headed by the mother, and almost 5 million lived with the father only. The rapid rise in numbers of this type of family is partly due to the number of children born to unmarried women (U.S. Census Bureau, 2008).

Because many divorced couples remarry, many children live in a **reconstituted or blended family**. Other terms that describe these families are *recoupled*, *refamilied*, and *binuclear*. These terms designate families that bring together children of one or both former marriages or associations, as well as children born of the new marriage. They are the "his, hers, and ours" children.

An increasing number of households include grandparents or are headed by a grandmother or grandfather. In 2002, 5.6 million children were living in a household where a grandparent was present (U.S. Census Bureau, 2002). These adults provide valuable assistance, particularly in families that have experienced a divorce. They can emotionally support children during difficult times, perhaps add some income, and provide child care. In some cases, the grandparent becomes the only adult in the household if both parents are unable to care for the children.

Another family form that is becoming more visible is the **multiracial family**, where the parents come from different ethnic groups. The 2000 census found that 7 million (2.4 percent) of Americans described themselves as multiracial because they came from families that mix people of two or more ethnic groups. In addition, multiracial families are created when parents choose to adopt a child from a racial or ethnic group different from their own.

A fairly recent development is the **single-gender family** composed of gay or lesbian couples. Some of the children in these relationships are the result of previous marriages to heterosexual partners. More liberal adoption laws have allowed some children to be adopted into these families, while other children are the result of artificial insemination.

In addition to understanding family forms, it is important to note that existing families change as members grow and develop, or as their circumstances shift. The first child may have grown up in a nuclear family, but his sibling is being reared by a single parent. A child whose divorced mother remarries may suddenly find herself with several new siblings. Whatever the form, the family is the first and, therefore, the most important determinant in children's development.

single-gender family
two adults of the same gender plus children

EFFECT OF HOME ENVIRONMENT ON CHILDREN

In the past it was assumed that the optimum environment for children's development was the two-parent family, one in which the father went to work and the mother stayed home to care for the children. However, social scientists are reexamining that idea because fewer families still fit that pattern. In many households both parents work outside the home.

Children in the United States live under a variety of family environmental circumstances. The following are a few of the statistics according to the U.S Census Bureau in 2002:

- 69 percent of children lived with both parents
- 23 percent of children lived with only their mother
- 5 percent of children lived with only their father
- 8 percent of children lived with a grandparent present

Some past research seemed to favor the intact, two-parent family as the best situation for the optimum development of children (McLanahan, 1997; Simons, 1996). It was believed that children who grow up with two loving parents who nurtured them from birth do better in school and are less likely to use drugs or get arrested when they become teenagers. The advantages these children enjoy stem from the fact that two adults share child-rearing tasks. Each parent can support the other or even take on tasks that may be difficult for one of them. Two-parent families often have a financial advantage over other family forms. In many of these families, both parents are wage earners, allowing them to provide better housing, health care, and education for their offspring. When the mother is proud of her work, children have a role model for making their own choices in adulthood. However, all of these positives for the intact family neither guarantee optimum development of children nor eliminate the possibility that other family forms can offer many of the same benefits.

Many children grow up in a household with either their father or their mother.

Newer research (McKeever 2009) indicates that the most important factor in children's success in life is growing up in a stable household whether it's a one- or two-parent household. Kevin McKeever challenged the conventional idea that two-parent households are always the best, with the exception of black two-parent families, where children did score better on reading and math tests than those living in single-parent homes. McKeever also found that a single parent marrying or moving in with a partner can be just as disruptive to children as divorce.

Children who attend child care have some advantages as well. They can participate in supervised activities and enjoy new experiences. They can make friends within a wider circle than that of their neighborhood. They learn to get along with adults other than their parents. Children who stay by themselves after school may also feel they have advantages. Many relish the freedom to come home and do what they want. They grow in independence and self-esteem as they master emergency situations or do household chores.

In spite of the advantages, there remains concern over the tremendous stress that many working parents feel. Their most frequently voiced complaint is that they never have enough time. Working parents do not have enough time to do housework, to spend with the children, or for each other. Fatigue and stress may cause family friction or result in adults taking out their frustrations on the children. Children may feel isolated because the adults have little energy left for being parents. Children may also feel abandoned, or sense that their parents care more about work than about them. If children do not attend child care but stay home alone after school, they may feel lonely and sometimes frightened.

Approximately 50 percent of children under the age of 18 are affected by divorce, adding another kind of stress to their lives. Newer research, however, shows that the negative effects of divorce have been exaggerated (Melamed, 2009). Children's reactions vary in degree depending upon three factors: the quality of their relationship with each parent before separation, the intensity and duration of parental conflict, and the parents' ability to focus on the needs of their children. There are also some age-related differences in children's reactions. Preschoolers are more concerned about maintaining relationships with both parents. In middle childhood, children

"Radio, Dad, me, brother, brother, Mom." Kevin, age 5.

tend to assume responsibility for the divorce and have unrealistic expectations of their own ability to affect their parents' behavior. They may believe they can get their parents back together again. High school children tend to relate the divorce to their own identity and their ability to maintain relationships and make wise life choices (Kurdek, 1989). However, if contact is maintained with both parents, these children do as well as those in an intact family.

Probably the most serious difficulty for the single-parent family, especially when headed by the mother, is low economic status. Women still receive lower salaries than men, often causing these families to live at or below the poverty level. Single parents often suffer from "role overload" as they try to nurture their children, offer sensible discipline, and provide adequate financial support. Stressors increase with more than one child or when illness strikes.

Frequently, when the words "single parent" are used, people assume that they apply to mothers. However, a growing number of men are granted custody of children. According to a 2002 count by the U.S. Bureau of the Census, there were 3,297,000 single-father households. When fathers are motivated to provide a loving, nurturing environment, both boys and girls in father-only families do as well as those living with their mothers (*Ebony*, 1995).

One reason that children do well in a father-headed household is that they respond well to the male as an authority figure, and are less likely to get into trouble. Finally, the income level of a father-led family is more likely to be higher than that of a single mother. The children benefit from a higher standard of living.

Sometimes single parents resolve some of the problems of caring for their youngsters alone by moving in with their own parents. Although there

"My family." Elizabeth, age 10.

are advantages to this arrangement, there are also additional stresses on the adults and children. One study surveying children in various family configurations found that those living with both grandparents had more behavior problems—such as dependence, disobedience, and aggression. They were also found to have poorer language skills (Hawkins & Eggebeen, 1991). This is less true in cultural or ethnic groups where the extended family structure is more commonplace. The adults in these families find ways to mitigate the problems of several generations living under one roof.

When divorced adults find new spouses, the remarriage and resulting blended family are usually seen as an opportunity to start over and to resolve the difficulties of a previous union or single parenting. For the children, the experience can be positive, negative, or mixed. If the children have been living with their mother, the economic situation improves. Boys can receive support from the presence of a stepfather, especially if he takes a personal interest in them. When the father remarries, there may be a more equal sharing of household chores and routines. Children in blended families often find they have more models and choices. In addition, they may gain an opportunity to live in new places and have new experiences. All of these are positives.

Many adjustments are difficult, however, and vary with the ages of the children. Younger children suffer more from loss of a close relationship with both parents. Some children continue to have problems of identity and self-worth in blended families. School-age children may go through a period of lower academic achievement.

Nearly 7 million (2.4 percent) of Americans listed their families as multiracial in the 2000 census (Burrello, 2004). Many children are proud of their dual heritage and feel good about themselves when they are young, and their world consists mostly of the home and family. Unfortunately, when they go to school or out into the community, these children may become targets of discrimination. Where the family lives may be a determinant. Many mixed families choose to live in large urban areas or culturally diverse neighborhoods where they will be accepted. The economic status and educational background of the parents may also determine a family's comfort in a particular community. It is easier if they fit in economically. There is also a growing number of magazines and books that help parents raise children in a biracial family.

One of the biggest problems for children growing up in a multiracial family is developing their own identity. The children must learn to define themselves as being of one group or another, or even a melding of the two. They may be pressured by parents or other adults to accept their identity as one ethnic group, and are sometimes discouraged from associating with children outside of one of their background groups. However, there are strengths of multiracial families not necessarily shared by mono-race families. Parents of multiracial families try to preserve the richness of customs and languages of both cultures. (Burrello, 2004) They teach their children to practice patience when others ask questions about their heritage. They demonstrate that races can coexist not only in neighborhoods, but also in the same home. When these children are encouraged to accept their multiracial origins, they usually develop a positive self-image.

Single-gender families may also be targets of discrimination. Although homosexuality is no longer considered a pathological state, many people still view these relationships with hostility. In spite of this, "children raised by lesbian or gay parents do not differ from children raised by heterosexual parents in terms of mental health, peer relations, or gender role behavior" (Ariel, 2009). Children in single-gender families are particularly cherished because of the choices involved in conception, whether by using a donor or through adoption. There are also more services available to help families who have to work continually to create strong family bonds within their community.

Although family composition does have an effect on children's development, the essential ingredients for emotionally healthy children can be found in any group. Successful families have the following common characteristics:

- They are affectionate. Members express their love and caring for one another.
- They have a sense of place. They either have a stable environment or they have a commitment to their place of origin.
- They pass on their cultural heritage.
- They connect with posterity. They honor their elders.
- They promote and perpetuate family rituals. Parents pass on traditions from their own past and encourage a sense of family continuity.
- They communicate with one another.
- They respect differences among their members.

As you can see, the ingredients for an effective family can exist no matter who makes up the group. Remember that as you work with children and families in your child care center.

Poverty

According to the Children's Defense Fund (2004), one in six children lived in families where the annual income is below the government poverty level. The number rose from 11.6 million in 1999 to 12.1 million in 2002. Female-headed households are most likely to live in poverty, either totally without child support from the father or receiving amounts that are inadequate to bolster the family income. The impact of poverty on children can be devastating, affecting them for the rest of their lives.

Children living in substandard conditions are likely to suffer from malnutrition and disease, are subject to abuse or neglect, and are injured or die more frequently from accidents than children in better environments. Poor children frequently live in housing where they are exposed to lead poisoning due to drinking water from lead-soldered pipes or breathing lead paint dust.

In addition to health risks, children in some low-income neighborhoods fall behind in academic achievement because their schools are poorly equipped and maintained, class sizes are large, and the teachers are poorly paid and may be undermotivated.

"My family and TV." Rachel, age 5.

Perhaps the most devastating of all is the toll that poverty takes on children's psychosocial development. Middle childhood is a time when children become acutely aware of their circumstances compared to those they see portrayed in movies or on television. When their own neighborhoods are rundown and dangerous, they can develop feelings of hopelessness and depression. Children can be helped to overcome these odds by developing resilience. Staff members of child care programs can model being resilient adults themselves to help children. Children learn resilience when they develop strong relationships with mentors (Day, 2006).

HELPING CHILDREN AND THEIR PARENTS

Probably your most important function as a caregiver is to support the bond between parents and their children. Working parents agonize over how they can provide the best kind of upbringing for their children and still earn a living. They are sad they cannot spend as much time with their family as they would like. Many find it hard to get back to being a parent at the end of the day after the pressures of their job. You can help them bridge the gap between their daytime activities and their role as parents. The keyword is Communicate! If you see the parents frequently, talk with them. If you seldom see some parents, you will have to find other means to communicate. Parent handbooks or newsletters provide an opportunity to present aspects of the program, make suggestions for parent–child activities, or announce coming events. A bulletin board in an entry area where all parents will see it can be used to provide information and also to display children's artwork or photos of children. Some centers set up their own website and have e-mail addresses for the staff. Parents can log on to the website to get information about the program, coming events, or special services. Staff members can receive inquiries from parents by e-mail and answer in the same way. You can also use telephone calls to keep in contact with parents. It is important to take the time to ask parents how they see their child's experience in child care or to check on a child who has been absent. Sometimes phone calls can be a means to say "Hello, I've missed seeing you for a while." That may open up a dialogue that will be invaluable in your ongoing relationship with that parent.

Some centers have found a parent survey to be an effective way to reach parents to determine their concerns or needs. Ask parents what they need to know about the program or their children's development. Additional questions might determine other ways that the center could support parents. Once the information has been gathered, staff can decide on ways to respond.

Parents appreciate knowing about any changes in their children since they left them in the morning. They want to know if their children are troubled or ill or are showing changes in behavior. You and the parents can then work together to determine causes and bring about needed change. And communication is not only one way. Ask parents to let you know when there are variations in the home situation or when they notice changes in their children.

Another way to keep in contact with parents is through a family journal. Every child is provided with a notebook in which both caregivers and parents can write notes to one another. The caregiver can direct inquiries such as "What has John been reading at home lately? He tells me he loves to read at home" or "Tell me the favorite things your child likes to do on weekends." The notebook can become a valuable contact tool as well as a record of a child's progress.

Schedule social events that allow parents to get to know staff members and other parents in a relaxed, fun situation. Many parents would welcome a potluck dinner on a Friday evening when they can meet their children at the center and have a meal. As an added bonus, make it a multicultural dinner, with everyone bringing a dish specific to his or her culture or a traditional family recipe. As the participants share recipes and discuss, everyone should gain an appreciation for how many families are alike even though their backgrounds are radically different.

Help parents see their children's behavior realistically. Working parents often feel guilty about leaving their children in the care of others. When problems arise, they immediately think, "If I didn't have to work, these things wouldn't happen." That may or may not be so. Help them to understand that some behaviors are developmentally predictable. Children will go through these stages whether the parent works or not. Often, time alone will resolve the situation. Sometimes simple changes within the family work miracles.

Encourage parents to use their *own* knowledge of their children to bring about changes. Do not be too quick to offer advice based on your own experiences. Your family and your child may be quite different. Instead, help parents think through the problem and come up with their own solutions. Discuss your observations of the child's behaviors, and ask them what happens at home. Encourage them to consider the causes, and let

It is important for teachers to support the bond between parents and their children.

them suggest ways to alleviate the problem. Obviously, if they have no suggestions, you can voice your own.

Recognize that parents sometimes express anger toward you as an outlet for their own fatigue. Try not to take it personally. Anger may be a way of expressing guilt about not having more time or energy to spend with their child. In addition, the cost of child care consumes a large portion of one parent's income. Parents may be feeling "I am paying a lot of money for this care. The least you can do is to see that he gets his homework done." If you understand the reasons for parents' frustrations, you can deal with them more easily. Recognition of fatigue helps. Most parents will respond to "It sounds like you have had a really hard day" or "Yes, it is hard to get him to do his homework. Do you have any suggestions as to how I can be any more successful?" Accept differences in family organizations. Examine your own prejudices about what makes a family. If you grew up in a happy, intact family, you may see that as the only alternative. Instead, be open to recognizing the strengths of each family you work with. It will help if you increase your knowledge about the changes that have taken place in the last decade by reading further in the books listed at the end of this chapter.

Encourage families to share their cultural and ethnic traditions with your center. This will be especially important to children in multiracial families. Visit the children's community and talk to the residents. Learn about the different cultures through books, pictures, music, and observation. Actively involve the parents by asking them to share stories, songs, drawings, and experiences that portray important aspects of their culture. One of the best times to involve parents is during holidays. Some parents may be able to spend time in the classroom showing children the way they celebrate. Others may be willing to bring in books, toys, or artifacts that are typical of their background. Still others may welcome an opportunity to get together at a workshop to make presents or decorations for the holiday.

Help all children increase their self-esteem. As you read earlier parts of this chapter, you learned that this is more vital for children in some families than in others. But caregivers know that children who feel good about themselves have a better chance of getting along and of becoming happy, functioning adults. So be aware of ways you can let children know they are liked and successful. A later chapter provides specific strategies and activities.

As a child care worker, you share the responsibility for children's welfare and education not only with parents, but also with elementary school teachers. In a model situation, each of you would have close contact with the other. However, this does not always happen. Although you may see parents daily when they deliver or pick up the child, you seldom have contact with elementary school personnel. If your child care center is located on a public school campus, it is easier to bring about a close working relationship. If your center is outside a school, it is harder to establish a liaison with teachers. When it is impossible for you to work directly with teachers, you can monitor the child's progress in other ways. Ask parents how their children are doing in school. Make sure you know what homework children have each day, and encourage them to get it done. Be aware of when report cards come out, and inquire how children did.

Bulletin boards can provide important information for parents.

Know when to refer parents for outside help. Find out what is available in your community so you can suggest resources. Make referrals when the service needed is not something your center can provide, such as medical or social services. Make referrals when the problem with the child or within the family is acute or longstanding.

Establishing a close relationship with parents can bring about immense rewards for you and the families you work with. Parents will find they are not alone in trying to provide the best for their children. You will find that getting to know parents adds to your ability to help their children.

SUMMARY

- As society has changed, the definition of a family has evolved. Several types of families are now recognized: the nuclear family, the extended family, single-parent families, and single-gender families.

- Divorced parents remarry and combine their families, sometimes conceiving additional children. Multiracial families may combine persons from widely different races or cultures.

- Single-gender couples have been able to incorporate children into their partnerships.

- The nuclear family no longer always has a stay-at-home mother who cares for the children while the father goes to work. Both parents frequently work, leaving children to care for themselves or be cared for by others.

- Single-parent families are often compared unfavorably with two-parent families. More recent information indicates that children do equally well with a single parent.

  Divorce can have a profound effect on children's lives, but new research indicates that children's reactions depend on the quality of their relationship with each parent before separation, the intensity of parental conflict, and parents' ability to focus on their needs.

- Probably the most serious difficulty for the single-parent family, especially when headed by the mother, is low economic status.
- Although adults see remarriage as an opportunity to start over, children in blended families may experience some difficulties.
- Children of multiracial marriages and single-gender couples may be the targets of discrimination.
- Close contact between parents, school, and caregivers is vital. Working parents suffer stresses and pressures. Caregivers can help by being understanding.

KEY TERMS

extended family   reconstituted or   single-parent family
multiracial family   blended family
nuclear (intact) family   single-gender family

REVIEW QUESTIONS

1. How has the definition of the word "family" changed?

2. List and describe three family forms.

3. What is the most common serious difficulty for the single-parent family headed by a woman?

4. What are the advantages to children when a parent remarries?

5. What are the challenges and opportunities faced by children in multiracial families?

6. List three characteristics of an effective family.

7. What are the advantages and disadvantages for children who live with a father-only household?

8. How does poverty affect children?

9. List some ways that child care staff members can share the responsibility for children's welfare with parents and elementary school teachers.

10. What is your most important function as a caregiver?

Case Study

For Mrs. Jolie and her family, the day begins long before it gets light. She and her children are on early, tight schedules to get to their various daytime commitments. Mrs. Jolie must travel 40 miles to her job as a middle school teacher and must leave the house at 6:45. Often her oldest daughter leaves even earlier, at 6:30, for before-school activities at her high school. Victor, age 10, is supposed to be picked up at 6:55 by the transporter service his mother has hired. This morning when it doesn't arrive, he tries to reach his mother, but she is still en route to her school. At 7:20 he calls the key leader at his child care center. Chris, the leader, tells him not to panic and to keep cool, and they will work to contact his mother. He assures Victor that his mom will have a solution. Chris leaves a message for Mrs. Jolie at her school's office. She returns his call immediately on arriving at the school, and quickly arranges other transportation for Victor.

Mrs. Jolie was really upset that this happened and said she felt guilty she had to leave her children to go to work. She has been divorced for only six months and knows that it has been hard on the children.

1. How would you assess the children's ability to cope with a divorce and a working mother?

2. Is there anything that Mrs. Jolie can do to prevent another upsetting incident like this?

3. What can you say to Mrs. Jolie?

STUDENT ACTIVITIES

1. Prepare a collage depicting your own family. You can do this on a large piece of poster board using cutout pictures, words, and phrases from magazines. Display this collage to your class. Ask class members to discuss the family portrayed in the collage, and verify or refute your classmates' impressions.

2. Visit a child care center when parents are arriving to pick up their children. Write a short paper on your impressions of parent–teacher–child relationships.

3. Bring to class an object that is meaningful to your family and representative of some aspect of your culture. It can be a picture, poem, story, an article of clothing, or a handcrafted object. Show it to classmates and discuss its significance to you. Following the completion of all the presentations, discuss what you have learned. Have you learned something new about your own or another classmate's culture?

4. Interview a single parent and a family with both a mother and a father. Ask them to describe the situations that create the most stress for them

and their children. Are there similarities between the two families? What are the differences?

5. Log on to the Web Resources listed below for this chapter. What kinds of information are available for child care workers? What is there for parents? How would you use the information to help the families in your program?

SUGGESTED READINGS

Brand, S. (1996). Making parent involvement a reality: Helping teachers develop partnerships. *Young Children*, 51(2), 76–81.

Kornbluh, K. (2008). Parent trap: Working parents have twenty-two fewer hours a week to spend with their kids than they did thirty years ago. *The Atlantic Monthly*, 291, Jan–Feb. 2003.

McLanahan, S. (1994). *Growing up with a single parent*. Cambridge: Harvard University Press.

Miller, P. A., Ryan, P., & Morrison, W. (1999). Practical strategies for helping children of divorce in today's classroom. *Childhood Education*, 75(5), 285–289.

Morrison, G. M., Storino, M. H., Robertson, L. M., Weissglass T., & Dondero, A. (2000). The protective function of after-school programming and parent education and support for students at risk for substance abuse. *Evaluation and Program Planning*, 23, 365–371.

Smith, E. (2007) The role of afterschool settings in positive youth development. *Journal of Adolescent Health*, 41, 219–220.

Wallerstein, J. (1993). Children after divorce. *Human development*. Guilford, CT: Duskin.

Wolpert, E. (1999). *Start seeing diversity: The basic guide to an anti-bias classroom*. St. Paul, MN: Redleaf.

WEB RESOURCES

http://www.childadvocate.net
The Child Advocate serves the needs of children, families, and professionals while addressing mental health, medical, education, legal, and legislative issues.

http://www.actionforchildren.org
The Action for Children site provides a wide variety of services to parents and child care centers.

REFERENCES

Ariel, J. (2003). Gay and lesbian families. Retrieved from Internet, 2009.

Berger, K. S. (2000). *The developing person through childhood and adolescence* (5th ed.). New York: Worth.

Burrello, K. N. (2004). What are the strengths of interracial families? Virginia, Diversity Training Group, Inc., 2004.

Children's Defense Fund. (2004). *The state of America's children, 2004*. Washington, DC.

Day, A. (2006). The power of social support: Mentoring and resilience. Reclaiming child and youth, 14(4), 196–198.

Hawkins, A. J., & Eggebeen, D. J. (1991). Are fathers fungible? *Journal of Marriage and the Family*, 51, 958–972.

Howard, J. (1978). *Families*. New York: Simon and Schuster.

Kurdek, L. (1989). Relationship quality for newly married husbands and wives: Marital history, stepchildren and individual predictors. *Journal of Marriage and the Family*, 52, 1053–1064.

McKeever, K. (2009). Single parents do as well as two. *Ohio State University news release*, August 31, 2009.

McLanahan, S. S. (1997). Parent absence or poverty: Which matters more? In G.J. Duncan & J. Brooks-Gunn (Eds.). *Consequences of Growing Up Poor*. New York: Russell Sage Foundation.

Melamed, J. Esq. (2009). Mediating Divorce Agreement. Retrieved from Internet, 2009.

Simons, R. L. (1996). *Understanding Differences between Divorced and Intact Families*. Thousand Oaks, CA: Sage.

Single fathers: Doing it all. (1995). *Ebony*, 50, 60.

U.S. Bureau of the Census. (2002, March). *Children's living arrangements and characteristics: Washington, DC*.

SECTION 2

How Children Grow and Develop

49

4

Development in Middle Childhood: Physical

CHILD DEVELOPMENT AND THE LEARNING ENVIRONMENT

The years between ages five and twelve bring about changes in children that make them more independent of adult assistance in the conduct of their daily activities. Children master new physical skills fairly easily when they have opportunities to practice those skills. Children's health is improved, and illnesses and death occur less frequently than during infancy and preschool years or later in adolescence.

Gender differences in physical development and ability are minimal. Most children feel competent to manage their school and home lives, and they want to perform in ways that earn recognition from adults.

A knowledge of the universal, predictable stages of growth as well as an understanding of individual patterns of timing are absolutely essential for anyone involved in planning and operating a child care program. The quality of a program may depend on a variety of factors, but a major determinant is the extent to which activities and procedures are appropriate for the developmental level of participating children. The learning environment and program activities should be based on an assessment of children's cognitive, social, emotional, and physical abilities at each stage of their development. The program should also provide challenges to promote further development. Knowledge of child development enables adults to choose effective techniques for guiding an individual child's behavior and planning strategies for group interactions. Further, an understanding of child development enables child care leaders to communicate more effectively with parents about a child's progress.

The study of human development examines how individuals grow and change over a lifetime, how they remain the same, and how some individuals may vary from typical

LEARNING OUTCOMES

After reading this chapter, you should be able to:

✔ Discuss the importance of understanding child development, and the differences between development and learning.

✔ Understand major changes and variations in physical growth patterns among children.

✔ State the causes of obesity and how child care staff members can help children and families.

✔ Describe the chronic health conditions children suffer.

✔ Describe the motor skills children develop during middle childhood.

What physical skills are these children using?

nature
a variety of characteristics that are inherited from parents

nurture
all the experiences and influences people are exposed to from the moment of conception on throughout a lifetime

maturation
progression of changes that takes place as people age

learning
processes by which environmental influences and experiences bring about permanent changes in thinking, feeling and behavior

patterns. Several characteristics of individuals are programmed by genetic makeup at the time of conception, whereas other traits result from environmental conditions and experiences. The relative importance of one over the other, known as "*nature vs. nurture,*" is a topic for debate among developmental researchers.

Nature refers to a variety of characteristics—such as eye color and body type—that are inherited from parents. Physical limitations and certain diseases are also inherited, as well as some personality characteristics such as activity level or verbal ability. **Nurture** refers to all the experiences and influences people are exposed to from the moment of conception throughout their lifetime.

The dichotomy of influences on human development is also portrayed as "maturation vs. learning." **Maturation** indicates the progression of changes that takes place as people age. **Learning** refers to the processes by which environmental influences and experiences bring about permanent changes in thinking, feeling, and behavior.

The basic question is the same no matter what labels are used. How much of development and human behavior results from genetic inheritance, and how much is the result of all of life's experiences? Most developmentalists believe that both are important and that, in fact, the interaction between them is the determining factor in a person's pattern of growth.

PHYSICAL DEVELOPMENT

Middle childhood is a time when children grow more slowly than they did in the preschool years, and they will not experience another growth spurt until they approach adolescence.

School-age children master many physical skills.

Height and Weight

A typical six-year-old is at least three and a half feet tall and weighs between 40 and 50 pounds (National Center for Health Statistics, 2008). Up to the age of nine, boys and girls are about the same size, but then girls start to pull ahead in both height and weight. Around age nine or ten, girls begin a growth spurt that precedes adolescence. By the end of the elementary years, girls are generally taller and heavier than boys. School-age children seem slimmer than they did during the preschool years because their body proportions change, and they begin to look more like adults. Their arms and legs get longer, their torsos elongate, and their faces are thinner.

Yet there are wide variations in their appearance. Variations in body size could be due to malnutrition. Children who are well nourished will be taller than their contemporaries growing up in poverty. Genetics also plays a large part in determining size and rate of maturity. Although adults may understand that variations in size and timing of maturity are normal, it is often difficult for children to accept these differences. Physical development can affect peer relationships because children often choose friends who have a pleasing appearance and are physically, academically, or socially capable (Hartup, 1983). Children who are shorter, taller, or heavier than their peers, as well as those who are less capable, may face rejection.

The onset of puberty and the beginning of menstrual periods—as well as how their peers perceive them—affect children's self-image. According to Chris Hayward (2003), some girls reach menarche as early as 12.2 years. An article by Chumlea et al. (2003) reported that 10 percent of girls start to menstruate before 11 years of age, and 90 percent are menstruating by 12.43 years. This is accompanied by physical changes such as the development of breasts and the appearance of pubic hair. These girls report more emotional problems than others, including depression, anxiety, and disruption of social interactions with their peers.

OBESITY

Obesity is a growing problem among children and can seriously affect a child emotionally as well as physically. A 2008 study done by the American Academy of Child & Adolescent Psychiatry (AACAP) found that between 16 and 33 percent of children and adolescents are obese. Whether a child is overweight rather than just childishly chubby can be determined by figuring the ratio of weight to height, a measure called body-mass index or **BMI**. BMI is found by dividing weight in kilograms by height in meters squared (BMI = kg/m^2). This number can be interpreted using charts provided by the Centers for Disease Control and Prevention (CDC) and should take into account differences in age and sex. Further assessment should include determining whether a child has excess fat by doing a skin-fold test, evaluating diet, physical activity, and family history (CDC, 2009).

Overweight children are subject to several health risks, including higher blood pressure and blood cholesterol levels. These children may also have orthopedic or respiratory problems. As obesity rates climb, the onset of diabetes in childhood has become more prevalent in young children and adolescents. The CDC reported in 2005 that one in every 400 to 600 children and adolescents had type 1 diabetes. The risk is that obese children will become overweight adults, prone to the same problems, with the added probability of developing gallbladder disease, arthritis, and some forms of cancer (Sothern & Gordon, 2003).

In addition, serious psychological distress can occur in obese children. Low self-esteem increases the risk of anxiety, sadness, loneliness, and depression, and makes these children more vulnerable to engaging in high-risk behaviors such as drug and alcohol abuse. Their unhappiness leads them to further curtail participation in sports or other activities with their peers; overeating becomes a way to compensate for their sadness (Eckart, 2007).

Thus, patterns are established that carry over into adulthood; overweight children frequently become overweight adults (University of Iowa, 2004). It is estimated that 60 to 80 percent of obese children become overweight adults (Lucas, 1991). Stigmatization and discrimination against obese people has been documented in employment and educational opportunities (Puhl & Brownell, 2001).

Causes of Obesity

There is no one cause of obesity; rather, it results from an interaction between several possible conditions. Patterns are often established in infancy and continue into adulthood.

- **Heredity.** Several factors that contribute to obesity are inherited: body type, height and bone structure, the amount and distribution of fat, metabolic rate, and activity level.

obesity
high BMI number

BMI
body mass index; a measure of the ratio of weight to height

A child who is overweight rather than just childishly chubby can be determined by figuring the ratio of weight to height, a measure called body mass index or BMI.

- **Activity level.** Children who are more active are less likely to be overweight because they burn more calories. Although activity level is influenced by heredity, an individual's willingness to engage in active play also affects weight. For some children, the unavailability of safe places to play will also be a factor.
- **Television watching.** Children younger than age eight spend two and a half hours a day watching TV. Older children, ages eight and up, watch four and a half hours of TV a day (Overweight and Obesity, 2007). Children are not only inactive when they watch television, they are also bombarded with commercials for foods that are high in fat and sugar. These are the foods they choose to snack on while they watch television.
- **Sedentary activities.** Some children spend a lot of their out-of-school time using mobile phones and pagers to text their friends, or using the computer to play games, e-mail friends, or log on to social networking or blog sites.
- **High-calorie foods.** Overweight children are not necessarily over-eaters. However, much of the food they consume is high in calories. Many children take in large quantities of high-calorie soft drinks, chips, high-fat hamburgers, and french fries. Often, too, parents give in to their children's demands for the high-calorie snack foods shown on television ads.
- **Attitudes toward food.** In some families, children are encouraged to consume large portions of food as a measure of the family's prosperity or a parent's love for their children. Often, too, food becomes a symbol for love and comfort, causing children to overeat when they are stressed or unhappy. Parents who offer special foods as a reward or comfort set up a lifelong habit that can lead to obesity.
- **Specific event.** A traumatic event in a child's life can be a precipitating factor in the onset of increased weight gain. Hospitalization, parental divorce, the death of someone close to the child, or even a move to a new neighborhood all can cause distress, along with the need for a substitute gratification in the form of food.
- **Physiological problems.** A small number of cases of obesity in children can be traced to abnormalities in the growth process or metabolism (Lowrey, 1986). Obesity is only one part of the problem that usually includes disturbances in normal physical and mental growth. Only about 1 percent of childhood obesity can be attributed to this cause, however.

Implications for Child Care Staff Members

Within any group of school-age children, particularly if there is a wide age span, there will be children of many sizes, shapes, and stages of development. Children compare their own appearance with their peers, and as a result often think they are too tall, too little, too heavy, or too thin. In addition, children who vary noticeably from their peers tend to get teased and labeled with unflattering names. Differing from the norm can cause a great deal of anguish and loss of self-esteem.

- An important task for adults who have responsibility for children's welfare is to assure them they are accepted no matter how they look, and to help their peers be accepting. Further, children need to know that they will change as they grow and develop.
- Caregivers should be especially sensitive to girls who have reached early puberty. They may need to help girls accept their body differences as well as providing the equipment these girls may require.
- Obese children need special attention to help them change their eating patterns and activity level. They can learn about good nutrition and how to prepare good-tasting, low-calorie foods. See Chapter 15 for ideas on this topic that can be used in child care. Although increased activity is the best way to lose weight, obese children have a difficult time participating in active sports or games. Other children often reject them as team members and tease them if they try to join in games. It is important to encourage obese children to start somewhere: walking to school, bicycling, or participating in the exercises suggested in Chapter 15.
- The children's families need help to change the environment that created the obesity, whether in the foods they eat, in parental interactions, or in the kinds of activities children are encouraged to engage in. Remember that talking about food and weight is a sensitive issue for many parents. Therefore, in a nonjudgmental way, provide parents with information about nutrition. Help them find ways to discipline or reward their children other than with food. Also, make suggestions for active things the family can do together.
- Caregivers are responsible for planning and preparing nutritious snacks that are not high in fat, salt, or sugar. Use the Food Guide Pyramid as a basis for choosing appropriate snacks.

HEALTH CONDITIONS

During middle childhood, children may suffer from a variety of health conditions. The number of children with chronic health conditions has dramatically increased in the past four decades (Perrin, Bloom & Gortmaker, 2007). A chronic health condition is one that limits usual daily activities or qualifies the child for Supplemental Security Income (SSI). One million children were receiving SSI in 2005; 20 percent of these had mental retardation, 46 percent had other mental conditions, and 34 percent had various physical conditions. Asthma affects 9 percent of children and adolescents in the United States, doubling the number since the 1980s. Approximately 6 percent of school-age children are diagnosed with attention-deficit/hyperactivity disorder (ADHD).

Conditions that are not chronic but are prevalent during the school years are communicable diseases and hearing, vision, or ambulatory limitations. Early sexual behavior leads to preadolescent pregnancies and sexually transmitted diseases, including HIV and AIDS. Drug and alcohol abuse also can occur at the elementary school level.

Poverty contributes to the poor health status of many children. According to the Children's Defense Fund (2004), 12.1 million children under age 18 were living in poverty in 2002. Nearly 14 percent of these children have no health insurance coverage. Because of their living conditions, they are subject to poor nutrition, inadequate prevention care, and little treatment for chronic conditions.

Implications for Child Care Staff Members

Caregivers can do a great deal to help children learn to maintain a healthy lifestyle and help parents take responsibility for ensuring that their children's health needs are met.

- Help children evaluate the messages they receive from their environment concerning health. Provide activities that encourage them to question images of people having fun while smoking cigarettes, eating "junk" foods, or consuming alcoholic beverages.
- Include program activities that stress good nutrition. Allow children to participate in choosing and preparing food.
- Offer only nutritious meals and snacks. Offer supplementary nutrition to children who may be undernourished.
- Provide space within the physical facility for activities that encourage health and fitness.
- Model behavior that demonstrates fitness. Do not smoke or consume non-nutritious foods.
- Become informed about community health services and resources. Refer parents to appropriate facilities.

MOTOR SKILLS

During the elementary school period, children develop a wide variety of motor skills, particularly when they have ample opportunities to practice and are encouraged to try new things. Five-year-olds endlessly practice running, jumping, and throwing. Gradually their timing and coordination increase, enabling them to become noticeably more proficient. They soon learn to judge the time when they should swing a bat in order to hit a ball or estimate the distance a ball will travel when thrown in order to catch it. Along with developing physical skills, children also acquire new ways to get along with their peers and begin to understand the importance of rules. The interaction of these developing abilities accounts for the popularity of sports during middle childhood.

Gross-Motor Skills

Several skills that children acquire in middle childhood occur in play activities typical of this period. Developmentally appropriate practices for school-age children should include opportunities to develop both gross- and fine-motor skills (Albrecht & Plantz, 1993).

- **Running.** By age five or six, most children have mastered the form and power required to run. They have learned to start, stop, and turn, and can integrate these movements into their play activities.
- **Jumping.** Jumping requires a complex set of skills including balance, maintenance of equilibrium, and form. Jumping is usually not attempted by children until they have become fairly proficient in basic locomotion, but by age five most children have a good mastery of jumping skills.
- **Throwing.** At age five or six, there is a perceptible change in children's ability to throw. They learn to transfer their weight from one foot to the other during the act of throwing. This weight shift, coupled with a horizontal movement of the arms and body, allows children to efficiently propel a ball forward. Most six-year-olds are able to perform an overhand throw.

Further practice and refinement of gross-motor skills allow children to participate in the popular activities of childhood: swimming, biking, roller skating, ice skating, jumping rope, baseball, and basketball.

Fine-Motor Skills

During middle childhood, most children master a variety of tasks requiring the use of small muscles. They learn to cut easily with scissors; draw, write or print accurately; and sew or knit. As their coordination increases further, they can learn to play musical instruments, engage in hobbies such as model making, or play games requiring fine-motor skills such as jacks.

Differences in Motor Skills

Boys and girls are fairly equal in their physical abilities during the middle childhood years, except that boys have greater forearm strength and girls have greater flexibility. Boys are often better at baseball, while girls excel in gymnastics. More and more girls are willing to try sports like baseball and,when given ample opportunities to practice, they, too, can catch and throw a ball accurately and hit well. Likewise, with training, boys can do well in activities that require flexibility, such as gymnastics.

Certain motor skills do not depend on the amount of practice a youngster engages in. Some motor skills depend on body size, brain maturation, or inherent talents. A good example of a skill dependent on brain maturation is reaction time—the length of time it takes to respond to a particular stimulus. An example of this is when a child can swing a baseball bat in time to hit the ball. A child's brain continues to mature into adolescence; therefore, older children usually do better where this skill is necessary.

Inherent traits are also important in determining how well a particular child performs a motor skill. Body size, particularly height, gives some children an advantage when playing basketball. Children also vary in their ability to coordinate body movements. Some children find it easy to kick a soccer ball with accuracy, while others find it almost impossible. Heredity accounts for children's basic skill at these activities, but practice and experience can increase their proficiency.

"I like to play baseball." Lark, age 8.

With practice, children can participate in difficult sport activities.

Implications for Child Care Staff Members

Middle childhood is a time when children want to feel competent at whatever they do. In school they must use small muscles to be successful, while out of school they need well-developed gross-motor skills to participate in the sports, vigorous games, and strenuous individual activities that are so much a part of the school-age years. Because practice and experience help children enhance their inherited abilities and acquire new skills, it is extremely important that child care offer as many opportunities as possible. Child care leaders can:

- Provide a wide variety of activities requiring different skills and skills at varying levels.
- Allow children ample time to practice and refine new skills.
- Encourage both genders to participate in all activities.
- Offer children encouragement for their efforts rather than praise their achievements.
- Encourage children to teach their skills to others.
- Discourage competition.

SUMMARY

- A knowledge of the universal predictable stages of growth, as well as an understanding of individual patterns of timing, are essential for anyone involved in planning and operating a child care program.

- Human growth is affected both by maturation and learning. Maturation refers to a variety of inherited abilities, characteristics, and limits. Learning refers to environmental influences and experiences that change thinking, feeling, and behavior.

- Children grow more slowly during middle childhood than they did in the preschool years.

- Obesity is a growing problem among children, and can affect a child emotionally as well as physically.

- Causes of obesity are heredity, activity level, types of food consumed, and attitudes toward food. In addition, specific events and psychological problems can trigger overeating.

- Child care leaders can help children accept the way they look and understand that as they grow, they will change.

- School-age children may suffer from a variety of health conditions, both chronic and non-chronic.

- During middle childhood, children rapidly acquire a variety of new gross-motor and fine-motor skills.

- Child care leaders can provide many opportunities for children to participate in a wide variety of activities requiring the use of large or small muscles.

KEY TERMS

BMI   maturation   nurture
learning   nature   obesity

REVIEW QUESTIONS

1. Why is it important for child care leaders to have a knowledge of the predictable stages of growth and an understanding of individual patterns of timing?

2. Differentiate between maturation and growth.

3. What is another way to describe the dichotomy of influences on human development?

4. How much will an average well-nourished child gain in weight and height per year? The typical 10-year-old will weigh _____ pounds and be _____ inches tall.

5. Boys and girls are about the same size for part of the middle childhood years. At what age do girls begin to increase in size faster than boys?

6. List the causes of obesity in children.

7. In what ways can child care personnel help children whose body size differ from the norm or who are obese?

8. List eight motor skills developed by children during middle childhood. In what ways do children use these skills in their daily lives at school or at home?

9. In what ways do the motor skills of boys and girls differ?

10. What can child care leaders do to help children enhance their inherited abilities and acquire more skills?

Case Study

Nine-year-old Ian is often called names by some of the other children. They refer to him as "Tubby," "Fatso," or "Lardo." He gets very angry and starts hitting, although sometimes he ends up crying in frustration. His caregiver has noticed that he seems to have an ample supply of snacks that he carries in his backpack—often chips and candy bars. He wants to have those for snack time rather than the food provided by the center. When his request is refused, he stomps away from the table and refuses to eat anything. Occasionally, he is seen sneaking food from his locker.

1. How would you respond when Ian stomps away from the table?

2. What can you say to his parents?

3. What can you do to help Ian change his eating pattern at child care?

STUDENT ACTIVITIES

1. Ask the children in your child care group to draw pictures of themselves and one best friend. Do they show themselves as taller or shorter than the friend? Is there any noticeable difference between the attractiveness of their own image and that of the friend?

2. Write a paragraph describing your appearance when you were six. Include the kinds of activities you engaged in during your out-of-school time. Next, describe yourself when you were 11. In what ways did your development follow the description in this chapter? In what ways did it differ?

3. Watch two hours of Saturday morning children's television programs. Count and list the commercials for food that are shown. How many ads promote high-fat, high-sugar, or high-salt foods? Do they show children having fun while consuming these foods? Discuss the impact these commercials might have on children.

4. Survey the neighborhood near your home or child care center. Are there places where children can play outdoors? How do you think the environment affects the children who live there? What could be done to increase opportunities for physical activities? Share your information with your classmates.

SUGGESTED READINGS

American Academy of Pediatrics, Author. (2006). A Parent's guide to childhood obesity: A roadmap to health. American Academy of Pediatrics.

Gartrell, D. (2007). Guidance matters; "You really worked hard on your picture." Guiding with encouragement. *Young Children*, 62(3), 58–59.

Hubbard, V. S. (1995). Future directions in obesity research. In Lilian W. Y. Cheung & Julius B. Bichmond (Eds.), *Child health, nutrition, and physical activity*. Champaign, IL: Human Kinetics.

Rimm, S. Sr. & Rimm, E. (2004). *Rescuing the Emotional Lives of Overweight Children*. PA: Rodale, Inc.

Smith, J. C. (1999). *Understanding Childhood Obesity*. Mississippi: University Press.

WEB RESOURCES

http://www.childobesity.com
Resources for parents and health professionals.

http://www.aacap.org
Discusses the problems, causes, risks and management of childhood obesity.

http://www.eric.ed.gov
ERIC Clearinghouse on Elementary and Early Childhood Education (EBIC.EECE): digital based library of educational research.

REFERENCES

Albrecht, K., & Plantz, M. (1993). *Developmentally Appropriate Practice in School-Age Child Care Programs.* Dubuque, IA: Kendall/Hunt.

American Academy of Child & Adolescent Psych (2008). Obesity in Children and Teens. Retrieved for the Internet http://www.aacap.org, 2009.

American Dietetic Association (1999). Dietary guidance for healthy children aged 2 to 11 years. *Journal of the American Dietetic Association*, 99, 93–100.

Blackwell, D. L., Vickerie, J. I., & Wondimy, E. A. (2003). Summary health statistics for U.S. children. National Health Interview Survey. National Center for Health Statistics. *Vital Health Statistics* 10, 213.

CDC (Centers for Disease Control and Prevention) (2002). About BMI for children and Teens. http://www.cdc.gov/healthy weight/assessing/bmi/childrens_bmi/about_childrens_bmi.htm.

CDC (2005). National Diabetes Fact Sheet. Retrieved from the Internet, http://www.cdc.gov/pubs/pdf/ndfs.2007.pdf.

Children's Defense Fund (2004). *The state of America's children, 2004.* Washington, DC: Author.

Chumlea, W. C., Schubert, C. M., Roche, A. F., Kulin, H. E., Lee, P. A., Himes, J. H., & Sun, S. S. (2003). Age at menarche and racial comparison in US girls. *Journal of American Pediatrics*, 111(1), 110–113.

Eckert, E. (2007). To Be the Fat Kid. Retrieved from the Internet, http://www.associatedcontent.com/article/221465

Gortmaker, S. L., Dietz, W. H., Sobol, A. M., & Wehler, C. A. (1987). Increasing pediatric obesity in the United States. *American Journal of Diseases of Children*, 141, 535–540.

Hartup, W. (1983). Peer relations. In Paul H. Mussen (Ed.), *Handbook of Child Psychology: Vol. 4. Socialization, Personality and Social Development.* New York: John Wiley & Sons.

Hayward, C. (2003). *Gender Differences at Puberty.* New York: Cambridge University Press.

National Center for Health Statistics (NCHS). Data from Fels Research Institute, Yellow Springs, Ohio.

Lucas, A. (1991). Eating disorders. In M. Lewis (Ed.), *Child and Adolescent Psychiatry: A Comprehensive Textbook.* Baltimore: Williams & Wilkins.

Overweight and Obesity (2007). Betrieved from http://www.revolutionhealth.com, October 2007.

Perrin, J. M., Bloom, S. R., Gortmaker, S. L., (2007). The increase of childhood chronic conditions in the United States. *Journal of the American Medical Association*, 297(24), June 27, 2007.

Puhl, B., & Brownell, K.D., (2001). Bias, Discrimination, and Obesity. *Obesity Research*, 9, 788–805.

Serdula, M., Ivory, D., Coates, B., Freedman, D., Williamson, D., & Byers, T. (1993). Do obese children become obese adults? A review of the literature. *Preventive Medicine*, 22, 167–177.

Sothern, M. & Gordon, S. (2003). Prevention of obesity in children: a critical challenge for medical professionals. *Clinical Pediatrics*, 42, 101–111.

5

Development in Middle Childhood: Cognitive

COGNITIVE THEORIES

Cognitive theories are used to explain all the mental processes that enable children to think or acquire knowledge and the way these processes affect how they perceive and understand their experiences. How individual children function depends partly on hereditary factors and partly on the children's experiences. As children's brains grow and mature, they are able to use different cognitive skills to gather and process information.

The thinking processes of school-age children are markedly different from those of preschoolers. By middle childhood, children can selectively focus on tasks; that is, they are able to screen out distractions and concentrate on the relevant parts of the information at hand. This capacity helps them to remember and to reason in logical steps to solve a problem. School-age children also learn strategies for increasing memory. These are called **storage strategies**. With these strategies, children rehearse the information, organize it into memorable units, or use mnemonic devices such as rhymes or mental images to aid in remembering. Language develops rapidly and is used to communicate ideas, interact with others, and develop the competencies required by the society in which children live. All these abilities enable school-age children to perform tasks beyond the reach of younger children.

This chapter will examine the major theorists who contributed to an understanding of how children's cognitive development proceeds. These include: Jean Piaget, who contributed an understanding of how children think and learn; several behaviorists who understood the impact of behavior modification through rewards and punishment; and Vygotsky's social learning theory, which stressed the importance of different societies' values and makeup.

LEARNING OUTCOMES

After reading this chapter, you should be able to:

✔ Discuss the major principles of several cognitive theories.

✔ List the concerns expressed by critics of each theory as well as the points of agreement.

✔ Describe the ways in which child care leaders can use each theory to enhance children's development.

✔ Discuss the ways in which children develop and use language, including second language learning.

Children's thinking changes, and they are able to use logic to solve problems.

JEAN PIAGET

The Swiss psychologist Jean Piaget was an important contributor to the understanding of how children think and learn. He began his work with children by helping to develop the first intelligence test. Piaget's task was to interview children and find the age at which most children could answer the test questions correctly. Instead, Piaget became curious about children's incorrect responses to items on the test, and he observed that children who were the same age gave similar answers. This observation began a lifelong search into understanding children's thought processes and how these processes change with age.

Piaget (1952) concluded that cognitive development follows predictable patterns through four major stages. Each stage has certain characteristics that form the basis for how children approach and process intellectual tasks. Everyone proceeds through these stages at his or her own rate—some slower, some faster—but everyone goes through them. Each stage is built on the skills of the previous stage. Piaget called the period from birth to two years the **sensorimotor period**. During this time, infants use all their senses to explore and learn about the world around them. They put objects in their mouths, become attentive to sounds, poke or pat objects, react to tastes, and follow out-of-reach objects with their eyes. The information they gather is experience based: they can understand only what they experience directly. They retain limited memory of an object or experience when the object is removed or the experience ended.

By contrast, preschool children, aged two to seven, are in the **preoperational period** during which they can begin to think symbolically.

storage strategies
methods children use to increase their memory

sensorimotor period
Piaget's first period, in which infants use all their senses to explore and learn about the world around them

preoperational period
ability to begin to think symbolically and to remember experiences and objects independently of the immediate encounter

They can remember experiences and objects independently of the immediate encounter. This is evident in their rapidly developing ability to use language. Words help them remember past events or talk about an object. They also begin to engage in pretend play, not always needing the real props to support the play. Preschool children can play out elaborate scenarios in which they relive familiar interactions with parents or with siblings.

Piaget observed that during the preoperational period children often come to the wrong conclusions. He believed that this was because they could not perform "operations." By operations Piaget meant the ability to internalize an action—that is, carry it out in the mind and understand it can go in one direction or reverse into the opposite direction. The preoperational child cannot perform these operations.

Piaget observed the difficulty children had with one of his conservation experiments. He placed two identical cylinders with equal amounts of liquid before four-year-olds. He then added two cylinders: one tall and slim, the other short. He poured the liquid from one glass into the tall cylinder and from the other into the short one. When asked which glass had more, most children would indicate the taller one. They could not mentally reverse the event to realize that, when poured back into the original containers, the amounts were equal. In addition to an inability to imagine reversibility, children at this age can focus on only one dimension of a form at a time. In the case of the liquids, they focused on the height of the fluid in the glasses. Piaget called this **centering**.

Another characteristic of preoperational children is that they believe everyone thinks and acts the same way they do. They are egocentric—incapable of understanding how others think or feel.

Between the ages of seven and 11, children are in the **concrete operations** stage. They begin to think symbolically and can imagine reversing processes. The word "concrete" means that children can carry out this process only when the information is presented concretely.

If a child is asked how many pieces of fruit there are if she has two apples and a friend gives her one, she will be able to figure out the answer. She can imagine two apples and then one additional one. She has experienced apples, can imagine them, and can execute the solution. It would be somewhat more difficult for her to figure out the answer to the question "What is half of a dozen?"

During this period children become less egocentric and much more social. Increased language skills enable them to interact more effectively with their peers and to begin to understand the views of others. The need to be a part of a group or to have friends requires discussion and negotiations over play activities. In the process, children learn that others do not always think or feel the same way they do.

Piaget's last stage, **formal operations**, occurs between the ages of 11 and 15. During this period adolescents are able to consider hypothetical problems without concrete examples. They also are not limited by having to consider the here and now, but can imagine situations they have not yet experienced or that are abstract. Thus, adolescents begin to ponder questions about the effects of global warming or the importance of preserving

centering
Piaget's observation that young children focus on only one dimension of a form at a time

concrete operations
ability to think symbolically and to reverse processes when information is presented concretely

formal operations
ability to consider hypothetical problems without concrete examples

wilderness areas for future generations to enjoy. They question the wisdom of using war as a way to resolve conflicts or what to do about the starving peoples of less-developed countries.

Several general principles underlie the concepts of Piaget's theory, and these are important to fully understand his perception of how children think and learn.

- Children are active participants in the development of their own intelligence. Piaget believed that children actually *construct* their knowledge of the world through their activities. Experiences are the raw ingredients from which children organize and structure their knowledge, implying that the process takes place within the child rather than being transmitted from the outside. Through experimenting with objects and experiences in their environment, children actually create their own intelligence.
- The development of intelligence is the result of a progression through stages. Each stage builds a foundation for the next one. There is no finite division of the stages because each stage may carry vestiges of the previous period. Thus, school-age children may function at a preschool level at times or in certain situations.
- Due to differences in maturation rates, individuals progress through the stages at different rates. However, each individual goes through the same stages in the same order.

Evaluation of Piaget's Theory

Piaget's ideas changed the perception of children's intellectual development, focusing more on how children come to know rather than on what they know (K. S. Berger, 2000). Yet there are criticisms from those who point to the formal nature of his experiments. These critics state that when children are watched closely in everyday situations, different interpretations of their abilities are possible. Some skills that Piaget relegates to later stages are clearly present in earlier ones. Therefore, critics contend that Piaget must have been wrong about just how early some cognitive skills develop.

Those who have looked closely at Piagetian theory also express concern that children's abilities are not homogeneous within a given stage. In fact, children enter each stage gradually, with vestiges of the previous stage remaining for a period of time. Additional factors affect children's ability to think consistently at an expected level for their stage of development. Hereditary differences in abilities and aptitudes, as well as timing of maturation, play an important part. Environmental factors—the kinds of experiences children are exposed to and the education they receive—also influence the rate of intellectual development.

Criticisms of Piaget's theory do not negate the importance of his ideas, however. It is commonly accepted that children proceed developmentally from one stage to the next, changing their thinking processes as their maturity and experiences dictate. They continue to learn, taking in new information, organizing it, and deciding how it fits in with previous information.

Implications for Child Care Staff Members

Piaget never claimed to be an educator, yet his theory is widely used to formulate educational programs for children. His theory provides a framework from which appropriate learning experiences can be designed. It enables educators to:

- Provide many different objects and experiences for children to explore so they can incorporate them into their symbolic thinking process later on. There needs to be a balance between unstructured materials and guided ones. Art materials, sand and water, and building materials are examples of unstructured activities. Experiences such as cooking, in which children must follow a recipe, and classifying or seriating a group of objects are guided activities.
- Plan activities that are age-appropriate for the level of ability of most members of the group. In addition, teachers can add activities that meet the needs of individual children.
- Allow plenty of time for children to explore freely and engage in play activities. Through play children have an opportunity to test out their own ideas and find out what is true and what is not.
- Provide experiences that allow children to solve their own problems and make decisions.
- Set up situations in which children can exchange ideas, thus learning that others may think differently than themselves.

BEHAVIORIST LEARNING THEORY

American psychologist John Watson (1967) saw the need for a more precise study of psychology. He believed that, in order to be true science, hypotheses should be tested and measured. The only way that could be done was to measure those things that could be observed: behaviors and words rather than feelings or thoughts. His concepts were popular because they differed from the prevalent psychoanalytic theory of the time.

Watson studied Ivan Pavlov's (1960) **classical conditioning** experiments with animals and used those ideas to formulate his own theory of human conditioning. In classical conditioning, a stimulus (anything that elicits a response, either a reflex or voluntary action) is repeatedly followed by a specific response (behavior). Dogs salivate when they see their food. Pavlov added a ringing bell along with the presentation of the food. After several repetitions, the dogs would salivate when they heard the bell. The result was a connection that allowed the response to occur without the need for stimulus. Another example is a person's response to a favorite food. When presented with that food, the sight and the smell cause a person to salivate in preparation for tasting. When viewing pictures of that food in a magazine or on television, the person often has the same reaction—salivating.

Watson was also influenced by the writings of physician and philosopher John Locke (1959) who was regarded as one of the most influential

classical conditioning
conditioning brought about by proximity of stimulus and response

of the British Enlightenment period. Locke saw human infants as a *tabula rasa*, a blank tablet on which life experiences write a script. According to Watson, human behavior could be shaped by controlling the events to which children were exposed and offering rewards for proper responses. Give children appropriate rewards and the desired behavior will follow. A parent who says "You are being so patient waiting while I pay for our groceries" is giving an appropriate reward to her child.

B. F. Skinner (1953) used both Watson's and Locke's (1959) ideas to formulate his theory. He proposed that infants are "empty organisms" that can be filled with carefully controlled experiences. He agreed that behavior can be changed by conditioning, but saw another type of conditioning that plays a larger role. He called it **operant conditioning**. Children play an active part by operating or acting on their environment and are reinforced for their behaviors. When a behavior is followed by a pleasant response (reward), it is likely to be repeated. If the consequence of a behavior is unpleasant, it is not likely to be repeated. Therefore, a system of positive or negative reinforcers can shape an individual's behavior. Teachers who tell children they have done a good job putting away their materials are using a positive reinforcer. At the next cleanup time, the children are more likely to go about the task willingly.

Albert Bandura (1977) contributed another dimension to the understanding of how learning takes place. He states that some behaviors cannot be explained as a simple conditioned response to a direct stimulus, but occur through less direct learning. He believes children observe others behaving in given ways, and then pattern their own behavior accordingly. This type of social learning is more likely to occur when a person is uncertain or unsure in a situation, and when the object of observation is admired or seen as powerful. Called **modeling**, it is a technique that parents and teachers use to increase the likelihood of acceptable behavior in children. In other words, parents model the behavior they expect of children. It may also explain why four-year-olds pretend to be Superman or teenagers want to dress like their favorite rock star. They are imitating the behavior of people they admire.

operant conditioning
the process by which children act upon their environment and are reinforced for their behaviors

modeling
adults exhibit the behaviors that are expected of children

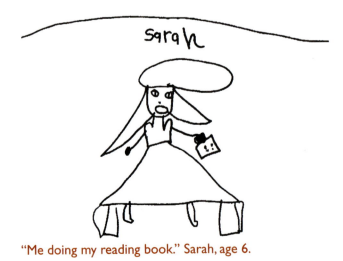

"Me doing my reading book." Sarah, age 6.

Social learning changes as individuals mature. Children are attentive to the behaviors of others, store the information for future retrieval, possibly mentally rehearse the behavior, and then use the information when needed. The consequences of behaviors are also noted. Children can then test out alternative behaviors and choose the one with the best outcome. A school-age child observes that when she gets mad and leaves a game, her friends do not ask her to play next time. She will try to curb her anger in order to be included in the future.

Evaluation of Behaviorism

Learning theories have contributed a great deal to the study of how behaviors are shaped (Berger, 2000). The emphasis on the connection between stimulus and the resulting observable response allows a different interpretation of some kinds of behaviors. Previous notions that behavior is the result of deep-seated emotional problems could be revised by observing the environmental causes of some behaviors. Behavior can then be changed by changing the response from the environment. As an example, when adults praise children for acceptable behavior rather than focusing on punishing unacceptable behavior, children can change. A statement like "Thank you for sitting quietly at story time, Jamal" often proves more effective than saying "Sit down and be quiet or I'll have to remove you from the story area." After a few repetitions, Jamal will likely cease his disruption.

Learning theory has also contributed to a more scientific study of human development. Researchers are pressured to refine their hypotheses, define their terms, devise tests for their hypotheses that can be duplicated, and avoid reliance on concepts they cannot test. Conversely, there are valid criticisms of learning theory. The emphasis on observable behavior and external influences does not take into account the inner life of children. Some behaviors result from complex relationships between biological maturation, an individual's thought processes, and the struggle to make sense of new experiences. Considering observable behaviors only creates an incomplete picture of the wide range of influences on human behavior.

When behaviorist learning theory was first proposed, researchers made claims that behavior modification through a system of rewards and punishments was manipulative. Present day critics still voice the same concerns, and also object to the kinds of reinforcers that parents or teachers sometimes use.

Implications for Child Care Staff Members

Behaviorist theory provides some specific guidelines for adults who work with children.

- Carefully arrange the learning environment. Because the importance of the environment is stressed in behaviorist learning theory, anyone who works with children can use this information to arrange the setting to bring about positive responses. The placement of

Children learn many skills by using computers.

furniture, the ways in which activities are presented, and how adults interact with children, all have to be carefully considered with expected results in mind.

- Use appropriate reinforcers to bring about desired results. Carefully consider the implications of reinforcers, and choose those that will enhance positive, rather than negative, behaviors.
- Model the behavior that you expect of children.
- Provide opportunities for social learning to take place among peers. Children are powerful models and can have extensive influence on one another.
- Help children find behaviors alternative to those that generate negative responses from others.

SOCIOCULTURAL THEORY

Lev Vygotsky (1978, 1987), writing in the early 1900s, was a pioneer in the study of sociocultural influences on learning. Only recently have his writings become available. Vygotsky's theory assumes that social interaction and children's direct participation in authentic cultural activities are necessary for their optimum development. Several main ideas follow this basic assumption.

Cross-Cultural Variation

Cultures differ in the kinds of opportunities they provide for children to develop the competencies they need. Every culture has hopes and expectations for the children growing up within it. These expectations are expressed in terms of competencies or things children need to know or be able to do. A child in rural China will be encouraged to learn vastly different skills from one living in a small village in Alaska.

Vygotsky believed that knowledge and skills are taught by the older and more mature members of a group. In daily interactions within families, school, child care center, and neighborhood groups, children are constantly being shown models or being told directly. Children in rural China work beside their parents, learning how to nurture the crops or perform the daily tasks necessary for their existence. In many rural areas of Alaska, children are considered most competent when they master hunting and gathering skills (Sternberg & Grigorenko, 2004).

Scaffolding

scaffold
support system that supports children as they move from one intellectual level to the next

Children constantly add to their knowledge and skills through learning and play activities (Berger, 2009). Vygotsky saw that this was possible because of the presence of a support system or **scaffold** in the form of the social environment. Both parents and teachers plan a series of activities from simple to more complex, thus allowing children to acquire the knowledge and tools they need in manageable steps. The scaffold may also be a suggestion or question. It might include encouragement to continue the task even though the child is frustrated. Another name for this kind of learning is "guided participation," in which the adult is available to encourage and suggest ways for children to move to the next level of learning. An example is a child who cannot complete a difficult puzzle. The teacher may place a puzzle piece close to where it fits or may suggest looking for pieces of a particular color. Another example is the parent who helps a child learn to ride a two-wheeler bike. The adult puts on training wheels, holds the handlebars, and runs beside the child. As the child's confidence grows, the adult releases the handlebars but remains close by. The final step may be removal of the training wheels.

Other family members may also provide the scaffold for learning new skills. Children may watch older siblings performing a task, then try to imitate the behavior. Sometimes the older brother or sister shows the younger siblings how to do something, then encourages them to attempt the task. When children go to child care or enter school, peers or older children are often part of the cooperative learning environment supporting growth. When children work together on tasks, the less skilled child has an opportunity to learn from the more skilled participant.

Zone of Proximal Development

The **zone of proximal development** is the hypothetical environment in which learning and development take place (Coffey, 2009). It can be further described as the region between what children can learn by themselves and what they can learn through the guidance and tutoring of a more competent member of society. Through carefully chosen and planned activities, children gradually move from assisted performance to independent performance. Crucial to this process are sensitivity to each child's level of competence and a means to encourage them to move to the next level. When teachers or parents help children acquire a new skill, they may begin with a demonstration, then carefully guide them through the steps and encourage them as they perform on their own.

zone of proximal development
the hypothetical environment in which learning and development take place

Evaluation of Sociocultural Theory

Sociocultural theory has added a new dimension to the study of children's development, particularly in understanding diversity (Berger, 2009). It has increased knowledge of the ways in which cognitive development varies depending on the values and makeup of different societies. It further emphasizes the importance of understanding each culture's values and beliefs and their effect on children's competencies. Some parents prefer the teacher or caregiver to be in control and direct everything that happens in the learning environment. Others are more comfortable with allowing children to have more control over their own learning experiences. (Gonzalez-Mena, 2001).

One limitation of sociocultural theory is that it does not take into account developmental processes that are not social. Some processes are the result of biological maturation.

Which theorist said that children learn from each other?

Another limitation is that Vygotsky did not consider how much children affect their own learning environment. According to Barbara Rogoff (2003), children often choose their own activities or mentors. They often reject or resist help and support from parents or teachers.

Implications for Child Care Staff Members

Most child care centers serve children who come from more than one cultural group and who, as adults, will live in an increasingly diverse society. It is important, therefore, that they learn to function comfortably in a multicultural environment without losing their own cultural identity. Child care staff members can help them achieve that goal in the following ways:

- Learn more about different cultures and be sensitive to cultural values, ways of interacting, and linguistic differences.
- Include families, integrating their values and culture into teaching and learning experiences.
- Learn about families' expectations for their children.
- Encourage children to learn about and appreciate cultures other than their own.
- Help children to acquire the competencies that are important in their culture as well as those that are necessary in broader society.
- Carefully choose and plan activities that gradually move children from assisted performance to independent performance.
- Cultivate each child's communication skills as an important tool of learning.
- Establish a meaningful relationship with every child, because much learning takes place through the interaction between adult and child.
- Encourage cooperative learning in small groups so children can learn from each other.

INTELLIGENCE AND LEARNING

Attempts to understand and measure intelligence have existed for many years. Tests were developed to try to quantify intelligence in relation to chronological age. Items on tests such as the Stanford-Binet focus on general knowledge, reasoning ability, mathematical skill, memory, vocabulary, and spatial perception. More recently, theories of multiple intelligences have interested professionals concerned with the education of young children. Robert Sternberg (1996) delineates three types of intelligence: academic (measured by achievement or IQ tests); creative (measured by imaginative undertakings); and practical (seen in everyday tasks and interactions). Howard Gardner (1983) describes seven distinct intelligences: body-kinesthetic, spatial, linguistic, logical-mathematical, musical, interpersonal (social understanding), and intrapersonal (self-understanding). Later, Gardner (1999) added naturalist intelligence, the ability to recognize and classify features of the environment, as an eighth intelligence.

Other intelligences have been considered by Gardner and his colleagues, including spiritual, existential, and moral intelligence. These were ultimately excluded since they did not meet all his criteria. According to Gardner, everyone has a basic aptitude for each of the intelligences, but most people are stronger in one area than in other areas. A person may have exceptional musical ability but limited spatial skill, and therefore gets lost easily.

Implications for Child Care Staff Members

Theories of multiple intelligences are important to anyone who works with children because they help us understand why some children do so well in some areas but have difficulty in others. They also explain why learning experiences should provide children with the opportunity to use all their senses and express their abilities in a variety of ways (Gardner, 1991). Many schools focus primarily on the tasks measured by standard tests of achievement. This does not allow children to develop other facets of intelligence. Child care personnel can encourage children to develop more than one intelligence by implementing the following suggestions:

- Understand that each child is unique and may be gifted in one area but not in others.
- Let children choose their own methods of learning and work at their own pace (intrapersonal).
- Use cooperative learning that includes feedback from others (intrapersonal).
- Provide a variety of experiences allowing children to use their senses in different ways (kinesthetic).
- Encourage children to use language in word games, crossword puzzles, or debates (linguistic).
- Foster the ability to visualize by providing the opportunity to work puzzles, draw maps, and work mazes (spatial).
- Provide games that require strategy planning or resolving problems (logical-mathematical).
- Help children use music in a variety of activities: writing songs, playing instruments, and creating musical plays (musical).
- Use the outdoors as another classroom by introducing science projects, creating a nature area, or nurturing animals (naturalist).

LANGUAGE

Middle childhood is a time when the ability to use language to enhance cognitive skills and to manipulate social situations increases rapidly. Children acquire as many as 20 words a day, achieving a vocabulary of 40,000 words by the fifth grade (Anglin, 1993). The list of words they understand and use may include some they have not experienced directly but understand through reading, conversation, television, and computers. They deduce the meaning of a word through knowledge of the context in which it is used.

School-age children define words differently from the way they did as preschoolers. When asked to define a word, preschool children give examples that are based on perceptions. "An orange is something to eat that tastes good." A school-age child will likely be more logical by saying "It's a fruit." Preschoolers also define words by using action-based statements, whereas older children analyze the relationship to other words. A four-year-old will say, "Under something is where I hide my toys from my brother." A nine-year-old might say, "Under is the opposite of over" (Holzman, 1983).

Children practice their language skills by trying to refine grammatical construction. By age six ,most children understand and use grammar correctly, but during middle childhood further improvement takes place. Preschool children acquire new language constructions by adapting what they have previously learned. They discover that "ed" is added to make a verb past tense and therefore say, "He goed." Gradually, school-age children learn the variations of verb forms and use them correctly. Older children may not always use correct grammar even though they know it. In conversation with their peers, for instance, they may say, "Me and my mom had a fight." In school they are able to say correctly, "My mom and I had a fight."

School-age children become adept at pragmatic uses of language. They choose words, modify sentences, or change voice inflections to fit the listener in a particular situation. They may use simpler words and shorter sentences when talking to a younger sibling than they would with their friends. The best example of pragmatic use of language is seen in the jokes told by elementary school children. In order to be successful humorists, they need to recognize what the listener will think is funny and to remember the exact words (Yasilove, 1978).

Further indication that school-age children use language pragmatically is the switch to different forms as the occasion dictates. When making a request of possibly reluctant adults, they are careful to use a polite form of request, "Could I please go to the movie with Rachel?" A more extensive switch in language is called **code-switching** .This means a complete change of form when addressing adults from that used when addressing cohorts. It "involves a change in tone, gestures, pronunciation, sentence length, vocabulary and sometimes language itself" (Berger 2009).

They may use **elaborated code**, sometimes called formal code, in the classroom, and change to a **restricted code**, called informal, on the playground (Berger,2009). Elaborated code has a more extensive vocabulary and is grammatically correct and longer. In contrast, restricted code is more limited and may rely on gestures and voice intonation to communicate meaning.

Although they are required to use standard English in the classroom, children also learn the idiosyncrasies of speech specific to their ethnic group or in common usage in their particular region of the country. Some forms differ in minor ways, such as regional accents or colloquialisms in common usage. Certain speech patterns or accents are so distinctive that they can identify the region where a person lives or grew up. A Southern accent is easily distinguished from a Texas drawl. Another variation is Black English, or Ebonics, which uses double negatives: "Nobody couldn't come to the party." Children for whom English is not their primary language

code-switching
a complete change of language form when addressing adults and when talking to other children

elaborated code
a communication that uses a more extensive vocabulary, is correct grammatically, and is longer

restricted code
communications that are more limited and may rely on gestures and voice intonation to convey meaning

face even greater problems. These children must use a language they may barely understand, causing them to fall behind in school. They may also be mercilessly teased by other children for their accents or misuse of words.

Second Language Development

The influx of refugees and immigrants into the United States has rapidly increased the number of children who are second language learners. They speak a native language at home and learn English in their out-of-home experiences. Research points out the cognitive, cultural, and economic advantages of bilingualism. Bilingual children have a whole new world open up to them and will be better prepared to understand others, themselves and their own language (Brown, 2009). , Hence, children who have the opportunity to speak two languages should be encouraged to maintain both. Cognitively, school-age children can understand that others may perceive them as different if their language is not that of the majority. They fear they will become the targets of teasing, and this affects their self-concept.

Some basic principles have been drawn from theory and research on second language acquisition (McLaughlin, 1995). The first is that it is rare for both languages to be perfectly balanced. As a child learns a second language, one language will be predominant. The more the second language is used, the less the native (home) language will be used, and hence both languages may appear less proficient. This is a temporary imbalance, and most bilingual children will reach age-level proficiency in their dominant language given adequate opportunities for use.

The thinking processes of school-age children are markedly different from those of preschoolers.

The second principle is that of the normalcy of code-switching. Young children tend to insert single items from one language into the other (McClure, 1977) primarily to resolve ambiguities and clarify statements. A Spanish-speaking child might say, "My abuela [grandmother] came to visit." "Abuela" is the familiar word associated with the grandmother. By around age nine, however, children tend to switch phrases or sentences. They will switch languages to convey social meanings following the manner in which they hear them switched at home and in the community. A child may say "Hey, that's cool, man" when talking to peers, but when addressing a teacher say "That's really nice." Third, there are different cultural patterns in the use of language. The communication patterns of some cultures do not encourage children to participate verbally in activities. Their home culture interprets this as calling attention to oneself or showing one's knowledge, which is regarded as an arrogant form of behavior (Philips, 1972). Finally, children internalize a second language more readily if they are asked to engage in meaningful activities that require using the language. They also need good models for language use and should have opportunities to experiment with language as they learn correct phrases and intonation.

Implications for Child Care Staff Members

The importance of language in children's development cannot be overestimated. Good language skills are essential for success in school, and children who can communicate their needs and feelings clearly get along better with their peers and adults. Perhaps even more important, good language skills are needed for many of the jobs these youngsters will pursue in the future.

- Provide a wide variety of reading materials: books, magazines, comic books, and newspapers.
- Read to children frequently and encourage them to read alone or with others.
- Plan a variety of activities and experiences that help children expand their vocabularies and their ability to communicate clearly with others. Remember that listening is a part of communicating.
- Model correct English when speaking to children, and accept children's forms of speech. Remember that the goal is for the child to communicate, not adhere to rigid rules about language. Do not correct grammar or pronunciation when children are communicating: respond to the content.
- Use demonstrations, modeling, and role-playing to communicate the meaning of language. The more visuals presented to limited English speakers, the more likely they will comprehend what is being presented to them.
- Invite parents of children with different cultural backgrounds to provide activities and information about their culture such as language, food, and special customs.
- Develop buddy and peer groups that will be supportive and provide feedback to the second language learner.

- Provide opportunities for children to use their primary language in ways that enhance their self-esteem. Encourage them to teach useful words or phrases to others. Allow them to use their speech forms in creative ways when writing stories, plays, or poetry.
- Include written or oral language in culturally based activities.
- Encourage children to use the computer to write and illustrate their own stories.

SUMMARY

- Swiss psychologist Piaget was a major contributor to the understanding of how children think and learn. Piaget believed that intelligence is the result of progression through four stages.

- Watson's behaviorist theory focused on the connection between a stimulus and a response as seen in classical conditioning.

- Skinner started with Watson's ideas but went a step further, proposing another type of conditioning—operant conditioning.

- Bandura saw that some behaviors occur as a result of less direct teaching, through observation of a model and subsequent imitation of that behavior.

- Sociocultural theory, proposed by Vygotsky, assumed that social interaction and children's direct participation in authentic cultural activities are necessary for optimum development.

- More recent attempts to understand intelligence have elicited theories of multiple intelligences.

- Middle childhood is a time when the ability to use language to enhance cognitive skills and manipulate social situations increases rapidly.

- Many children speak a non-English primary language in their home and therefore are at various levels of proficiency in using English.

KEY TERMS

centering	formal operations	scaffold
classical conditioning	modeling	sensorimotor period
code-switching	operant conditioning	storage strategies
concrete operations	preoperational period	zone of proximal
elaborated code	restricted code	development

REVIEW QUESTIONS

1. Why did Piaget observe that during the preoperational period children often come to the wrong conclusions?

2. Between ages seven and 11, children progress to the stage of concrete operations. What new abilities have they acquired?

3. State three applications of Piagetian theory in a school-age child care setting.

4. How does operant conditioning, proposed by Skinner, differ from the social learning theory of Bandura?

5. What are some criticisms of behaviorist theory?

6. How is behaviorist theory used when planning an appropriate environment for school-age children?

7. What is meant by scaffolding?

8. What is meant by the zone of proximal development?

9. How can child care leaders use Vygotsky's ideas in a multicultural community?

10. State three ways child care leaders can help children increase their language skills.

11. List the eight intelligences delineated by Gardner.

12. Describe the role of the caregiver as it pertains to children who are learning English as a second language. Consider curriculum, peer interaction on behalf of the second language learner, and your own interactions with the child.

Case Study

Angela and Jennine wanted to learn to knit so they could make scarves for their dads. Their child care leader, Nancy, promised to show them how because she had been knitting since she was very young. She told them to buy some number six needles and a ball of yarn in the color they liked.

They came to the after-school program the next day, eager to get started. Nancy cast on the stitches on each of their needles because she felt it would be hard enough for them to learn the stitch without starting with casting on. She demonstrated knitting for each of them, then guided their hands through several stitches. Angela was quickly ready to proceed on her own, but Jennine was having trouble. She would forget which way to wrap the yarn around the needle or how to pull the stitch through. Nancy again guided her hands, but Jennine still had problems and became increasingly frustrated. Then, Nancy remembered that she had a knitting instruction book in the cupboard, which showed the step-by-step process. She got it out and propped the page in front of Jennine. Jennine studied it and then cautiously tried each step. Finally she understood and was exuberant that she was successful at last.

1. Why do you think Angela found the instructions Nancy gave her easy to follow? Why was it difficult for Jennine?

2. How would you describe the methods that Nancy used to teach the girls?

3. What does this tell you about other learning experiences that you provide for the children in your group?

STUDENT ACTIVITIES

1. Observe a group of school-age children. Can you recognize any models the children are using to pattern their own behavior? Are the models real people (familiar adults or their peers) or characters from television, films, or computer games? Why do you think they have chosen these particular models? In small groups, share your observations with classmates. Discuss the preceding questions.

2. Visit an after-school program serving children from ages five to 11. Record the number of times the adults use positive reinforcers. What types of reinforcers seem to be most effective with this age level? Did they encourage repetition of the behavior? What negative reinforcers were used? Did they discourage the behavior? Share your findings with classmates and compile a list of responses that seem effective when working with school-age children.

3. In small group discussions, ask members to relate their own methods of working with children to one of the theories described in this chapter. Do they prefer one theory over the others? Or do they tend to use an eclectic approach, employing several different theories?

4. Plan two activities for a group of nine-year-olds that will help them increase their vocabulary. Share your plans with classmates.

5. Present a demonstration of an activity using only visual gestures and materials to convey your meaning. In small groups, discuss the difficulties of learning concepts and instructions without understanding of the language being spoken. (It would be ideal to have someone who speaks another language, unknown by the majority of the classmates, do this presentation in their native language followed by small group discussion.)

SUGGESTED READINGS

Moore, T. (1999). Bringing diversity into your center. *Child Care Information Exchange*, 126 (March/April), 35–37.

WEB RESOURCES

http://en.wikipedia.org/wiki/Multiple_intelligence
   Gardner's Multiple Intelligences: Explanation of Gardner's categories of intelligence.

http://www.childdevelopmentinstitute.org
   Child Development Institute: Information on child development, parenting, family life, and learning.

REFERENCES

Anglin, J. M. (1993). Vocabulary development: a morphological analysis. *Monographs of the Society for Research in Child Development*, 58 (10, Serial No. 238).

Bandura, A. (1977). *Social Learning Theory*. Englewood Cliffs, NJ: Prentice Hall.

Berger, K. S. (2009). *The Developing Person Through Childhood and Adolescence* (5th ed.). New York: Worth.

Bernstein, B. (1971, 1973). *Class, Codes, and Control*. Vols. 1, 2. London: Routledge and Kegan Paul.

Brown, Skilla, (2009). Parlez-Vous Francais? The Case for the Bilingual Child. Retrieved from the Internet, http://www.education.com/magazine/articles/Case_Bilingual Child.

Coffey, Heather (2009). Zone of proximal development. Retrieved from the Internet http://www.learnnc.org/lp/pages/5075.

Gardner, Howard (1983). *Frames of Mind: The Theory of Multiple Intelligences*. New York: Basic Books.

Gardner, H. (1991). *The Unschooled Mind: How Children Think and How Schools Should Teach*. New York: Basic Books.

Gardner, H. (1999). *Intelligence Reframed: Multiple Intelligences for the 21st Century*. New York: Basic Books.

Gonzalez-Mena, Janet (2001). *Multicultural Issues in Child Care*, 3rd ed. Mountain View, CA: Mayfield Publishing Company.

Hakuta, K., & Pease-Alvarez, L. (1992). Enriching our view of bilingualism and bilingual education. *Educational Researcher*, 21, 4–6.

Holzman, M. (1983). *The Language of Children: Development in Home and in School*. Englewood Cliffs, NJ: Prentice Hall.

Locke, J. (1959). *Essay Concerning Human Understanding*. Collated and annotated by A. C. Fraser. New York: Dover.

McClure, E. F. (1977). *Aspects of Code-Switching in the Discourse of Bilingual Mexican-American Children*. (Tech. Rep. No. 44.) Cambridge: Berancek and Newman.

McLaughlin, B. (1995). *Fostering Second Language Development in Young Children: Principles and Practices*. Washington, DC: National Center for Research on Cultural Diversity and Second Language Learning.

Pavlov, I. (1960). *Conditioned Reflexes: An Investigation of the Physiological Activity of the Cerebral Cortex*. (G. V. Anrep, Ed. and Trans.) New York: Dover.

Philips, S. (1972). Participant structures and communicative competence: Warm Springs children in community and the classroom. In C. B. Cazden, V. P. John, & D. Hymes (eds.), *Function of language in the classroom*. New York: Teachers College.

Piaget, J. (1952). *The Origins of Intelligence in Children*. (M. Cook, Trans.). New York: International Universities Press.

Rogoff, Barbara (2003). *The Cultural Nature of Human Development*. New York: Oxford University Press.

Skinner, B. F. (1953). *Science and Human Behavior*. New York: Macmillan.

Sternberg, R. J. (1996). *Successful Intelligence*. New York: Simon & Schuster.

Sternberg, Robert J. & Grigorenko, Elena, (eds) (2004). Culture and competence: Contexts of life success. Washington, D.C.: American Psychological Association.

Vygotsky, L. S. (1978). *Mind in Society: The Development of Higher Psychological Processes*. Cambridge: Harvard University Press.

Vygotsky, L. S. (1987). *Thinking and Speech*. (N. Minick, Trans.). New York: Plenum.

Watson, J. B. (1967). *Behaviorism* (rev. ed.). Chicago: University of Chicago Press. (Original publication dated 1924).

Yasilove, D. (1978). The effect of riddle-structure on children's comprehension and appreciation of riddles. Doctoral dissertation. New York University. *Dissertation Abstracts International, 36,* 6.

Yoon, K. (1992). New perspective on intrasentential code-switching: A study of Korean-English switching. *Applied Psycholinguistics, 13,* 433–449.

6

Development in Middle Childhood: Psychosocial and Moral

THEORIES OF PSYCHOSOCIAL DEVELOPMENT

The world of children between the ages of five and 12 expands as they enter school and begin to experience the environment outside their homes. Increased physical and cognitive skills allow them more independence to explore their neighborhoods, visit friends' homes, and use community facilities such as playgrounds or clubs. In the process, they have many adventures and encounter new people. Parents are often unaware of and have little control over the kinds of challenges their children face as they maneuver this new territory. How children manage depends largely on how they feel about themselves and the moral values they have learned within their families. There are several theories used to explain how children develop their sense of identity and learn to be successful members of a society.

Psychoanalytic Theory and Sigmund Freud

Sigmund Freud (1938) was an Austrian doctor and the founder of the psychoanalytic theory of human behavior. While working with people diagnosed as "hysterics," Freud developed the theory that irrational behaviors have underlying causes stemming from unconscious sexual and aggressive drives that he called *libido*. He saw the psyche as having three parts: the **id**, the source of pleasure-seeking drives; the **ego**, or the rational aspect of personality; and the **superego**, which controls behavior through the development of a conscience. Freud also proposed that the id is present at birth, whereas the ego and superego develop as one progresses through stages of development. In the process, the ego functions as a mediating force between the desire to seek

83

Increased physical and cognitive skills allow school age children the independence to explore their neighborhoods and use community facilities such as playgrounds.

id
in psychoanalytic theory, the part of the personality that is the source of pleasure-seeking drives

ego
in psychoanalytic theory, the rational aspect of personality

superego
in psychoanalytic theory, the part of the personality that controls behavior through the development of conscience

oral period
Freud's term for the first stage, in which the infant gains pleasure through sucking

anal period
Freud's second stage, in which children increase body awareness and focus of attention is on the anus as a source of pleasure

phallic period
Freud's third stage, in which the genital areas are the focus of pleasure and children become aware of physical differences

latency period
Freud's fourth stage, in which children's sexual urges are unobtrusive, and energies are directed toward school activities and sports

pleasure and the need to yield to the demands of parents and society. Each stage brings with it conflicts that a child must resolve. How well a child manages this is determined by the skills and competencies acquired along the way. Freud delineated five stages of development: The first two are the **oral period** and the **anal period**. Both are concerned with children under the age of three. Freud's third stage, the *phallic*, begins at age three and covers school-age children up to the age of six. The later two stages are *latency* and *adolescence*. A discussion of these later three stages follows.

Stage 3. Phallic: Third to Sixth Year

During the **phallic period**, the genital areas are the focus of pleasure, and children become aware of physical differences between boys and girls. It is also during this period that children develop attachments to the parent of the opposite sex; boys are attracted to their mothers, and girls to their fathers. Eventually they learn that they must control these feelings and resolve the conflict by identifying with the parent of the same sex. This leads to development of gender identity and sexual orientation, as well as internalization of family moral values.

Stage 4. Latency: Seventh to Eleventh Year

The **latency period**, as the name implies, is a period of latent or quiet feelings. Children's sexual urges are unobtrusive; their energies are directed toward school activities and sports. During this period children develop competencies and refine their self-images.

Stage 5. Adolescence: Twelfth Year to Adulthood

Adolescence brings changes in sexual organs and physical transformations in the appearance of both males and females. Strong sexual urges cause the adolescent to struggle with how to satisfy those urges in socially acceptable and safe ways. Adolescents reexamine the moral values they incorporated during earlier stages, testing these values against those of their peers, their religion, and society.

Evaluation of Psychoanalytic Theory

Many of Freud's ideas are so widely accepted that they are no longer attributed to psychoanalytic origins (Berger, 2000). There is general agreement that unconscious drives affect some behaviors, although the source of those drives may not be attributed to sexual urges, as Freud proposed. Modified aspects of psychoanalytic theory are evident in research and popular writings about the importance of attachment between mother and infant, gender identity, parental discipline, moral development, and adolescent development.

Some facets of psychosexual theory, however, are no longer considered valid. There is little support for Freud's belief that the way in which conflicts during the oral and anal phases are resolved result in specific personality traits. An even more important criticism of psychoanalytic theory is that it was based on Freud's experiences with white, middle- or upper-class patients. Present day developmental theory emphasizes that a person's heredity, life events, and culture have a greater effect on personality and behavior than the conflicts that occur in childhood. There is also little support for Freud's belief in the struggle between the id and the superego. The strongest criticism of psychoanalytic theory is that it cannot be proven through controlled scientific research. Freudian theory is very much a part of the historical process of understanding human behavior and has affected much of modern thinking about children's development. However, the theory should not be interpreted literally.

Psychosocial Theory and Erik Erikson

Erik Erikson (1963) studied psychoanalytic theory in Vienna with Anna Freud, the daughter of Sigmund Freud. Erikson later moved to Boston, where he started a psychoanalytic practice. Erikson's work included children from a wide variety of backgrounds. Some were from middle-class, professional families, others from poor families, and some were delinquent children. At first he found it difficult to apply psychoanalytic principles to his work with children who were not typically middle-class, but eventually he found some common characteristics in all children. Erikson expanded Freud's stages of development to encompass the entire life span, with each stage characterized by a challenge or developmental crisis.

Erikson's first five stages of childhood are similar to those of Freud. They are (1) **trust vs. mistrust**; (2) **autonomy vs. shame and doubt**;

---

adolescence
Freud's fifth stage, in which there are changes in sexual organs and in appearance, accompanied by strong sexual urges

trust vs. mistrust
Erikson's first stage, in which babies learn to trust that others will take care of their basic needs and that others can be depended upon

autonomy vs. shame and doubt
Erikson's second stage, in which the focus is to become independent by gaining control over bodily functions

Erikson's emphasis is on a person's relationship to the social environment rather than on the body.

initiative vs. guilt
Erikson's third stage, in which children attempt new activities that can result in either pride (initiative) or guilt when unsuccessful

industry vs. inferiority
Erikson's fourth stage, in which children expend all their energies on mastering new skills at home, in school, on the playground, and in their neighborhoods

identity vs. role confusion
Erikson's fifth stage, in which adolescents search for their identity as individuals in a society

(3) **initiative vs. guilt**; (4) **industry vs. inferiority**; and (5) **identity vs. role confusion**. Erikson delineated three additional stages that follow the childhood years and extend into adulthood: intimacy vs. isolation, generativity vs. stagnation, and integrity vs. despair.

The significant difference between Freud and Erikson, however, lies in Erikson's emphasis on a person's relationship to the social environment rather than on the body. He called his ideas the psychosocial theory of development. At each stage of development, the resolution of a crisis depends on the interaction between the individual's personality characteristics and the support and guidance provided by the social environment. How successful or unsuccessful a person is in resolving these crises depends a great deal on competencies and the support and guidance that parents and society provide. The first two stages cover birth to age three, while Stages 3–5 include school-age children. A discussion of those stages follows.

Stage 3. Initiative vs. Guilt: Third to Sixth Year

During this period children want to attempt many tasks they observe their parents or other adults performing. They sometimes attempt activities that are beyond their capabilities or are outside the limits set by their parents. If their caregivers provide support and guidance, the result will be feelings of success and pride in their own initiative. If they are unsuccessful, children will be left with feelings of guilt.

Stage 4. Industry vs. Inferiority: Seventh to Eleventh Year

During this middle-childhood period children expend their energies on mastering new skills at home, in school, on the playground, and in their neighborhoods. When they are successful, they acquire the tools they will need for important societal tasks, such as getting a job and getting along with others. When they are unsuccessful, feelings of inferiority set a pattern for possible failure throughout life.

Stage 5. Identity vs. Role Confusion: Adolescence

This period is highlighted by adolescents' search for identity as individuals in a society. They must balance a desire to establish their own uniqueness with a need to conform to the standards set by the society or culture in which they live. Rebelliousness may lead to role confusion, while strict conformity may lead to a stifling of individuality.

Evaluation of Psychosocial Theory

Erikson's perception of human development is more widely accepted than psychoanalytic theory even though it is based on Freud's ideas (2005). Erikson's writings are more contemporary and not based on the Victorian morality of Freud's time. Many ideas taken from Erikson are currently applied to issues regarding the care of infants, parenting problems, the care of children in groups, and the training of caregivers. The chart "Comparison of Freud and Erikson Age-Level Stages" shows the similarities and differences in the two theories.

Comparison of Freud and Erikson Age-Level Stages

Approximate Age	Freud	Erikson
3–6	Phallic stage	Initiative vs. guilt
	Oedipal situation	Attempt adult activities
	Identification with same-sex parent	Gaining independence
7–11	Superego, conscience	Overstep parental limits, feel guilty
	Latency	Industry vs. inferiority
	Quiet period, less sexual tension	Becoming competent is important
	Psychic energy goes into learning skills	Can feel inferior if unsuccessful
		Identity vs. role confusion
Adolescence	Genital	Considering own identity
	Seeking sexual stimulation and gratification	Establishing ethnic and career identities

Implications for Child Care Staff Members

Two themes are present in both Freudian and Eriksonian ideas about how children develop: the significance of childhood stages in the formation of personality, and the importance of the manner in which adults respond to children's behavior during each of the stages. These concepts lead to several specific implications for people working with school-age children:

- Remember that adults are active participants in helping children resolve the conflicts inherent in each of the stages of development. Provide guidance and support so the conflicts can be resolved in ways that enhance children's self-image.
- Include families in decisions concerning a child's problem behaviors. These behaviors have been formed within the context of family interactions, and changing them will be facilitated with cooperation from family members.
- Support children's need for competence by providing opportunities for them to acquire new social skills and practice already acquired skills.
- Support children's need for independence by allowing them freedom to make choices and do things without adult intervention. Let them plan and carry out many of their own activities. Also, let them make their own rules within limits that do not interfere with others' rights.
- Let children know their competence and responsibility are valued.

MORAL DEVELOPMENT

The process of acquiring and using moral values and attitudes continues throughout life. At each step of development, children learn that certain behaviors are acceptable, whereas others evoke disapproval and rejection. The years of middle childhood are particularly fertile ground for learning the lessons taught by family, culture, and society for several reasons. First, peer relationships become extremely important, sometimes taking precedence over family. Children want to be part of a peer group, so they learn to negotiate, compromise, and "play by the rules." Second, they have already acquired cognitive skills that allow them to think logically and even abstractly. They understand concepts of right and wrong and can consider moral issues related to their own behaviors. Finally, their world has expanded beyond the family into the school and the neighborhood. Toward the end of middle childhood, children begin to look at broad moral issues that affect others: human rights, the destructiveness of war, ecological devastation, and global hunger.

Jean Piaget

As discussed in Chapter 5, Piaget's (1932) primary concern was the cognitive development of children, but he was also interested in how children

Writing is an important societal task to be mastered.

begin to understand justice and develop a respect for social order. He believed that children's understanding of rules goes through stages as their thinking processes change. In the earliest stage, the preschool and early school-age years, children believe that rules are created by an all-powerful authority figure and that they are not to be changed. He called this stage **moral realism**, in which justice equates to whatever the authority decides at a particular time. By age seven or eight, children reach another level. During this period they interact with their peers differently, often with give-and-take reciprocity. They also alter their ideas about authority, recognizing that punishments may be fair or unfair, depending on the transgression committed. As children approach adolescence, around age 11 or 12, a new stage emerges. Piaget called this stage **moral relativism**. At this level, children can be more flexible, change rules, and discuss moral issues.

Lawrence Kohlberg

The most complete theory of children's moral development was proposed by Lawrence Kohlberg, who used Piaget's theories as a starting point for developing his own theory of moral development. Kohlberg (1963) believed that children's moral thinking developed in stages, along with the development of cognitive skills. As cognitive processes changed, the ability to consider moral questions also changed. To test his theory, he presented children with a set of hypothetical stories about moral dilemmas that required decisions involving human life, property rights, or human needs.

moral realism
a stage of moral development in which children believe that rules are determined by an authority figure and they are not to be changed

moral relativism
a stage of moral development in which children view punishments as fair or unfair, are more flexible in their thinking, and can discuss moral issues

He examined children's responses to these situations and concluded that children proceed through the following three levels of moral reasoning:

Level I. Preconventional: Emphasis on Punishment and Rewards, Ages Four to 10

Stage 1. Might makes right.   At this level behavior is labeled good or bad based entirely on the consequences of an action. Children obey authority in order to avoid punishment. "If you do that, you'll get in trouble."

Stage 2. Satisfy your own needs.   People take care of their own needs first and occasionally the needs of others. Children believe that if they are nice to others, others will be nice to them. "I'll invite you to my birthday party if you let me play with you."

Level II. Conventional: Emphasis on Social Rules of the Individual's Family, Group, or Nation, Ages 10 to 13

Stage 3. Interpersonal concordance.   Good behavior is behavior that others approve of and reward. Approval is more important than any other kind of compensation. Children value conformity to stereotyped images of majority behavior. A significant change occurs during this stage: Children recognize intent that is attached to behavior. "He didn't really mean to ruin your building. He was just trying to help."

Stage 4. Law and order.   Emphasis is on authority and obedience to the laws set down by those in power to maintain social order. Right behavior means doing one's duty, showing respect for authority, and recognizing the need to maintain the social order. "It's not right to take things that don't belong to you. Besides, you might get arrested."

Level III. Postconventional: Emphasis on Universal Moral Values and Principles, Age 13 and Older

Stage 5. Social contract.   People understand that laws and rules exist to ensure individual rights, and see right action in terms of standards that society has examined and agreed on. Aside from what has been democratically agreed on, right is also a matter of personal values and opinions. Laws might be changed if a consensus can be reached: "I think we should change the rules of this game so the little kids can play."

Stage 6. Universal principles.   People behave according to universal ethical principles. These principles are abstract, like the "golden rule," and involve a basic right for everyone to be treated equally and with dignity: "I don't think anybody should be discriminated against. Everyone should be able to live where he wants or go to school where she wants."

Kohlberg found that individuals progress through the moral hierarchy very slowly. He found that most school-age children function at Stage 1 or 2. He held that children must be at the cognitive level of adolescents to make moral decisions comparable to Stage 3. Only then will they begin to consider another person's intent before judging behavior as right or

preconventional
Kohlberg's first stage of moral development, in which there is an emphasis on punishment and rewards

conventional
Kohlberg's second stage of moral development, in which there is an emphasis on the social rules of the family, group, or nation

postconventional
Kohlberg's third stage of moral development, in which there is an emphasis on moral values and principles

"Me." Nicole, age 7.

wrong. Once they reach that level of thinking, they may be able to proceed to question authority and laws in terms of faithfulness to maintaining basic human rights. Each stage must be experienced before progressing to the next level, and no level can be skipped.

Some individuals may become fixed at a certain level and never move on to a higher one.

Evaluation of Kohlberg's Theory

Although Kohlberg's stages of moral development were originally praised by developmentalists as a way of understanding moral education, several researchers took a closer look.

Carol Gilligan (1982) noted that Kohlberg's scheme was validated on a group of only males, ages 10, 13, and 16. When women were tested, they scored lower than males; women on average were at Stage 3, and men at Stage 4. Moral development at Stage 3 is at an interpersonal level, with the emphasis on gaining approval for good behavior. Stage 4 represents a more objective acceptance of rules. Gilligan argues that girls develop what she calls a **morality of caring,** whereas boys judge right and wrong in terms of a **morality of justice**. She further holds that girls are reluctant to judge right and wrong in absolutes because they are socialized to be caring and nurturing. When faced with making choices, boys immediately determine what is right or wrong followed by a clear solution, whereas girls try to find a variety of alternatives.

One researcher tested Gilligan's ideas and came to a different conclusion. Lawrence Walker (1988) found that during middle childhood, both boys and girls tended to seek justice when faced with a moral dilemma. Both boys and girls tended to be more affected by cultural and educational differences than by their biological differences when there were social issues to be resolved.

Elliot Turiel (2002) pointed out that Kohlberg used hypothetical situations, not the daily circumstances children typically confront. When Turiel used real test situations more closely resembling children's own experiences, he found that children could reason better about familiar settings. When playing games, for instance, they functioned at a higher level of moral thinking. Turiel also found that when children had a chance to discuss issues repeatedly, they made wiser decisions.

A further criticism of Kohlberg's theory is that his stages reflect Western values and cannot be applied to other cultures. B.V. Reid (1984, 1989), studying Samoan and European families in New Zealand, found that the needs of family members sometimes take precedence over observing moral principles that apply to everyone.

morality of caring
Gilligan's theory that girls are socialized to be caring and nurturing and reluctant to judge right and wrong in absolutes

morality of justice
Gilligan's theory that boys will determine what is right or wrong and then follow it with a clear solution when faced with making choices

Implications for Child Care Staff Members

Because middle childhood is a period when children are learning to find their way in the world outside their home, it is important to facilitate their ability to live within society's rules and get along with others. They should also be encouraged to develop their own moral compass that helps them care about others and lays the foundation for the next stage of moral development. Child care workers can play an important part by:

- examining their own moral principles and how these may influence the children in their care
- providing children with both male and female caregivers
- involving children in solving moral dilemmas that occur in their everyday experiences, giving them opportunities to discuss the possible solutions and consequences of each decision, and allowing them to find new ways of approaching moral dilemmas
- providing children with opportunities to interact with children and adults of different age groups, thus exposing them to higher levels of moral functioning
- creating an environment in which individual and family value systems are accepted. (It is easy to accept value systems similar to one's own; it takes more practice to accept those that are different.)
- modeling the kind of behavior expected of children, and behaving in ways that are fair and just rather than imposing arbitrary rules with no relation to values
- allowing the children to help form the language of the program rules

SUMMARY

- Freud's psychoanalytic theory of development saw the psyche as having three parts: the id, the ego, and the superego, with the ego facilitating the struggle between the pleasure-seeking id and the conscience-driven superego.

- Erikson based his theory on psychoanalytic principles but felt that the resolution of the conflicts between the id and the superego takes place in the context of the social environment.

- Piaget observed that moral development continues throughout life and related it to the development of cognitive abilities.

- Kohlberg used Piaget's ideas as a starting point to develop the most complete theory of children's moral development. He posited three levels of moral reasoning with two stages at each level, and related moral development to the acquisition of cognitive skills.

- Gilligan noted that Kohlberg's theory focused only on boys, and argued that girls develop a morality of caring, whereas boys develop a morality of justice.

- Turiel contends that Kohlberg's test situations were hypothetical, not the day-to-day dilemmas children actually faced and could understand.

KEY TERMS

adolescence	ego	latency period
anal period	id	moral realism
autonomy vs. shame and doubt	identity vs. role confusion	moral relativism
	industry vs. inferiority	morality of caring
conventional	initiative vs. guilt	morality of justice

oral period   postconventional   superego
phallic period   preconventional   trust vs. mistrust

REVIEW QUESTIONS

1. Freud saw the psyche as having three parts. List and define each.

2. How is Erikson's theory related to Freud's ideas? How is it different?

3. Briefly describe children's development according to Erikson during the following stages: initiative vs. guilt; industry vs. inferiority; and identity vs. role confusion.

4. State some criticisms of psychoanalytic theory.

5. What are some ways child care leaders can apply Freudian and Eriksonian theory to their work with children and families?

6. Piaget cited two stages in children's development of a sense of justice and respect for social order. What are they?

7. Kohlberg proposed three levels of moral reasoning. He called Level I, age four to 10, preconventional. State and describe Stages 1 and 2 at this level.

8. Why did Kohlberg believe that school-age children would find it difficult to make moral decisions having to do with a person's intent behind a behavior?

9. What was the basis for Gilligan's criticism of Kohlberg's theory?

10. Another researcher who criticized Kohlberg's findings was Turiel. What were his concerns?

Case Study

Joaquin is a caregiver for a group of eight-year-olds. He would like to change the way some children react when there are problems among them. Danisha, the youngest boy in the group, never does anything wrong, but when someone else misbehaves, he loudly says, "You're going to get in trouble for that." Emily maintains control over her two friends by threatening, "I won't invite you to my birthday party if you don't do what I want!" Joaquin understands that Danisha is trying to be good and wants Joaquin to notice him, but also to punish the wrong-doers. Emily maintains control by doing what generations of children have done: withholding a promised pleasure. Joaquin knows these behaviors are not healthy for any of the children and wants to help them change.

1. Why are the children reacting this way?

2. Joaquin wants to reinforce the importance of rules as well as to help the children move on to a higher plane of morality. What could he say to the children?

3. When you are faced with helping children make decisions about good or bad behavior, what do you want them to learn?

STUDENT ACTIVITIES

1. Ask several school-age children to discuss some moral dilemmas they are likely to face in their everyday lives. The following are some possible scenarios, but you can make up your own:
   a. You and your friend go to the store to buy some candy. You notice that your friend puts a candy bar in his pocket, but pays for a package of gum. What should you do?
   b. Your friend's little sister wants to play a game with the two of you, but you know that it will be too difficult for her. What will you do? (Write down the children's responses and put them into one of Kohlberg's stages. Share the results with your classmates during your next class.)

2. Ask your family members how they handled the following situations when you were growing up:
   a. Questions about gender differences
   b. Sibling rivalry
   c. Adolescent relationships

3. Were their methods influenced by psychoanalytic thinking? If so, in what way?

SUGGESTED READINGS

Crain, William C. (2005) *Theories of Development: Concepts and Applications* (5th ed.). Upper Saddle River, NJ: Prentice Hall.

Danis, A., Bernard, J. & Leproux, C. (2000). Shared picture-book reading: A sequential analysis of adult-child verbal interactions. *British Journal of Developmental Psychology*.

Sapp, F., Lee, K & Muir, D. (2000). The sojourner experience of Yemeni American high school students: An ethnographic portrait. *Harvard Educational Review*, 71, 390–415.

WEB RESOURCES

http://www.piaget.org/
John Piaget Society. An online source of information and relevant publications for Piaget.

For more information about the theorists in this chapter, go to **http://wikipedia.com or http://Ask.com**

REFERENCES

Berger, Kathleen S. (2005). *The developing person through childhood and adolescence* (7th ed.). New York: Worth.

Erikson, E. H. (1963). *Childhood and Society* (2nd ed.). New York: Norton.

Freud, S. (1938). *The Basic Writings of Sigmund Freud.* (A. A. Brill, Ed. and Trans.). New York: Modern Library.

Gilligan, C. (1982). *In a Different Voice: Psychological Theory and Women's Development.* Cambridge: Harvard University Press.

Kohlberg, L. (1963). Development of children's orientation towards a
    moral order (Part 1). Sequence in the development of moral thought.
    Vita Humana, 6, 11–36.

Piaget, J. (1932). *The Moral Judgment of the Child*. (M. Gabin, Trans.). New
    York: Free Press.

Reid, B. V. (1984). An anthropological reinterpretation of Kohlberg's
    stages of moral development. *Human Development*, 27, 56–74.

Reid, B. V. (1989). Socialization for moral reasoning: Maternal strategies
    of Samoans and Europeans in New Zealand. In Jaan Valsiner (Ed.),
    Child Development in Cultural Context. Toronto: Hogrefe and Huber.

Turiel, Elliot (2002). *The Culture of Morality: Social Development, Context,
    and Conflict*. New York: Cambridge University Press.

Walker, Lawrence, (1988). The development of moral reasoning. Annals of
    child Development, 5, 33–78.

7

Helping Children Develop Social Competence

SOCIAL COMPETENCE

Making and keeping friends is of major importance to children during middle childhood. Those who lack social skills do not have friends, may become bullies, exhibit aggressive or passive behavior, face difficulties in school, and have emotional problems. On the other hand, children with good social skills have lots of friends, get better grades, and will probably function more effectively as adults (Ferrer-Chancy & Fugate 2008). Middle childhood is an optimal time to help children develop the skills they need to get along with others. At this stage, childen have begun to develop empathy and can consider how others think and feel. At times they are willing to give up gratification of their own needs to do what a friend wants. They are learning self-control and take responsibility for behaving in ways that do not conflict with others' rights. Child care professionals are in a unique position to help children develop positive behaviors.

In the past, teaching relationship skills was left to the family, but now it is included more often in the curriculum of schools and child care programs. In fact, some professionals believe it should be the fourth "*R*," along with reading, writing, and arithmetic. There are several reasons for this change. Many family members do not communicate with one another because they are so busy and on different schedules. The parents put in long hours at work, and the children have school and extracurricular activities or are in after-school care. Families may be separated, or they may move frequently, losing neighborhood stability. Models for how to work out long-term relationships are not readily available. Many marriages end in divorce, and grandparents who are still married may live far away. The child care setting is an ideal place to help children learn how to make and

LEARNING OUTCOMES

After reading this chapter, you should be able to:

✔ Discuss strategies for helping children make and keep friends.

✔ State the steps used to help children resolve conflicts.

✔ Describe children's development of their self-image.

✔ Relate the ways in which children learn cooperative behavior.

✔ Discuss verbal and other strategies for helping children change their behavior.

✔ Describe behaviors and issues related to caring for students with special needs, which can create problems for individuals and the group.

97

keep friends. The atmosphere in a child care center is less structured and more relaxed than in the school classroom. There is time for group discussions or individual conversations. Learning activities can be organized into games or other fun things to do with friends.

Strategies to Help Children Make Friends

Young children are egocentric, more focused on their own needs than on those of others. This makes it difficult for them to form friendships. They need to observe how their behaviors affect others and how to change in order to be liked and have friends. The following are a few strategies to employ:

- Identify social strengths and weaknesses in children. What are the ways they interact successfully with others and what do they do that results in rejection?
- Coach children to find more effective ways of behaving toward friends. Ask what behavior causes friends to dislike or reject them. Discuss alternative behaviors and urge them to try them.
- Praise children when they are successful interacting with others.
- Teach children how to react to others who are mean to them or bully or tease them. Children can stay calm, ignore the behavior, or use appropriate comebacks.
- Model good social skills as you interact with colleagues and parents. The children will observe you and want to use you as a model for their own behavior.
- Discuss with children the characteristics that foster friendships. Encourage them to discuss a time they had fun with a friend and what made it enjoyable. How did they and their friend act toward each other?
- Talk about the meaning of respect and how important it is in relationships.
- Take part in plays and other dramatic activities that help them understand what it feels like to be bullied.
- Use games to teach social skills. The following section provides several suggestions.

Activities That Develop Friendships

Make a Friend
Purposes:

- practice interaction skills
- demonstrate approaches to other children

Facilitate mini-dramas of role-playing, in which each child plans what he or she would do to make a friend. Play out the scene. At the end of the scene, discuss what happened and how the participants might have felt. Possible scenarios are the following:

- You are playing a game of basketball with your friends, and a kid you do not know stands at the side watching. Your friends think he is too little to play.
- A new girl comes into your classroom. She has just moved into the neighborhood from another part of the city. Your best friend whispers that she is "kinda ugly 'cause she's too fat."
- A new family moves into the house next door to yours. You see that they have twins who look about your age. You are a little shy, but would like to have somebody next door to play with.

OK, We'll Do It
Purposes:

- develop negotiation skills
- learn to postpone personal gratification
- practice making joint decisions

Divide the children into groups of three. Tell them to pretend their group can choose to do one of the following: see a movie, go out for pizza, or buy a new computer game. Ask each to relate his reasons for choosing one over the others. They can choose only one, so they will have to decide which it will be. When each group has made a choice, ask them to discuss how well their group worked together. What was the most difficult part of the process? How did they finally reach a decision?

Best Friends Are _____
Purposes:

- identify characteristics of friendships
- practice communicating
- appreciation for friends

At group time, tell the children that the topic for discussion is "What makes a friend?" You might relate that when you were their age, you had a best friend, and one of the things you liked about that person was ____. Encourage them to tell one thing they like about one of their friends. Write down the characteristics they describe either on a chalkboard or a piece of paper. Encourage each child to add to the discussion while the rest of the group listens. Read the list and ask them to think about how many of the characteristics they have themselves. Conclude the discussion with ways they can become more like the best friend they want for themselves.

CONFLICT RESOLUTION

Children are growing up in a world where they witness violence almost every day. They learn ways of dealing with conflict by watching the adults they see at home, in their neighborhoods, on TV and in media, and at

What do you think is happening between these children?

school. Often adults behave in ways they do not want children to imitate. Yet children often "try on" behaviors they observe in others and only gradually learn to resolve conflicts in more effective ways. Preschool children will call on adults to intervene in resolving disputes. School-age children gradually learn to negotiate a compromise, bargain, or use humor to lessen angry feelings. However, at times those strategies do not work, and children resort to fighting. The fighting may escalate, and children may be seriously hurt or even killed. According to the Children's Defense Fund (2009), each day nine children and teens die from gunfire.

Violence is a confrontational and harmful way of settling disputes. The violent act can be physical, verbal, or emotional. These methods of settling disputes are counterproductive. Violence often escalates until serious injury or death results. However, violence is only one of the styles people use to resolve conflicts. Avoidance is frequently used: When confronted with a difficult situation, a person turns away, withdraws completely, or remains silent. This method does not resolve the conflict but just internalizes angry feelings. After repeated incidents, the anger may intensify until it erupts either in violent behavior or displays of anger out of proportion to a particular situation. The most effective way of dealing with conflicts is through problem solving, yet many people, both adults and children, find this difficult to do. Child care leaders can help children proceed through the necessary steps to resolve their conflicts so that each participant feels validated and empowered. All parties should be satisfied that they have been heard, that their feelings have been considered, and that the solution is mutually agreeable. When all parties are gathered, the adult can facilitate a discussion that takes the children through the following steps:

1. *Decide to resolve the conflict.* All the children involved in the dispute must agree to solve the problem. "I am willing to try to settle this argument." Set some ground rules:
   - Each child is committed to solving the problem.
   - Name-calling and put-downs are not permitted.
   - Each child will be truthful.
   - An option is for each child to take a cooling-down period at the peace table where they draw pictures of the participants in the conflict and what happened.

2. Each child relates what happened.
   - Use "I" messages. "I get mad when you . . ." "I am unhappy when . . ." "I feel sad when . . ."
   - Describe exactly what happened.
   - Relate how each felt about the incident.
   - Listen to what the other person has to say.

   Example: "I was waiting for my turn at the tape player, but she grabbed it. I got mad because she does that all the time." "I had been waiting a long time, and I didn't know she was, too. I was surprised she got so mad at me."

3. Each child states what he or she needs to resolve the conflict.
   - Be specific; use "I" messages.
   - Listen to the other person's needs.

   Example: "I just want to have a turn so that I can play the music I like." "I don't always want to hear what she likes."

4. Explore possible ways of solving the conflict.
   - Brainstorm options.
   - Evaluate the suggestions.
   - Decide which option will be satisfactory to both parties.

   Example: "Let's think of ways to solve this problem." "Will that solution satisfy both of you?"

5. After an interval, get the children together to determine whether the solution is working or whether a new approach should be considered.

   Example: "How has it been working to have a sign-up sheet and a timer for using the tape player?" The adults in an after-school program can be powerful motivators to help children change their behavior, enabling them to become part of a group, feel good about themselves, and achieve their personal goals. The process may be difficult along the way, but it helps to remember that change takes time and effort.

Strategies for Conflict Resolution

Reading nonverbal cues, seeing another person's point of view, and practicing conflict negotiation are skills that children can learn in addition to the steps for conflict resolution. Adults can use various strategies, such as the following, to help children learn these additional skills:

- Increase children's ability to read nonverbal cues from others. Sometimes a look or gesture is misinterpreted, and an argument ensues. When an altercation takes place, encourage the participants to discuss what they saw and what they thought it meant. If there has been a misunderstanding, help them clarify their meanings. Does ignoring an invitation to play just mean "I didn't hear you," or does it mean "I don't want to play right now. Go away"? Does an angry look mean "He's mad at me about something" or that he just had a bad day at school?

- Help children to see that others may have a different viewpoint. Use discussions to let all children express their own perspectives or state their own needs. One way to accomplish this is to involve children in planning parts of the program. They may all have good ideas based on their own interests or what is most important to them. Accept and value each contribution, even though it may not be put into action.

- Provide many opportunities for children to learn by trial and error. They have to practice conflict negotiation and ways to cooperate with one another.

- Encourage children with frequent conflict difficulties to draft a conflict plan. The plan might include a description of the kinds of conflicts, the child's usual behavior, and how they might change their behavior. The plan's final statement should include a future date to evaluate how it is working. A conflict plan might look like the following drawn up by John: "I sometimes get mad when other kids won't let me play. When that happens, I start calling them names. Next time I will try to remember to either suggest how I can be a part of their play or find someone else to be with. I will try these methods; then look at how successful they've been in two weeks."

Activities to Encourage Conflict Resolution

Silent Stories
Purposes:

- practice in reading nonverbal cues
- increase understanding that others have different points of view

Have children work in pairs. Tell them to use nonverbal ways to tell their partner something about themselves. For instance, they can use gestures to convey their age or things they are interested in. They can use facial expressions to indicate something that makes them mad or sad. Set a time limit of five or 10 minutes. At the end of that time, each child tries to relate to the other they have learned. Have them clarify any misinformation and discuss another way they might have conveyed the information.

Cultural Scenes
Purposes:

- practice observational skills
- understand the similarities and differences in the ways families carry out familiar routines
- appreciate the similarities and differences in cultures

Ask three or four children from the same culture to enact a typical scene from their culture. Allow them time by themselves to talk about what they will do. Examples might include a dinnertime routine, a visit from grandparents, or a birthday celebration.

The remainder of the group observes the enactment, paying attention to procedures and the things people say. When the enactment is finished, allow the audience group time to ask questions of the participants.

Lead a discussion of their observations, focusing on how some of the audience saw things the others did not, and how actions or words were interpreted differently.

Shopping Trip
Purposes:

- practice working together as a group
- develop decision-making skills
- resolve conflicts effectively

Divide your class into groups of three. Give each group a catalog. Tell them they have $100 to spend buying presents for a boy and girl who are both nine years old. Explain that they all must agree on what to buy. Set a time limit. When they make their decision, they can cut out the pictures and paste them on a sheet of paper.

Have each group share their choices. Ask children about the problems they encountered and how they resolved them. Why did they make the choices they did?

Build a Tower
Purposes:

- cultivate creativity
- develop leadership qualities
- encourage verbal and nonverbal communication

Divide your class into groups of three or four. Pass out 20 pieces of heavy paper and a roll of tape to each group. Tell them to construct a tower using only these supplies. (You can add another dimension by telling them they cannot talk while working on the project.) Set a time limit of 10 or 15 minutes.

Have each group show their tower. Discuss how they managed to complete their tower. Was one person the leader? Did anyone feel excluded? What kinds of nonverbal communications did they use? Is it easy or difficult to understand nonverbal messages?

Brainstorming
Purposes:

- foster divergent thinking skills
- strengthen the ability to negotiate conflicts
- amplify group cohesiveness

Tell the children that many great inventions result from a group of people getting together to create something new. You might remind them that it takes numerous scientists and engineers to design and build space vehicles. Divide them into groups of four, and tell them they are going to invent a new bicycle. Give each group a piece of paper, and have them designate one member to write down ideas. When they have several designs, ask them to choose one to be built. Set a time limit of 10 minutes.

Let each group relate their ideas to the entire group. Discuss the value or difficulties of creating as a group. How did they decide on the design to be built?

Picture Problems
Purposes:

- increase ability to understand (decode) nonverbal communications in pictures
- recognize and accept others' points of view
- practice in group decision making

Glue pictures of people in a problem situation onto the front of a large manila envelope. You can find pictures in magazines, coloring books, discarded books, and posters. Have children work in groups of three. Give each group a picture and some paper. Ask them to reach an agreement about the problem portrayed in the picture and write it down. Have them put their paper into the envelope, and pass it on to the next group until all groups have looked at all the pictures. Allow three minutes for each picture.

Collect the envelopes. Read each of the descriptions. Discuss how different groups saw the problem differently.

Fighting Fair
Purposes:

- practice resolving conflicts effectively
- foster independence
- expand self-esteem

When two children start to fight or argue, send them to a quiet corner of the room. Tell them to have a three-minute time-out. During that time, instruct them to work out a solution to their conflict. Set a three-minute timer, and when the timer goes off, ask them to tell you their solution and then implement it. Praise them for success.

Role-Playing

Purposes:

- resolve conflicts
- develop understanding of others' feelings
- evaluate solutions to conflicts

Set the stage by describing a situation that creates conflicts. The problem may be between two boys or two girls, a male and a female, or a child and an adult. Assign children to the roles. Tell them to act out the situation, then reverse their roles. The male takes the female part, and the child takes the adult part.

Stop the play before a resolution is reached, and ask the rest of the children to suggest a solution. Continue the play as the actors find a solution, possibly using one suggested by the audience. Ask the actors to discuss their feelings while the action was taking place. Talk about the play after it is finished, discussing whether the problem could have been prevented or whether the solution was satisfactory to both parties.

SELF-IMAGE

Self-image has two components: our perceptions of ourselves and the perceptions conveyed to us by others. Throughout a lifetime, self-image changes as physical abilities evolve, cognitive functions change, and interactions with others are refined. During middle childhood, self-image is tied closely to feelings of competence. Children compare themselves to their contemporaries in terms of physical abilities, academic success, ability to manage behavior, physical appearance, or popularity with their peers. Their evaluations of themselves are sometimes realistic and at other times radically unrealistic. In addition, adult attitudes and behaviors play a significant role in how children feel about themselves. When adults react positively to them, children feel they are valued and therefore have self-worth.

> **self-image**
> our perception of ourselves plus the perceptions conveyed by others

How children feel about themselves has a direct effect on their behavior. If they like themselves and see that others react positively to them, they behave in ways that gain further approval. If children have negative perceptions of themselves, they may use unpopular tactics to gain attention or satisfy their needs. This solidifies their perception of themselves as someone who is unlikable or cannot succeed. Therefore, it is essential that anyone who works with children conveys attitudes that help, rather than hinder, children in the development of their identity and self-esteem.

Strategies for Enhancing Self-Esteem

- Develop a genuine interest in every child. Find opportunities to spend time with children individually. Get to know them, listen to them, and try to understand their concerns. Offer help when needed, but also support their ability to find their own solutions to problems.

- Recognize every child's unique qualities, and respect their differences. Eliminate prejudice or bias in your own thinking or in the behaviors of the children. Ensure that all activities are nonracist and nonbiased.
- Support self-esteem by involving children in intrinsically meaningful activities. Plan challenging projects in which children and adults work together, and children develop skills and gain knowledge. As they acquire skills and feel more competent, children's belief in their own self-worth increases.
- Conduct group meetings that allow all children to ask questions, express concerns, discuss problems, or make plans. During group meetings, there should be a free exchange with no put-downs. Each child's contribution should receive respect and consideration, and children should learn to consider all sides of an issue.
- Provide many ways for children to succeed. Offer a variety of activities appropriate for children at different developmental levels. In this way, all children will be able to choose, according to their needs, some activities that are easy for them and others that offer a challenge. Writing and illustrating a simple story is a fairly easy task for nine- or 10-year-olds. Older children might tackle the more difficult task of writing a play complete with dialogue.

Activities That Foster Self-Esteem

Greetings
Purposes:

- foster respect and recognition of each child's unique qualities
- develop a feeling of belonging to a group

Welcome each child who comes into your group. Every day, when children enter your room, greet them and spend a minute or so chatting. If any children enter during a group time, stop, greet them, and then help them find a place in the group. Tell them what the group has been doing. Continue the contacts when children are ill. Telephone them at home to find out how they are feeling and when they will return.

Interior Decoration
Purposes:

- cultivate students' feelings of responsibility for and control over their environment
- strengthen the ability to negotiate differences in ideas, needs, and preferences

In a group meeting, discuss plans for children making the room their own. Ask for ideas about what they want to have in "their room." Write down all the ideas on a chalkboard or a large piece of paper. If needed, suggest additional ideas: a class mural, a rearrangement of the furniture, a room sign or logo, or decorative containers for storage. Ask for discussion on the most important or the most feasible ideas, and vote on which ones to implement. Tell the children that they will reevaluate the plan at a specific time in the future.

Getting to Know You
Purposes:

- develop friendship skills
- increase awareness of similarities and differences between people

Encourage children to get to know others in the classroom. Make a class roster with children's names and pictures, or create a class book with a page for each child. Information on the page can include a picture, the names of family members, the child's birthday, the child's likes and dislikes, or whatever she chooses to say about herself. Leave the book in a place where classmates and parents can look through it.

For a more extensive project, have the children make an individual book all about themselves. The purpose of this book is to provide helpful information for the adults who work with these children. (See the textbook website for reproducible pages that can be used for this purpose.)

Puppet Talk
Purposes:

- foster development of language skills
- increase organizational skills
- provide an outlet for the expression of ideas and feelings
- explore fairy tales and stories from other cultures

Set up a puppet stage. Provide books of fairy tales, fables, or stories from other cultures. Assist children in writing scripts using the stories from the books as the framework or using a story of their own devising. Provide materials and instructions for making puppets. Chapter 11 has some suggestions for making puppets.

TV Talk
Purposes:

- foster development of language skills
- increase each child's feelings of self-worth

Provide a setting where children can interview their classmates. Secure a microphone, or make one, using a piece of wooden dowel for the handle. Make two slits in the form of a cross on a tennis ball. Slip the ball over the end of the dowel. If you wish, you can spray it with black paint. When the "microphone" is ready, help the children structure an interview. Suggest a few questions they can ask, then allow them to devise their own format. It may also help if you suggest they watch television interviews beforehand.

If a tape recorder is available, have them tape their own interview, then play it back. Ask them to evaluate the interview. What did they find out about the person being interviewed? What other questions might have been asked?

Silhouettes
Purposes:

- strengthen their ability to work together
- develop appreciation for similarities and differences
- increase feelings of self-esteem

Have children work in pairs. Tape large pieces of paper onto a wall. Darken the room and provide a bright light. (A strong, steadily held flashlight or a high-intensity lamp will work.) Ask one person to sit sideways in front of the paper while the partner outlines a facial silhouette. Children can sign and color their silhouettes. Display the portraits.

Getting to Know Me
Purposes:

- increase self-esteem
- understand how people are alike and different
- communicate each person's uniqueness to others
- develop appreciation for others' individual traits

Ask children to bring things from home that are special to them and represent who they are. These may be things they like to collect, photos of special people, or mementos of special occasions in their life. The objects must be small enough to fit into a shoe box. Provide each child with a box and distribute materials they can use to decorate their box. Wallpaper pieces, wrapping paper, construction paper, collage materials, paint, marking pens, and pictures from magazines are examples. Allow time at group meetings for each child to show the items from his box and explain why they have special meaning to him.

Family Tree
Purposes:

- increase self-esteem
- develop appreciation for family differences
- increase communication with family members
- develop pride in one's family

Instruct children to gather as much information as possible about their family. Who are their parents' parents? How about their grandparents' parents? How many aunts, uncles, and cousins can they discover? Help them draw up a family tree. They can include the names or pictures of the people in their families.

Older children can use the computer software program listed at the end of this chapter to gather family information. Caregivers should be sensitive to the fact that some children may live with foster parents. If so, this is not an appropriate activity for the group.

COOPERATION

Cooperation with others does not come easily to children. As infants, toddlers, and young preschoolers, they are intensely egocentric. During those years their main concern is satisfying their own needs and achieving their own goals with little focus on the needs of others.

Gradually, during middle childhood, cognitive development enables children to see others more clearly, and they begin to understand that others have needs too. When others' needs conflict with their own, children learn to compromise and cooperate in order to have friends. They also find they can achieve common goals by working together. Key factors in helping children learn cooperative behaviors are supportive parents and well-qualified child care staff members.

Strategies for Increasing Cooperative Behavior

"My dad." Vince, age 7.

- One of the most powerful strategies adults can use to teach children to be more cooperative is *modeling* or what parents call "setting a good example." When they see adults helping others, showing kindness

Space for school-age child care should be designed to accommodate groups of varying sizes.

or compassion, and assisting others to achieve their goals, children understand how it can be done. They have a model to follow when confronted with situations in their own daily activities. Conversely, children also imitate selfishness, cruelty, and uncooperative behaviors they observe in adults.

- Another important strategy is emphasizing cooperation rather than competition. During middle childhood, children are striving to succeed at whatever they attempt and constantly comparing themselves to others. They want to be "the best, the first, or the fastest." Some competitiveness is inevitable because many of the sports that are popular among youngsters are based on someone winning and someone losing. This cannot be avoided, but it can be minimized by child care staff members. The staff members can recognize each child for his or her participation during the game, rather than praising only the winner. In addition, there should also be games that do not involve someone emerging as the winner. Several of the games described in Chapter 10 require cooperation, and there is no real victor.

- Space for school-age child care should be designed to accommodate groups of varying sizes. When children play in proximity to others, they must compromise or engage in negotiations concerning the use of space or materials. Space should not be so limited, however, that children feel crowded, for that causes tension and squabbling. Within the workspace, materials should be close at hand, adequate in number for all to share, and stored in an uncluttered manner. In this way, children can work comfortably and with fewer conflicts.

- Staff members can help children develop more cooperative behavior by leading discussions about sharing, fairness, taking turns, and negotiating when working together. They can use examples from daily occurrences or hypothetical situations. As an example, fairness is an important issue for school-age children, and conflicts over what is fair occur frequently. A sensitive child care leader uses these situations to discuss what happened, why a situation may have seemed unfair, or what the children can do differently next time. It is also important to help children become aware that sometimes one child or another has needs that may seem to take precedence over her own. Equity does not always mean fairness, but implies that meeting each child's needs to the greatest extent possible. Equity should be part of the philosophical approach to school-age care.

- In child care groups where the children are of different age levels or have special needs, there are many opportunities to help children be more cooperative. Staff members can encourage capable children to take on responsibilities commensurate with their abilities for helping younger or special-needs children with activities, games, projects, or even homework. Both children and adults gain from this arrangement.

- Include activities that require children to work cooperatively toward a common goal. A good example is the production of a play. An entire group could work on this type of project, with some children writing the script and others making costumes, taking roles, designing stage sets, or directing the final presentation. Another example is producing a newsletter. Children must work together to gather news, write articles, decide on a format, and print and distribute the paper. Both of the newsletter and play projects require a great deal of discussion, negotiation, and compromise and can be effective techniques to help children develop these skills.

Activities That Require Cooperation

Sculpture
Purposes:

- provide opportunity for sharing ideas
- increase ability to work under time pressure
- strengthen problem-solving skills

Divide the class into groups of three. Give each group a pile of toothpicks, some glue, a piece of Styrofoam, and some small corks. Instruct them to make a single sculpture. The ground rules are that they each child gets to help decide what to make and to participate in the construction. Set a time limit. (You can also use other objects: clay, Tinkertoys, beads, recycled materials, etc.) Have each group share their experience in creating the sculpture.

Discuss how the groups decided what to make. What were the problems they encountered? How did they resolve the problems?

Storytelling
Purposes:

- develop language skills, both talking and listening
- create a group fantasy with a beginning, a middle, and an end

Tell the children they are going to write a story together. Use a tape recorder to record it. Designate one child to start the story with a few sentences, then point to another child to continue. Allow any child to pass if he or she chooses not to add to the story. Set a time limit for bringing the story to an end.

Rewind the tape and listen to the story. Ask the children what they thought of their tale. Would it have been different if just one person had told it? If so, how? Transcribe the story, asking the children to contribute some illustrations to accompany the printed pages, and put it together in book form. Place the book in the reading area so children can read the story themselves.

Y'All Come Up
Purposes:

- increase awareness of others' feelings
- foster group cohesiveness
- practice problem solving

This game is the opposite of "King of the Hill," in which the object is to keep others from getting to the top of the hill. In this game, one child stands at the top of a hill and one by one asks others to join him. The purpose is to get everyone onto the hill without anyone falling off. (If no hill is available, use a very low table.)

Discuss what the children had to do to keep everyone together at the top of the hill. How did it make them feel to be included? How did it make them feel if they fell off and could not be included?

Class Caring Project
Purposes:

- increase cooperative behavior
- foster feelings of empathy for others

Involve the entire group in planning and implementing a caring project. It can be raising money for a worthy cause, getting involved in a community cleanup drive, or visiting a retirement home. Allow the children to research community needs and then choose a project. Have them plan ways to implement their ideas. Encourage them to assign tasks and coordinate ways to follow through. When they complete the project, evaluate what they learned and what they might have done differently.

These are some of the ways you can encourage children to feel better about themselves and learn to function effectively in a group. However, in spite of all your efforts, you may find that some children are still

Hitting or hurting another person is never an acceptable response to anger.

troublesome to themselves and their peers. These children may need extra thought and care.

CHANGING CHILDREN'S BEHAVIOR

Helping children reverse recurring cycles of behavior that interfere with reaching the goals they set for themselves is one of the most important tasks for teachers in before- and after-school programs. The task is two-fold: to stop harmful or destructive behaviors and to encourage children to act in ways that others approve of, thus enhancing their self-esteem.

Stopping destructive behavior begins with a clear understanding by both children and adults about which behaviors are acceptable and which are not. Adults must state their demands clearly, describing what the child can do and cannot do, when, and how often. "You may never hit. Use words to tell him how you feel or what you want." Another example is "I expect you to put away your materials where they belong each time you use them. Do not leave anything on the floor to get stepped on or broken." A parent might say, "I want you to take out the trash and put it in the outside can without spilling any. Do it every Friday before it gets dark."

Avoid cliché statements of expectations. "Shape up," "Try harder," and "Get a life" are examples of clichés that have no real meaning for children. How do they shape up? What can they do to try harder? How can they get a life?

Making an unspecific demand is a similar mistake adults frequently make. "I want you all to behave when we go to the museum." Children may have concepts of what behaving means, which are very different from those of the adult who made the statement. Adults can be more helpful by stating exactly what kinds of behavior they expect and why that behavior is important: "I want you all to stay together with the group so that no one gets lost."

Expectations may also be stated in the form of rules. Both families and child care programs have rules that they expect children to abide by. There are three kinds of rules. First, there are **non-negotiable rules**, which are not open for discussion or negotiation. Mandatory rules apply to actions that can be harmful to others or destructive to property. An example might be "No hitting."

Second, there are **negotiable rules** that offer choices. The child has the option of choosing one of a limited number of alternatives. "You can choose to do your homework now or as soon as we finish dinner and before any TV." When using this strategy, it is important to be sure the child is mature enough to make the decision.

One teacher configured negotiable and non-negotiable rules differently. She defined a line of acceptable and unacceptable behaviors. Acceptable was above the line and unacceptable below. Acceptable behaviors could allow children choices, while unacceptable behaviors were forbidden.

non-negotiable rules rules that are used for actions that can be harmful to others or destructive to property and that are not open for discussion

negotiable rules rules that are based on choices

optional rules
things that children can reasonably control themselves

logical consequence
a tool for changing behavior, in which the result of a child's misbehavior is related to the behavior

If necessary, an adult can offer to help the child in considering the possible consequences of each choice. A discussion with a child who uses unacceptable behavior will help him make better choices in the future.

Finally, **optional rules** are the things that children can reasonably control themselves. An example might be that the parent wants the child to finish her homework before dinner, but the child wants to rest first and do homework later. If the child has shown responsibility in other situations, she should be allowed to choose the time for doing homework as long as she gets it done before going to bed.

Every infraction must be dealt with every time the behavior occurs to make a rule effective. When misbehavior occurs, restate the rule or expectation firmly and in a way that shows that you mean it: "The rule is no hitting when you are mad at somebody. I expect you to use words to tell him how you feel." Sometimes it is tempting to ignore infractions because of caregiver fatigue or discouragement. However, ignoring misbehavior sends the wrong message to a child. Behaviorist theory teaches that intermittent response to misbehavior is a positive reinforcement, increasing the possibility that the behavior will increase—or at least will not decrease.

A *time-out* is a frequent response to children who exhibit unacceptable behavior, such as aggression toward another child. The child is removed from an activity area and expected to sit by himself for a specified period of time. He is allowed to cool off and told to think about what he has done. The advantage to this method is that it prevents the child from further harming another child, and he does not get attention for his inappropriate behavior, which would reinforce it. The disadvantage of this method is that leaving the child alone while he is experiencing strong emotions may result in his becoming more resentful toward both adults and other children. Time-outs alone do nothing to help the child learn to express his emotions more effectively, resolve conflicts, or build relationship skills.

To be effective, a time-out has to be followed by a discussion with an adult. The child should be asked to describe what started her behavior and to explore what she was feeling at the time. Further discussion can help her to find alternative ways of either preventing similar situations in the future or reacting to them differently should they occur.

Another method of changing children's behavior is to follow misbehavior with a **logical consequence**. This does not mean punishment. A logical consequence is intended to help the child learn, whereas punishment is a forceful way to stop behavior. To be an effective tool for changing behavior, this method has to be related to the specific misbehavior. If a child deliberately makes a mess while painting, it is logical to expect him to clean it up. The consequence for misbehavior should be stated in a calm but firm way that emphasizes the child's ability to be responsible for his own actions. "I expect you to clean up all that paint you have just poured onto the floor. You can get a bucket of water and a sponge in the kitchen. You might bring some paper towels, too, in case you need them."

Reinforcing positive behavior is another method of changing children's behavior. This method is based on behaviorist theory, which states that when behaviors are followed by a pleasant response, that behavior will likely be repeated. Therefore, children should be rewarded when they are observed behaving in ways that are expected by adults.

The rewards can be extrinsic, coming from the environment in the form of a treat, better grades, or a special privilege. Verbal praise and positive feedback are even more effective because they enhance children's intrinsic interest. When the praise and feedback are later removed, children continue to show interest in work (Belsky, 2008). Intrinsic rewards come from within the individual and include feeling good about oneself or feeling capable of achieving a goal.

Positive reinforcers are most effective when children are first trying out new ways of functioning. The reinforcer should immediately follow the desired behavior every time the action is observed. When the behavior seems to be fairly well established, the rewards can be applied less frequently. Eventually, the reward will not be necessary. An example frequently used by both parents and teachers is "I appreciate the way you helped with the cleanup today. It really helps me to get it done more quickly."

Strategies for Changing Behaviors

Children want to behave in acceptable ways but often find their conflicting emotions or lack of experience cause them to act in ways that elicit negative responses from others. If they do not learn another way of behaving, they may be labeled "bad, naughty, or mean." They may even take on that label themselves and wear it as a badge of importance.

"I can be the baddest of the bad." Adults can reverse this process by trying to understand why a child is acting in a particular way and find ways to help her use more acceptable methods to achieve what she wants or needs. Child care staff members can

- try to understand the motivation behind troubling behavior. Is the child trying to get attention? Is he feeling insecure? Is he attempting to boost his self-esteem? Once the behavior is understood, staff members can take appropriate measures to bring about changes. Find methods to give attention, offer support to an insecure child, and boost self-esteem in acceptable ways.
- help children develop an honest sense of their own competence. Point out their special abilities and help them accept the things they may not do so well.
- help children learn to praise themselves. "You should feel proud of yourself for telling Kevin how you felt when he ruined your block building instead of hitting him."
- allow children to express their feelings in ways that are not hurtful to others. Some children may not be able to put their feelings into words. A discussion with a caring adult sometimes helps them find acceptable ways to relieve the feelings. Some children may need active ways to relieve feelings, particularly anger. Provide them with pillows to pound or a place to run.

"Me, when I'm mad." Ricky, age 9.

- model acceptable behavior toward other adults and toward children. Adults who are sensitive to others' needs show children how to behave in similar circumstances. Caregivers who help coworkers or express empathy when another is having difficulty demonstrate appropriate ways to interact and the positive results that follow.
- help children devise additional methods to act on their feelings of empathy by discussing possible ways to behave. Their own limited experiences may not be enough for children to know what to do, and fear of failing may prevent them from acting. "Let's think of some ways to help a friend who is having a difficult day."
- encourage children to put their feelings into words. They may not have acquired the vocabulary to describe feelings or may not have been encouraged to express emotions with words. "Tell her it makes you feel really bad when she calls you names."
- create a nonaggressive environment. Physically, provide plenty of spaces to play and enough age-appropriate materials so children can engage in activities with minimal conflict. Socially, adults and children should focus on supporting and respecting others, offering encouragement when needed. Wherever possible, make it clear that aggressive behavior gets negative results.
- be consistent. Staff members must communicate with each other on how behaviors are to be handled.

COMMUNICATIONS THAT HELP CHANGE BEHAVIOR

The ways in which adults respond verbally to children's behavior can either increase the likelihood of repetitions or bring about changes in behavior. It is normal to become exasperated with children's behavior, particularly at the end of a difficult day. The tendency is to respond with anger, generalizations, or labeling. At one time or another, most adults have made comments such as, "Jason, why are you always getting into fights?" or "Rachel, you're such a loudmouth." These kinds of verbal responses may momentarily relieve the adult's angry feelings, but they do nothing to help the child change. In fact, they may bring about the opposite result, a tendency for the child to repeat the behavior. The child knows how to irritate the adult and takes pleasure in doing it again; or the child may feel that the negative label gives him status among his peers. Child care leaders can learn to respond in ways that are appropriate to the situation, and that will help children gradually change their behavior.

Acknowledge Children's Feelings

Often adults respond to children's expressions of their feelings by denying their existence or trying to change the feelings. Constant denial of feelings or a rush to force them to change makes children distrust their own inner senses.

Example Jennifer has been lying on the book area pillows since she got off the bus from school. Her child care leader wants her to get involved and asks why she does not find something to do. Jennifer answers by saying: "Can't you see I'm tired?" Inappropriate response:

Adult: "How can you be tired when you haven't done anything yet?"

An appropriate response might be:

Adult: "Yes, I know some days at school are tiring. You decide when you're rested and ready to do something."

Describe the Situation

Children are sometimes unaware of all aspects of a situation. They are concentrating on achieving their own goals and are oblivious to anything else.

Example It is cleanup time before a field trip, and there are still materials that have not been put away. Inappropriate response:

Adult: "You guys haven't finished cleaning up, so maybe you won't be ready to go on the trip. Why are you always such slobs?"

An appropriate response might be:

Adult: "I can still see some puzzles on the table and some paints that need to go into the sink. The bus will be here in five minutes, so let's all be ready."

Help Children Recognize How Their Behavior Affects Others

Until children reach a stage of maturity at which they are less egocentric, they often fail to understand that what they do affects others.

Example Two girls are beginning to dress up with some costumes that are kept in a large trunk. Shari pulls out a white dress and says she wants to be a princess and wear it. Leanne looks at her and tells her she can't be a princess because she is too fat. Inappropriate response:

Adult: "Hey, you girls. No name calling."

An appropriate response might be:

Adult: "Shari, how did it make you feel when Leanne said you couldn't be a princess because you're too fat?"

Another appropriate response:

Adult: "Leanne, when you call Shari fat it really hurts her feelings. Did you notice how she quickly put away the dress and looked like she was about to cry?"

BEHAVIORS THAT CREATE PROBLEMS FOR THE INDIVIDUAL OR THE GROUP

Even with knowledge of child development and good intentions, child care staff members often find they are baffled by the behavior of one or more children in their group.

These are the children who exhibit similar behaviors to other children, but what they do has increased intensity and are therefore potentially harmful. There may be a child who is not just aggressive when the situation warrants it, but who bullies other children, seemingly for no reason. Another child may spend a good portion of her time alone and resist any attempts to be included in group activities. Still another may be in a perpetual whirl of motion, hardly stopping long enough to have contact with either adults or children. Each of these children desperately needs, and probably wants, help to become a part of the group and to accepted by others.

The Overly Aggressive Child

Nearly every group includes at least one child who seems to be angry all the time and dislikes both children and adults. Although he often complains that others are picking on him, in reality he is usually teasing other children. At times he may resort to outbursts of physical aggression or verbal attacks. This may be a child who has experienced many failures. He may be feeling powerless and only feels good when he is bullying others. He may also come from a harsh and punitive family background that provides very little nurturing.

Child care leaders can become the significant adults in this child's life, helping him change his behavior. They can

- win his trust by showing him they care about him.
- make sure he understands the rules and standards for behavior in the child care setting.
- be consistent with disciplinary actions. Always follow unacceptable behavior with an appropriate action such as a time-out or the removal of a privilege.

"I am mad when my mom spanks me." Kevin, age 5.

- try to anticipate situations that are likely to cause his outbursts. Suggest alternative actions, activities, or situations.
- acknowledge and reinforce acceptable behavior whenever possible . Do not overdo, but give praise when it is warranted. Include a description of the behavior to be repeated: "I'm happy to see that you were able to wait your turn without pushing."
- encourage intrinsic motivation for appropriate behavior. "You should feel proud of yourself for solving your problem with Juan by listening to what he had to say and working out a solution."

The Quiet Child

The quiet or withdrawn child is often overlooked in a group because she is hardly noticed. She does not create problems, does what she is told, but stays by herself. Sometimes she may appear to be depressed or anxious. Behind this behavior the child may just be shy or feel she is not competent to do the things others do. She may also be afraid of rejection by other children. Child care staff members can

- capitalize on her interests, initially allowing her to pursue them in seclusion. Gradually encourage her to talk about her interests with one other child, then with two children. From there, it may be possible to move her into related activities in a small group of children.
- involve her in puppetry either alone or with a small group. She may be able to participate behind the stage or by acting through the puppet.
- practice pretend telephone conversations. Start by engaging her in a conversation with you. Choose a topic that is likely to interest her. "I know you have a dog at home named George. I certainly like that name. Tell me about him." Encourage further conversation by additional prompting. "What are some of your favorite things you and George do together?" Encourage her to practice with another child. Suggest topics for the conversation, such as telling one another about favorite things they do on weekends or their favorite movie.
- plan activities that will allow this child to be successful. Acknowledge her achievements by describing the behavior that allowed her to succeed. "You were really creative when you figured out how to make a curtain for the puppet theater. That was good thinking!"
- make specific suggestions about things to say to other children or things she can do to enter into group activities. Acknowledge her efforts when she is successful, pointing out what she did that worked.

The Overactive Child

The overactive child creates a lot of problems for teachers and caregivers. During group times, he fidgets, talks loudly, or pokes whoever sits next to him. He never settles down to an activity but moves randomly from one to another. His path through the room may be marked by a trail of destruction.

When asked to wait his turn for a snack or during games, he gets very angry. He has a hard time making or keeping friends because he is often argumentative or manipulative. This may be acting-out behavior due to stress factors, such as a disrupted family life or not enough attention from his parents.

Some of these children may be classified as suffering from attention-deficit hyperactive disorder (ADHD, which will be discussed in the next section), but others may just be overactive. When attempts to moderate the behavior are unsuccessful, it is important to encourage the parents to get a professional evaluation. Before referring an overly active child, however, some modifications can help him control his own behavior. Child care staff members can

- be consistent about rules. Make sure the child understands the rules and enforce them after every misbehavior.
- anticipate unstructured times that are likely to create problems. Examples of these times are when the group moves from indoors to outdoors or in the transition between an activity-oriented period to a snack period. Give plenty of warning that one period is ending and another will begin. Assign this child a specific task during the transition time; have him help prepare the snack and pass it out, or let him hold the door while the other children go outside.
- give this child plenty of support. Seat him nearby at group times, accompany him to an activity, and help him get started.
- help him acquire social skills. Suggest ways he might enter into others' play. Remind him of expected behavior while with other children.
- praise him for times he exercises impulse control. "I saw that you were able to stop yourself that time. You must be proud of yourself for that."
- avoid using negative statements whenever possible. Say "You can build your buildings over here" rather than "Don't knock down Sean's block building."
- encourage physical exercise to use up excess energy. Physical activity also helps stimulate beneficial hormones in the child, which bring about greater calmness.
- simplify your environment. Consider whether there are ways you can eliminate clutter and disorder in the classroom. Are materials easily accessible without having to pull out other materials? Do materials get put back in their places so they are available the next time they are needed?

Attention-Deficit Hyperactive Disorder (ADHD)

Children with true hyperactive disorders display many of the same behaviors as children who are classified as merely overactive. The difference may lie in the intensity or frequency of the behaviors. Diagnosing Attention-Deficit Hyperactive Disorder (ADHD) can be achieved by several methods. Computer imaging of the brain shows smaller basal ganglia and reduced frontal lobe activity in children with ADHD. Basal ganglia affect routine behaviors, and the frontal lobes affect the ability to organize, pay attention, control impulses, and inhibit responses to sensory stimulation (Health Communities, 2001).

In addition to brain scans, observation and evaluation of a child's behavior are still necessary to make an accurate diagnosis. The behaviors that ADHD children most exhibit are distractibility, impatience, impulsivity, and a short attention span. They may also perform acts without an awareness of the consequences or risks.

ADHD is diagnosed six times more often in boys than in girls and occurs in 3 percent to 7 percent of children (Bing Health 2007). This is partly due to the fact that girls who have ADHD daydream, whereas boys act up or talk loudly during class. Girls don't interrupt class routines the ways boys do.

The causes of ADHD seem to be related to neurobiology and genetics. There is some evidence that the use of cigarettes and alcohol during pregnancy or high levels of lead in the environment may be contributing factors (Bing Health, 2007). Since diet restrictions seem to alleviate some symptoms, sugar and food additives may play a part in causing ADHD. Since the disorder runs in families, genetics strongly influences who will be diagnosed with ADHD.

The most frequent treatment for ADHD is the use of several drugs, most often Ritalin. Dexedrine and Cylert are also used. These medications increase the production of the neurotransmitters dopamine and norepinephrine, resulting in increased attention and less restlessness. It may also be effective to decrease the amount of food additives in children's diets. Some diagnosticians also recommend adding vitamin B_1 and magnesium. The suggestions made for managing the behavior of overly active children given in the previous section apply to the child with ADHD as well and are not repeated here. In addition, child care staff members can refer the family to reliable sources for testing and diagnosis. The child care leader can

- make sure the child takes medication as recommended if it is prescribed as a treatment.
- maintain close and supportive contact with the family to continue to evaluate the child's progress and condition.
- give positive reinforcement for the child's attempts to control behavior.

Helping Children with Other Special Needs

Child care leaders may encounter a wide range of special needs when working with children. Certainly a child who comes to the before- and after-school program after experiencing a night of parental fighting, who has had no breakfast, or is temporarily disabled because of a sprained ankle has special needs. This discussion about children with special needs refers, however, to the child who has a diagnosed disability that interferes significantly with his or her development. Some children have learning disabilities that impact their ability to succeed in the school setting when doing reading, writing, or math activities. Others may have a physical problem such as cerebral palsy, which forces them to walk with a limp, wear a brace, or even rely on a walker. There are many diagnosed disabilities—far too many to mention in this textbook. This discussion will be of a more general nature on how to work with children with disabilities. It may be necessary for a caregiver to receive specialized knowledge and training about specific disabilities when children with those disabilities enroll in the child care program.

The child care leader should realize that each child is unique, including those with disabilities. For example, children with autism may share some common characteristics, but for each child there is some uniqueness. The severity of the disability and how he manages the challenge varies from one child to the next.

Inclusionary Settings

Historically, children with disabilities did not receive an education in the traditional school setting and consequently were not a part of traditional before- and after-school child care programs. In December 2004, President George W. Bush signed into law the Individuals with Disabilities Education Act (IDEA). The law specifies that states must adopt criteria for determining whether a child has a specific learning disability. This determination must be made by the child's parents and a team of qualified professionals. Consequently, these children are being more fully included in regular classrooms and child care programs. **Inclusion** refers to placing children with diagnosed disabilities in settings with same age peers. Sometimes children who are fully included in the school setting receive support through the use of classroom assistants. Often these same supports do not exist for the child in a nonacademic setting. Consequently this may pose additional challenges for child care leaders.

An effective child care leader learns about each individual child. He learns about the child's interests, the child's basic temperament, and how to work with the child. The same basic skills of learning about and working with **typically developing** children—that is, children without disabilities—also apply to working with children with special needs. Therefore, the first skill needed by the child care leader working with special-needs children is to develop a positive attitude about the child. The leader must think of this child as if she or he were any other child in the child care program. Think of the child first, then the disability.

When adults model openness and acceptance of children with disabilities, they have a positive influence on the attitudes of other children in the child care program. School-age children may be blunt and ultimately hurtful with their comments as they notice physical differences in children who look or act differently from the majority. Children may exclude the child with disabilities and may even taunt or tease the child. There should be a zero tolerance attitude on teasing. Caregivers can help children gain understanding and acceptance of children who are different from them in a variety of ways. Leaders can teach children that different does not mean bad and that it is okay to be curious but not to be mean. The strategies described earlier for helping children develop their identity and self-esteem

inclusion
placing children with disabilities in settings with same-age peers

typically developing
children without disabilities

are also effective for children with special needs. In addition, caregivers can use the strategies listed for helping children learn cooperative behaviors.

A second skill used by an effective child care leader is to establish a working relationship with the parents and be included in the parent-teacher-caregiver team that supports the child. Assure parents of confidentiality regarding the information they share about their child's disability. Consider the following questions to discuss with parents about a child's abilities and needs:

- "What are the child's current abilities related to movement, cognition, communication, and social interaction?
- What motivates the child to explore his environment and interact with others?
- Which children in the program have similar interests to the child and could play with him in cooperative learning groups?
- What tends to overstimulate or even frighten the child?
- What barriers currently exist that impede the child's access to materials, equipment, and peers?
- What are the parent's current goals for the child in the before- and after-school program?" (Flynn & Kieff, 2002).

This information will be helpful to the child care leader when planning activities and in thinking about the specific **accommodations** to make in order to take care of the child and help the child feel successful. Children with identified special needs will have an **Individualized Education Plan (IEP)** with specific goals and objectives. The goals represent what a team of professionals and the parents think the child can accomplish in his areas of disability in a year's time. Objectives are more specific, measurable tasks that demonstrate the child's progress toward the goal. The IEP is developed for the child in the educational setting, but many of these objectives may apply to the child care setting. A goal may be for the child to give eye contact when someone is talking to him. Another goal might be for him to follow through 80 percent of the time when given verbal instructions. A social goal may be to take a role in cooperative play situations.

Accommodations are the modifications made to activities and routines to meet the needs and goals of the child with special needs. These accommodations may be related to the child's IEP goals. A child with autism may not be able to pick up on instructions given to the entire group or the nonverbal cues that it is time to transition to another activity. An accommodation would be to provide cue cards that can be handed to the child to read or to enlist the help of a peer to guide the child in a transition. A child with a physical impairment may not be able to run while playing a game of soccer with the other teammates. An accommodation would be to involve the child in keeping score or, perhaps, designate her as the person who throws the ball back onto the field when it goes out of bounds. Once children get to know the strengths and challenges of the child with disabilities, they can be involved in developing accommodations. They may decide to change how the game of soccer is played so that all can be included. The leader may have to start this problem solving. "Sylvia really is interested in playing soccer. How can we change the game so she can use her walker on the field and still play?"

accommodations
changes that are necessary when planning activities to include special-needs children

Individualized Education Plan (IEP)
set of goals determined by a team of professionals and parents to reflect what the child should accomplish within a year's time

What are some possible physical accommodations to fully include this child?

It will be important to determine whether the child's needs match the program goals and objectives. Under the Individuals with Disabilities Education Act (2004) a child with disabilities must be included in your program unless

- the child's condition poses a direct threat to the other children or your staff and the direct threat cannot be eliminated through reasonable accommodations.
- the child's condition would require architectural changes that cannot readily be achieved.
- the child's requirement for special equipment or services would impose an undue burden or fundamentally alter the nature of the program and there were no reasonable alternatives.
- the child's condition would require changes in policies, practices, or procedures, which would fundamentally alter the nature of the program.

A third skill to enable leaders to be effective when working with children with disabilities is consistency. Most children, typical and atypical, do best when the daily routine is consistent. Routines give structure and stability to children who may not be very adaptable or struggle with self-regulation and need to know what to expect. Create consistency by learning how challenges or difficult behaviors are handled at home and in school.

The Child with Autism

One of the disabilities that caregivers of school-age children may encounter in a before- and after-school program is autism. Autism is a complex set of disorders that affect about one-half million people in the United States today. About 10 to 15 out of every 10,000 people, depending on the diagnosis criteria used, will be diagnosed with the disease. An additional 12 to 20 per 10,000 have autistic-like features. Three boys to one girl have the disorder (Landy, 2009). The term *autism* is sometimes used to describe several related disorders that are included under the heading of pervasive developmental disorder (PDD). The term is also used to refer to a child who cannot be specifically diagnosed but has severe impairment in behaviors. The standard reference *Diagnostic and Statistical Manual* (DSM) (2000) lists the following categories:

- *Autistic Disorder*. Limited social interaction, language, and imaginative play observed in children, usually before the age of three. There may also be stereotyped interests and repetitive behaviors.
- *Asperger's Disorder*. Impaired social interactions, restricted interests and activities. No significant general delay in language. These children test in the average or above-average intelligence levels.
- *Childhood Disintegrative Disorder*. Normal development in the first two years, then loss of previously acquired skills. Children who fall within the general spectrum of pervasive developmental disorders may seem relatively normal for the first two years or so, then parents or caretakers notice changes that may include a delay in

speech or inappropriate use of words. As an example, many of these children refer to themselves by their name, rather than "I." Or they may repeat the words of TV commercials without seeming to attach any significance to them. Often these children do not want to be held or cuddled and avoid eye contact with others. They seem incapable of spontaneous play and do not initiate pretend games. Their behavior ranges from overactive to very passive and may include aggression toward others or themselves. Changes in routine often bring on temper tantrums.

However, children with autism can be vary widely with their own unique characteristics and personalities. Some may be only mildly affected, for they make eye contact, display a variety of emotions, and have the ability to communicate. Their abilities to learn may fluctuate from day to day, depending on external stimuli and the level of anxiety the child is feeling. These children may also process information in unique ways, perhaps using mental images rather than words to process and remember information. They may have above-average verbal or memory skills but encounter great difficulty engaging in imaginative activities with others. As autistic children grow older, some learn to compensate for and cope with their disability, becoming productive adults who can earn college degrees, obtain meaningful work, and establish families.

Caregivers can help children with autism and their families if they

- refer parents to programs that can provide evaluation and intervention measures. There is evidence that early intervention (during the preschool years) is the most effective; but even later intervention can help children learn to live with their disability. Some children with autism need to be in a small, specially designed program, whereas others benefit from inclusion in regular programs.
- provide a structured environment for children with pervasive developmental disorder. They need to know what to expect in terms of routines and be given time to manage transitions.
- understand and make use of each child's unique way of learning. Design learning activities that allow each individual to process information in his own way. For instance, use pictures as well as words to describe a process to follow for an activity.
- use positive reinforcement. This helps children understand what they are doing that is right and increases their self-esteem.
- are flexible and willing to change approaches. Evaluate what you are doing on a regular basis, and find an alternative approach if one is needed to achieve the desired results.
- use good communication skills yourself, and encourage children to use words. Sometimes helping a child use even a single word to express a need or emotion can lead to greater ability.
- support parents. Living with a child who has autism can be extremely stressful, and parents need to be able to talk to others about their concerns. Be willing to listen without being judgmental. Parents also may need help finding more effective ways to manage their child at home through educational services or support groups.

SUMMARY

- During middle childhood, children want to have friends. Those who lack social skills have a difficult time and may be either aggressive or passive, perform poorly academically, and have emotional problems. Those who have good social skills will have lots of friends, get better grades, and probably function effectively as adults.

- Children often learn to resolve conflicts by observing adults at home, in their neighborhoods, in movies, on TV, and at school but can gradually learn to negotiate a compromise, bargain, or use humor to deflect anger.

- Self-image has two parts: our perceptions of ourselves and the perceptions conveyed to us by others.

- Cooperation with others does not come easily to children. Gradually, during middle childhood, they learn that others have needs and that they must compromise and cooperate to have friends.

- The ways adults respond verbally to children's behavior can either increase or decrease the likelihood of repetitions and bring about changes in behavior.

- Some children exhibit behaviors that create problems for themselves or the group.

- The overactive child may be suffering from Attention-Deficit Hyperactive Disorder (ADHD) and should be evaluated. Appropriate treatment should be prescribed.

- Since passage of the Individuals with Disabilities Education Act, children with special needs are sometimes fully included in before- and after-school programs. Autism is one of the disabilities child care leaders may encounter in children in the before- and after-school child care program. The term "autism" covers a complex set of disorders, sometimes also called pervasive developmental disorders.

KEY TERMS

accommodations	logical consequence	optional rules
inclusion	negotiable rules	self-image
Individualized Education Plan (IEP)	non-negotiable rules	typically developing

REVIEW QUESTIONS

1. State four reasons why professionals advocate teaching children how to relate to others.

2. List and explain the steps in problem solving.

3. State three strategies for helping children learn to resolve conflicts effectively.

4. List five things an adult can do to help children increase their self-esteem.

5. What are some causes of overaggressive behavior in children?

6. Describe the behavior of an overly active child. What might be the cause of this behavior?

7. This chapter suggests that reinforcing positive behavior is effective for changing how children relate to others. Describe this method.

8. One of the strategies for helping children increase their self-esteem is to involve them in projects where children and adults can work together. How does this affect how they feel about themselves?

9. Why is it important to help children increase their ability to read non-verbal cues?

10. Describe one activity you could use to foster social competence.

11. What are three things that are important to learn about a child with disabilities entering the program?

12. What is the difference between learning about the child with disabilities and learning about the disability?

Case Study

The room where Rowan's child care group meets has only one computer, which is much sought after by all the children. This afternoon Mei wants to e-mail her friend in China and is eager to get started. Three other children are clamoring to get online as well. They each have urgent things they want to do. Emily has a homework assignment, Gregory wants to finish a game he started the day before, and Xavier just wants to explore some information about stars, his newest interest. They all begin squabbling, each declaring he or she should be first. Rowan is so tired of the fighting over the one computer that she would like to just get rid of it, but she knows the children benefit by using it. Her assistant thinks they should all be told that no one can use the computer until they learn to share.

1. Do you agree with the assistant's advice that none of them should be allowed to use the computer until they learn to share? If you disagree, why?

2. If you were Rowan, what would be the first thing you would do to resolve the problem?

3. Can you think of a plan that would prevent problems like this in the future?

STUDENT ACTIVITIES

1. In class, practice problem solving using the steps listed in this chapter. Work in pairs, with each member of the pair assuming one side of a controversy. Choose one of the following situations, or describe one from your own experience.

   a. Two caregivers share a room. One never cleans up thoroughly when an activity is finished, so at the end of the day the room is in chaos.

   b. On the playground, one caregiver spends a lot of time with individual children rather than supervising the group. The other adult is left to intervene when altercations occur, stimulate additional activities, and generally manage a large group of children.

   Share the results with classmates. Was the process easy or difficult? Were you able to use "I" messages when telling what happened? Did each of the partners feel satisfied with the resolution?

2. Work with one of your classmates to determine whether your perception of yourself is the same as or different from how others see you. First, write down five words that describe your partner. Next, write five words that describe you. Compare your partner's list with your own. Did each of you agree when describing the other? How close was your self-evaluation to the way your partner described you? How does this activity contribute to your understanding of the complexity of self-image in children?

3. Interview a caregiver. What methods does he or she use to promote children's ability to cooperate with one another?

4. Imagine that you have just enrolled a first-grade child with autism in your program. Develop a plan for learning about the child and his disability. What strategies will you use to ensure the child is included in small group activities and is accepted and respected by the other children?

SUGGESTED READINGS

American Academy of Child and Adolescent Psychiatry, (2008). Bullying, 80, May 2008.

Coloroso, B. (2003). *The Bully, the Bullied, and the Bystander*. New York: HarperCollins.

Frankel, E.B. (2004). Supporting inclusive care and education for young children with special needs and their families: An international perspective. *Childhood Education*, 80 (6), 310–316.

Gallagher, K.C.(2005). Brain research and early childhood development: A primer for DAP. *Young Children* 60 (4), 12–20.

Jones, N.P. (2005). Big jobs: Planning for competence. *Young Children*, 60 (2), 86–93.

Szabo, Liz, (2010). Youngest is class get ADHD label. *USA Today*, August 17, 2010.

Winerip, Michael, (2010). A school district that takes the isolation out of autism. *The New York Times*, August 8, 2010.

WEB RESOURCES

http://www.ada.gov
Americans with Disabilities Act (ADA). This website offers information and technical assistance on the ADA.

http://www.autism-society.org
Autism Society of America. Multiple links to information for helping children with autism.

http://idea.ed.gov
Individuals with Disabilities Education Act (IDEA). Information and resources for IDEA.

http://www.naar.org
National Alliance for Autism Research. A nonprofit organization dedicated to finding the causes, prevention, treatment, and ultimately a cure for the autism spectrum of disorders.

REFERENCES

Americans with Disabilities Education Act (ADA), (2004). United States Department of Justice.

Arcia, E., & Conners, C. K. (1998). Gender differences in *ADHD? Journal of Developmental and Behavioral Pediatrics*, 19 (2), 77–83.

Belsky, Jay (2008). Rewards are better than punishments: Here's why. *Psychology Today*, September 25, 2008.

Children's Defense Fund. (2009). *The State of America's Children, 2009.* Washington, DC: Author.

DMS-V-TR. (2000). *Diagnostic and Statistical Manual of Mental Disorders,* 4th ed. American Psychiatric Association, Washington DC: American Psychiatric Press.

Ferrer-Chancy, M. & Fugate, A. (2008). The importance of friendship for school-age children. Retrieved from the Internet http://www.edis.ifas. ufl.edu/fy545.

Flynn, L. L., & Kieff, J. (2002). Including everyone in outdoor play. *Young Children,* 57(3), 20–26.

Health Communities (2001). Attention-Deficit Hyperactivity Disorder (ADHD) cause and risk.

Safer, D. J. & Krager, J. M. (1994). The increased rate of stimulant treatment for hyperactive/inattentive students in secondary schools. *Pediatrics*, 94,462–464.

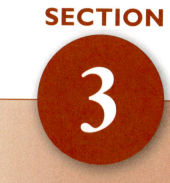

SECTION

3

The Background

8

Program Planning

DEVELOPING PROGRAM GOALS

One of the best ways to design a program is to gather everyone together who has a stake in program outcomes. These stakeholders could be staff members, parents, community agency personnel, and school personnel. Organize a dialogue around the questions "What do children need to learn in this setting? What do young people need to be successful?" Stakeholders can inform their discussions by examining the research on school-age programs to learn about their outcomes for children. The research brief on *After School Programs in the 21st Century* by the Harvard Family Research Project (2008) is a good place to begin. Stakeholders can also read the literature of well-known organizations such as the National Association for the Education of Young Children and the National Institute on Out-of-School Time to determine elements of quality programming for school-age children. These can be found at www.naeyc.org and www.niost.org. The conclusions of the stakeholders' dialogue will probably include ideas such as providing a safe place for children with opportunities to: explore cultural and gender issues, improve academic success, get assistance with homework, acquire social competence skills, develop meaningful relationships with adults and children, pursue their own interests, and learn to appreciate good nutrition and fitness. Other questions might ask whether any of these goals are being met in other environments, such as the home, school, church, temple, or community. Participants in this discussion should also decide which goals should take priority and whether the child care center has the resources to meet the goals. Finally, question how the goals can complement what is going on in other places in the children's lives or how they can compensate for what is *not* happening.

LEARNING OUTCOMES

After reading this chapter, you should be able to:

✔ Describe how to begin the process of developing program goals.

✔ Explain the difference between a holistic vs. an academic approach to programming.

✔ Discuss the two general aspects of developmentally appropriate practices and the three kinds of knowledge necessary for child care leaders to understand.

✔ Describe planning for children with varying cultural and linguistic backgrounds.

✔ Discuss the importance of planning, and some common planning approaches and guidelines.

✔ Describe some approaches to organizing an after-school program.

✔ Discuss the planning of summer programs.

APPROACHES TO PROGRAM PLANNING

Early developmental research led to the conclusion that the most successful programs for young children should be based on the premise that the optimal conditions for developmental changes occur with an active child in an active environment. Studies by both Jean Piaget (1952) and Lev Vygotsky (1978) pointed to the importance of children's interactions with their environment and the impact of the social environment on development. Piaget stressed the predictable stages of qualitative changes in a child's thinking that allow him to construct knowledge through interactions with his environment. Vygotsky believed that thinking changes as a result of instruction or support (scaffolding) from the environment and as language skills increase.

The ongoing debate among early childhood professionals asks the questions, "Which is better, an academic, or a holistic approach to providing before and after school age child care? Or is the best approach one that is both academic and holistic?" An **academic approach** to programming involves determining outcomes related to school performance that can be measured, and then planning a program to help children reach those goals. A **holistic approach** allows the curriculum to focus on the development of the whole child, and evolves based on children's individual and group abilities and interests. This approach does not mean that the curriculum is unplanned, but that it includes a basic structure from which many possible variations can emerge: This is also called an **emergent curriculum**. The structure is formed through the knowledge caregivers have of children's abilities and interests, through having a wide variety of materials and activities available for use as needed, and through encouraging children to be involved in planning.

In addition to this debate about the approach to planning are discussions that center on the range of academic, social, and other knowledge and skills children will need to develop to succeed later on as adults. A summary of the research on after-school programs over the last 10 years by the Harvard Family Research Project (2008) has resulted in some answers to these questions. The project's findings confirm that after-school programs can improve children's academic performance as well as their social and communications skills, decrease delinquency, and contribute to healthier lifestyles through increased knowledge about nutrition and exercise. A critical factor in achieving these successful outcomes is quality programming that provides a wide variety of enriching opportunities for children to be exposed to new ideas, challenges, and people while addressing children's interests and needs. The research studies indicate that the outcomes are a result of balancing academic support with engaging, fun, and structured activities in a variety of real-world contexts.

More recently, Sue Bredekamp and Carol Copple (2009), editors of *Developmentally Appropriate Practice in Early Childhood Programs Serving Children from Birth through Age 8, 3rd edition* (2009), have provided us with an approach to programming for young children that is recommended by

---

academic approach
an approach to programming that involves determining outcomes related to school performance that can be measured and then planning a program to help children achieve those goals

holistic approach
a curriculum that focuses on the development of the whole child and evolves from children's individual and group abilities and interests

emergent curriculum
activities that are planned as a result of caregivers noting the current interests of children or that develop as children play

the National Association for the Education of Young Children (NAEYC). This resource is more commonly known as DAP. It provides teachers and caregivers with guidelines for practices that are most effective in promoting children's learning and development. Developmentally appropriate practice is grounded in research on child development and learning, as well as in the knowledge of proven effective teaching practices in early education.

DEVELOPMENTALLY APPROPRIATE PRACTICE

According to Bredekamp and Copple (2009), developmentally appropriate school-age child care programs should be tailored to the age and developmental status of the children they serve, and should respond to the social and cultural contexts in which children live. Bredekamp and Copple further state: "Developmentally appropriate practice means ensuring that goals and experiences are suited to children's learning and development and challenging enough to promote their progress and interest" (xii). Therefore, there are two core considerations for caregivers as they make decisions in their work with children. One is knowledge of children's development and learning, and the second is determining challenging and achievable goals for children.

Knowledge of Children's Development and Learning

Child care leaders base decisions in every aspect of their work with children on their understanding of how children develop and what children know and can do. There are three kinds of knowledge for child care leaders to consider:

- Knowledge of child development and learning and age-related characteristics of children
- Knowledge of each individual child in the child care program
- Knowledge of each child within the context of his family, community, and culture

Caregivers are knowledgeable about the universal, predictable growth and changes that occur in children, and make predictions about what children are capable of doing and learning. They are intentional about designing an environment and planning activities that will optimize the physical, cognitive, social, and emotional development of children. Quality programs must address the fact that children change tremendously in middle childhood, and there are great variations in the rate and type of change in all developmental areas. Even within an individual child there is great variation from one stage to another or within a stage of development. Children who are five to seven years of age differ from those approaching adolescence in terms of what they know and are able to do. The youngest children may need more direction and motivators. The oldest children want more autonomy and adult-like responsibilities. Caregivers understand that middle childhood is a period in which children become independent of their parents and increasingly want to be accepted by their peers. As they strive for independence from their parents, children look to other adults to guide them through the process of adjusting to the outside world.

Caregivers of school-age children are knowledgeable about the development and learning of each child in their program. They learn about each child through observations, meaningful conversations with the children, examining children's work, and conversations with the family. Children differ in their rate of development, their interests, skills, and abilities. For example, as caregivers plan to promote children's development of friendships, they might notice that one child does not play with other children, another seems to have lots of friends, and yet another watches children in play as if she wants to join in but does not know how. The program planners will be intentional as they plan for the development of each of these children.

Caregivers are knowledgeable of the social and cultural context in which children live. Each child comes from a home and community with values, beliefs, language, experiences, and behavioral expectations that are unique. For example, children may live in low-income or affluent families, with a single parent, or in a household where the dominant speaking language is not English. Program planners will consider the experiences of each child as they decide what is meaningful and relevant curriculum that can promote all children's development and learning.

Promote Development Through Challenging and Achievable Goals

School-age child care programs have goals for the children in their care based on the philosophy and goals of the particular program. Additionally, child care leaders develop challenging and achievable goals as a result of knowing the developmental status of the children in their care, and understanding what the children can understand and are able to do. Child care leaders are intentional in creating an environment and planning teaching strategies and activities directed toward these goals.

When child care leaders know their children well, they are more attuned to capturing "teachable moments." These moments come when children's excitement over something they have learned or experienced suggests the possibility of planning a new activity or project or having a meaningful conversation with adults or peers. With a wide variety of materials available, caregivers can help children explore these ideas. The emphasis is on developing and broadening the children's expressed interests.

Consider the goal of fostering children's peer relationships. Friendships with one or two others and a sense of belonging to a group are essential to children's self-esteem. Adults can facilitate peer relationships by supporting children's developing social skills. Staff members are intentional in initiating activities that encourage children to discuss the causes of conflicts and ways to resolve them and capturing teachable moments when conflicts arise. Additionally, developmentally appropriate child care programs use both mixed-age and same-age grouping to help children develop relationships with their peers according to their own developmental needs. Staff members should use positive guidance strategies to help children achieve self regulation—that is, inner control and self-discipline. Adults need to encourage children to resolve their own differences, listen to children, and encourage them to verbalize their feelings. Positive guidance also means that staff can help children behave productively by describing problem situations and encouraging group problem solving.

A goal for children might be to help them develop their self-concept. Child care leaders recognize the need for independence in this process. Children want to feel successful and gain control over their own actions. Child care leaders can help achieve this sense of success by letting children direct their own activities and having supportive staff who allow independence, but offer guidance as needed.

Children should also be challenged to increase their cognitive abilities. Caregivers should provide varied and interesting activities that are neither too easy nor too difficult for their developmental level. Those planning developmentally appropriate programs should not overlook the importance of physical competence and well-being. Children should have a wide variety of activities in which they can practice skills requiring both large- and small-muscle coordination. Intentional child care leaders can encourage children to develop sound attitudes and practices to ensure their own health and safety. Children should have opportunities to learn what constitutes fitness, how to maintain health, and what to include in a healthy diet.

A program goal might be for children to become more aware of others and less egocentric. They can be challenged to explore their community and grapple with societal issues. This is also an opportunity to understand diversity and develop attitudes that respect differences. The youngest children can read books and experience the arts from different cultures. The oldest children may be ready to discuss global issues, including ecological conservation or social ills such as discriminatory practices. They may even become involved in activities to try to resolve some of these problems.

PLANNING FOR CULTURAL AND LINGUISTIC DIVERSITY

One area of knowledge caregivers should have is knowledge of each child within the context of his family, community and culture. Children come from varied backgrounds and cultures. The 2008 census found that 22% of all children in the United States are in immigrant families. (Mather, 2009). Children's sense of self-worth stems partly from their experiences within the family and their community and their ability to master the skills expected of them in those settings. They will learn best if the expectations and values of their school or child care are congruent with those of their family and community. As an example, children who can communicate well with their family or neighborhood friends in a language other than English may find it difficult to be understood or learn in other environments. To this end, the NAEYC has published a position statement entitled "Responding

Children's sense of self-worth stems partly from their varied backgrounds and cultures.

to linguistic and cultural diversity—Recommendations for effective early childhood education" (1996). It states that developmentally appropriate programs should recognize that all children are cognitively, linguistically, and emotionally connected to the language and culture of their home.

The 2009 Developmentally Appropriate Practice (NAEYC) states: "When children are in a group setting outside the home, what makes sense to them, how they use language to interact, and how they experience this new world depend on the social and cultural contexts to which they are accustomed". As previously stated, this means that the teacher must consider the developmental level of each child when planning activities and daily routines. It also means considering the child as a member of a family, living in a cultural community that has its own expectations for learning and behavior.

Another aspect of cultural and linguistic diversity is embodied in the 1996 NAEYC statement:

Acknowledge that children can demonstrate their knowledge and capabilities in many ways.

This statement recognizes that children have acquired many cognitive skills and knowledge before entering school or child care. They should be able to demonstrate those skills using their home language and then begin to build on that base while learning English. They may be able to learn English, but learning more complex cognitive skills requires an integrated approach. Children learn more easily when they are given instruction in their primary language and when their language is used and respected.

Additional recommendations focus on establishing reciprocal relationships with families. NAEYC suggests that parents become actively involved in the early learning program, that teachers help parents become knowl-edgeable about the cognitive value of knowing more than one language, and that programs support the family's cultural values. A study on develop-ing literacy in second-language learners (August & Shanahan, 2006) points strongly to the importance of parents helping children succeed academi-cally by providing home literacy experiences and opportunities. When children have lots of opportunities to read and be read to in their home or in a group setting, they will develop literacy in a second language more easily (Krashen, 1992). Classroom computers may also provide opportuni-ties to learn with the child's home language or to begin learning a second language. Check http://www.languagegames.org.

The NAEYC recommendations also suggest supporting and preserv-ing children's home language. This can be done by an adult speaking the language and also by providing many examples of the language within the environment. Books, bulletin boards, CDs and tape recordings, labels on materials, and signs are all ways to incorporate the home language into the environment. If caregivers do not speak the child's language, they can learn words and phrases from that language as well as create an environment with the words and phrases displayed. In addition to designing the environ-ment to reflect different languages, children who speak the same language can be grouped together at times to work on specific projects. However, it is important to ensure that these children do not become isolated and are incorporated into other groups as well.

Anti-bias Education

Since the publication of *Anti-Bias Curriculum: Tools for Empowering Young Children* (Derman-Sparks & the ABC Task Force, 1989), early childhood educators have been embracing **anti-bias education** in their work with children and families. Now, more than 20 years later, this work has been built on and refined in *Anti-Bias Education for Young Children and Ourselves*, (Derman-Sparks & Edwards, 2010). According to the authors, "the under-lying intentions remain the same – to support children's full development in our multiracial, multilingual, multicultural world and to give them the tools to stand up to prejudice, stereotyping, bias, and eventually to in-stitutional 'isms.' We are called upon to integrate core goals of anti-bias education in developmentally appropriate ways throughout our children's educational journey" (p. vii).

Derman-Sparks and Edwards (2010) have identified four core goals for anti-bias education. All four goals work together, apply to all children, and influence every aspect of early childhood programs. When implemented, these goals work together to provide a safe, supportive community for all children.

- Each child will demonstrate self-awareness, confidence, family pride, and a positive social identity.
- Each child will express comfort and joy with human diversity; ac-curate language for human differences; and deep, caring human connections.

anti-bias education
An educational approach that supports children's full development in our multiracial, multilingual, multicultural world and gives them the tools to stand up to prejudice, stereotyping, bias, and eventually to institutional "isms"

- Each child will increasingly recognize unfairness, have language to describe unfairness, and understand that unfairness hurts.
- Each child will demonstrate empowerment and the skills to act, with others and alone, against prejudice and/or discriminatory actions.

One of the anti-bias education principles cited by Derman-Sparks and Edwards (2010 is that "anti-bias education avoids the pitfall of tourist curriculum" (8). The "tourist approach" teaches children about other cultural groups through holiday celebrations, ethnic art activities, and cooking ethnic foods. These groups are not talked about again until the same time the following year or when there is another culturally related holiday. In contrast, an anti-bias approach reflects the children and families in the program. It takes into account all children's developmental levels, their interests, and their concerns, and consistently identifies opportunities to learn about differences and similarities of culture, racial identity, abilities, gender, family structures, and economic class.

At an early age children become aware of differences among people. Four-year-olds notice and begin to ask about the differences between boys and girls, why one child has dark skin, why another speaks with an accent, or why another cannot walk and has to be in a wheelchair. By the time they reach middle childhood, children may stop asking the questions because adults are embarrassed or do not know how to answer them. The result can be the development of prejudices or stereotypes. In a bias-free environment, Derman-Sparks (1987) says, "children should be free to ask questions about any subject, to use their own ideas in problem-solving, to engage in real dialogue with adults, to make choices, and to have some say in their daily school life" (8).

One of the ways to promote anti-bias education is to start with the child care environment by including

- photos of children and families that reflect the racial and ethnic makeup of the group
- images of both men and women doing a variety of jobs, not just those that are typically associated with a certain gender
- images of people with disabilities performing jobs or interacting with others in recreational settings
- toys and materials that include books reflecting diversity of gender roles and ethnic differences, people with disabilities, and diverse family structures; books that include different languages, either through stories or alphabets; dramatic play materials that encourage children to engage in common everyday tasks without concern for gender roles; implements and tools used by different ethnic groups, such as cooking equipment, holiday decorations, clothes, or personal objects; art materials that can be used to depict people of different skin tones or that are representative of different cultures; small toys and manipulatives that depict racial diversity
- opportunities for children to see or hear different languages through signs, labels, story tapes, or songs
- musical activities that include music from other cultures

THE IMPORTANCE OF PLANNING

If you think of yourself as a spontaneous and flexible person, you may wonder whether you really need to plan. Nevertheless, when you work with children, looking ahead is absolutely essential. Without it, a day can lead to chaos, unhappy children, and irritable adults.

Planning ensures that you can provide a variety of play opportunities that will attract and stimulate children and enhance their development. **Curriculum** is a plan of activities that accomplishes the goals of a program. Caregivers should provide a balance between old and new activities. Some should be familiar things children like to do over and over again. Others should be new things to spark their interest.

Planning ahead allows you to gather the materials needed to carry out an activity. Knowing a day or week in advance what you will need allows you time to find, purchase, or prepare whatever you will require. When children have to wait while you collect supplies, they get restless. Then, when you are ready, they may no longer be receptive.

Planning lessens the number of conflicts between children. A group of children can engage in free play for periods of time, but eventually differences arise. During the three hours or so that children are in after-school care, some free play, along with planned activities, keeps children busy and involved. Petty arguments and irritability will decrease.

Plans allow staff members to divide responsibilities. Everyone should know specifically what they will be required to do during a period of time.

> **curriculum**
> a plan of activities that accomplishes the goals of a program

Planning ensures that you can provide a variety of play opportunities that will attract and stimulate children and enhance their development.

Some may have responsibility for playground supervision and others for setting up activities in the classrooms. Every step of the day—including transitions, activities, snack, and free play—should be planned ahead of time.

The most important function of program planning is to ensure that both the short- and long-term goals of the program are met. Short-term goals are those that can be achieved during a single day, a week, or even, perhaps, a month. Long-term goals are those that will not be achieved until a fairly long period of time has passed. This span may cover several months or even a school year. Children need to feel successful through the completion of short projects or at the end of a single activity. But they also should be learning to carry through activities that will not bring rewards until a considerable period of time has passed.

Planning also helps staff members apply the guidelines for developmentally appropriate practices and incorporate goals of anti-bias education. As each day's activities are decided, they can be measured against the guidelines. Will they allow children to develop their physical skills? Are there opportunities for creative expression? Is there a balance between staff-initiated activities and time for child-initiated ones? Are there activities at different levels of difficulty so children at diverse developmental levels can participate and feel successful?

Plans allow you to keep parents and the school administration informed of program activities. Make written plans so this information is readily accessible. Post your plans on a bulletin board for parents. Provide copies for the administrative person at your school or center.

PLANNING THE INTEGRATED CURRICULUM

integrated curriculum
the linking of two or more subject areas such as literacy and math, or linking an academic subject to the community or vocations

Planning an integrated curriculum is one approach to meeting the goals of school-age child care program. An **integrated curriculum** is the linking of two or more subject areas such as literacy and math, or linking an academic subject to the community or vocations. This is accomplished by providing meaningful experiences that allow children to develop a variety of skills and knowledge that lead to the understanding of relationships and how things fit together. A school-age program is an ideal place to provide children with such meaningful experiences because it can allow for the necessary time for integration. An integrated curriculum activity has two or more primary goals. For example, an art activity could have the goal of teaching children painting techniques. Another goal would be to link the activity with someone in the community who paints pictures. The artist could visit the classroom and paint alongside the children. This activity could be further integrated with a literacy goal of doing research about the techniques of a specific artist, such as Jackson Pollock, Diego Rivera, or Vincent van Gogh. Often it requires more than one child care leader to implement an integrated curriculum. In this example, one caregiver might be responsible for the art activity and inviting an artist, while a second caregiver could plan the artist research activity. One resource for research would be http://www.gettingtoknow.com.

A key component to integrated curriculum is that children make connections between one subject and another. In this example, literacy, art, and the community are connected. Children can experience the connections between research, personal techniques and creativity, and local and historical artists.

THE PROJECT APPROACH TO PLANNING

Another way of meeting the goals of the program is through the use of the **project approach**. Lilian Katz (1994) defines project as an in-depth investigation of a topic worth learning about. The investigation is undertaken by a small group of children, the entire class or an individual child. It is a research-based project focused on finding answers about a topic posed either by the children, the teacher, or the teacher working with the children. Projects provide sustained involvement of children, can engage parents, and are an opportunity to integrate the curriculum components of science, math, social studies, and literacy while challenging children. They evolve as a result of child care leaders reflecting on what they know about the interests, capabilities, and cultural context of the children in a group. The implementation of a project undergoes three phases: beginning the project, investigation, and concluding the project (Helm & Beneke, 2003).

project approach
an in-depth investigation of a topic worth learning more about

Consider the situation in which a child care leader observes that children have an interest in motorcycles. The leader begins the project, phase I, by providing a variety of books, magazines, and pictures on the subject for children to explore. If their interest persists, he may decide to continue the project. He asks the children, "What do you know about motorcycles?" and "What do you want to find out about motorcycles?" The children's ideas are written on a large piece of paper and posted in the classroom. Then in phase II, children investigate motorcycles. The leader plans to have a parent bring his motorcycle to the center and the children study the motorcycle, noting the details of its design. They create observational drawings for later use. The leader invites the parent to talk about the motorcycle. Video and digital cameras are used to document the investigation. The topic can be further investigated by going on a field trip to a motorcycle shop, or parents can be encouraged to take their children to visit one. The field trip will result in more observational drawings and pictures by the children. Later the children's observation drawings, video footage, and digital pictures will be used to continue discussion about motorcycles. From these discussions, children can begin making and playing with a pretend motorcycle shop. Children refer to their drawings and the pictures of the motorcycle and replicate its components out of materials such as paper plates, toilet paper rolls, tape, and boxes. (Note: In one such investigation, the caregiver provided a sawhorse to be the frame of the motorcycle.) In phase III, the leader concludes the project by asking the children, "What did you learn about motorcycles?" Pictures and the caregiver's written observations of children's conversations and work acquired throughout the project document the learning experience. These can be organized to create a class book or poster presentation of the project.

GUIDELINES FOR PLANNING: WHAT SHOULD BE INCLUDED IN A CHILD CARE PROGRAM?

Start with the Routine Things You and the Children Do Every Day

Plan who will pick up children at their schools, and know what the children will do when they first arrive at their after-school setting. Decide who will take roll, when you will have the snack, who will supervise the playground, and what activities will be ready. These activities may seem trivial, but they are not. Children enjoy a predictable environment, and predictable environments support children's development of self-regulation. Carefully planning your schedule makes the day run more smoothly for both adults and children.

Capitalize on Children's Interests

Some children may want to continue themes they are working on at school, whereas others may have some current interests unrelated to school.

Holidays, too, create excitement that can generate ideas. Television or movies may also pique interests you can use. Sometimes one child has a special interest that can be shared with others. Use this child's interest to generate enthusiasm in others as they work together on projects.

Increase Children's Awareness of and Respect for Cultural Diversity

Plan activities to help children embrace that they live in a society that includes peoples of many races, colors, and religions. This philosophy can be conveyed through books, holiday celebrations, art activities, toys, building projects, games, and festivals. Make these topics an integral part of your program, not just something you do on special occasions. Ask parents for help. Use the children as resources for customs that are representative of their culture.

Include opportunities for language-minority children to share their language with others. An example might be to have one child read or tell a story with another child translating as the tale progresses. Learn and use words from the minority language during the day's activities.

Foster Children's Desire to Become Competent

Provide choices for children by creating space for a wide variety of activities for individual children or small and large groups with more self-selected activities than staff-selected activities. Let children help with daily routine tasks that allow them to use real tools. Teach them to cut up fruit for snack time. Let them answer the telephone and take messages. Include them in the maintenance of their environment.

Plan projects that use tools and technology. Show them how to use a saw, hammer, and drill for woodworking projects. Let them measure with a T square, a tape measure, or a yardstick. Work with children to use digital cameras, CD players, video cameras, and computers.

Encourage Children's Natural Play Interests

Keep a store of props that inspire music, drama, and dancing. Help children also to be more competent with the fads that sweep through groups of children. Yo-yos, roller skates, and skateboards are not just "time wasters" but allow children to develop their skills. Use these interests to foster their physical development and greater self-esteem.

Plan a Balance of Activities with Enough Choices for Children

Include both group and individual activities. Provide quiet times interspersed with active play. Allow time for activities the children themselves initiate and conduct as well as those you choose and direct. Provide a variety of choices to allow for different interests and levels of capability and give children something to do.

Include Some Activities That Will Recreate Everyday Experiences

Remember that children who spend after-school hours in child care will miss these kinds of experiences. Take children with you to do the shopping for snacks or for a special art project. Arrange trips to local businesses. Take walks around your community.

After a day at school, children need more active play opportunities.

Allow Time to Meet the Special Needs of School-Age Children

Let the children be alone or give them time to do what they want. Provide opportunities for them to make new friends or spend time with existing friends. Some children may even need time to rest or just do nothing.

Plan How Transitions Will Be Accomplished

Transitions are times when all or part of the group change places or activities. The morning arrival and end-of-the-day departure are also transitions. Each of these transitions should be thoughtfully planned to prevent chaos and help children develop self-control and self-direction. Plan ahead by setting up curriculum areas so the next activity is ready as soon as the children move. For instance, when going from group time to individual activities, tell the children what is available and have them choose what they are going to do before they leave the group area. In that way, they can move directly to an activity. Minimize waiting time or times when children have nothing to do. Provide books, videos, or tapes for those times when children have to wait for others to be ready to move to the next activity or when a parent is late for pickup. Alert the children that a change will be taking place, allowing them time to finish whatever activity or task in which they have been engaged. "You have five minutes to finish up your project, then it will be time for cleanup."

Involve the children in cleanup. Assign areas of responsibility and give them guidelines for what needs to be done. "Put all the blocks back on the shelf, matching the sizes and shapes." "The leftover snacks can go into the refrigerator, wipe off the tables, and throw away the paper cups and napkins."

Suggest an activity to avoid boredom on field trips. Sing songs, play games, or provide a snack. Children will find the time less stressful when they are occupied.

Additional Guidelines for Planning

- Be sure that all activities are developmentally appropriate. Know what children are capable of doing. Plan activities that allow success but also offer a challenge.
- Vary the settings for activities. Try painting outdoors or put on a play under a tree.
- Be flexible. If your plans are not working, change them. Or allow children to decide they want to do something different from what you had planned.
- Encourage adult/child and child/child interactions. Set up activities sometimes so you can be involved with children. At other times, encourage children to work together.
- Help children change their attitudes about male/female stereotyping. Beware of falling into the trap of unconsciously planning different activities for boys and for girls. Encourage them instead to try all activities.

ORGANIZING THE AFTER-SCHOOL PROGRAM

There are several approaches to organizing the program for your after-school group. The following are types that have proved successful in different situations. No one is more effective than the other. The appropriateness of each depends on many factors: your goals for children, the children involved, the physical layout of your space, the materials available to you, and the ratio of children to adults. You may even use several types for greater variety, so try what works for you.

Independent Projects

Many children have abundant ideas about what they want to do. Their own enthusiasms lead them to be involved in reading, making maps, constructing models, or collecting. These children will work diligently by themselves. Some children want to continue alone on a project they began with a group. They may follow a group project to grow crystals with a study of how crystals are used in tools, industrial equipment, or even jewelry.

Often you will initiate an idea for a project based on the interests or needs of a particular child. A child may talk about a visit to a local planetarium with her grandparents. You can suggest a variety of related activities about stars and the solar system. Another child may need encouragement to use language. Begin with making simple puppets, then a puppet theater. Few children will be able to resist staging their own plays.

It is important to allow as much freedom to pursue individual interests as possible. Children should feel they can still do the kinds of things they might do if they were at home. Other children will cherish this opportunity to do things that they cannot do at home. All you have to do is allow enough time, provide the materials, and offer guidance when needed.

Group Activities

In order to foster group unity, at times you want all the children to engage in the same activity. A group may work on a single project that has many parts. Each part will be completed by small groups of children. An example might be preparing a drama to present at a parent meeting. Some children can write the script, some make costumes, and others build the scenery. Then, new groups can be formed to delegate acting parts, rehearse, change scenes, and arrange lighting. This is a typical example of a long-term project that might be many months in the making.

Sometimes limitations on space or equipment may dictate your decision to have all children doing the same thing at the same time. If you have limited space indoors for extensive projects, you may have to divide your group with some children on the playground while others work in the classroom. Some child care facilities have one room set aside for a specific activity such as arts and crafts. In this case, children may have to sign up to use the special room, or groups might be scheduled for designated times.

Groups may have a variety of configurations. Some may consist of children who are close to one another in age or ability. Others may have a mixture of ages and proficiencies. When there are wide differences in ages such as from five- to 12-year-olds in a class, plan some things for the younger children and others for those approaching adolescence. Each age level has different developmental abilities and interests. At other times, a mixed group allows opportunities for the older children to help the younger ones.

This can add to the older children's self-esteem and to the competence of the younger ones.

Whatever the reason for grouping children together for an activity, make sure these activities build on previous skills or interests. Also ensure that these experiences further the goals of your program.

Interest Centers

An interest center is a space carefully arranged to accommodate the activity for which it will be used. A variety of interest centers throughout the room allows children to move freely from one to another. This encourages exploration in different areas of the curriculum. Typical interest centers found in child care environments are block building, science, art, reading, music, cooking, computers, dramatic play, and games. Within each of these areas, basic materials are always available to the children. Some materials are changed from time to time to add new interest and stimulation. A block area might contain a selection of standard wooden blocks, animals, cars, or signs. At times you might add people, trees, boats, airplanes, or colored blocks. Styrofoam sheets, flat wood pieces, or metal forms also invite new kinds of play. Stock an art area with paper, crayons, marking pens, scissors, and paste. For variety, add different colors, sizes, or shapes of paper. Consider using paper punches, staplers, various kinds of tape, rulers, calculators, and templates.

Field Trips

Field trips can consist of a simple walk around the block or an all-day trip to the beach. Both should be planned carefully, although obviously a walk takes less planning than an all-day excursion. Start by deciding on the purpose of the trip. A walk can reinforce a project to map your neighborhood or collect material for a nature collage. A trip to the beach can include collecting shells or studying wave patterns as the tide changes. As with all other activities, fit this into the overall pattern of activities.

Plan each detail so both you and the children know what to expect. Obtain permission slips from parents for car or bus trips. Arrange for lunch and transportation. Make sure there are enough adults to properly supervise the children. Discuss the arrangements with your administrator and other staff members. Tell the children where they are going, what they will do, and what the rules will be. (Make sure you visit the site ahead of time so you will know what to expect and can plan appropriately.) Have the children wear recognizable clothing such as a special T-shirt or a large name tag that includes the program's information.

Plan further with the children so they will get maximum benefit from the trip. For instance, if they are going to the beach to gather shells for a collection, prepare ahead. Read books, look at pictures, and talk about different kinds of shells they might find. If you are fortunate to have a video or digital camera, take it along to record interesting finds and to document where the shells were found or what the children saw in tide pools.

Do a follow-up when you return to the center at the end of the day or when they come back to the center on the following day. Ask children to share what they collected and tell about what they saw. They should also be encouraged to relate what they learned from the trip, what they liked best, and perhaps even how would they change the trip if they went again. You can then create a book documenting the field trip by having each child draw a picture and briefly write about the trip.

Clubs

Clubs are ongoing groups organized around common interests of the participants. When they belong to a club, children have the opportunity to pursue a topic or an interest in depth. They learn to set goals for themselves, solve problems, and cooperate with others on common goals. Some club activities may require them to do extensive research and then to communicate their findings to others, thus developing skills that are part of scientific endeavors. Typical club topics are photography, calligraphy, cooking, magic, collecting (shells, rocks, or stamps), stitchery, space, drama, or sports. Within any group of children, there are likely to be other ideas as well. Appoint a leader for the group, either a staff member or an outside volunteer. Sometimes a parent, community resident, or senior citizen will have a special interest and be willing to share information with the club. Many high school students need to participate in service learning as part of their curriculum. They would make good leaders for a group. Decide how many members the group can accommodate, and ask interested children to sign up.

Clubs can provide children with the experience of making a long-term commitment. When they sign up for a club, they state they are willing to spend a specified period of time with the group. This may be as short as one month or as long as four to six months.

Clubs also give children the opportunity to be a part of a small unit within the larger child care group. This can foster friendships built on a mutual interest. In addition, club participation helps children learn to govern themselves as they set rules and elect officers for their organization. This is particularly important to the older children, the 12- to 14-year-olds.

At the end of the period, encourage children to share what they have learned with others. This can be in the form of an exhibit, a presentation, or a demonstration. Whenever possible, invite parents to participate in these events. Schedule a presentation for a parent meeting. Draw parents' attention to a display when they come to pick up their children. The children can also write about the club's activities for your center's newsletter.

Spontaneous Activities

You should have a store of activities ready for unexpected situations. One of your aides calls in sick, the weather turns cold and rainy, another group stays too long on the playground, or the CD player breaks down. All of

Have a store of activities ready that can be used when unexpected situations occur.

these and many other emergencies will happen, so it helps to be well prepared.

Know some games you can use to keep a group occupied. "Twenty Questions" is an old standby that everyone enjoys. Learn some others as well. Every caregiver should have a store of songs children like to sing. They often want the same ones over and over, but occasionally introduce a new one. You might consider learning some stories or making up your own, and telling these with appropriate dramatics.

Have some materials you can bring out for rainy or snowy days when you have to be indoors. These materials should be a selection of things you do not put out every day. A new game, special books, or unusual art materials are some of the possibilities. Indoor days could also allow children to spontaneously organize activities such as dramatizing a familiar story or dancing to music.

Some spontaneous activities will be child-initiated. In order for child-initiated activities to occur, adults must be willing to follow children's lead, and the environment must have a variety of easily accessible materials. This kind of play is most often seen in the dramatic play center, where children engage in elaborate imaginary or real-life scenarios.

A wide selection of costumes and accessories affords children the opportunity to work through troublesome feelings, learn social skills, and increase their ability to communicate clearly. Dramatic play also takes place with blocks and additions such as animals, human figures, cars, airplanes, and rockets. Children also engage in spontaneous activities outdoors, but here too, they need time and materials to allow them to fully explore their fantasies. The adventure playgrounds seen in some public parks capitalize on this idea by providing boards, boxes, hammers and nails, and pipes. Children can use these to construct objects they need for their play.

Community Involvement

You can use community resources to provide children with a wider range of activities. Instead of duplicating classes or facilities that are available elsewhere, use these to enrich your program. This kind of reaching out also gives children less of a feeling of isolation from the kinds of experiences their school friends might be having.

Some of the possible situations are the following:

- A Girl or Boy Scout troop could meet at your site so your children could attend.
- A local swimming pool might offer reduced rates for children when they are supervised by their own teachers or caregivers.
- A nearby volunteer nature center might offer to sponsor activities your children could attend.
- Have resources come to the center. For example, organizations that train dogs for the blind could come for a talk and bring a dog.
- Your children could attend community classes sponsored by the local school district or recreation department in return for having an extra adult to supervise.

Join other sites within your child care organization for some activities.

Service Learning Projects

Involvement in the community may include service learning projects. For instance, your children could get involved in beautifying their neighborhood. They can grow plants from seeds, make them available to residents, and even offer to plant them if needed. Environmental issues have become extremely important. Children can plan to clean up beach debris and then try to find the source of the debris. They might meet with local organizations to explain why the community should become involved and keep the area clean in the future. As part of their science curriculum they can take water samples from a nearby stream and analyze the pollutants it contains. They might follow up by writing to their local government agencies to inform them of the problem. Recycling is also a popular cause. Children can set up bins to receive materials and then take them to a redemption center. Do not forget the possibility of children lobbying their governmental representatives over issues affecting children. They can write letters, make posters, distribute flyers, or appear at hearings. Service learning is a valuable participation experience for children and should not be missed just because they are in child care. Check the website http://childreninc.org/service-learning.html for more ideas.

MAKING A SCHEDULE

A good program is more than just a series of activities. The structure of those activities within the context of the day allows children to enjoy their time in child care. Allow plenty of time for each activity, but not so much that children get bored.

From reading the previous pages you know what goes into a typical day with children. Start by writing down the specific goals for your program. Make a list of everything you do each day, then add things that have to be done less frequently. Examine the goals for the program and individual children. Notice where they fit into your activities. Make any necessary changes to be sure you are working toward the goals. Next, estimate how much time to allow for each activity. As you put your schedule into effect, you will probably revise it a few times.

A typical schedule for a before- and after-school program may look like the following:

6:00 AM

Children arrive individually. Breakfast is available for children who are hungry. Some children may want to finish homework; others may want to finish a project from a previous day. Still others may want to work quietly at an art center or read. A few may be wide awake and need to run off energy outdoors.

8:15 AM

Children complete whatever they are doing and prepare to go to school.

8:30 AM

Children board the bus for their elementary schools.

When children return to the center at the end of the day, they may follow this schedule:

3:00 PM

Children arrive in a group on the bus. Some may be hungry and need a snack. Others may want to rest a bit before joining activities. Still others may need to spend time with their caregiver to talk about what happened at school.

3:15 PM

Most children want to be outdoors after a day of sitting in school. Schedule outdoor free play, exercises, organized games, or sports.

4:00 PM

Group time, music, planning, discussions, problem solving.

4:15 PM

Indoors for a variety of activities and interest centers: homework, clubs, individual projects, reading, cooking, or talking with friends.

5:30 PM

Finish activities, straighten environment, and collect belongings. Children may read alone or in a group until parents arrive.

Your job as a teacher or child care worker should be enjoyable and exciting. Planning helps avoid many of the frustrations that make that difficult to achieve.

SUMMER PROGRAMS

Summer brings about a variety of changes in a child care program. Staff members may change, additional people may be needed, or the number of hours they work might be longer. The number and ages of children can also change, particularly if the program has been sharing space with a Head Start program or public school. The weather changes and that affects what happens. In some locales, it is too hot, too rainy, or too smoggy for children to engage in certain activities. Perhaps the most important change is that there is more time to participate in activities so the schedule can be more relaxed. There should be no need to rush children from one activity to another. Therefore, the summer curriculum should not be a duplicate of the rest of the year but should add new dimensions to the program. The following are some suggestions for an all-day summer program:

Involve Children in Planning

The children may have wonderful ideas about how to use the longer days of summer. They may want to establish clubs, plan weeks around a theme, or suggest an overnight camping trip. Set up a suggestion box so that they can share their ideas about ways to make the program more interesting. Conduct a survey during group time. Print out short questions such as "What is your favorite thing to do?" or "What is one thing you would really like to add to our program?" or "What would you like to learn about?" Allow the children time to think about their answers and reply in writing. Collect the responses and report back about what they suggested. Choose several to implement during the summer.

Rearrange the Environment

A plan to spruce up the environment is a good project for when the weather is too hot to play outdoors. Spend group time discussing ways the children would like to change the room arrangement. Choose a plan, then assign groups of children to work on specific areas. When the children have had time to function in the new surroundings, evaluate the plan and revise it if necessary.

Long-Term Projects

Blocks of time can be set aside for projects that take place over days, weeks, or even the entire summer. A group of children can write a script for a play or adapt an existing story. Some can make costumes, others design and construct the sets, and some can learn the lines and rehearse the play. An integrated curriculum approach can be applied to a puppet play—writing the play, constructing the stage, and making puppets. What makes this different from the same activity during the school year is that it can be done at a leisurely pace in the summer so children can have a more in-depth experience.

Sports

If the weather permits, children can have time to practice and refine their skills at a favorite sport. Find a volunteer who can coach them on ways to improve. Schedule games with neighboring child care or summer camp programs. Have children plan and present a sports fair with demonstrations of equipment, accessories, and games. If a pool is available, have them design and produce a water ballet.

Field Trips

Summer is the perfect time for field trips. What better time to spend the whole day at the beach exploring tide pools, making sand castles, or cooling off in the surf? Other suggestions for all-day field trips appear in previous pages, but the difference in the summer is that more time can be allowed for the visit. A trip to the zoo can include a picnic lunch planned and prepared by some of the children. A trip to the museum may include time to watch a film on a particular artist.

Gardening and Cooking

Plant a garden with summer vegetables and herbs. Some plants, like carrots or radishes, grow fairly quickly, but others can be speeded up by using already sprouted plants from a nursery. Have the children research the growing time for each variety, then choose plants that will have different times for harvesting. When the plants have matured, the children can pick a few at a time, then incorporate them into recipes to be served at lunch or snack time. Provide cookbooks and gardening guides, or use the Internet for the necessary research.

Allow Quiet Time

The long stimulating days of a summer program can cause some children to become fatigued. Therefore, it is important to allow time for them to read quietly by themselves or spend time with friends talking or "hanging out." Make certain the environment has inviting places for these activities: a cozy reading corner or secluded places where several children can be together.

Read Aloud

Choose a long book that all the children will enjoy, and read it aloud to the group. Choose a stopping place each day that will create some suspense. Ask the children what they think is going to happen next. At the beginning of the next day's session, ask them to recall what had just happened in the book when the reading ended.

Plan Special Events

Include the children in planning for a special event. This may entail making costumes, decorating the environment, finding equipment, and inviting parents or others to participate. Some ideas for special events include: a carnival, a scavenger hunt day, a mystery day requiring detective skills, kite flying, Olympics, and a backwards day. Each of these events can require several days of preparations and should include an assessment of the success following the day.

Organize a Fund-Raising Event

Ask the children to decide the kind of event to be planned, how much money they might bring in, and whether it is within the school or out in the community. When figuring potential profit, they must consider the cost of any materials they might need. Suggestions for fund-raisers are selling popcorn, cookies, or unused toys or games brought from home. After completing the event, let the children figure out the profit and decide what to purchase; then take them shopping.

Community Facilities

Take advantage of community facilities to enrich the children's summer program. Many libraries having reading programs. Participating children are encouraged to read a specific number of books and receive an award for doing so. The library may also have group reading times that the children can attend.

Museums may also have summer discovery programs children can attend. Some have classes in science, astronomy, archeology, biology, and art where children can have hands-on experiences.

The children may take classes (for additional fees) at local riding stables, dance studios, swimming pools, tennis courts, or art studios.

SUMMARY

- A current debate among early childhood professionals concerns which approach to programming is better: academic, holistic approach, or a combination of academic and holistic.

- Developmentally appropriate practices are tailored to the age and developmental status of the children and youth they serve and are responsive to the social and cultural contexts in which children live.

- Caregivers make decisions based on their knowledge of the development and learning of children, the specific development of the individual children in the program, and the social and cultural contexts in which the children live.

- Children should be challenged with achievable goals that promote their development and learning.

- Guidelines for developmentally appropriate practices address all areas of an effective child care program for school-age children.

- The NAEYC has made recommendations for working with children whose home language is other than English

- NAEYC recommends that programs support children's home language by providing examples of the language in the environment.

- An anti-bias education incorporates the positive intent of multiculturalism and uses activities and materials that depict how people are similar and different.

- Integrated curriculum and the project approach are two ways to guide children into more in-depth investigations while addressing more than one curriculum area.

- Planning is essential to a good child care program.

- Foster children's desire to be competent by teaching them how to do real jobs using real tools and technology.

- There are several ways to present activities: independent projects, group activities, interest centers, field trips, clubs, spontaneous activities, and community projects.

- When drawing up a schedule, allow adequate time for each activity but not so much time that children get bored.

- Summer programs allow for different activities that make use of the longer days.

KEY TERMS

academic approach	emergent curriculum	integrated curriculum
anti-bias education	holistic approach	project approach
curriculum		

REVIEW QUESTIONS

1. Define developmentally appropriate practice. What three kinds of knowledge should a child care leader consider when planning for children?

2. What are the goals of anti-bias education?

3. What is the primary role of staff members in a child care program? How should they adjust their interactions from the youngest children to the oldest?

4. State five reasons for intentional planning when working with school-age children.

5. Defend the statement "Staff members should have paid planning time each day."

6. How can you include children in your planning?

7. In what ways can parents help you plan a good program?

8. Suggest three activities you can include to increase children's desire to become competent.

9. List three approaches to presenting activities.

10. How can children who attend child care become more involved in their community?

Case Study

Gilles and Marissa have both been assigned to a group of 10- to 12-year-olds in a YMCA after-school program. Marissa was a preschool teacher and has a degree in early childhood education. Gilles worked for many years as an assistant teacher in a fourth-grade classroom. They have widely differing opinions about how their program should be planned. Marissa believes they should rely to a great extent on what the children want to learn or do, and develop the curriculum from there. Gilles has read the curriculum guidelines of the local school district and thinks they should be reinforcing what the schools teach. He points to the fact that at the nearby school many of the children attend, reading and math scores are extremely low. He says it is their job to help the children increase their academic skills so they will be able to go on to the next grade level.

1. How would you describe their different approaches to curriculum planning?

2. How can they resolve their differences so they can work together and the children can gain the maximum benefit?

3. Can you think of a way to combine the two approaches?

STUDENT ACTIVITIES

1. Talk to a group of school-age children. Find out what they are interested in by asking what they do after school, what they read, or what they watch on television. Is there a difference between boys' interests and girls' interests? Are there age-level differences?

2. Write a short paragraph about what you liked to do when you were between six and 10 years old. How did you get started with these interests? Did your parents encourage them? Did your friends?

3. Survey your community to determine what resources are available that might be used for a school-age child care group. Is there a wide variety, or are there limited resources?

SUGGESTED READINGS

Bergstrom, J. M. (1990). *School's out.* Berkeley: Ten Speed.

Boutte, G., Van Scoy, I., & Hendley, S. (1996). Multicultural and nonsexist prop boxes. *Young Children,* 52(1), 34–39.

Espinosa, L. (2008). Challenging common myths about young children language learners. No. 8. FCD Policy Brief Advancing PK-3. Foundations of Child Development.

Espinosa, L. (2010). *Getting It RIGHT For Young Children from Diverse Backgrounds; Applying Research to Improve Practice.* Washington, DC: National Association for the Education of Young Children.

Helm, J. H. & Katz, L. G. (2001). *Young Investigators: The Project Approach in the Early Years.* New York, NY: Teachers College Press.

Kindler, A.L. (2002). Survey of the state's limited English proficient students and available educational programs and services: 2000–2001 summary report. Washington, DC: National Clearinghouse for English Language Acqusition.

Lewis, B. (1995). *Kid's Guide to Service Programs.* Minneapolis: Free Spirit.

National Center for Education Statistics. (2004). The condition of education, 2004. (Retrieved December 2009, from http://nces.ed.gov/programs/coe.)

WEB RESOURCES

http://www.naeyc.org/files/naeyc/file/positions/PSDAP.pdf
National Association for the Education of Young Children: full text of Developmentally Appropriate Practice position statement

http://naeyc.org/yc/
Current and past issues of *Young Children,* the professional journal published by the National Association for the Education of Young Children.

http://niost.org
National Institute on Out-of School Time: provides current statistics and information about school-age child care.

REFERENCES

August, D. & T. Shanahan, eds. (2006). Executive Summary. Developing literacy in second-language learners: Report of the national literacy panel on language-minority children and youth. Mahwah, NJ.: Lawrence Erlbaum Associates, Publishers.

Bredekamp, S. & Copple, C. eds. (2009). *Developmentally Appropriate Practice in Early Childhood Programs Serving Children from Birth through Age 8,* 3rd ed. Washington, DC: NAEYC.

Derman-Sparks, L. & the ABC Task Force (1989). *Anti-Bias Curriculum: Tool for Empowering Young Children,* Washington DC: NAEYC.

Derman-Sparks, L. & Edwards, J.O. (2010). *Anti-Bias Education for Young Children and Ourselves.* Washington, DC: NAEYC.

Harvard Family Research Project. (2008). *After school programs in the 21st Century*. no. 10. Cambridge, MA: Harvard Graduate School of Education.

Helm, J. H. & Beneke S, eds.(2003) *The Power of Project Meeting Contemporary Challenges in Early Childhood Classrooms—Strategies and Solutions*. Washington, DC: NAEYC.

Katz, L. G. (1994). *The Project Approach*. Champaign, IL: ERIC Clearinghouse on Elementary and Early Childhood Education.

Krashen, S. (1992). *Fundamentals of Language Education*. Torrance, CA: Laredo.

Mather, M. (2009). Children in immigrant families chart new path. Washington, DC: Population Reference Bureau.

NAEYC Position Statement (2009). Developmentally appropriate practice in early childhood programs serving children from birth through age 8. NAEYC: Washington, DC.

NAEYC Position Statement: Responding to linguistic and cultural diversity—Recommendations for effective early childhood education. (1996). *Young Children*, 51(2), 4–12.

Piaget, J. (1952). *The Origin of Intelligence in Children*. (M. Cook, Trans.). New York: International Universities Press.

Vygotsky, L. (1978). *Mind in Society: The Development of Higher Psychological Processes*. Cambridge: Harvard University Press.

9

Creating an Environment

HOW THE ENVIRONMENT ENHANCES DEVELOPMENT

The physical environment is the basic component of a child care program—the foundation for everything that happens there. The best program activities, materials, or equipment are less effective if the physical setting does not meet the needs of the children for whom it is designed. The physical setting should be developmentally appropriate, supporting and enhancing all areas of children's development: physical, cognitive, emotional, and social. The environment should encourage children to participate in activities that will further their development, not discourage them.

Earlier chapters indicated that children's physical development proceeds rapidly during middle childhood, although fine-motor control lags slightly behind gross-motor control. Indoor areas can be planned to provide children with opportunities to increase both these skills. To develop fine-motor control, children need space where they can work puzzles, do art projects, build with small blocks, or construct models. There should also be space for dancing or active games that will increase gross-motor control and eye-hand coordination. Outdoor areas provide many opportunities for gross-motor activities such as running, jumping, and throwing. Child care leaders should provide a variety of activities that progressively enhance physical development. As children become more adept at using their large muscles, they should have a place where they can play hopscotch, baseball, or soccer, and swim, bike, or skate. Space can also be provided for activities that increase small-muscle control. Planting seeds in a garden bed, creating nature collages, and modeling with clay are some examples.

LEARNING OUTCOMES

After reading this chapter, you should be able to:

✔ Describe ways in which the physical environment enhances development.

✔ State general guidelines for planning indoor and outdoor space.

✔ Draw a plan for a child care room with an adjoining playground.

✔ Discuss ways to adapt the environment when space must be shared.

A developmentally appropriate child care environment provides many places where children can enhance their cognitive abilities. In Chapter 5, you read that Piaget and Vygotsky believed that children need to be active participants in the development of their own intelligence. To achieve that goal, their environment must invite participation and offer a wide variety of choices. Children must be free to explore and discover, to hypothesize and experiment, in order to increase their knowledge about the world around them. Each area must include space in which children can work comfortably and have their materials close at hand.

You need storage space to keep ongoing projects safe or to display the children's work. Social skills and language are also components of cognitive development. Work areas should be conducive to verbal interactions among the children. Round tables for some activities and enclosed spaces for others encourage children to talk to one another. Comfortable places for reading also encourage children to increase language skills.

During middle childhood, peer relationships and a sense of belonging to a group become extremely important. Children will usually find places where they can get together, but an effective child care environment will structure places that foster both a group rapport and friendships between children. The setting needs to have a space where all the children can gather at one time for activities or discussions. The environment should also include places where two friends can just hang out and talk. Spaces for clubs also allow children to form relationships and share interests within a small group.

DEVELOPING THE PLAN

The originators of child care centers seldom have the luxury of choosing or building a facility that fits the program they envision. Most often, after-school programs are housed in extra classrooms, multipurpose rooms, cafeterias, or gyms. However, within any physical space, it is possible to create an environment that welcomes children, makes them feel safe and secure, and enhances their development. It just takes more thought and ingenuity in some situations than in others.

If you are not sure where to start, get a feel for how children play. Watch them playing in your neighborhood, at a park, or on a school playground. Note how the children group themselves. Do they all play in one large group, or do two or three children do something together? You probably will notice that the groups are small and that children tend to stake out their own territories. They meet in specific places each day and continue play activities together. Watch, also, how they change their space whenever they can. Many will use boxes for forts, some will build tree houses from scrap lumber, while others will pitch tents so they can be alone. Some children add materials to already existing structures to suit their own needs. They place a wide board on the jungle gym to make a platform for their space ship or enclose a climbing structure with large packing boxes for a clubhouse.

Consider the characteristics of your particular group of children. Their diversity should be reflected in your environment. Look at their age level.

Are they all about the same age or do ages vary? What skills and abilities do they have in common? What are their interests? Is there a predominant ethnic group? Do some children have special needs? Each of these factors should be considered when planning your environment.

Next, think of the goals of your program. Your space should allow children to do the things stated in your goals. If you want children to be able to work independently, you must provide a place where they can do that. If you want to encourage a group feeling, you need a space where the whole group can gather or do things together. If your goal is for children to develop their physical skills, you must provide space and equipment where that can happen.

When you have followed the preceding suggestions, you should have a fairly good idea of your constituents—the children who will use your environment. In addition, your goals tell you what you want these children to be able to do. It is up to you to set the stage where children and activities can mesh. The following general considerations will guide you in planning both indoor and outdoor space.

OVERALL DESIGN OF INDOOR SPACE

Make the indoor space attractive and homelike. Add color. Place flowers on a shelf or table, and hang artwork done by the children on the walls. Paint some of the furniture an interesting color, and put a colorful rug in a corner to set off that space with a touch of brightness. Try changing the lighting. A harsh light is somewhat jarring and distracting; a softer light might create a more relaxed atmosphere.

Well-planned indoor space allows for both individual and group activities.

Set up boundaries for activities. A corner of the room invites privacy, and you can make it more secluded with a free-standing rack for books. A table and shelves can define space where individual projects are to take place. A rug tells children this is a place for floor activities. A large space that is left open can accommodate group meetings.

Areas should be used consistently for the same purpose. The block area should be used for block building, not active games; the quiet area for reading or quiet talking, not loud music activities. That is not to say these can never be changed. Change them when the need arises. If a space is not working as planned, discuss it with the children and be open to their suggestions as to how to rearrange the area.

Leave pathways for easy access to all activities and to entrances and exits. Look at the most likely traffic patterns children might use to move around the room or from indoors to outdoors. Arrange work areas so they are undisturbed by children tramping through them.

Make each area readily identifiable by children, staff members, and parents. The kinds of materials you place there, the furniture, or the arrangement should inform everyone of that area's purpose. Some programs go so far as to place signs at these areas—a good idea, perhaps, but you can convey the purpose just as effectively with the materials and equipment.

Remember that some activities go well together and can be placed next to one another, while others clash and diminish the usefulness of each. Dramatic play may be incorporated into block building, so these two activity areas can be in proximity. On the other hand, children trying to read quietly in a corner will be disturbed by noisy construction projects, so these two areas should be some distance from one another.

Minimize crowding in activity areas by allowing enough space for large group functions and limiting the number of children who can work comfortably at other areas. An open area where the entire group can meet should be spacious enough so children are not pushing right up next to one another. In the activity areas, avoid crowding by making it clear that only a specified number of children can participate at an activity at any one time. Four chairs at a table indicate that four people can sit there. The children may attempt to add chairs, but you can remind them of the limitation and direct them to another area.

What Should Be Included?

Several guidelines will help you to plan indoor space. Consider each one as you plot out the placement of furniture and equipment.

There should be enough space so that children can move about safely. Check the licensing regulations in your state to determine the number of square feet per child you will need. Add enough tables, chairs, shelves, and cabinets to accommodate your program. Leave enough room so children do not bump into furniture or trip on equipment.

Include places where children can work on individual or group projects. They will probably need a table, some chairs, and a place to keep their work until it is completed.

This area may also include a place where completed work can be displayed.

Have a place where the children can keep their belongings. Children will come to you from school carrying backpacks, lunch boxes, and jackets. Everyone should have a cubby, shelf, or box in which to deposit these articles until they are ready to go home.

Make room for messy activities near a water supply. Many art projects such as clay, painting, or papier-mâché will require a ready supply of water. Cooking projects, too, tend to be messy. These two areas can be adjacent and share a sink for water.

Set aside an area for quiet reading, resting, or just talking with friends. An enclosed corner as just described will serve this purpose. Furnish it with a low sofa, beanbag chairs, large pillows, and a soft rug. Add books and magazines.

Keep distance between activities that clash, such as reading and noisy construction activities.

Leave an open area where your whole group can be together at times. Many schools leave the center of a room for this purpose. This space can also be used for large-muscle activities indoors when you cannot go outside. You can dance or do exercises or gymnastics when the space is unobstructed.

Remember to arrange a place where children can complete their homework. Have computers and printers available for homework. Provide access to the Internet. A table and chairs in a quiet area of the room are needed for this area. Make sure the lighting is adequate so children can see well. Some children will be able to work together at one table, whereas others may need their own work place. You may have to set up a small individual table for the child who needs to work alone.

If you can, provide high spaces and low spaces. Many centers with limited floor space resort to a double-decker approach. Imagine a climbing structure that could serve as a dramatic play area in the upper level with a quiet hideaway underneath. The upper level might even become a stage for dramatic productions.

Designate places to hang artwork, display photographs, or feature news items. This area can be a bulletin board near the entrance so parents can also enjoy it. If you do not have a bulletin board, use picture gum or masking tape to attach items to the wall.

Provide adequate storage. This area should include both closed cupboards and some that are accessible to the children. Use closed cupboards for the things you do not use all the time. Examples are special art or project supplies, games, table activities, or books. Some materials should be on open shelves or cupboards so children can use them as they wish. Always keep a basic assortment of art materials readily available. Change these periodically with those you have stored away.

If your curriculum includes club activities, arrange a place for children to meet. Let the children decorate the space and add a sign with the club name. Furnish the club area with whatever is needed for their particular activity. A collector's club will need a table and chairs. A drama club could use a stage and a place to store props.

If your group includes some older children (children between the ages of 10 and 13), design a special place for them. A separate room would be best, but if you cannot provide that, set up a corner for them. Make it their special place in which younger children are not allowed. The equipment for this area might include a tape recorder or radio, model kits and games, beanbag chairs, or large pillows. If the room size permits, add a Ping-Pong, air hockey, or pool table.

Do not forget the adults when you design your indoor space. Arrange a place where you can prepare materials and keep any records that are required by the program administrators. In addition, you will need a cupboard or drawer where you can keep your personal belongings.

Parents, too, must be considered. Provide a place for sign-in/sign-out sheets and mailboxes for notes to individual families. In addition, you might install a bulletin board where you can post schedules, pictures of the children, reminders of upcoming events, or any other items of interest to all the parents. Also, designate a space for lost-and-found articles.

Now that you know what must be included, you can conceptualize the placement of activity areas. Try using a scale drawing of your room. Mark the doors and windows and designate the areas. Check that you have included an area for each activity in your program plan. Try to imagine yourself and the children living in the space. When you actually place furniture and storage cabinets in the environment, walk through it again, thinking about how it will function. If you are satisfied, try it with your group of children. After a period of time, evaluate your arrangement and get input from the children. Do not be afraid to change it, however. As long as everything is movable and not built-in, you can reorganize it. Be flexible.

When You Have to Share Indoor Space

You may not have the luxury of a space that can be set up and left intact at the end of each day. It can be overwhelming to have to arrange your environment at the beginning of each day, but with a bit of preplanning and some imagination, it can be done. If you use adaptable materials and have movable cabinets, your task can be managed. The following are some suggestions that have worked for other programs, but each space may require you to devise your own strategies.

Set up interest centers each day. This process will be easier if you plan ahead by having all the materials you need in a basket, a large box, ice-cream cartons, or shoe boxes. Carry these to the table or area where children will use them.

Install large casters or wheels on cupboards, bulletin boards, or dividers used to designate areas. Sometimes it helps to label these to specify their use. Put locks on the cupboards.

Design furniture that can be taken apart when it must be put away at the end of the day. Buy or construct modular furniture made from sturdy,

Designate places to hang artwork, display photographs, or feature news items.

lightweight building material such as tri-wall. Add large vinyl pillows and vinyl beanbag chairs for reading or listening areas.

A large pegboard on wheels is adaptable for many uses. It can be a convenient place to hang woodworking tools or art supplies. It can also divide one work area from another. (You can divide spaces with folding screens, sheets, or blankets, as well.) Have some shelves that are also equipped with casters, and use these for art materials, games, block accessories, and science materials.

Use plastic stackable containers for the children's belongings.

Carpet squares can define an activity area if there is no rug. This will make the floor more comfortable as well as designate a space. Carpet pieces can often be obtained inexpensively from carpet stores or carpet installers.

Allow children to rearrange the indoor environment. They may be able to see possibilities that adults have not considered. Before starting, however, discuss with them the kinds of activities that must be provided for, and then have them offer suggestions. Compile the children's suggestions and let them vote on which ones will be implemented. Draw up a plan and execute the changes. Evaluate how the plan is working after a trial period.

Work together with other occupants of your space so everyone has an understanding of what can and cannot be done. Meet with the principal or building administrator on a regular basis to reinforce mutual commitments to serving children and their families and to resolve any problems that arise. Maintain contact with teachers to determine ways in which the goals of the child care center can complement those of the school. Set up an agreement with school secretaries about the use of office equipment and the telephone. Establish an explicit understanding with the janitors about who is responsible for cleaning and taking out the trash and who will clean up when others use the space.

OVERALL DESIGN OF OUTDOOR SPACE

It is rare that child care staff members are able to design a new playground. Most have to adapt an existing facility to suit the needs of their program and the children they serve. Whether starting from scratch or adapting an existing playground, it helps to visit other child care centers, parks, or schools to see how others have planned play spaces for children. Note how the children use both the open spaces and any permanent equipment. Are some not used at all? What kinds of equipment attract the greatest number of children or hold their interest the longest? What kinds of play occur? What do children do in the open spaces? This valuable information will be useful when planning child care outdoor areas.

The next step is to take an inventory of everything in the outdoor space that will be available to the center. Map out areas that cannot be changed and indicate the places that are open. Brainstorm ideas for the space with other staff members. If children are already enrolled in the center, get their input. They may have wonderful suggestions for what they would like to have. Make a priority list of what will be needed and figure the cost of each item. If financial resources are limited, plan to purchase first items that are likely to be used the most or that have the greatest capability for multiple uses. Are there things that staff members or parents can build or install, thus decreasing the cost?

Consider providing natural or "green" playscapes, areas where children can experience nature. Richard Louv (2005) coined the phrase "nature-deficit disorder." He referred to the fact that many children never go outside and even express fear of "nature." Often when these children do go outside, they are still connected to their electronic gadgets. R.D. Bixler, et. al (1994) also wrote that children express fear of snakes, insects, and

Children use both open spaces and permanent equipment to play.

even plants in natural areas. In addition, some children say that their parents don't feel it is safe for them to play outdoors in their neighborhoods or go into wild areas. Louv concludes that the absence of nature in many children's lives increases the possibility of problems such as obesity, depression, stress, and attention-deficit disorders. Randy White (2004) supports that belief. A later section in this chapter on "What Should Be Included" lists ways that a natural playscape can be created.

Clarify program goals that will be supported by the outdoor environment. What is it you want children to be able to do as a result of using the space? Remember that outdoor space is not just for helping children develop physical skills but can help them grow cognitively and socially as well. Outdoor play can involve problem solving, investigating, observing, listening, matching/naming objects, and predicting, to name just a few cognitive skills. Socially, outdoor play can help children learn to cooperate, share, develop friendships, engage in group fantasy play, and foster group cohesiveness.

A playground should be based on a knowledge of child development. Review the chapters on development at the beginning of this textbook to remind you of what school-age children are like. They are extremely active and like to have lots of space to run, jump, and throw. They want to be competent at any activities that require physical agility and need places where they can practice their skills. They want to have places where they can be with their peers, either one-on-one or with a group.

Design your space with children's special needs in mind. If the group includes children with physical limitations, include spaces to which they will have access. Some possibilities are to include paved pathways that are wide enough for a wheelchair, a raised sandbox or a sand table, wheelchair-accessible areas for throwing balls, and climbing equipment with a transfer station, allowing a child to go from chair to climber. Many playground equipment companies will offer advice on how to adapt their pieces to fit the needs of children with disabilities.

"Me on the bars." Mariah, age 10.

Safety

Children's safety is a top priority for all child care centers and therefore is treated here as a separate subject to consider when planning or renovating outdoor play areas. The process should begin with a survey of the area to be used. Do a **safety audit** of existing structures by comparing them to standards, guidelines, and laws set by federal and state agencies. Find information on these guidelines from the following sources:

> United States Consumer Product Safety Commission: *Handbook for Public Playground Safety* (1988)
> 4330 East-West Highway
> Bethesda, MD 20814-4408
> Phone: 301-504-6816
> FAX: 301-504-0124 or 301-504-0025
> e-mail: info@cpsc.com; http://www.cpsc.gov.

> National Program for Playground Safety
> University of Northern Iowa
> Cedar Falls, IA 50614-0614
> Phone: 800-544-PLAY or 319-273-2416
> FAX: 319-273-7308
> e-mail: playground-safety@uni.edu; http://www.uni.edu/playground.

> Americans with Disabilities Act of 1990 (**ADA**) — the *Americans with Disabilities Act Accessibility Guidelines* (ADAAG)
> Phone: 800-514-1301 (voice)
> 800-514-0383 (TTY)
> http://www.ada.gov.

> American Alliance for Health, Physical Education, Recreation and Dance (AALR)
> 1900 Association Drive
> Reston, VA 22091-1598
> Phone: 800-213-7193
> http://www.aahperd.org.

> American Society for Testing & Materials (ATSM)
> 100 Barr Harbor Drive
> West Conshohocken, PA 19428-2959
> Phone: 610-832-9585
> FAX: 610-832-9555
> http://www.astm.org.

Check also with your state-licensing bureau for regulations affecting playground space and equipment. Your state also may have laws pertaining to playground safety. Arkansas, California, Connecticut, Florida, Illinois, Michigan, New Jersey, North Carolina, Oklahoma, Oregon, Rhode Island, Tennessee, Texas, Utah, and Virginia all have such laws. Others have proposals in process. Familiarize yourself with these laws before making a final playground audit. You can obtain information about laws from your state attorney general's office.

safety audit
survey of all playground structures in comparison to standards, guidelines, and laws set by federal and state agencies

ADA
Americans with Disabilities Act

Two level structures encourage diverse activities.

Additional guidelines you can use for planning a safe outdoor environment for children follow:

- Make sure the equipment is appropriate for the ages of the children who will be using it. Your knowledge of developmental stages and abilities should help determine whether equipment is too easy or too difficult.
- Do a daily environmental inspection, looking for bottles, cans, animal waste, standing water, or anything else that may create a hazard. Include a survey of equipment, looking for rust, splintering wood, or exposed bolts.
- Choose cushioned surfaces for beneath equipment as a fall zone. Do not use asphalt, black top, grass, packed dirt, or concrete. Choose pea gravel, sand, or hardwood fiber/mulch. The height of the equipment will determine the depth of the material used. Usually 12 inches of loose fill will be adequate for equipment up to 8 feet in height. If synthetic material is used, the manufacturer will recommend the depth.
- Make sure all climbing equipment meets consumer safety standards. Steps on ladders should be in good condition, and handrails should have appropriate grip sizes. Protective barriers should be at least 38 inches high for school-age children.
- Swings should have soft seats, and only two should be placed in one framework. They should be positioned at least 24 inches apart at the base of the seats and 30 inches from any supports.
- There should be a cushioned fall zone 20 feet in front and 20 feet in back of the pivot height of the swing. The cushioned zone should also extend 6 feet to each side of the support structure.
- Slides should be securely anchored. The steps should have firm handrails and provide good traction. Drainage holes in the steps will prevent moisture that makes them slippery. Make sure there is no space between the slide platform and the bed where strings from clothing can catch. If the slides are metal, they should be in a shaded area.

- Seesaws should be designed with secure handles of a size that school-age children can grip easily. There should be a soft bumper under the seat, and all pivot points should be covered.
- Ensure that all areas with potential hazards are easily supervised and can be seen from various vantage points. Be sure no trees or other structures block your view.
- All entrances to the playground should have secure, self-latching gates.
- Always provide adequate supervision when children are using playground equipment. You must have an adult nearby who is attending what the children are doing. That person must be aware of the rules for using the equipment and capable of enforcing the rules when necessary.

What Should Be Included?

The following items will provide a guideline for things to include in your outdoor space.

single purpose equipment
play equipment that can be used for only one kind of play

multipurpose equipment
equipment that has many possibilities for play activities

Include both single purpose and multipurpose equipment. Most children love the old standbys: swings, jungle gyms, climbing rope, and a sandbox. Swings are **single purpose equipment**: they can be used only for swinging. A climbing structure can be **multipurpose equipment**, having many different kinds of play possibilities. A sandbox seems to be single purpose at first glance. You immediately think that it is just for digging, but children can find almost endless ways to incorporate other kinds of play into this area. They build dams, cook elaborate foods, and search for dinosaur bones, to name just a few.

Add some materials so children can construct their own equipment. Large blocks, boards, cartons, cable spools, and sawhorses present interesting possibilities. Consider using tires, inner tubes, logs, and sheets of wood or cardboard. These are materials for "adventure playgrounds" that are actually available in some parts of the country. Children can be marvelously inventive in what they can devise.

As needed, bring out equipment to stimulate new play ideas. Balls, rackets, hoops, hockey sticks, jump ropes, tumbling mats, and horseshoes are just a few choices. (Do not forget a pump for rejuvenating deflated balls.) You might add chalk for sidewalk games, yo-yos, and batons, depending on the children's interests. In different kinds of weather there are additional items to use. When it is hot, bring out a hose, buckets, sprinklers, a small pool, and boats. For areas that get snow, provide shovels, sleds, and snow saucers.

Include areas where children can have some privacy. A playhouse, park bench, tree house, sunflower house, willow dome, or even a secluded corner under a tree can be a place where children can gather to chat with a friend or just be alone.

Allow spaces for special activities, some protected from inclement weather. Some games need a hard surface, others require dirt. Set aside a safe place away from pathways where children can practice skateboarding or roller skating. Use a covered area for art or table activities that can be enjoyed when the sun is hot or even when it rains.

Have a variety of surfaces in your playground. Include grass, dirt, cement or asphalt, sand, or wood chip areas for added interest. In addition to these surfaces, it is nice to leave some planted areas in the yard. Trees, flowers, shrubs, or a garden area add a pleasing touch to any yard.

Provide an opportunity for children to learn about and gain respect for their natural environment. Growing urban areas have almost obliterated any wild and natural places for children to play. The playground of a child care center can allow children to explore the outdoors within a relatively safe setting. Create an area that contains unmanicured grass, bushes, plants, some rocks, a small hill, some trees, and a birdbath and feeder. Add a garden where children can grow vegetables or flowers, plant flowers that will attract butterflies or hummingbirds, and include wild grasses or plants native to the area. Show children how to plant a square of sunflowers to make a sunflower house. In addition, allow children to construct their own play spaces or private hideaways with tree limbs, willow branches, boards, boxes, and large tires. Children will strengthen their appreciation of the outdoors if they share the responsibility for maintaining the area.

Remember to have a water outlet in the yard, both a drinking fountain and hose faucet. Active children get thirsty, and water is needed for many art projects. If hoses are added, children will be able to build dams in the sandbox, learn how water sculptures any area where it runs freely, maintain a garden, or observe how sunlight shining through sprinkler spray makes a rainbow.

The outdoor area of a child care center may be the only opportunity some of today's children have to engage in free, active play. Many live in apartments or areas where they cannot play outside their houses because it is not safe. In addition, many will get home after dark. Therefore, you should put as much thought into the kinds of activities you provide for children outdoors as you do for inside time. Play outdoors is not just a chance to run around and let off steam but also an opportunity for additional learning and the acquisition of skills.

When You Have to Share Outdoor Space

If you have to share outdoor space with other programs or with neighborhood children, you have an additional challenge. You probably will not be able to change the environment, but you can add your own movable play equipment. Bring out easels and painting materials, a box of balls or other sports equipment, digging tools in a crate, or games to play on the grass. You will have to look at the possibilities of the space available and add whatever you can.

Allow your children to mingle with others using the space. It would be difficult if your children felt different from neighborhood youngsters in a park just because they were in child care. Establish clear rules about where the children can go and what they can do, but allow as much freedom of movement as you safely can.

The playground of a child care center can allow children to explore the outdoors within a relatively safe setting.

Environment affects us all in subtle ways. A good atmosphere will encourage children to be relaxed and engage in productive play. Poor conditions may result in upset children who cannot settle down to sustained activities. Design your child care space with thought, and be willing to change it as needed. You and your children will be glad you did.

SUMMARY

- The physical space of a developmentally appropriate environment will support and enhance all areas of children's development: physical, cognitive, and social.

- Children's safety should be a top priority for all child care centers. Planners should obtain guidelines, regulations, and laws that govern playgrounds.

- When you have to share indoor space, you can organize materials in easy-to-carry boxes or crates, install casters on all furniture, use shelves or pegboards to divide work areas, use carpet pieces to delineate a space, allow children to set up the environment, and work with other occupants to avoid misunderstandings.

- Before you begin to draft a design for a playground, visit a variety of places where children play: other child care centers, school playgrounds, or parks. Then plan your playground based on what you know about children.

- Plan natural playscapes that allow children the freedom to play outdoors.

- When you have to share outdoor space with other programs, add movable equipment, allow children to mingle with others using the area, and establish clear rules about what children can and cannot do.

KEY TERMS

ADA
multipurpose equipment

safety audit
single purpose equipment

REVIEW QUESTIONS

1. List five general guidelines to remember when planning indoor space.

2. Indicate which of the following activities can be placed next to one another: block building, music, art, science, cooking, karate club, homework, drama practice, woodworking, wood sculpting, reading, table games.

3. State five things to be included in indoor space.

4. List three possible storage containers for children's belongings. Can you suggest any others?

5. Describe the arrangement of an art area.

6. What are the requirements for a space where children can do their homework?

7. What is meant by single purpose and multipurpose equipment? Give examples of each.

8. Why is it important to provide wild spaces for children in an outdoor play area?

9. List some equipment you might take outside to stimulate new play ideas.

10. In what ways can you adapt both indoor and outdoor equipment when you have to share space with other programs?

Dion and Hazel have been hired to be co-leaders in a new child care center in an upscale urban area. As they start to plan, they realize they have quite different ideas about what should be in the room. In addition, the director tells them she wants the room to convey the high academic standards in which she believes. The parents who have already enrolled their children are well educated and want their children to be successful in school.

Case Study

1. If you were responsible for planning this environment, where would you start?

2. How can you take into consideration the differing ideas of the two caregivers, the concerns of the director, and the demands of the parents?

3. Is there a way to make the environment flexible so that it can be changed if needed?

STUDENT ACTIVITIES

1. Obtain several catalogs from companies that supply playground equipment. Select a climbing apparatus and three other articles for a school-age playground. In class, explain your choice in a group of two other students. Compile the list of choices from each group member, then negotiate and agree on buying only three items.

2. Visit three child care sites that are under different auspices: church, recreation program, school district, community organization, or privately owned. Record the kinds of furniture and equipment available in their indoor space. Share your findings with your classmates.

3. Draw a floor plan of an ideal indoor space for a group of 20 children from ages six to 11. Use the list of things to include in an indoor environment discussed in this chapter. How might you have to adapt your plan to accommodate a child in a wheelchair?

SUGGESTED READINGS

Cornell, J. (1998). *Sharing Nature with Children 20th Anniversary Edition.* Nevada City, CA: Dawn Publications.

Keeler, R. (2008). *Natural Playscapes.* Redmond, Washington: ChildCare Exchange.

Keeler, R. with Sharon Young (2010). *Outdoor Classroom Coordinator.* Exchange, Jan/Feb 2010. Redmond, Washington: ChildCare Exchange.

Marotz, L. R (2012). *Health, Safety, and Nutrition for the Young Child* (8th ed.). Belmont, CA: Wadsworth Cengage Learning.

Nabhan, G. P., & Trimble, S. (1994). *The Geography of Childhood: Why Children Need Wild Places.* Boston, MA: Beacon.

Rivkin, Mary S. (1995). *The Great Outdoors, Restoring Children's Right to Play Outside.* Washington, DC: National Association for the Education of Young Children.

Sutterby, J., & Frost, J. (2002). Making playgrounds fit for children and children fit for playgrounds. *Young Children* 57(3), 36–41.

Ward, Jennifer, (2008). *I Love Dirt.* Boston, MA: Trumpeter.

White, Randy (2004). Adults are from earth; children are from the moon . . . Designing for children: A complex challenge. Retrieved from the Internet January 15, 2010. http://www.whitehutchinson.com/children/articles/earthmoon.shtml.

Wilson, R. A., Kilmer, S. J., & Knauerhase, V. (1996). Developing an environmental outdoor play space. *Young Children*, 51(6), 56–61.

WEB RESOURCES

http://www.uni.edu/playground
National Program for Playground Safety: Guidelines for safe playgrounds, online training for child care professionals.

http://www.NSC.org
National Safety Council: List of safety recommendations.

REFERENCES

Bixler, R. D., Carlisle, C. L., Hammitt, W. E., & Floyd, M. F. (1994). Observed fears and discomforts among urban students on field trips to wildland areas. *Journal of Environmental Education*, 26(1), 24–33

Louv, Richard, (2005). *Last Child in the Woods. Saving Our Children from Nature-Deficit Disorder.* Chapel Hill, NC: Algonquin Books.

White, Randy (2008). Benefits of nature for children. Retrieved from th Internet, January, 2010. http://www.whitehutchinson.com. Go to Child Care, Head Start & Children's Play and Learning Environments. Click on Benefits of Nature for Children.

The Curriculum

10

Games and Other Fun Things to Do

HOW GAMES CAN ENHANCE DEVELOPMENT

Games offer children a change of pace after a day in school. Their choice of activity in the after-school hours, though, will depend on their energy level and personality. Some children have a lot of energy after sitting down all day and need to be active. Others are tired and want to rest. Some children are gregarious and ready for playing in groups, while others want to be by themselves and choose activities they can do alone. Fortunately, games offer a wide variety of options. They can be intensely vigorous or played quietly. Children can participate in large or small groups, or one child can play alone.

Games provide many opportunities for children to practice their physical skills. Although boys and girls have nearly equal motor skills, boys have greater forearm strength, and girls possess greater overall flexibility. Children's body size, coordination, and inherited talent also affect their agility. As a result, they often select games at which they can excel; boys often prefer basketball or baseball, and girls may choose gymnastics. Some girls want to be involved in group games, and they might choose volleyball. Encourage children to try new activities by emphasizing the fun of participating rather than the degree to which they are successful.

Children learn to work together when they play games. By middle childhood, most understand that rules are for everyone and that they must abide by the rules to be a part of a group. Typically, they often spend more time discussing and negotiating the rules of a game than they do actually playing. In the process, however, they learn about fairness, how to take turns, and to accept that each person can be a leader or a follower. In addition, they experience the fun of a group effort.

Games reinforce and extend children's cognitive skills. They use logic when they have to plan the next move in

LEARNING OUTCOMES

After reading this chapter, you should be able to:

✔ Discuss why games should be part of a child care curriculum.

✔ Understand how to establish a safe environment for games.

✔ Plan and implement a variety of games for outdoor and indoor play.

✔ List some guidelines for making games fun.

✔ Discuss the use of computers as adjunct learning tools.

checkers or a series of strategies in chess. "If I do this . . . then next I do that . . . this will happen." Many games involve problem solving as well. A marvelous example is a game called Jenga®. The game begins with a completed tower, 18 levels with three blocks at each level. Each player removes one block and places it on the top of the tower without toppling the structure. It takes a great deal of looking, thinking, and predicting before deciding which block can be safely removed. Trivial Pursuit® encourages children to remember facts. Dice games such as Yahtzee® require math skills.

Children can gain an appreciation for their own or other cultures by playing games of different countries. In doing so, children learn that games are often played as part of celebrations, on holidays, or to bring groups of people together in a common activity. They will also find that, in some cultures, games teach children the skills they need for survival. Figure 10–1 on page 187 and Figure 10–2 on page 196 are two examples of games. There are many other cross-cultural games available on the Internet; one such site is http://wilderdom.com/games/MulticulturalExperientialActivities.html.

Some children will view games as an opportunity to win or to be the best in order to enhance their self-esteem. You may not be able to eliminate this tendency toward competitiveness entirely because it is so much a part of children's environment at school, on television, and in the news. However, you can minimize this tendency by including noncompetitive games and games that encourage creativity. Also, reinforce children for their efforts and their skills rather than for being best or first. A poem by Matt Zwerling, published in the January 1991 issue of *Young Children*, addresses the matter of competition. He wrote:

Child's Play

I watched the relay races today,
First grade recess
Filled with teachers' whistles and students' squeals,
With shouts and seeming delight.
The winning team screamed and jumped,
Gave high-fives and handslaps just like on t.v.
One winner clenched his fists and put on a game face,
Almost grim, Will Clark in the Series
Giving high-fists and raising arms in triumph.
The other team slowly walked away; And I thought this really is the beginning. Surely, surely, there is a better way. How can there be losers in children's play?

GAMES AND SAFETY

You will find a section on planning a safe outdoor environment in Chapter 9, but some specifics need to be considered when children are engaged in games or other outdoor activities. School-age children often overestimate their competence and attempt feats that are beyond their capabilities. They also compare themselves with their peers and want to be the best at whatever they do. You can witness this tendency by watching a group of boys on skateboards and observing the risks they take. The following guidelines will help prevent serious accidents to the children in your care:

- Set clear rules for using all equipment, and make sure the children know the rules. Ensure that the rules are vigorously enforced.
- Never allow children to use equipment in inappropriate or unsafe ways or engage in an activity that is potentially injurious.
- Before planning any vigorous activity, consider all the ways children might get hurt, and eliminate the most serious hazards. When the activity is introduced, make the children aware of possible hazards, ask them to suggest ways to prevent injury, and add additional cautionary measures if necessary.
- Provide the appropriate safety equipment for sports activities—such as knee and elbow pads, helmets, and catcher's mitts.
- Have enough adults to supervise the activities and maintain the required ratio of adults to children. Train staff to position themselves where they can see the widest area under their supervision and to be vigilant at all times.
- Apprise every staff member of the center's policies and procedures for managing accidents. There should be a written statement easily accessible to each classroom that includes procedures for dealing with an accident, telephone numbers for nearby emergency services, and information regarding notification of parents.
- All staff members should know first-aid procedures. Staff should be able to treat minor injuries such as scrapes or bruises and should recognize when an injury requires medical attention.
- Staff members should carry out a follow-up after an accident, reviewing the causes and making suggestions to prevent a similar mishap in the future.
- Do a follow-up with the children. Children may be upset by the accident and need to be comforted. They may want to know what happened and why. Make sure the discussions with children are low key but factual and honest, focusing on ways to prevent the same kind of injury in the future. Never tell children the accident would not have happened "if John had only listened to me when I told him to stop." Honestly describe what happened. "John was going too fast around the skateboard area and wasn't able to make the turn."

OUTDOOR GAMES

Generations of children have played outdoor games. If you look at pictures painted several centuries ago, you are likely to find children playing some of the same games they still play today. Pieter Brueghel's paintings done in the 16th century, for instance, include children playing blind-man's bluff, hide-and-seek, and drop the handkerchief. The street games played on the sidewalks of New York, in other large cities, and in other countries have been passed down from parent to child, with each generation adding

Set clear rules to enforce safety and make sure children know all the rules.

its own variations. Most of these games are noncompetitive but designed to test the player's skills. This section will remind you of some of the old favorites and provide you with some new ideas.

Activities

Jump Rope
Purposes:

- develop physical coordination
- promote cooperation to maintain rhythm
- enhance language development, especially for children learning a second language

Jumping rope is often done to a rhythmical song or chant. The beat sets the timing for jumps and counts the number of times the individual jumps before making an error.

In other chants, words direct the individual to perform different motions while continuing to jump.

Cinderella,
Dressed in yellow,
Went upstairs to kiss a fellow,
By mistake, she kissed a snake,
How many doctors did it take?
1,2,3, . . .

Teddy bear, teddy bear, touch the ground,
Teddy bear, teddy bear, turn around,
Teddy bear, teddy bear, jump real high,
Teddy bear, teddy bear, pat your thigh.

Hopscotch
Purposes:

- develop balance and large-muscle strength
- encourage play by traditional rules
- increase eye-hand coordination necessary for aiming

A hopscotch board is visible on the floor of the forum in Rome, indicating that generations of children have played the game. In Italy, the game is called "heaven and earth," earth being the starting point and heaven the finish.

Draw the traditional pattern for hopscotch. Vary the rules by hopping with the stone held on the back of the hand. Or hop without the stone, but with the eyes closed.

Instead of the usual rules for hopscotch, try some variations. Set up a set of six squares, three on each side. Number them from one to six. Have children jump through the squares in sequence with a stone held between

Hopscotch   Hopscotch Variation

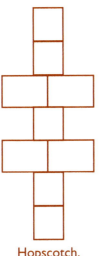

5	6
4	3
1	2

Hopscotch.   Hopscotch Variation.

their shoes. They must jump with both feet together like a kangaroo. If the stone is dropped, that player loses her turn.

Sock Ball
Purposes:

- develop eye-hand coordination
- reinforce playing by rules

Push a tennis ball or sponge ball into the toe end of a tube sock. Tie a knot close to the ball. Children can toss this ball back and forth holding the open end. Vary the throws: twirl the sock before throwing or toss it underhand. To make catching more difficult, especially for older children, rule that they can catch the ball only by the tail.

Leapfrog Race
Purposes:

- foster trust in others and group cohesiveness
- develop large-muscle coordination

Have the children line up single file in two separate lines. At the starting signal, the first player in each line crouches down on hands and knees. The next player jumps over his back and then becomes a second back. The third player must leap over two backs before becoming the third back. This continues until all players have had a turn. When the first player has jumped over all his teammates' backs and is at the head of the line again, he stands up. Each player at the end of the line follows the same procedure until all players are standing. The first team to have all players standing wins.

Stalker

Place of Origin: **Botswana**
Skills: Large motor and listening skills
Ages: 7 and older
Players: 7 or more
Materials: Two scarves for blindfolds; watch or timer

About the Game

The *springbok* is an animal similar to a gazelle, but it is found only in southern Africa. Like many games from this region, this one is about a real-life skill: hunting. For centuries children have played this game imitating adult Bushmen stalking a springbok. Through play, children learn the lifelong skills of good hunters: patience, concentration, eye-hand coordination.

Playing the Game

- Have all the players form a circle. Choose two players to start the game: one will be the HUNTER, the other the SPRINGBOK. Blindfold them both and then spin them around. Have one player announce for the hunt to begin.
- Moving quietly within the circle, the HUNTER tries to catch the SPRINGBOK, while the SPRINGBOK tries to avoid the HUNTER. Players forming the circle can either remain silent or make animal noises to distract the HUNTER and SPRINGBOK. No one is allowed to touch the HUNTER and SPRINGBOK.

Ending the Game

After a set period of time, if the HUNTER fails to catch the SPRINGBOK, the "animal" wins and a new HUNTER is brought out. If the SPRINGBOK is caught, two new players take over.

From *The Multicultural Game Book* by Louise Orlando. Copyright 1994 by Scholastic Inc. Reproduced by permission.

Catch the Dragon's Tail
Purposes:

- promote group cooperation
- practice being leaders and followers
- increase gross-motor skills

Eight or 10 children line up, one behind the other. The last person in the line tucks a handkerchief in the back of her belt. At the start signal, the dragon begins chasing its own tail. The object is for the person at the head of the line to snatch the handkerchief. When the head finally gets the handkerchief, he becomes the tail. The second in line then becomes the new head.

FIGURE 10–1 Stalker game.

From The Multicultural Game Book by Louise Orlando. Copyright 1994 by Scholastic Inc. Reproduced by permission.

A version of this game is played in China, where the dragon is a symbol of good fortune. The game is often played at Chinese New Year celebrations. In the Chinese version, the children line up, putting their hands on the shoulders of the person in front. The first person is the head and the last one the tail. The tail calls out: "1, 2, 3, dragon." The head leads, running and twisting, trying to catch its tail. If the body of the dragon breaks, the dragon dies. The head then moves to the end of the line, becoming the tail. The game continues with a new head leading until everyone is too tired to play.

PomPom Paddle Ball
Purposes:

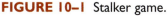

- develop eye-hand coordination
- provide practice in pair cooperation

Make paddles using five-inch lengths of broom handle or dowel. Drill a hole in one end of the handle. (Do this with the wood securely held in a vise.) Using wire cutters, cut the hook off a wire coat hanger just below the twisted part. Shape the remaining wire into a triangle. Pull a knee-high nylon stocking over the triangle. Secure the end with a bit of tape. Push the two ends of the wire into the handle.

Make a pompom by looping yarn around a six-inch piece of cardboard. Use enough yarn to make a small ball. Slip the yarn off the cardboard, then secure the middle with a piece of yarn. Clip all the ends and shape it into a ball.

Children can play in pairs, tossing the pompom back and forth. Or vary the game by having children form two lines facing each other. A group of six children works best. Have them toss the pompom back and forth between the two teams.

Obstacle Course

Purposes:

- develop gross-motor skills
- foster self-confidence by presenting increasingly difficult tasks

Set up an obstacle course using whatever equipment you have available. Place a sign showing the number at each station so children can proceed in sequence. Start with easy tasks and make them increasingly difficult. However, be sure that all activities are safe and all the children can complete most of the tasks. Some suggestions are:

- walk through a ladder that is lying flat on the ground
- crawl through a tunnel made of tables or large cardboard cartons
- balance on a balance beam or walk on the edging of a sandbox
- jump in and out of a staggered series of tires lying flat on the ground
- jump from wooden packing boxes of several heights
- swing from a knotted rope
- climb a rope net
- shinny down the fireman's pole of a jungle gym

Snake

This game is played by children in Ghana, where there are many different kinds of snakes.

Purposes:

- develop coordination
- provide practice in cooperating with others
- increase gross-motor skills

One person is chosen to be the snake. The snake goes to his home, an area that is large enough to fit several children. When given a signal (blow a whistle), the snake comes out of his home and tries to tag other players. Anyone the snake catches holds hands with her and tries to catch others. The original snake is the head and determines who will be tagged next. The end person, or "tail," can also tag players.

If the snake's body breaks, the group must return to its home and start again. Free players can try to break the snake's body, forcing the snake to return home. The game ends when all the players have been caught or when everyone is totally out of breath.

Tug of War

At one time, tug of war was a portrayal of the battle between the forces of good and evil. In Burma, the battle represents the natural occurrences of rain or drought. The custom is to allow rain to win.

In Korea villagers play the game to determine which village will have the best harvest.

This version is played in Afghanistan.

Purposes:

- develop gross-motor skills
- increase coordination
- provide practice in balancing
- increase the ability to plan strategies

Provide the players with a three-foot-long piece of doweling.

The players draw a line on the ground and stand on opposite sides. Each player clutches the dowel. The object of the game is to pull the other person across the line.

The Hunter

This game, often played in Saudi Arabia, resembles hide and seek but with a variation.

Purposes:

- develop gross-motor skills
- develop a sense of cooperation

The game is played by five or 10 children, with one person chosen to be the hunter ("it").

The hunter counts to 10 with his eyes closed so the others can run and hide. Then the hunter starts searching. When the hunter finds someone, that child tries to escape and the hunter chases her. The hunter must catch all the children or can say "clear," and start over. If the hunter catches all the children, he joins the other children, and the last one caught becomes the hunter.

Sardines

This game is frequently played in Germany.

Purposes:

- increase observation skills
- develop the ability to cooperate with others

Any number of children can play.

The person who is "it" hides while the others have their eyes closed, then the others try to find her. Whenever a child finds the person who is "it," he hides with the "it."

Soon only one person is left searching for the others. That person becomes the next "it."

ACTIVE GAMES THAT CAN BE PLAYED INDOORS

You should know a few active indoor games children can play when the weather prohibits outdoor play. Even on warm days, children sometimes need to move around while inside. The following are some games that can be played indoors, but you can set them up outdoors if you wish.

Activities

Beanbag Bowling

Purposes:

- practice in taking turns
- cooperation needed to set up pins after each turn

You will need one or two beanbags and four to 10 tall, slim cans. Pringles® cans work best, but you can also use tennis ball cans. In addition, you need a smooth, shiny floor or a long piece of plastic carpet cover. Place the cans in one of the configurations shown below. Each child sits at the end of the "alley," then slides the bean bag toward the pins. Children can keep score, adding up the number of pins knocked down at each turn.

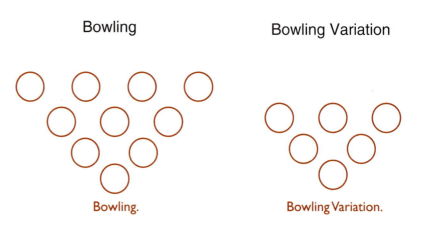

Bowling   Bowling Variation

Bowling.   Bowling Variation.

For a variation of this game, use cylindrical floor blocks for the pins and a soft ball. Players roll the ball, knocking over as many pins as possible.

String Ball Bowling

Purposes:

- increase eye-hand coordination
- increase ability to reproduce a pattern when resetting the pins
- increase math skills
- develop teamwork and cooperation

A version of this game was played in France many years ago. It was brought to the United States by Dutch settlers and developed into the modern game of bowling.

Use a hollow ball, either a tennis or racket ball. In addition, you will need duct tape, string, and cans or plastic bottles. Cut a small slit in the ball. Have children knot one end of a six-foot length of string and push the knot into the slit. Tape the string to the top of a doorway, letting the ball clear the floor by about three inches. Find ten plastic bottles of the same size. Spray paint them all the same color. Pour 1½ inches of water into each. Replace their caps securely. Set the bottles in a triangle, leaving space on either side of the doorway. Players swing the ball around the pins on either side and hit them from the back.

Bean Bag Shuffleboard
Purposes:

- practice motor skills of throwing, pushing
- improve math skills: writing numbers, adding
- taking turns, scorekeeper and player

Use masking tape or chalk to mark off a court on an area of smooth floor. The court should be a large triangle, sectioned into six segments. Number each segment, giving the smallest segment the highest score. Children sit on the floor at the large end of the triangle and slide their bean bag along the floor. Each child has two turns. Each can keep his own score, or a scorekeeper can be appointed. After a set number of turns, total the scores.

In a variation of this game, a broomstick or long dowel can be used as a shuffleboard stick. Instead of sitting, children stand, then push the bean bag with the stick.

Shuffleboard

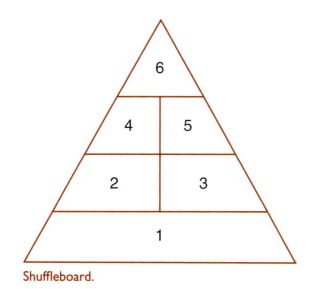

Shuffleboard.

Ping-Pong Jai Alai
Purposes:

- refine eye-hand coordination
- encourage cooperation when working in pairs

Provide a Ping-Pong ball and tall can for each child. A Pringles® can, tennis ball can, or large frozen juice can is suitable. Children drop or toss the ball with one hand, then try to catch it in the can. You can vary the game by suggesting they let the ball bounce two or three times before catching it.

Children might also work in pairs, with one child releasing the ball while the other catches. The catcher then puts the ball in play for her partner.

Indoor Basketball
Purposes:

- strengthen eye-hand coordination
- rehearse turn-taking

You will need the inner ring of an eight-inch embroidery hoop, heavy tape, and a NERF ball. Have children tape the hoop to the wall as high as their arms can reach. To play the game, each player gets three chances per turn to make a basket.

Box Marble Shoot
Purposes:

- develop small muscles of hands and fingers
- increase math skills: number recognition and addition

For this game you need a shoe box, felt marking pens, scissors, and marbles. Draw five arches on one side of the box. Make one large arch, two medium, and two short. Mark number values above each arch and cut out the arches. Each player gets three marbles and several turns to complete the game. Players shoot their marbles, trying to get them through the slots. At the end of a set number of turns, each player totals her score.

Kulit K'rang

Children in Indonesia play this game with small shells.
Purposes:

- develop eye-hand coordination
- increase reaction time
- predict where pieces will fall

The players sit in a circle around a bowl. Each player is given an equal (10–16) number of playing pieces (dried beans, peanuts, pebbles, or sea-shells). Leave about 20 pieces in the bowl. Each player places his pieces on the floor in front of him. The first player puts a piece on the back of his hand, then tosses it in the air. He must grab another piece from his pile, then catch the falling piece. If he successfully catches the falling piece, he takes one piece from the bowl. If unsuccessful, he must put one piece in the bowl.

Play continues until the bowl is empty or all the players are out of pieces. The player who finally has the most pieces wins the game.

INDOOR GAMES

There are many commercial games you can use in child care. Ask the children what they like to play at home. Remember the games you enjoyed when you were a child. Visit toy or game stores to find appropriate games for school-age children. In addition to commercial board games, there are some that you and the children can make. Also, encourage the children to think of their own ideas for games. Once you begin, new ideas will be generated.

Introduce children to simple card games; these are inexpensive because they only require a deck of cards. Some are described here, but you can find others in the books suggested at the end of this chapter.

Activities

Three-Dimensional Tic-Tac-Toe
Purposes:

- develop ability to recognize spatial relationships
- use deduction; predict results when moves are made

Mark off a 9 by 9-inch square on a piece of tag board. Leave a small border around the edges. Divide the square into nine 3-inch squares. Cut a toilet paper tube into five ¾-inch rings. Cut the heads off 10 wooden matches. Glue or tie pairs of matches together in the shape of an X. Children can use felt markers to color the tube circles one color and the match Xs another. Players take turns, one using the Xs and the other the Os. Each places his token on a square. The purpose is to get three of his tokens in a row down, across, or diagonally.

Memory Game
Purposes:

- practice the ability to match like symbols
- develop the ability to remember placement of objects in space

Find 20 pairs of pictures. You can use playing cards from two decks or secure your own matching pictures. Use identical photos or glue matching magazine pictures to cards. They should all be the same size and with no identifiable marks, patterns, or colors on the back. Two to four children can play this game.

Mix the cards, then place them face down on a table. Players take turns selecting two cards at a time. Show the cards to the other players. If the cards are a matching pair, the player keeps them. If not, they are placed back in their original spot. The next player then has a turn. The game ends when all the pictures have been picked up. The player with the most pairs is the winner.

Twenty Pairs
Purposes:

- practice ability to match like pairs
- accept that it is all right to lose

This game can be played by three or more and requires a pack of 52 cards.

Remove one queen from the deck, then deal the remainder to the players. The goal of the game is to get rid of one's cards by getting matched pairs and laying them on the table.

Each player picks up and examines her cards. She can discard any matching pairs by placing them face down on the table. If she has three cards of the same value, she can discard only two of them.

To begin the game, the player to the left of the dealer fans out his cards and offers them face down to the next player on his left. That player takes one card and incorporates it into his hand. If he now has a pair, he places it face down on the table. He, in turn, offers his cards to the next player. The procedure continues around the table until all the players have managed to pair and discard their cards. One person is left holding the odd queen.

Rotation Dice
Purposes:

- practice in taking turns
- enhance math skills: set recognition, adding

Two or more players can play the game, and all you need is a pair of dice.

Each player takes turns trying to get a specified number on each throw. There are 11 rounds to the game. In the first round each player tries for a 2. In the second, each tries for a 3. In the third round, each tries for a 4. Succeeding rounds follow the sequence to the last round when the sum of both dice must be 12.

If a player succeeds in throwing the number she is trying for, she gets that number of points. For instance, if she is trying for a 5 and succeeds, she can add five points to her score. If she does not succeed in throwing the number she needs, she ends that turn with no points. At the end of the 11th round, the scores are totaled, and the player with the most points wins.

Tic-Tac-Toe Dice
Purposes:

- strengthen math concepts: writing numbers, number recognition, adding

Two or more players can play. You need two dice, a scorecard, and pencil for each child. The score grid can be drawn on a piece of paper or a 3 by 5-inch card. Each grid should have 12 squares.

In each of the spaces, write the numbers from 1 to 12. Start with the upper-left square with one proceeding down the first column. Write 5 at the top of the second column, go down to 8. Write 9 at the top of the last column with 12 at the bottom-right corner.

Each player throws the dice only once each turn. On each play, players cross out a number or numbers on the scorecard. They can cross out a total or each of the two numbers. Players also can cross out any combination of numbers that equals the total on the dice. As an example, if a 5 and a 2 are thrown, the following combinations can be crossed out: 6 and 1; 5 and 2; 4 and 3; or 1, 2, and 4. The first person to cross out all the numbers is the winner.

Solitaire
Purposes:

Card games that one plays alone are called "solitaire" in the United States. In England these games are called "patience."

- increase ability to concentrate
- reinforce ability to count accurately
- practice recognition of symbols for suits

Shuffle a deck of cards. Deal out seven cards in a line, with the first card face up and the others face down. Deal out the line again with the

Tic-Tac-Toe

1	5	9
2	6	10
3	7	11
4	8	12

Tic-tac-toe.

Nim

PLACE OF ORIGIN: **China**
Skills: Counting, creative thinking and planning skills
Ages: 8 and older
Players: 2
Materials: 21 toothpicks, beans, or other small markers

About the Game
This is the thousand-year-old Chinese game of nim. It doesn't have any set patterns or rules. Here, however, is one way it might be played.

Playing the Game
- Players will need 21 toothpicks or other small game pieces. Arrange the sticks in one row as shown in the picture.
- Taking turns, the players pick up 1, 2, or 3 sticks at a time.

Winning the Game
The player to pick up the last stick loses.
From *The Multicultural Game Book* by Louise Orlando. Copyright 1994 by Scholastic Inc. Reproduced by permission.

FIGURE 10–2 Nim game.

second card face up and the others face down. Follow this pattern starting consecutively with the third, fourth, fifth, sixth, and seventh cards.

If an ace is showing, remove it and put it above the line of cards. Turn over the card under it, or if it was the first card, replace it with one from the deck. The object of the game is to fill each of the suits from the ace to the king in a line (pile) above the game line.

Remove three cards at a time from the remainder of the deck, looking only at the top card. Play a black card on a red card, sequencing the numbers from largest to smallest. Cards can be removed from one pile to place on another, thus freeing the bottom card. The game ends when all four suits have been filled or there are no more plays possible from the remaining deck cards.

Ajaqaq

During the dark winters Canadian Eskimos play a variety of games to pass the time. At one time they believed that playing this game would make the sun return earlier.

Purposes:
- develop fine-motor skills
- increase eye-hand coordination

Give each player a curtain ring or similar weighted ring about 2 inches in diameter, an 8-inch stick, and 20 inches of string. Tie one end of the string to the ring and the other around the end of the stick. Hold the stick in one hand. Flip the ring in the air, then try to catch it on the end of the stick.

All Ears
Purposes:

- develop listening skills
- associate sound with familiar objects
- discriminate similar sounds from one another

This is a game for a group of children. All you need are several objects that make a sound.

Sit where the children cannot see you (behind a shelf or a hanging bedsheet). Make a sound with each of the objects. Players guess what the object is or what action made the sound.

Some ideas for making a sound:

- shake a rattle
- bounce a ball
- pour water
- cut a piece of paper with scissors
- staple two pieces of paper together
- open a can of soda that has a pull tab
- snap your fingers
- crumple a piece of cellophane
- blow up a balloon until it pops
- rub two pieces of sandpaper together
- saw a piece of wood
- pound a nail into a piece of wood
- bite an apple
- unwrap a candy bar
- rotate a hand eggbeater
- jingle some coins together

At the end of the game, ask the children to think of other objects that can make a sound. Add some of those to your next game.

GUIDELINES FOR HAVING FUN WITH GAMES

Before introducing any game to children, play it yourself. Know how to start the game and how to determine the first player. Although you want children to read the rules of a game, you should be familiar with them.

Introduce new games periodically. Although children like to play the same games over and over, they also need to keep extending themselves. Once they master a game, there may be little challenge left. Therefore, look for new games. Talk to other caregivers to get ideas.

Encourage children to invent their own games. **All** games start with an idea of something that would be fun. Let them make their own board games, develop new ways to play outdoor games, and think of different ways to use available materials.

Help children feel competent when they gain new skills. Provide **authentic feedback** by describing their real accomplishments. Praise their efforts to improve their own performance, for being able to solve a problem, or for being a committed team player.

Encourage children to share their own favorite games with the group. Suggest that they bring games that are part of their cultural background.

authentic feedback
a description of a child's
real accomplishments

Encourage youngsters to try increasingly difficult tasks. Once they have mastered one task, they are often more willing to try harder ones. Encourage them to do so, but do not pressure them. Praise them for their efforts.

Stress cooperation rather than competition. You cannot avoid having a winner and a loser when playing some games. Children need to learn they do not win all the time. Some of the challenge in playing certain games is to see who can be first or fastest. However, you do not want children to view winning as the primary focus of games. Therefore, do not set up contests or give prizes. Instead, praise all the children for their participation, their sportsmanship, and their efforts.

Be flexible about rules. Many games have an accompanying set of rules; however, young children like to change rules or develop their own. Allow them to do so when all the players agree. Enjoy physical activity yourself. Feel the joy children experience when they run, catch balls, or shoot baskets.

Remember the games you especially enjoyed in childhood. Teach the children how to play them; your enthusiasm will be contagious.

Enjoy the challenge of indoor games. Sit down and play solitaire or try Trivial Pursuit® with some friends. Try some of the other games described in this chapter. Above all, have fun.

COMPUTERS

Computers and access to the Internet are very much a part of daily lives in the workplace, at home, and in schools. Adults will need to have strong computer skills to be successful. It makes sense, then, to have computers available in the child care setting, since children spend so much time there. However, questions arise about how available the computer should be—any time the children want or at scheduled times. Should the newer hand-held devices and video games also be allowed? Professionals also frequently ask who will monitor computer use.

There is a lot of support for the use of computers as **adjunct learning tools** or additional means that are not a part of traditional reading programs. The Internet and educational software can offer multimedia presentations that enhance children's literacy. Children hear a book read while viewing the words along with pictures or animations. These may motivate reluctant readers to improve their listening skills as well as their ability to read words. There are some excellent websites available for literacy.

adjunct learning tools
additional ways to learn that are not part of traditional curriculum activities

- Story Place is available both in English and Spanish and for preschool and elementary levels.

  http://www.storyplace.org

- The Kennedy Center Storyline shows the book along with the text. This encourages children to read along.

  http://www.kennedy-center.org/multimedia/storytimeonline

A computer is a marvelous research tool when children have a home-work assignment, when they are interested in a particular topic, or when they just want to find information. With the click of a mouse, they can access a wealth of information. Sometimes there is so much that children become overwhelmed. There are specific search engines geared to elementary-age children with age-appropriate material, including graphs, diagrams, and charts they can understand.

- Yahooligans has wonderful slide shows and news articles for children.

  http://www.yahooligans.com

- The Internet Public Library for Kids allows children to ask questions and then discover the answers.

  http://www.ipl.org/div/kidspace

- A Math Dictionary For Kids is an interactive dictionary that explains over 500 common mathematical terms. It also allows children to manipulate objects in order to understand concepts.

  http://www.amathdictionaryforkids.com

- The Exploratorium Online covers a wide variety of topics.

  http://www.exploratorium.edu/explore/online.html

- Ben's Guide to U.S. Government For Kids has interesting information and activities about the U.S. government presented in a way that is attractive to children.

  http://bensguide.gpo.gov

One important reason to include computers in after-school programs is that some children may not have any other access to this technology. In affluent communities computers are likely to be in every classroom, and children may very well have their own computer at home. For children in poorer neighborhoods, the after-school program may be their only source to learn how to use this tool. Even though a school district may have computers, after-school programs can allow children more open-ended computer time than they receive in the classroom. Girls use computers in different ways than boys. They see a computer as a means to making friendships and communicating with others through e-mails while boys use them for violent games Slayton (2000). Computer use changes as children get older. Girls are less likely to take advanced level computing classes in high school or to enter high tech fields as adults. The child care setting can begin to change this disparity by encouraging both boys and girls to find new uses for the computer.

The question of Internet safety should be carefully considered. Curious children who are adept at "surfing the net" can get into websites that give them misinformation or put them in dangerous positions. Software programs can filter Internet access to sites you do not want children to explore. Warn children not to reveal information about themselves, such as their home address, phone number or e-mail address, to anyone online. Tell children not to order games or buy anything online without their parents' permission. All sources of information should be screened by a staff member as a reliable source for children to use. You should also solicit

Computers can be a vital element of learning if they are integrated into the total curriculum.

active participation from staff, parents, and children to decide on how much access will be available to children and ways to prevent problems.

Choose software programs carefully, reviewing them before introducing them to the children. So many games available for computers either are violent or teach children values you may not want to promote. In a 1996 position statement, NAEYC stated that principles of developmentally appropriate practice should be applied. NAEYC believes that "in any given situation, a professional judgment by the teacher is required to determine if a specific use of technology is age appropriate, individually appropriate, and culturally appropriate" (NAEYC, 1996). You can also find reviews of software and help in choosing appropriate programs on the Internet at the following websites:

Superkids™ Educational Software Review—reviews new software. Includes games to increase vocabulary and increase logic and reasoning.

http://www.superkids.com

Juniornet—site designed primarily to provide easy e-mail access to children and includes interactive games.

http://www.juniornet.com

Knowledge Adventure®—has a wide range of software from different sources as well as a special page for educators. Includes product reviews and demonstration programs that can be downloaded.
http://www.knowledgeadventure.com

Guidelines for Caregivers

Although this section on computers has been placed in the chapter titled "Games and Other Fun Things to Do," that should not be construed as meaning that computers are not an important tool for learning. Computers can be a vital element of learning if they are integrated into the total curriculum. Teachers and child care personnel often use the term **integrated learning** to describe the use of interrelated disciplines such as language, math, or science to achieve a goal. This occurs most often in a project approach where children work on self-initiated projects individually or in a group. The explorations to complete the project may entail the use of a word processor to write letters, stories, poems, or reports. Even children who are just learning to write can be adept at this, because they can delete and rewrite easily, without the difficulties entailed with laboriously handwriting words. Children an use the Internet to research information to include in a report or to follow additional areas of interest.

In order for children to make the most effective use of computers, teachers or caregivers must play several roles depending on the children's level of competence.

Instructor: When computers first come into the program, children will need time to become familiar and comfortable with the hardware (the computer) and software (the programs). At this time teachers must take the most active role, guiding the children through the various steps necessary to explore the new medium.

Coach: As children gain experience, the adult can begin to withdraw active participation, allowing children to work independently or rely on peers to provide help as needed. The adult becomes a facilitator, providing support when needed or ensuring appropriate behavior.

Model: Children will more likely use computers as an important tool for learning if they see teachers or caregivers using them. The adult can demonstrate the ease with which a story can be recorded on the computer or classroom materials and charts can be produced.

> **integrated learning**
> the use of interrelated disciplines such as language, math, or science to achieve a goal

SUMMARY

- After long hours at school, children need a change of pace that allows them to be active or spend time alone.

- Games allow children to practice motor skills, to work together, or to reinforce or extend cognitive skills.

- Know the laws and guidelines governing safety in child care settings.

- Many popular outdoor games have been played by generations of children.

- Games should be fun, and having a set of guidelines will ensure that result.

- Computers can be an important addition to the after-school program, allowing children to write their own stories or poems and to research information for school projects.

- Adults must be aware of the safety and appropriateness of software programs available to the children

KEY TERMS

adjunct learning tools   authentic feedback   integrated learning

REVIEW QUESTIONS

1. What are the factors that affect children's choice of active games?

2. How can you help children to feel competent when they gain new skills?

3. What should you do to ensure the safety of children when they engage in vigorous outdoor play?

4. Name three academic skills that are reinforced when children play table games.

5. List four outdoor games.

6. Name three indoor games that allow children to move around.

7. Briefly describe how 20 pairs is played.

8. List eight guidelines for having fun with games.

Case Study

Ryan, Joel, and Trevor were playing on the outdoor climbing structure. They were pretending they were on a spaceship heading to Mars. They went up and down one of the ladder sections, saying they needed to check on the equipment. Trevor and Joel were rushing to be first down the ladder, pushing and shoving each other. Trevor lost his footing and fell to the ground. Although there was a ground cover of safety mats, Trevor was momentarily unconscious and had a cut on his forehead where he hit something as he fell. The cut was bleeding, but Trevor wasn't crying. Their caregiver, Anthony, knelt over Trevor without moving him and waited for him to recover consciousness. It took only a few seconds, but all the children were standing around looking very anxious. When it was safe to do so, Anthony picked up Trevor and carried him to the office so his mother could be called. The director took care of the cut on Trevor's forehead.

1. Is there a way this accident could have been prevented?

2. What would you say to Joel?

3. How would you explain the accident and Trevor's injuries to the children?

STUDENT ACTIVITIES

1. Visit an after-school program. Interview two children about their favorite games. Ask them the following questions:

    a. What is your favorite game?
    b. What do you like best about that game?
    c. What do you dislike about it?

2. Summarize your findings. Were there any games mentioned by several children? Why do you think those games were popular? Share your findings with the class.

3. Choose one of the indoor or outdoor games listed in this chapter. Teach the game to a group of school-age children. Was it successful? If not, why?

4. Make one of the games described in this chapter. Try it out with a group of adults and children together. Did both adults and children enjoy the game? How do you think the participants benefited from playing the game?

5. Interview a senior citizen. Ask him or her to describe a favorite childhood game. Why was it a favorite?

SUGGESTED READINGS

Barbarash, L. (1999). *Multicultural Games*. Champaign, IL: Human Kinetics Press.

Braman , A.N. (2002). *Kids Around the World Play! The Best Fun and Games from Many Lands*. New York: Wiley.

Haugland, S. W. (1999, November). What role should technology play in young children's learning? *Young Children*, 54(6), 26-34.

Kirchner, G. (2000). *Children's Games from Around the World*. (2nd ed.) Boston, MA: Allyn and Bacon.

MacColl, G. (2007). *The Book of Card Games for Children*. New York: Workman Publishing.

Stassevich, V., Stemmler, P., Shotwell, R., & Wirth, M. (1989). *Ready-To-Use Activities for Before and After School Programs*. West Nyack, NY: The Center for Applied Research in Education.

WEB RESOURCES

http://www.sikids.com
Sports Illustrated online magazine for kids. Information about teams and athletes, plus games and activities to increase interest in sports.

http://www.exploratorium.edu
How knowledge of science can increase sports skills. Hands-on activities and answers to frequently asked questions.

REFERENCES

National Association for the Education of Young Children. (1996, November). NAEYC position statement: Technology and young children—Ages three through eight. *Young Children*, 51(6), 11–16.

Slayton, K. (2000). Gender equity gap in high tech. A report presented to a chapter of the Americasn Association of University Women.

Zwerling, M. (1991). More food for thought, Child's play. *Young Children*, 46(2), 82.

11

Imagination and the Arts

ROLE OF THE ARTS IN SUPPORTING DEVELOPMENT

Watch a group of children as they paint at easels, dance with scarves, or listen to music. Notice their expressions of concentration, joy, or relaxation. You cannot help but conclude that creative activities satisfy children in a way few other experiences can. Children enjoy the arts because everyone can be successful. There is no right or wrong answer or just one way of doing things. They also find creative activities enable them to communicate things they might not be able to put into words. They can use bright colors when they are happy or subdued colors to show sadness. They often feel more relaxed after they pound, roll, or cut clay to release pent-up emotions. They learn what their bodies can do when they dance to music. They relive and re-make their own experiences with puppets or in plays.

Art can be shared with others or experienced privately. Painting alone lets a child express feelings or ideas that might not be easy to put into words. Group painting on a mural entails planning, compromise, sharing, and cooperation—all of which are important social skills. Listening to music alone can be a way to release tension and achieve a sense of inner peace, experience emotions vicariously, or just enjoy the sounds and rhythms. Even dancing can be enjoyed alone and offers opportunities to increase physical abilities such as large-muscle control and coordination. Group dancing can be a social activity requiring sensitivity to a partner or to the group. Patterned dances necessitate remembering sequences, an important cognitive skill.

Art, music, and drama can help children from diverse cultural and ethnic backgrounds gain a greater appreciation for their own culture and share their heritage with others. Children can view art created by prominent artists from different countries, or they can use the same materials. Some cultures use sand for painting, others paint with brilliant colors, while still others use only black media on white paper. Music can tell stories about a people, convey values or ideas, or use a rhythm that can be identified with a way of life. Children also can dramatize a folktale, write their own plays, or use puppets from different countries. Through each of these media, children learn how others live their lives. As a result, children should gain a greater tolerance for differences and a greater appreciation of similarities from one country to another.

Very young children use art experiences simply to try out materials. In preschool, children use all their senses to investigate the properties of art materials. They want to learn how colors mix together, how a paintbrush works, and how clay feels. They seldom know ahead of time what they are going to create. In kindergarten, children still enjoy just trying out materials for the pleasure of the experience, but they are beginning to realize they can express feelings and past occurrences as well. They sometimes decide to portray something specific, as Ryan did in his drawing shown below. "I'm going to draw a picture of me when I get in trouble for jumping on my mom's water bed." By the end of the elementary years, children can set goals for themselves and want recognition for their accomplishments. "I want to learn how to paint with oil paints."

The arts can provide children with a lifelong interest in all creative media. When children view others' creations, they are introduced to new ways of expressing ideas and feelings. When they study paintings or sculpture, they appreciate how artists use color and form to create something beautiful. While they listen to music, they hear how other people express emotions. When they watch a play, they share in others' experiences.

An important function of the arts is the opportunity to use both sides of the brain. There are two distinct hemispheres of the brain that serve different functions. This division or **lateralization** is most often associated with adults, but studies of children show that, even though there is an early tendency toward specialization, children's brains are still malleable

lateralization
specialization in function of the two hemispheres of the brain

"I'm getting in trouble 'cause I'm jumping on my mom's bed."
Ryan, age 7.

(Brooks & Obrzut, 1981). The left side of the brain specializes in language and logic, uses deductive thinking, and is associated with science and mathematics. The right side of the brain uses an intuitive approach associated with creative processes. Traditional education, and even society, tends to value left-side thinking, but children should be encouraged to use creative thinking as well. The arts present the perfect opportunity to do just that.

Most important of all, art is a perfect medium to help children develop **divergent thinking** and **convergent thinking**. Divergent thinking is a process of thought or perception that involves considering alternatives, taking a line of thought that is different from the usual. In art there are no right or wrong answers, and there is no single way to accomplish a creative task. L. O. Wilson (2004) listed eight characteristics of divergent thinkers: fluency, flexibility, elaboration, originality, complexity, risk taking, imagination and curiosity. Using divergent thinking, children can ask themselves "What if I used a different kind of paper for my picture?" or "I wonder if this would sound better in a different key or another instrument?" Convergent thinking is just the opposite. It means to gather facts and data from a variety of sources and then apply that information to solve a problem or achieve an objective. A child may want to express a feeling generated from a past experience. His thinking process will consider the various parts of the experience and consider the many ways in which this could be done: through a painting, a sculpture, a piece of music, and a dance. Through a process of considering and eliminating, he will decide which will serve his purpose most effectively.

When you plan any creative activities, start first with children's interests. Capitalize on these to formulate your program. Allow children to expand their interests or find new ways to express them. Find out also what they are learning in history or social studies at school, and plan activities that complement these school experiences. For some children, the creative activities they experience at child care will be all they have. Cutbacks in school districts' budgets or personnel often hit school art programs first. For these children, your program will become an even more important part of their lives. Let them enjoy one or more of the arts every single day.

The most effective art program will meet the needs of both the youngest children and the older ones. Younger children want plenty of opportunities to freely explore what they can do with materials. They should have lots of materials available at all times, and have time to use them in any way they want. The result of their efforts should be less important than the experience. As children get a little older and approach the end of their elementary years, they become more critical of what they produce. They want to learn how to use real tools to enhance their efforts. They appreciate the opportunity to learn techniques from real artists or people with special skills.

divergent thinking
a process of thought or perception that involves considering alternatives, taking a line of thought that is different from the usual

convergent thinking
a process of thought that narrows down many ideas into a single focused point

VISUAL ARTS

There are so many art activities youngsters enjoy that this chapter can give you ideas for just a few. Read the books listed at the end of this chapter, investigate what is available at your local library, and talk to other teachers or caregivers. Attend workshops sponsored by NAEYC or other professional

Look around for all different kinds of materials that can be used to construct, paint, or draw.

organizations. Look around at all the possible materials children can use to construct, paint, or draw. Save anything that might become part of your art program. You can also ask parents to donate materials that they might normally discard.

Activities

Clay and Other Kinds of Modeling Media
Purposes:

- develop fine-motor coordination
- enhance understanding of spatial relationships
- transform an idea into a three-dimensional object—from symbolic to concrete

Gray or terra cotta clay.   This is easy to use and can be dried in a kiln if one is available. Provide plastic forks or knives, small combs, garlic presses, and small pieces of sponge to vary the texture of sculptures. Add real sculpting tools for further interest.

Display pictures of Native American pottery. Tell children how pottery bowls can be made using long coils of clay. Demonstrate how to roll the clay into a long coil, then start winding a tight circle for the bottom. Continue winding, building on the base circle. Keep the bowl shape. When they reach desired height, the children can smooth the outside of the bowl with a sponge dipped in water. Allow the bowls to dry, then provide glazes so the children can paint on designs. Fire the bowls. Display the bowls.

Polymer clay.   This material is readily available but tends to be difficult to soften and work with. It comes in a variety of colors but will not harden for a permanent sculpture.

Dough.   This is fairly inexpensive, and you can vary the texture. (See Figure 11–1 for recipes.)

Papier-mâché.   This is made from paper strips or pieces plus liquid starch. Use a balloon for a base. (Caution: young school-agers may need adult help to blow up the balloon.) Dip the paper in the starch and lay it on the surface of the balloon. Overlap the pieces and make at least two layers. Let it dry thoroughly, and then prick the balloon. You should have a fairly solid round sphere. (The finished product can become the head or body of an animal. Use paper towel tubes as the legs and neck. This can also be used as a puppet head.)

For added interest, bring a Mexican piñata to class. Show the children that it has been made of a papier-mâché sphere similar to the ones they have made. Encourage them to make their own piñatas with balloons and papier-mâché. When the papier-mâché is dry, prick the balloon. Help the children cut a slit at the top of the sphere so that the piñatas can be filled with candy if desired. Pull out the balloon. Provide tissue paper in a variety of colors, scissors, a small brush, and liquid glue. Show the children how

Flour and Salt

4 cups flour
1 cup salt
Food coloring
Water to moisten
Mix the dry ingredients together. Add food coloring to water. Add water to dry mixture to achieve the desired texture. This dough will dry hard in the air and then can be painted. If a reusable dough is desired, add two tablespoons of cooking oil.

Sawdust Dough

2 cups sawdust
Liquid starch
1 cup flour or wheat paste
1 tablespoon glue (if flour is used)
Mix until the dough has a pliable consistency. Can be air dried and then painted.

Cornstarch Clay

1 cup cornstarch
1/3 cup vegetable oil
2/3 cup flour
Put cornstarch in a bowl and add oil. Mix well until starch has been absorbed. Gradually add flour until the mixture is thick and the desired consistency. Knead well for several minutes. Store in an airtight container.

Cooked Dough

1 cup flour
1/2 cup salt
2 teaspoons cream of tartar
1 cup water
1 tablespoon oil
1 teaspoon food coloring
Combine dry ingredients in a saucepan. Mix liquids and gradually add to dry ingredients. Cook over medium heat, stirring constantly until a ball forms. Remove from the heat and knead until the dough is smooth. (This is a very pliable dough that lasts for a long time.)

FIGURE 11–1 Variations of play dough.

to cut fringed strips from the tissue paper. Brush the sphere with the glue. Tell them to lay the strips evenly on the sphere, each strip slightly overlapping the previous one. Be sure to evenly cover the balloon with the strips. Remember to leave the slit visible if the piñata is to be filled.

Construction

Purposes:

- reinforce divergent thinking through exploring possibilities of found objects
- enhance understanding of spatial relationships
- develop fine-motor coordination

Styrofoam and pipe cleaners.   Use Styrofoam meat trays or packing pieces, heavy cardboard, or cork board as a base. Cut pipe cleaners into different lengths. Add additional peanut-shaped, round, or square Styrofoam package fillers for further interest.

Toothpicks, natural or colored.   Combine with small corks, drinking straws cut in different lengths, or small wooden beads. Lengths of copper or colored wire can be added. This sculpture can be freestanding or pushed into a base of Styrofoam.

Wood.   Use a flat piece of wood or heavy cardboard as a base. Add lumber scraps cut into interesting shapes, wooden beads, wooden buttons, tongue depressors, wood stir sticks, wood lathe scraps. (You can obtain many interesting shapes from a furniture manufacturer or a high school woodworking class.) Furnish white glue. For a variation, add pieces of tree bark, small twigs, or seed pods.

Recyclable cans.   Create "can creatures" using clean soda or juice cans. Provide construction paper in assorted colors, fluorescent paper, markers, scissors, white glue, and assorted objects (yarn, buttons, beads, feathers, etc.). Encourage children to imagine a "creature" with the can as the body. They can cut out feet or arms from the paper and make "hair" from fringed pieces of paper or yarn. Buttons or beads can become eyes or clothing decorations. Display the "creatures" when they are finished.

A variation of this type of construction uses chopsticks. Explain to the children that people in Asia use chopsticks instead of forks. (This activity might follow the preparation of a Chinese or Japanese meal.) Give each child a chopstick and a piece of polymer clay for a base. Provide feathers, yarn, construction paper, scraps of fabric, small movable plastic eyes, felt-tipped markers, scissors, and white glue. Encourage the children to use their imaginations to create interesting "people."

Sand casting.   Use a flat cardboard box filled with slightly damp sand for a mold. Mix a batch of plaster of Paris in a bucket. Children can make a free-form depression in the sand. Pour in plaster of Paris and let it set. For a variation, let them press shells or other objects into the sand. Remove the objects to leave an imprint before pouring the plaster.

Collage
Purposes:

- increase appreciation of the natural environment
- enhance sensitivity to differences in color, texture, and appearance of different materials
- develop fine-motor skills

Nature collage.   Have children collect natural objects outdoors or on a walk: leaves, twigs, bark, dried grass, seed pods, acorns, pinecones, feathers,

Provide a variety of colors so children can choose their own palette.

rocks. Give each child a base of heavy paper, tagboard, Styrofoam, or wood. Provide white glue for making the collage.

Paper collage.   Use small pieces of paper: wallpaper, gift wrap, greeting cards, paper doilies, construction paper, aluminum foil, or cellophane. Give each child a base of cardboard, heavy textured paper, or thin box top (from stationery or shoe box). Provide white glue.

Fabric collage.   Use small pieces of fabric: felt, lace, ribbon, yarn, buttons, colored beads, small silk flowers, and dried or paper flowers. Give each child a base of colored tagboard, construction paper, or a thin box top. Provide white glue.

Shape collage.   Provide children with a piece of drawing paper on which has been drawn one of the following shapes: a square, a triangle, a rectangle, a circle, an oval, or a parallelogram cut from construction or other kinds of paper. Challenge the children to create a picture with the shape as the base. Provide marking pens, paints, an assortment of paper and fabric pieces, scissors, and white glue.

Seed collage.   Provide an assortment of seeds in different colors and shapes. Give each child a piece of heavy paper, cardboard, tagboard, or wood for a base. Provide white glue and a small brush. Encourage them to create a picture using the seeds.

To stimulate interest in seed collage, display pictures of the New Year's Day parade floats in Pasadena, California. Explain that many of the colors that are seen on the floats are made from millions of seeds that are glued on to the base.

African Kente Cloth

Kente cloth is used for shirts, ties, and hats in many African countries. Display pictures of the cloth or obtain samples. Point out that the cloth is made up of simple geometric patterns on square or rectangular shapes. Supplies needed: construction paper of assorted colors, rulers, scissors, crayons, or marking pens. Display the cloths when they are finished along with pictures of Kente cloth.

Large Masks

Masks have been used for ceremonies to bring power and spiritual forces to the people who wear them. They often have intricate designs or carvings. Display pictures of ceremonial masks, or visit a museum that displays them.

You will need the following supplies: large pieces of tree bark or palm frond bases (large pieces of corrugated cardboard can also be used), scissors, white glue, construction paper in assorted colors, and found objects. Remind the children they can build up parts of their masks with construction paper pieces or add found objects to make the masks scarier.

Painting and Drawing
Purposes:

- increase language—new words relating to artistic endeavors
- provide opportunity to move from one intellectual level to another in a nonthreatening environment (scaffolding)
- increase awareness of cultural differences and similarities through appreciation for ethnic art

Crayon rubbings. Use any thin white paper over flat stones, leaves, sandpaper, corrugated paper, or cardboard shapes. Use the flat side of a crayon to cover the entire sheet of paper, picking up the design underneath.

Chalk painting. Cover a sheet of paper with a thin layer of liquid starch. Provide several colors of chalk, either sharpened to a point for a thin line, or blunted for a thick line. Use a rag, piece of paper towel, or fingers to mute or brush colors together.

Melted crayons. Use pieces of crayons without paper coverings. Allow children to smash crayons in a heavy bag with a mallet. They can then sprinkle crayon bits onto a piece of paper and cover it with a second sheet. Let them press the paper with a warm iron. Peel off the top sheet. You can vary the result by sprinkling crayon bits on paper and setting the paper in the hot sun to melt.

Tempera paint. Provide a variety of colors so children can choose their own palettes. Give them a choice of brushes: thin, fat, stiff, or soft. Provide a variety of textures of paper: rice paper, grocery bags, parchment, newsprint, or wallpaper. Try changing the shape of paper: long, thin rectangle; large or small oval; large or small square; triangle; hexagon. For added interest let them paint outdoors, on the floor, or at table easels.

Textile paint. Provide a variety of colors of textile paint (obtain from a fabric store). Give children a choice of fabrics of different colors, textures, and sizes.

Crepe paper paint. Use paper with a slick finish (finger paint paper or butcher paper). Provide each child with lengths of crepe paper streamers. Give each a squirt bottle of water. They can tear the crepe paper, lay it on the paper, and spray it with water. The colors will fade onto the paper, running together. If they tilt the paper, the colors will run down the paper.

Paint with different tools. Provide toothbrushes, feathers, roll-on deodorant bottles, small sponges, cotton balls, sponge-top bottles, cotton swabs, foam swabs (used for cleaning audio and video equipment), flexible spreaders (used in cake decorating), or squeeze bottles.

Oil-like paint. Mix one part powdered tempera with two parts liquid dishwashing detergent. Mix well until the mixture becomes thick and creamy. Use a small palette knife or craft stick to spread the paint on paper.

Field trip. Visit an artist's studio. Ask the artist to demonstrate some techniques to the children. Point out the safety precautions the artist uses.

Museum visit. Visit an art museum. Request a tour with a docent who can tell the children about the exhibits. Children will enjoy seeing how the artists painted people, landscapes, or abstract designs. As a variation, visit an art gallery to see special exhibits.

Display ethnic and cultural arts. Obtain paintings, sculptures, folk art, and illustrated books from different cultures. In conjunction with the displays, provide children with art materials that use the same colors or materials. Encourage them to produce their own ethnic art.

Example 1: Display Asian landscape paintings. Provide the children with long sheets of white paper and the subtle colors typical of these paintings: pale greens, tans, black, creamy beige, white, and orange or red for accents. Supply brushes with slim bristles. Encourage children to make their own landscapes of an imaginary view or of a place they have been to. (To add interest to this activity, play some Asian music while the children paint.) When they are finished, mount the pictures with a piece of bamboo at the top. Tie a black string to the bamboo and display the pictures.

Example 2: Display pictures of Native American sand paintings. Tell children to look at the designs that were used. Supply them with square pieces of cardboard, colored sand (obtain from pet stores or make your own by mixing powdered tempera with the sand), white glue, and small brushes. Instruct the children to draw a design on the paper, then paint glue on a part of the design that will be one color. Sprinkle the sand on that portion, and let it dry briefly before painting another section. Continue in this manner until the painting is complete. Display the paintings when they are completely dry.

Example 3: Show children paintings by Mexican artists. Tell them to observe the vibrant colors and color mixes that these artists use.

"Prince, ballerina, and the kids. They're at a dance." Stephanie, age 5.

Provide some bright paint: orange, red, yellow, pink, purple, black. Tell children to create their own picture, perhaps portraying an experience from their own lives. Display the pictures.

Equipment to Have Available

- aprons or old shirts
- brushes—various sizes and shapes
- boards for clay—Masonite, plastic, or wood
- drying racks
- easels—floor and table
- matting knife
- paper cutters—for single sheets and for large rolls of paper
- craft sticks, palette knives
- rags and towels for cleanup
- reproductions of fine art
- rulers, measuring tape
- scissors—assorted sizes, left- and right-handed
- sculpting tools, garlic press
- sponges—large and small, natural and manufactured
- staplers

Discussion

Enhance children's experience by helping them learn more about art. Discuss the following art topics with them:

- how things look: light, texture, color, position
- effect of using contrasting colors: light and dark, bright and dull
- two-dimensional surfaces: forms, variations in size and shape
- drawing techniques: line drawings, imaginative and decorative styles
- painting techniques: dry or wet brush, stippling, finger painting, color mixing
- new words: colors—ivory, crimson, burnt sienna, hot or cold, primary
- art professions: painter, sculptor, ceramist, illustrator, cartoonist, designer, museum director

MUSIC AND MOVEMENT

When children enter kindergarten, most are able to sing simple songs, although they may not always be on pitch. They have favorite songs and seem especially attuned to music with a pronounced rhythm. Given a few simple instruments, children will imitate rhythms they have heard or create their own. They also like to move to music, using their whole bodies or just their hands or feet. By the end of elementary school, most children

"Me dancing." Rachel, age 5.

have developed a good sense of rhythm and beat. They can remember and sing a large selection of songs and have added the new skill of being able to sing in harmony. Some are able to play instruments, and a few will be able to write down simple musical patterns or songs.

Music should be a part of every day. It does not have to take place at a formal music time but can be integrated into the daily routine. Start the day with a few songs, then have instruments available for children to use when they wish.

Take instruments outdoors on occasion so children can play or dance in a different environment. Occasionally play records or tapes during activity times.

Activities

Purposes:

- increase physical coordination
- develop listening skills
- provide an outlet for expression of feelings
- enhance appreciation of ethnic contributions to the arts

Musical styles.   Play different kinds of music: classical, lullaby, folk music, marches, gospel, rock, or jazz. Have the children identify each style, then ask them to compare two styles. How are they alike or different? Provide many opportunities for children to hear music, encouraging them to really listen to how the music is formed. Place tapes or CDs in a listening corner for children to enjoy at leisure.

As an added interest, play selections of music from different countries and cultures. Select reggae from Jamaica, opera from Italy, a mariachi band from Mexico, sitar music from India, balalaika music from Russia, flute music from the Andes, or Native American drum music. Ask the children to compare the sounds of the music. Why do they think the music is representative of the country?

Paint to music.   Play different kinds of music as children paint. Suggest they paint what they hear. Include ethnic music.

Dancing with props.   Add props to enhance movement: scarves, balloons, hoops, colored rope, streamers, or dress-up clothes.

Mirroring.   Provide a scarf for each child. Group them in pairs. Have one child act as leader, making movements using the scarf. A second child mirrors those movements. After a short period, change places.

Instruments.   Provide a variety of simple instruments: autoharp, drums, rhythm sticks, shakers, castanets, tambourines, and bells. Allow children to experiment with the sounds.

Provide the materials for children to make their own instruments. Several websites listed at the end of this chapter provide information on easy-to-make musical instruments.

Listening corner.   Set up a listening corner with a tape recorder or CD player and earphones.

Provide a selection of music. Change the tapes or CDs periodically.

Musical statues.   Play a tape or CD while children dance. Instruct them to "freeze" in whatever position they find themselves in when the music stops. Stop and start the music several times.

Shadow dancing.   On a sunny day, take the tape or CD player outdoors. Encourage children to dance, watching their own shadows as they move.

Video.   Let children view a video or DVD of dance segments. (Check your library or watch for television shows you can tape.) Discuss the kind of dance portrayed, then encourage children to dance to the video.

Visitor.   Invite a musician to your center to demonstrate techniques. If possible, allow children to try out the instrument. Include musicians who play instruments that are typical of a particular ethnic group or are representative of a country.

Equipment to Have Available

- autoharp(s)
- banjo
- blank tapes for recording
- books—song, poetry

Set up a listening corner with a tape recorder or CD player and earphones.

- dance props—tap shoes, tutus, scarves, streamers, canes, hoops, ropes
- earphones for listening center
- ethnic musical instruments—maracas, bongo drums, Chinese temple blocks
- guitar
- piano
- tape or CD player—assortment of tapes or CDs; select all kinds of music, including ethnic and holiday pieces
- recorders
- selection of percussion instruments—drums, rhythm sticks, shakers, castanets, tambourines, bells
- television monitor and videotape player

Discussion

Some concepts to discuss with children to enhance their learning:

- musical terms: tempo, pitch, dynamics (loud/soft)
- movement: walking, running, swaying, balance
- dance forms: ballet, folk, tap, interpretive, jazz
- instruments: names, how they produce sound, care of instruments
- listening: differentiating sounds, following musical directions or beat
- professions: teacher, lyricist, composer, conductor, performer, recording technician, arranger.

DRAMA

From a very early age children engage in dramatic play. Toddlers charm their parents by imitating actions or situations they observe around them. Preschoolers use dramatic play to try out what it feels like to be a grownup. They play at being mom or dad, doctors, firefighters, or teachers. As they get a little older, dramatic play becomes a way to conquer their feelings of being scared or helpless. Four-year-olds and young "school-agers" play at being monsters, Superman, or any current popular TV figure. During the middle childhood years, youngsters use dramatic play to consolidate and understand what they are learning in school and at home.

Although they may still dress up and act out situations, children also use small toys, blocks, or other materials to replay a trip to the fire station or other community facilities. They may also reenact what they see happening on television news or familiar shows.

Older children take a more organized approach to dramatic play. They want to write their own scripts, assign parts, make costumes, and stage plays. This activity provides a variety of opportunities to practice skills that youngsters try to develop during this period of their childhood. Writing a script entails listening to how people talk during conversations, writing words, and organizing a story line. Negotiations and compromise are necessary to ensure that all participants have an opportunity to contribute according to their own skills or interests.

The best kinds of dramatic play occur when children can play whatever they wish. Allow children many different opportunities to use their imaginations in both spontaneous and organized activities. Make materials available as their interests dictate.

Activities

Purposes:

- provide practice in negotiating and compromising during a group effort
- enhance the ability to set long-term goals and to postpone gratification
- increase the ability to portray ideas, feelings, and experiences through drama or using blocks

Puppets.   Design and make different kinds of puppets. Try shadow, finger, stick, papier-mâché, or sock puppets. Read about how puppets are constructed and used in other countries. (See Figure 11–2 for ideas.)

Puppet theater.   This can be permanent or impromptu. Older children can make a permanent theater using carpentry tools and plywood. Or make a theater from a large appliance box. An impromptu stage also can be as simple as a table covered with a blanket or a wall of large blocks.

Produce a puppet play.   Have children write a simple script or use a favorite story. Let them make the puppets and plan the production.

Drama kits.   Collect a variety of props children can use for dramatic play. Store them in related sets for different jobs: beautician, doctor, mechanic, or astronaut. (Listen for children's interests, then provide additional props suitable for play.)

Makeup.   Provide makeup (non-allergenic theatrical makeup, if possible) and mirrors. Allow children to try out ways to use makeup. Have tissues and cold cream for cleaning up when they are finished.

Blocks.   Provide both small and large blocks. Add accessories as children's interests dictate: cars, airplanes, boats, people, animals, trees, and signs. Add more materials: cardboard packing forms, Styrofoam pieces, plywood, or cardboard tubes.

Play.   Have children write and produce a play. They can also adapt a book or use a published play. (Check the library for suitable children's plays.)

Blocks give children the ability to portray ideas and experiences.

Papier-mâché Puppet
Materials needed:
>   dried papier-mâché sphere made on a balloon
>   length of cardboard tubing from paper towel roll
>   felt and cloth scraps
>   yarn, ribbons, buttons
>   marking pens
>   tempera or acrylic paint, small brushes
>   scissors, glue

Directions:
>   Cut a small opening in one side of the sphere. Gently push the cardboard tubing into the opening. Paint the face with flesh tones. Let the face dry overnight before adding features. Use yarn for making hair. Cut fabric or felt scraps for clothing, making it large enough to cover the child's hand. Decorate clothing with ribbons or buttons.

Sock Puppet
Materials needed:
>   clean sock, can be white or colored
>   buttons
>   eyes (you will find these in a hobby shop)
>   felt, fabric scraps
>   yarn, pipe cleaners, ribbons
>   scissors, glue

Directions:
>   Show children how to fit the sock over their hand and then make a moving mouth with thumb and fingers. Let them glue scrap materials onto puppet to create a face.

Shadow Puppets
Materials needed:
>   cardboard strips or craft sticks
>   construction paper
>   scissors
>   marking pens
>   staple gun

Directions:
>   Have children draw a figure on the construction paper, then cut it out. Staple the figure to the cardboard strip or craft stick.

FIGURE 11–2 Puppets.

Tell stories.   Encourage the children to tell their own stories with a beginning, a middle, and an end. During group time, have one child start a story with a few sentences. The next child takes up the story line and continues with a few more sentences. Each child must listen to all the previous storytellers in order to remember the gist of the story before continuing.

The last child has the most difficult part because she must bring the story to a close. As a variation, tape the story as the children tell it. Place the tape in the listening corner so the children can hear it again.

Read folktales. Folktales are stories that once were told by parents, grandparents, or community storytellers. Originally they were not written down, but passed on from generation to generation. Read folktales at group times or encourage small groups or pairs of children to read to one another.

Invite an adult storyteller to visit. Ask the adult to tell the children a story that was a favorite when he or she was a child. Encourage stories that have been part of a family tradition or culture.

Field trip. View a puppet play or children's drama. Look for professional performances at theaters or amateur performances at schools, community centers, or libraries.

Equipment to Have Available

- blocks—wooden floor blocks, large hollow blocks, small colored blocks
- block accessories—cars, boats, airplanes, people, animals, trees, signs
- boxes, shelves, racks for storing props
- carpentry tools—saw, measuring tape, yardstick, hammer, sander, nails
- dress-up clothes—skirts, dresses, capes, shoes, hats, wigs, scarves
- floor lights—standing lamps, spotlights
- mirrors—individual makeup mirrors, full-length mirrors
- puppet theater or materials for construction
- sewing tools—needles, thread, pins, scissors
- tape recorder
- window shade or curtains

Discussion

Some concepts to discuss with children:

- imagination: new ways to tell a story or express feelings
- props: how to make props and costumes for their productions
- scripts: books, poems, films, TV shows
- skills: skills needed to produce a drama
- puppets or marionettes: which one fits a particular character
- manipulating puppets to create a story
- dramatic professions: actor, writer, painter, producer, puppet master.

Not all children will grow up to be painters, sculptors, actors, musicians, or playwrights. However, you want them to learn that when they progress into the sometimes harried world of adulthood, the arts will provide continuing pleasure and relaxation. By having a variety of art activities available, all children can find one that suits their own individual needs and abilities. So, make art of all kinds an integral part of your day. Both you and the children will reap boundless benefits.

Art of all kinds should be an integral part of the child care day.

SUMMARY

- Creative activities satisfy children because all children can be successful, children can communicate nonverbally, and they can release emotions.
- Creative activities should be based on children's interests.
- The most effective art program will meet the needs of both the youngest children and the older ones.
- By kindergarten age children have a good sense of rhythm and can create their own songs. Some can play an instrument.
- Dramatic play helps children consolidate learning.
- Art of all kinds should be an integral part of the child care day.

KEY TERMS

convergent thinking   divergent thinking   lateralization

REVIEW QUESTIONS

1. This chapter stated that "creative experiences satisfy children in a way few other experiences can." Give three reasons for that statement.
2. In what way does a preschooler's use of art materials differ from that of a child approaching adolescence?
3. Give five examples of art activities appropriate for school-age children.
4. List three musical concepts to discuss with children to enhance their learning.

5. You want to encourage children in your child care group to enjoy more music. What kinds of equipment should you have available?

6. Relate the developmental steps in children's dramatic play from toddlers to older middle children.

7. List some accessories children might use with blocks for dramatic play.

Case Study

Hannah is a lively six-year-old. Her favorite activity is using whatever art materials are available each day, and she spends most of her inside time in the art area. However, she constantly wants reassurance and praise for her efforts. She will finish an interesting collage and then run to Susan asking her to look at it. Hannah will ask, "Do you like my picture? Do you think those colors go together?"

1. How would you respond to Hannah's "Do you like my picture"? Explain why you would answer in that way.

2. How would you react to her "Do these colors go together"?

3. Hannah spends most of her time at this one activity. Would you do anything to broaden her interests? If so, what?

STUDENT ACTIVITIES

1. Visit a library, museum, community center, and theater in your community. Ask about programs or resources they might have that would interest school-age children. Prepare a list to share with your classmates.

2. Plan and implement one of the activities suggested in this chapter. Write an evaluation of the experience. Were there things you could have done differently? If so, how?

3. Talk to teachers and caregivers in three different child care groups. Ask which creative activities their children most enjoy. Find out why they think those activities are so popular.

SUGGESTED READINGS

Baker, N. (2010). *Bug Zoo*. New York: May Media Group, LLc..

Carlson, L. (1993). *EcoArt*. Charlotte, VT: Williamson.

Cherry, C. (1990). *Creative Art for the Developing Child* (2nd ed.). Belmont, CA: David S. Lake.

Gomez, A. (1992). *Crafts of Many Cultures.* New York: Scholastic Professional.

Gordon, L. (2005). *Super Duper Art and Craft Activity Book*. San Francisco: Chronicle Books.

Gutwirth, V. (1997). A multicultural family study project for primary. *Young Children*, 52(2), 72–78.

Haas, C, & Friedman, A. (1990). *My Own Fun—Activities for Kids Ages 7–12.* Chicago: Chicago Review Press. (Available from School-Age Notes, Nashville).

Kohl, M., & Potter, J. (1993). *Science Arts: Discovering Science Through Art Experiences.* Bellingham, WA: Bright Ring.

Milford, S. (1990). *Adventures in Art, Art and Craft Experiences for 7- to 14-year-olds.* Charlotte, VT: Williamson.

Ringenberg, S. (2003). Music as a teaching tool: Creating story songs. *Young Children,* 58(5), 76–79.

Ryder, W. (1995). *Celebrating Diversity with Art, Thematic Projects for Every Month of the Year.* Glenview, IL: Scott Foresman.

Sierra, J. (1991). *Fantastic Theater, Puppets and Plays for Young Performers and Young Audiences.* New York: H. W. Wilson.

The Complete Book of Arts and Crafts, (1999). au. Columbus, OH: School Specialty Publishing.

Computer Software/Video

China: Home of the Dragon (Mac Windows CD-ROM). Orange Cherry/ New Media Schoolhouse. Intermediate, Advanced.

Let's Visit Mexico (Mac IBM CD-ROM). Fairfield, CT: Queue. Advanced.

Thinkin' Things Collection 1 (Mac IBM Windows MPC CD-ROM). Redmond, WA: Edmark. Primary, Intermediate.

Thinkin' Things Collection 2 (Mac IBM Windows MPC CD-ROM). Redmond WA: Edmark. Primary, Intermediate, Advanced.

Thinkin' Things Collection 3 (Mac MPC CD-ROM). Redmond, WA: Edmark. Intermediate, Advanced.

WEB RESOURCES

http://www.bestchildrensmusic.com
   Best children's music: list of best children's music, musical books, links to music education websites.

http://www.si.edu
   Smithsonian Museum site for educational resource guides, lesson plans, programs, and other resources.

http://www.moma.org
   Museum of Modern Art in New York has several click-on related sites. Education site offers programs and publications for children, their families, and their schools.

http://www.artsedge.kennedy-center.org
   Kennedy Center in New York supports art education for grades K-12. Includes ideas and lesson plans.

http://www.getty.edu
   Getty Museum in Los Angeles has a variety of programs for teachers and children, including guided visits to the center.

http://www.kinderart.com
   This site offers a wide variety of craft ideas.

http://www.nancymusic.com
Find homemade musical instruments at this site.

http://www.philtulga.com
Making musical instruments using math and measurement.

http://www.mudcat.org
Easy to make instruments.

REFERENCES

Sinha, S.; Bookheimer, S.; Gorg, M.; Badr, L.; & Grinstead, J. (2003). *Leftside of brain activates speech from birth*. Retrieved from the Internet, February 2010. http://www.scinecedaily.com/releases/2003/12/031204075435.htm

Wilson, L.O. (2004). Divergent thinking abilities. Retrieved from the Internet, February 2010. http://www.uwsp.edu/education/wilson/creativ/divergentthink.htm

12

Science and Math

SCIENCE AND MATH IN SCHOOL-AGE CHILD CARE

A goal of the National Science Foundation (2006) is to "cultivate a world-class, broadly inclusive science and engineering workforce, and expand the scientific literacy of all the citizens." Additionally, a summary of research in early childhood mathematics (Cross, Woods, & Schweingruber, 2009) states that the new demands of international competition require a workforce that is competent in and comfortable with mathematics. **Scientific literacy** means having knowledge of basic scientific facts, concepts, and vocabulary, so as to be able to follow news-related reports in the media and discuss science-related issues. Some of the science-related issues of today include global warming, becoming ecologically friendly, and biotechnology.

The National Science Educations Standards (National Research Council, 1996) describe someone who is scientifically literate as having the ability to describe, explain, and predict natural phenomena. Caregivers in school-age programs have the opportunity to support and advance children's scientific literacy. The attitudes and values established toward science in the early years will shape a person's development of scientific literacy as an adult.

Science and math are a part of children's daily life. The environmental context in which children live influences the theories they may form and the concepts they may learn. Children in the Midwest may learn about ice storms, thunderstorms, tornadoes, mosquitoes, fireflies, or growing field corn and soybeans. Children in southern California may learn about earthquakes, oceans, smog, garden snails, or growing strawberries, oranges, and avocadoes. Children who help a parent cook may engage in measuring the ingredients to make chocolate chip cookies and discovering the effects of putting the cookie batter in a hot oven.

LEARNING OUTCOMES

After reading this chapter, you should be able to:

✔ Discuss the importance of science and math in a school-age child care program.

✔ Describe how children engage in science and math activities as scientists and mathematicians.

✔ Explain how math and science are integrated, and why the process of science is important in school-age child care.

✔ Describe a science and math environment in a high quality child care program.

✔ Discuss the leader's role in supporting children's cognitive development through facilitation of science and math activities.

✔ Plan and implement appropriate science and math activities

Six-year-old Skylar was frequently seen with a stick in his hand. He would swing it like a bat to knock a flower from its plant, drag it in the dirt to make a path, or use it like a golf club to move small rocks. On a particular day he discovered a second stick. Both sticks were about 1 inch in diameter; one was about 2 feet long and the length of the other one was about 12 inches. As Skylar walked along, he began tapping the long stick with the shorter one. He tapped near his hand, at the middle of the stick and at the end. "Hey, look! This makes a different sound when I hit it in different places!" He then began systematically tapping up and down the stick, checking and noting the differences in the sounds.

scientific literacy
knowledge and understanding of science concepts and process

Children come to their school-age child care setting equipped with the daily learning experiences of their school's math and science curriculum. One aspect of caregiving is supporting the personal and educational experiences of children. Learning does not happen only during school hours. In fact, it is estimated that 40 percent of children's time is spent in informal or unstructured activity (National Science Foundation, 2006). Programs for school-age children are ideal places for children to expand their understanding of the science and math concepts they learned in school, as well as enhancing their experiences of science and math in their daily lives.

School-age children are naturally inquisitive and seem to have an insatiable thirst for knowledge. They try to understand the world around them as they spontaneously do things such as attempting various strategies for tossing rocks, stopping to investigate a slithering worm, or wondering why their crayons melted. Physically and cognitively, school-age children are at a developmental stage where they can act more intentionally on their environment as they question and test out their ideas and communicate their discoveries. Unlike the preschool-age child, the school-age child can engage in divergent thinking and consider alternative strategies and possibilities. School-age children are concrete learners—meaning they need hands-on experiences with real materials to learn.

All types of school-age programs can be arenas for children to learn about math and science. A summer park and recreation program can feature science investigations in the outdoor environment. A sports program can incorporate physics and math as children discover strategies for moving a ball through space, track distances, and keep score. Center-based before- and after-school programs can provide dedicated space and time for ongoing science investigations.

CHILDREN AS NATURAL SCIENTISTS

Children are often exposed to the traditional careers of firefighter, teacher, doctor, and so on; rarely are they introduced to the idea of being a scientist, an engineer, or a mathematician. Children can easily grow up with the

Six-year-old Ethan approached leader Parisa holding plastic farm animals in his hands, saying, "Parisa, I think that everything that is plastic floats and if it's not plastic it will sink." Parisa replied, "Ethan, how could you test your theory?" Ethan replied that he could fill the sink with water, and he promptly walked to the sink. Once the sink was filled with water, he tested his theory. He discovered that the items he had selected did float and concluded that his hypothesis was correct. Parisa, noticing this, said, "I wonder about other plastic things. Are all plastic things made the same way? Do they float also?" Ethan looked around the room and gathered a variety of plastic items again to test and refine his theory. He eventually concluded that some things made of plastic had air inside them, and that is what made them float.

stereotype of the mad scientist and determine that being a scientist isn't a career choice for them. Yet children already actively engage in these roles using the skills scientists and mathematicians employ.

What do scientists do? They explore, investigate, observe, record data, make hypotheses, develop theories, and draw conclusions. Scientists use mathematics as they measure quantities, temperature, volume, and distances. They make quantitative and qualitative comparisons, classify information, and create charts and graphs to represent their findings. From very early ages, children naturally explore and investigate, observe, ask questions, develop theories, test their theories, and draw conclusions. They develop their own theories of how the world works. According to Jean Piaget, this is known as **constructing knowledge**. They come to know concepts (construct knowledge) as a result of their own experiences and their own thinking about those experiences.

During middle childhood, children's ability to develop more logical theories increases as they shift from preoperational thinking into more concrete thinking where they see cause-and-effect relationships more realistically. The five-year-old sees relationships and draws conclusions but has difficulty grasping concepts such as reversibility or recognizing that quantities of matter remain unchanged. As children's cognitive abilities mature, they realize that things can change physical form and be transformed again, such as water becoming ice and then again becoming water.

Children's construction of knowledge is greatly enhanced by what Lev Vygotsky refers to as scaffolding. The discussion of sociocultural theory in Chapter 5 holds that children can experience cognitive development when they are supported by a skilled peer or adult who has the ability to scaffold their experiences. Scaffolding may occur through specific questioning that provokes thinking or guided participation that, in turn, helps the learner through the steps of a process and encourages the learner to think. Consider the activity, "Is it liquid or solid?" When left to their own devices and thinking, children may only explore the sensory aspects of materials, never exploring a substance from the perspective of thinking about it as liquid or solid. Through the scaffolding process,

constructing knowledge
children develop their own theories about how the world works

Is it liquid or solid?
(Messy but easy to clean up!)

Mix equal parts of water and cornstarch on small trays. Encourage the children to investigate this with their fingers. Be prepared to provide utensils, such as spoons, plastic knives, or spatulas, for further investigation. Discuss with the children the characteristics of a solid (holds its own shape) and the characteristics of a liquid (pourable, wet, takes the shape of its container). Encourage the children to hypothesize and form theories about the mixture and then to continue investigating to see if they can discover an answer to their question.

Hint: It is both. The cornstarch remains a solid. It does not dissolve in the water, but its particles are suspended in the water.

a knowledgeable peer or adult can discuss the characteristics of solids and liquids, guiding the science participants to more in-depth exploration and subsequent understanding.

Science activities allow children freedom to explore materials and carry out experiments in a nonthreatening atmosphere. Not only do children increase their scientific inquiry skills through these activities, they also gain confidence in seeking solutions to problems and opportunities to practice math skills. This investigative environment allows children the opportunity to take risks. They try new things, make mistakes, learn from their mistakes, and continue trying out new ideas.

Children gain new perspectives from scientific explorations.

Science activities also allow children to work together as they discover the concepts of physical, life, and earth sciences. They share ideas. They each bring their personal experiences and knowledge to the investigative process and thereby help one another as they brainstorm to develop theories, hypotheses, and strategies for experimentation, exploration, and documentation.

CHILDREN AS NATURAL MATHEMATICIANS

Children naturally have opportunities to use mathematics on a daily basis, and they will seek mathematical answers to their questions. Spontaneous activities occur, such as when children need to add scores when playing games or when they have to figure out how to divide a set of materials so everyone has an equal share. Preoperational children will count everything in sight once they learn how to count. They don't yet understand that the quantity of a set of objects stays the same when the objects are moved. According to Piaget this is a lack of conservation of number. Yet children enjoy the task of counting. Children between the ages of five and seven are in transition from preoperational thinking to concrete operations. Children in the stage of concrete operations are better able to conserve number if they have ample opportunity to work with materials to group and regroup them, and to experience and discover the relationships of different quantities. Child care leaders can give children guidance in counting correctly through scaffolding.

Life presents many opportunities for children to notice and respond to the physical characteristics of objects such as color, size, and shape. Children consider these characteristics to sort the objects into categories—also known as classification. Children classify when they identify the various shapes and sizes of blocks and put them in their appropriate places on shelves. Similarly, children are classifying when they put all the markers together, pencils in their own place, and scissors in another. Children may group objects together when investigating science. For example, they may group together objects that roll fast and others that roll slowly in an activity with inclined planes. Children represent the physical characteristics of objects when they paint or draw. When science investigations are explored through the project approach, children may engage in observational drawings of something they are studying. This requires them to notice the detailed characteristics of the objects.

Children in preoperational thinking (nonconservers) can manipulate small quantities of objects and solve problems. If a child is allowed to have five crackers for snack and only has taken four, the child can figure out how many more crackers he will need. Children in concrete operations can think about larger numbers and manipulate them to solve problems. When given a large group of items to count, they may group them in piles of 10s and then count by 10s to determine the total number of objects. Children with the task of setting the tables for snack can now recognize that there is a relationship between the number of tables, the number of chairs per table, and the total number of children. How many children are here for snack today? How many tables will we need to set up? We have eight tables with six chairs at each table; is that enough? How can we find out? Using advanced mathematics, children can further think about how to solve the problem if snack is served in shifts of three groups of children.

INTEGRATED MATH AND SCIENCE AS A PROCESS

Science, by its very nature, provides a rich opportunity for children to use their developing math and problem-solving skills. Children become active participants in the investigative process as they think of questions and manipulate materials, using mathematics to gain understanding of scientific principles. Although children can memorize facts, they do not gain a true understanding of scientific principles without having an actual hands-on experience. The *process* of science involves inquiry, experimentation, observation, and hypothesis testing. Children think of questions such as, "What if we raise the pendulum higher to try to knock down the blocks? How can we make the cars turn when they get to the end of the ramp? How can we make a river in the sandbox? What would happen if we mixed all these colors of paint together?" As children work to formulate answers to their questions, they discover the *content* of science—the scientific facts.

Children incorporate skills of comparing, classifying, and measuring to help organize and further their science discoveries. They may compare the sizes of earthworms, categorize animals according to their habitats, or measure ingredients when exploring the reaction of mixing vinegar and baking soda. Children use the language of math to communicate their ideas and discoveries to each other and to formulate new ideas. Key vocabulary such as "more," "bigger," "heavier," "faster," and "longer" can be heard from children as they investigate and ask questions such as, "How high is the pendulum? What is the elevation of the ramp? Does it make a difference in how far a car will travel?"

Think again about the activity, "Is it liquid or solid?" You can give children the opportunity to measure their own ingredients. They can calculate how much cornstarch and water is needed for the entire group. Once given the materials, they will have conversations that can't help but include mathematical language as they investigate and compare their cornstarch goop to that of others. They may want to predict what will happen if they add another teaspoon of water or cornstarch, and then experiment to discover the answer.

Child care leaders can guide children in organizing their discoveries in the form of charts, tables, and graphs. Children can document their hypotheses and discoveries by writing in their science journals. The mathematical skills of counting, noting attributes, and classifying can be integrated into nearly every science activity.

THE SCIENCE AND MATH ENVIRONMENT

Ideally, science and math materials are always available for children to explore as they work to expand their knowledge. An interest center can house the many treasures children bring to share, whether an insect, a special rock or shell, or the acorns that fell from their neighbor's tree. Often children will find something such as a praying mantis or a walking stick on the playground and want to share it with other children.

Two subscales of the *School-Age Care Environment Rating Scale* (Harm, Jacobs, & White, 1996) are math/reasoning activities and science/nature activities. For these subscales, the authors of the *SACERS* recommend the following practices for quality care of school-age children:

- Staff encourage children to practice math/reasoning skills in daily activities such as dividing snacks or recording scores for games.
- A variety of age-appropriate math/reasoning games and activities are accessible daily
- Include a variety of science and nature materials that are accessible daily.
- Staff encourage questions about science or natural phenomena and help children find answers.
- Staff extend children's interest and introduce new concepts such as recycling, conservation of water, and endangered species.

When the child care facility has a center devoted to science and math, then science experiments, observations, the recording of science findings,

Computers can add to children's ability to research information.

and other science and math activities can be a part of the daily choices. An area designated for science and math gives children and parents the message that science and math are important, integral parts of the curriculum. Plants, pets, and books add a visual, inviting appeal to such a center. Have standard math and science tools readily available to encourage children's spontaneous investigations. Include items such as rulers, meter sticks, measuring tapes, balances or scales, stopwatches, magnifying glasses, and insect containers. Children's science journals and materials on which to record information are other standard supplies for the science center.

The materials in the center can change from time to time to provide different learning opportunities. It is not necessary to spend large amounts of money on science and math equipment. You can use a variety of recycled materials. For example, disposable plastic containers can be used for collecting insects, and small water bottles with the bottoms cut off make great funnels. The activities suggested in this chapter present many opportunities for children to investigate; and the materials used are inexpensive.

ROLE OF THE LEADER IN SCIENCE AND MATH ACTIVITIES

The most important component of the science and math environment is the child care leader. School-age caregivers should recognize that their role is not to be the science and mathematics teacher; rather, their role is to support each child in the development of scientific literacy and help them become more comfortable and competent in using math. It is imperative that caregivers themselves have sufficient scientific inquiry and math skills. Caregivers cannot model, guide, and support children in the development of skills that they do not themselves possess. Caregivers have daily opportunities to provide meaningful experiences with science and math, and they should be intentional about guiding children in develping these skills.

Child care leaders who are intentional take an interest in the children's science discoveries and scaffold their experiences to encourage more in-depth explorations. They validate what children are learning, and consequently children believe that what they are doing is important.

divergent questions
questions that have no specific answer and require a child to think critically

The caregiver asks **divergent questions**. These are questions that have no specific answer and require the child to think critically. For example, in an incline plane activity, children explore propelling balls down a ramp. The children experiment with the elevation of the ramps and different sizes and weights of balls. Some divergent questions might be: "How can you figure out which ball can travel the fastest? The farthest? What do you think would happen if you changed the height of the ramp?" This type of questioning encourages children to think critically about science and math concepts, to act on their thinking, to form their own questions, to problem solve, and ultimately to construct knowledge and develop theories and conclusions. Be sure to give children time to mentally process the questions and discover their own answers. Avoid giving them the answers.

Child care leaders scaffold children's experiences. They need to know what children can do independently and what they can do with assistance. For example, they might model how to measure a distance or provide assistance in completing a task such as creating a graph to record information. Leaders must be careful not to take the lead in the discoveries but rather to follow the lead of the children, encouraging them to do the investigating. Keep in mind that children are developing their sense of industry and are forming an opinion about themselves as learners, as critical thinkers, as scientists, and as mathematicians.

When planning a science activity, the child care leader should have some ideas about the knowledge possibilities of the activity. Piaget identifies three types of knowledge: social, physical, and logicomathematical. **Social knowledge** is the information children cannot construct for themselves. What is its name (e.g., magnet, iron)? What are the scientific terms (magnetism, repel, attract)? **Physical knowledge** refers to how objects behave as a result of their characteristics. This is information that children learn as they explore. What does it do? How does it change? What does it feel or sound like? **Logicomathematical knowledge** refers to how objects compare to one another. This is also knowledge that children must construct as they discover similarities and differences, noting attributes. How are these objects alike? This knowledge enables children to classify and categorize information.

The science leader should have access to background information about an activity to guide children's thinking. Internet access can give some immediate information in the child care setting. When searching websites, look for links such as education, educators, kids, or activities. See the list of helpful websites at the end of this chapter. You can also make books from the library available. Often parents can provide a resource for background information, or they may be willing to get involved in the information-discovery process through their own Internet search or exploration.

Caregivers can also look for outside resources within the community, such as guest speakers or field trip opportunities (see Chapter 16). Parents and grandparents may be able to provide support to your science and math

social knowledge
information children cannot construct for themselves

physical knowledge
how objects behave as a result of their characteristics

logicomathematical knowledge
how objects compare to one another

Six-year-old Chanelle had just entered first grade. She had seen a news report about seal pups struggling in an oil spill and asked her child care leader, Michelle, about oil spills. Michelle set up an experiment with a tub of water and a small amount of dark motor oil on top so Chanelle could investigate what happens to things in the water. Chanelle choose several small, plastic animals to place in the water. She was surprised to see the oil cling to the animals. Her curiosity about seal pups continued when she returned home. That evening Chanelle and her father learned about seal pups on the Internet. The next day, Chanelle excitedly entered her child care program with a stack of papers in her hand, eager to tell Michelle all she had learned about seal pups with her dad.

programs by sharing what they do in their workplace or as a hobby. For example, a person who gardens can provide children and staff members with information about the importance of worms in a garden or how to test for soil acidity.

The science leader must also be a careful observer. By carefully observing children's interactions with their environment, the caregiver learns what children know and are able to do. The adult uses this knowledge to facilitate children's further learning by presenting additional materials and information. For example, a child working with a pendulum trying to knock down blocks may be unsuccessful because she consistently stacks the blocks out of the reach of the pendulum. The child tries many techniques in releasing the pendulum without success. When told, "I wonder if there is another place to stack the blocks," the child most likely will rethink the situation and change the placement of the blocks.

A final step in facilitating children's science experiences is for the leader to help them record their findings. True scientists record their findings, draw diagrams, and write about their experiments so they can share the information with others. In a school-age program, children can be encouraged to draw pictures and write (or dictate) what they have learned. They can write about their strategies, observations, and new theories and hypotheses. Documentation makes learning visible so parents and others can see what children are experiencing and learning in their child care setting. This also gives parents something to talk to their child about. Rather than, "What did you do today?" the parent might say, "I see that you are experimenting with . . . Tell me about it."

There are additional ways that child care leaders can document children's experiences. They can use a large piece of easel paper to write comments the children made during the exploration process or when working in a small group. This models the process of gathering information and recording it. You can also report science activities in a monthly newsletter. Collect drawings and written accounts and make them into a book for display. The use of technology helps track children's scientific inquiry process. Digital cameras and video camcorders can be used to document each step of the process: the gathering of evidence, setting up of experiments, trials and errors, and the outcomes of children's actions. Caregivers can assist older children in incorporating photos and video clips into computerized reports or PowerPoint® presentations. They can obtain help and equipment from parents if cameras, computers, and camcorders are not available to the child care program.

SCIENCE ACTIVITIES FOR SCHOOL-AGE CHILDREN

There is an abundance of curriculum ideas for school-age children that are accessible from the Internet or in activity books purchased at a bookstore or borrowed from the library. Child care leaders should be intentional as they select activities that will sustain children's participation, cause them to engage in scientific inquiry, and give them opportunities to construct knowledge about natural phenomena. Many activities on the Internet and in books will not meet these criteria and therefore will not be a good fit for a school-age program. Some may require unusual or expensive materials; be limited in the scope of what children can do, explore, and learn; require too much work on the part of the leader and little on the part of the child; or simply not be appropriate to the children's age or the group in the school age setting.

The following activities are not inclusive of everything child care leaders can implement; however they are presented so the reader can gain an understanding of what science and math activities could look like in a child care program. These activities may be short- or long-term projects, or they could be investigated through the project approach as described in Chapter 8. Find additional science activities with comprehensive lesson plans in Appendix B.

Physical Science: How Can I Make It Move?

On an adult level, physics is defined as the science of dealing with the properties, changes, and interactions of matter and energy. Children construct knowledge of physics by acting on the principle, "How can I make it move?" For example, a group of first-graders could use a variety of balls for rolling and a variety of objects to knock down, such as empty cans, milk cartons, or plastic bottles. The children can learn about the distance from the objects or the weights of the rolling ball and the objects being knocked over. They can experiment with placement of the objects. Math tools such as a scale and a meter stick will be valuable in making the connection between the science- and math-related concepts. To learn physics principles, children use actions such as pushing, sliding, rolling, tilting, pounding, and throwing, and materials such as sand, pendulums, magnets, balls, wheels, pulleys, marbles, paint, and water. Their manipulations cause immediate action that is visible and comprehensible. As children create movement, they can observe the results of their actions, continue the action so as to gain mastery, formulate theories, make changes in actions, and refine their original theory or formulate additional theories. These activities give children an opportunity to apply math through measurement of length or distance, speed, and weight. Physical science activities tend to hold children's interest the longest and have a vast amount of learning possibilities. Children are actively involved with the materials, can vary their actions, and the results of those actions are immediate.

Physical Science
Purposes:

- develop the scientific inquiry skills of observing, experimenting, and theorizing
- predict outcomes and formulate conclusions
- interact with materials and develop theories about physical phenomena
- develop a personal confidence as a scientist

Experiment with pendulums.   Suspend a cotton clothesline rope with a ball attached to the end of it from the ceiling, a doorway, or a swing set. Children can stack cardboard boxes or blocks and try to knock them down by swinging the pendulum. They will naturally experiment with the placement of the blocks and the positioning of the pendulum. Provide various sizes and weights of balls for additional exploration. Children can discover the relationships between the length of the pendulum, the height and placement of the objects, the size and weight of the object at the end of the pendulum, and the result of the force of the pendulum as it collides (or fails to collide) with the blocks.

Explore inclined planes.   Rain gutters cut into lengths of three, five, or 10 feet make great ramps for balls, marbles, water, and toy cars. Provide other materials for children to discover concepts about things that slide and roll. Incorporate Legos® for children to build cars. Have a scale available for children to weigh the load of the cargo of their cars and a meter stick for measuring the height and length of the incline as well as the distance the various objects travel. Children can discover the relationships between the height of the incline, its length, and the weight of the objects traveling down the plane.

Additional objects may be used for inclined planes, such as tubes from wrapping paper or mailing tubes. You can obtain large, durable tubes from businesses that lay carpeting. (Carpet is rolled up on them.) Cut cove molding into various lengths and add it to the block center. This can be an outdoor activity to provide children with ample opportunity for ongoing exploration of inclined planes.

Pieces of wood or cardboard can also be used as inclined plans. Provide fabric, wax paper, aluminum foil, and other textured materials to create varying degrees of friction.

Discover propelled objects (target practice).   Provide balls of different kinds and sizes and materials to roll at targets such as cardboard blocks, milk cartons, cardboard cylinders from paper rolls, or large juice cans. Children can discover the relationships between the placement of target objects, the kind and size of ball used, and the physical force with which it is propelled. Incorporate math by including measuring tools, paper, and pencils to record discoveries.

Use ping-pong balls with Velcro® attached and a fabric target such as felt. Children learn best when they can clearly see where their propelled ball has landed.
Toss beanbags onto a floor target.

Make a simple catapult with a plastic spoon and a wooden ruler. Attach the handle of the spoon firmly to the end of the ruler by wrapping a rubber band tightly around it. Propel small pom-pom balls to a target. To use the catapult, pull back on the bowl of the spoon with one hand, hold the ruler with the other hand, and release the spoon.

Explore magnetic force.   You can buy wand and horseshoe from toy stores. Small, inexpensive (but not very durable) circular magnets are available at stores that sell electronic equipment. Purchase strong internal magnets from a store that sells products for large farm animal care. (Internal magnets are used inside a cow to collect pieces of metal that the cow may ingest.) Incorporate measurement by noticing the distance between the magnets when they visibly repel or attract each other. Use magnets to drag through sand and search for particles of iron.Investigate a variety of metallic-looking objects to determine which ones contain iron. Use magnets around the classroom to search for metal with iron. (Use caution when investigating the room. Computer components, CDs, or computer programs can be damaged when magnets are placed on or near them.) Develop a collection of small items such as bolts and paper clips that are attracted to a magnet. Use this collection with the large magnets found on the inside of stereo speakers to build temporary sculptures that are held together by magnetism.

Use magnets to move objects. Place magnetic wands or internal magnets under the table or under a piece of Plexiglas®. Place lightweight objects such as paper clips on top of the table or Plexiglas®. Use the magnet to move the objects.

Additional Physical Science Activities

Other physical science activities could focus on:

- spatial awareness (fitting objects in, out, through, under, etc.)
- air (fans, blow dryers, homemade fans)
- construction (wood with hammers, nails, saws, screws, screw drivers, and hand drills)
- pulleys and wheels
- kitchen tools (scoops, basting bulbs, sifters, beaters, gadgets)
- opticals (binocular, magnifying glasses, kaleidoscopes)
- making, listening to, and identifying sounds
- light and shadows

Chemistry: How Can I Make It Change?

Chemistry deals with the properties, composition, and transformation of substances. Many chemical experiments require skills, equipment, and knowledge too advanced for the school-age child. Still, the child care leader can provide chemical exploration opportunities that are age appropriate and enable children to learn concepts of chemistry, furthering their scientific skills of theorizing, observing, and experimenting.

Observations of the physical characteristics of substances and explorations that create transformations are very appropriate chemistry for children of this age group. For example, children can explore transformation by mixing substances such as vinegar and baking soda, baking cookies or biscuits, or adding water to sand. Some of the art activities offered in Chapter 11, such as sand casting, provide children with opportunities to experience transformations. The child's natural tendency is to respond to the internal question, "How can I make it change?"

Chemistry
Purposes:

- further develop scientific skills of observation, hypothesizing, and drawing conclusions
- observe physical characteristics of substances and their transformations
- acquire awareness of chemistry in everyday life

Exploration of nature's tie-dyeing.   Provide various substances that can be combined with water to make a medium for dyeing fabrics. The spice turmeric makes a yellow-orange, coffee and tea make browns, and red cabbage or beets cooked in water create a reddish color. Children can also draw from their experiences of things that stain their clothing, such as mustard, chocolate, and grape juice. Provide various containers to explore substances that could dye fabrics. Give the children strips of muslin or some white, cotton fabric such as old T-shirts. Use a timer and track how the colors change over time.

An extension of this activity would be to try various types of fabrics. (Be sure to provide the children with smocks to protect their own clothing when doing this investigation!)

Experience the effects of heat on food.   Children can wash, cut, and prepare vegetables such as carrots, potatoes, or green beans. With adult supervision, they can cook these foods, noting the effect of heat on the taste, consistency, texture, and color of the vegetables. Children can use a timer to measure specific amounts of cooking time and notice what happens. Observe changes after one minute of cooking time, three minutes of cooking time, five minutes, and so on. These discoveries can be written in a chart format and later shared with parents or posted in the classroom. Other cooking activities might include melting cheese for nachos or grilled cheese sandwiches, or cooking eggs in a variety of styles (scrambled, poached, hard-boiled, over easy).

Investigate heat as a means of transformation.   Making things such as bread, biscuits, cookies, and pancakes gives children the opportunity to experience the effect of using substances such as yeast, baking soda, or baking powder. The sun is a natural way to use heat and see its effects. Guide children in an experiment melting leftover stubs of crayons. They can discover what time of day the sun most effectively melts the crayons, or what location in their play yard is the warmest. They can further investigate by putting crayons in various containers that reflect heat, limit air circulation, or contain heat. Children can also observe the effects of heat on discarded videos, CDs, and cassette tapes.

Other transformations to explore:

- condensation and evaporation (breathing on cold glass, investigating a puddle or melting ice over time)

- effects of freezing various liquids (ice cubes made of various substances, salted water)
- absorption (materials that do and do not absorb water)
- dissolving (substances that do and do not dissolve in water)
- color mixing

Life and Earth Science: How Do I Fit In and What Is My Role?

Environmental and life sciences involve the study of plants and animals. Earth science studies elements of the earth. Because all of these are interrelated, it is impossible to study one without investigating the others at least on some level. They may include an aspect of chemistry or physical science as well. When learning about plant life, it is also necessary to investigate soil, the sun, and water. Earth science investigations involve phenomena such as shadows, the heat of the sun, properties of water, weather, and compositions of rocks. You may recall that the effects of heat were considered in an activity in the chemistry section of this chapter. An investigation of shadows may more appropriately fall under the physical science section because it addresses the question "How can I make it move?" An investigation of weather that is interesting for children could require the children to be actively involved in learning how the weather affects them or studying weather predictions. The key to successful earth and life science activities is to develop them in a way that provides children with opportunities to act on the materials, observe characteristics, make predictions, and develop theories. Many of these activities lend themselves to a long-term, project-based approach .

Learning about the care of plants, animals, and the environment should not encourage experimentation that causes harm to something living. Children can develop a knowledge base about environmental issues and an understanding about their role in the care of living creatures and their life-support systems. Learning about the human body and its functions and care, including nutrition, is also included in this aspect of science (see Chapter 15). Children have a natural sense of wonder about the world. Life and some earth science discoveries focus on answering the question, "How do I fit in and what is my role?"

Life Science
Purposes:

- develop an understanding of the natural environment
- acquire the ability to nurture and care for living creatures
- observe the life cycles of plants and animals
- cultivate awareness of endangered species and the need to preserve them

Let children care for live animals.   A bird, gerbil, guinea pig, hamster, rabbit, snake, or fish are common choices for the child care center. Ask children to help choose the animal to be added to their classroom. Before introducing the animal, have children research what the animal eats

Biology involves the study of plants and animals. Earth science studies elements of the earth.

or drinks, what kind of environment it needs, and how to care for the animal. Consult with a local pet store and check with a veterinarian. Guide children in Internet searches to further their knowledge, and construct a habitat appropriate for that animal.

To stimulate scientific inquiry, encourage children to observe the animal. A hamster can generate questions about the types of vegetables the animal eats. Let children predict, then test the various choices by offering a selection of lettuce, carrots, celery, and spinach. Notice which vegetables the hamster prefers and which ones it will not eat. Be sure to read about hamsters and only offer your hamster food choices that are safe for it to eat.

Let children observe the life cycle of frogs.
Get some frog eggs or tadpoles from a stream, pond, or lake. Put them in an aquarium with plenty of pond water and a few pond plants. Feed the tadpoles extra food: goldfish food, boiled spinach or other leafy green vegetables. Observe their growth.

Encourage children to predict how long it will take for the tadpoles to turn into frogs. Let them chart the growth, noting the decrease in size of the tadpoles' tails and the appearance of legs. How close were they in their predictions?

Cultivate a garden outdoors.
Involve the children in a discussion of whether they want a vegetable or flower garden. Provide seed catalogs, books on plants, or magazines that have a gardening section. Take a trip to a local nursery.

Have children measure the amount of space that can be allotted for the garden, and research the types of plants that can be grown at different seasons of the year. Have them draw a plot plan, spacing the various plants according to what they have learned about plant requirements. Plant the garden. Children can keep measure and track the growth of the plants.

Keep potted plants in the classroom.   Include a variety of plants: those grown from seeds, from cuttings of mature plants, and from pits or tubers (avocado pits or sweet potatoes). Conduct an Internet search to learn about the requirements for plant growth.

Perform an experiment to determine how much sunlight a plant needs by planting a bean seed in each of 10 plastic cups filled with sterile potting soil. Place half of the cups at various distances from a window light source but not in direct sunlight. Cover the other cups or place them in complete darkness. Keep the soil in all the containers wet, but be careful not to overwater. Compare the growth of the two sets of plants once a week and chart their progress. Record the height and condition of the plants in each container.

Learn about endangered species and what can be done to prevent total extinction of these plants and animals.   Contact National Geographic, the National Wildlife Federation, or the Sierra Club to ask if they have DVDs, magazines, speakers, or other sources of information about endangered species. Guide children on an Internet search of the World Wildlife Fund to learn about endangered species.

Visit other websites, such as the following:

World Wildlife Fund
http://www.worldwildlife.org

The Nature Conservancy
http://nature.org

National Wildlife Federation
http://www.nwf.org

The Sierra Club National Headquarters
http://www.sierraclub.org/

If there is a wildlife preservation area in your vicinity, schedule a field trip. Observe and record the plants and animals found at the preserve. Follow the visit with a discussion of why it is important to save these plants and animals from extinction.

Earth Science
Purposes:

- cultivate curiosity about the Earth and the solar system
- encourage scientific inquiry
- increase knowledge of the principles of earth sciences

Explore the solar system.   Obtain posters or photos taken during space explorations. The National Aeronautics and Space Administration (NASA) has views of the Earth taken from outer space; pictures of astronauts at work;

and photos from space probes of Mars, Venus, Mercury, and Jupiter. The Jet Propulsion Laboratory in Pasadena, California, and the Smithsonian Air and Space Museum in Washington, DC, are also resources for materials on the solar system. Your local library may have books, CDs, or DVDs pertaining to space. Obtain books on space that children can read or browse through in the book corner. Provide a tape recorder or CD player and earphones if tapes or CDs are available. To stimulate children's interest in space and space travel, ask them to draw or paint a picture of what they think they would find if they were actually on one of the other planets. They might create another picture of things they would take with them on their trip to the planet. Display the pictures and ask children to discuss their choices, explaining why certain items would be necessary or desired.

Visit a planetarium, if possible. Your community may have one; but also find out if a nearby college or university has one.

Chart the weather for a month.   Provide a calendar form for each child or a large one for a bulletin board. Obtain a thermometer that records both temperature and barometer readings that can be placed outdoors. Have children record daily temperatures, barometer readings, and weather conditions. Ask them to bring in weather reports and predictions from daily newspapers or follow reports on the Internet. Have the children keep track of how many times the predictions are correct.

Have children search the Internet for more information about weather predicting and tracking. Good sources are:

American Meteorological Society Headquarters
http://www.ametsoc.org

National Oceanic and Atmospheric Administration, United States Deptartment of Commerce
http://www.noaa.gov

Weatherwise
http://www.weatherwise.org

Make a rain gauge.   Use clear plastic containers. Using a permanent marker, make a horizontal line at 1 inch, 2 inches, and so on, starting from the bottom of the container. Children can place the containers strategically outside to collect rain. If possible, purchase a real rain gauge to use as a comparison. After a rainfall, children can compare their results to the weather rainfall reports. Children can pour the water from the containers into measuring cups. They can discover how the quantities differ from container to container and develop theories as to why they are the same or different.

Additional Equipment to Have Available

- animal habitats; an incubator for hatching eggs
- ant farm with a supply of ants
- aquarium with books on tropical fish
- binoculars and bird identification books

- insect house, insect-capturing containers, butterfly net
- collections of shells, rocks, and fossils
- flashlights
- hair dryer, small vacuum, bicycle pump
- measuring tools such as scales, cups, rulers, protractors
- levers, inclined planes, pulleys, wheels
- magnets: bar and horseshoe, assorted sizes
- magnifying glasses, insect collections
- microscope with prepared and blank slides
- mirrors, plain and ground
- prisms, eyeglasses, gyroscopes, color wheels
- PVC pipe lengths, rain gutters, wood planks, wood blocks
- rock-polishing equipment, jewelry tools
- sun-sensitive papers and outlines
- telescope, books on astronomy, compass, a globe
- terrarium, seeds, potting soil, small pots
- indoor and outdoor thermometers
- computer, digital camera, video camera, DVD player

MATH IN SCHOOL-AGE CHILD CARE

Keep in mind that a primary function of a school-age program is to support children as they gain tools for living. Math is one of those tools. Children have the opportunity to experience and understand math concepts when they manipulate, count, and measure real objects. They need to hold

Children begin to understand math concepts when they manipulate objects.

objects in their hands, weigh, or count them so that the concepts of size and number are evident. The caregiver of school-age children will most likely be able to recall some of the math concepts he learned in school. Basic number computations of addition, subtraction, multiplication, and division, as well as concepts related to money, time, temperature, geometry, and measurement of lengths, volume, and weight are generally the concepts that come to mind. Real-life situations provide opportunities to problem solve by using math computations, including working with fractions and percentages. Children develop strategies for solving these problems. Additionally, children learn to organize their math thinking and to communicate in the language of math to express their ideas. It is noteworthy to point out that appropriate math in before- and after-school child care programs is not about the mechanics of the pencil and paper math practiced in school. It is about incorporating math in everyday life and giving children an opportunity to construct their own knowledge about mathematical concepts while supported by the child care leader.

MATH ACTIVITIES FOR SCHOOL-AGE CHILDREN

Math may be embedded in science activities, board games and activities or incorporated into the child care center's daily events, such as preparing for snack. The activities that follow represent the kinds of activities appropriate for school-age children. Additional activities are available in Appendix B. When selecting activities, intentional child care leaders consider what they know about child development and about the individual children in their care.

Number Concepts and Computation
Purposes:

- increase comfort and competency in the ability to count and carry out mathematical calculations
- practice using math skills in everyday life situations
- organize group, and regroup quantities according to common attributes

Games that involve math. A quality school-age program should include a variety of age-appropriate math and reasoning games of varying difficulties. In addition, children who are more experienced with games should be encouraged to teach others new games. (Harms, Jacobs, &: White, 1996). Monopoly® comes in a version for children from age nine and up; Monopoly Junior® is for ages five to eight. Yahtzee®, ages nine and up, involves counting, addition, money, and the exploration of probability. Scrabble® for children ages eight and up requires addition and multiplication in the score-keeping process. Battleship® is a two-person game that teaches children about coordinates and is geared for ages seven and up.

Review the various games discussed in Chapter 10 and identify which ones can easily incorporate math. Visit your local toy stores for games that involve the math concepts of counting and keeping score. When children must keep score they have opportunities to use addition and subtraction.

Eat a fraction snack.   Involve children in preparing sandwiches or foods that involve fractions. Cut the food into halves and fourths. Discuss these fractions and notice that the fractional parts come together to make the whole sandwich. Encourage children to notice things such as how many whole sandwiches can be made from eight fourths (8/4). Cut apples, oranges, celery, and carrots into sections. When eating snacks, children can be given half an apple. Have them cut it in half again, and discuss the fractions they are using. Write the fractions for the children to see. Encourage them to write their own fractions.

Dividing up a plate of food.   Children can participate in the daily division of food for snack. Create a "Math Team" to count the available items, and figure out how many can be given to each child. Another approach would be to have the team calculate how many of an item will be needed for the entire class. For example, if there are 35 children and each child can have four crackers, how many crackers will be needed all together? See a lesson plan activity for this in Appendix B.

Read the label.   Packaged foods provide a variety of information on their labels. Each label indicates how many servings are in the package. Give a team of two children a label to read and food to divide into the indicated servings. For example, a package of pretzels may serve three and a half people. The children can discuss how to divide the pretzels. An additional task would be to determine how many packages would be needed to serve the entire class, or to figure out how many people could be served with five packages, 10 packages, etc.

Measurement
Purposes:

- increase vocabulary and understanding of concepts related to measurement
- practice using various tools of measurement
- increase ability to see how measurement is used in everyday life

Weigh a variety of objects.   Set up a center with different types of scales: balance, electronic, and spring. Include many different objects the children can weigh or balance. Ask children to weigh the objects, compare them, and record their weights.

Encourage the children to experiment with the balance. How many objects of one kind on one side of the balance does it take to counterweight objects on the other side? After a few experiments with this activity, provide different objects and ask the children to estimate their weight before putting the object on the scale.

Measure length.   Secure a measuring tape to the floor or use two yard-sticks, end to end. Tell children to look at the divisions on the tape, pointing out the inch and feet marks. Have children lie down next to the tape. Ask one child to record each child's height in feet and inches. Provide children with meter sticks and have them measure again, this time in centimeters. Discuss how the meter sticks and the yardsticks are similar and different. Children can measure a friend by stacking same-sized cardboard blocks. Have children record each child's height in blocks.

Measuring time.   Stopwatches, digital clocks, clocks with hour and minute hands, and calendars are some of the tools used everyday to measure time. Involve children in the daily monitoring of the schedule. Use a clock or stopwatch to measure how much time is used for outdoor activities, taking turns while playing games, or how long until time for snacks. Children can record the time of day along with the number of children present. Remember to make clipboards, paper, and pencils readily available so children can record the information.

Involve children whenever possible in using the calendar in meaningful and purposeful ways. Post children's jobs and special events on a calendar. Use store-bought calendars or create a large calendar each month out of poster board for the children to use. Encourage children to use the calendar to determine how many days until the guest speaker will arrive, or how long until the field trip. Children will learn these concepts when they see their relevance to everyday life. There is no need to have a boring calendar time as a part of a whole-group period, such as when children recite, "Today is Monday, October 22, 2012."

Measuring temperature.   Children can use a large outdoor thermometer, such as those found in a gardening store, to measure temperature. Use different colors of masking tape to place at the edge of each 10-degree

At summer camp there was an old concrete swimming pool that had been converted to a sandbox. Seven-year-olds Josh and Kevin questioned the camp counselor, "Jennifer, how deep is the sand in the sandbox?" She replied, "I don't know. How could you find out?" They decided they could dig a hole and measure the depth of the hole. They spent the afternoon digging. After a while they came to a bed of rock. Jennifer supplied them with a yardstick and the boys concluded the sand was 17 inches deep. The next day, Josh approached Jennifer. "OK, I know that the sand was 17 inches deep where we dug. Is it 17 inches deep everywhere?" She replied, "I don't know. What is your prediction? How could you find out?" Josh predicted that it was different in other parts of the sandbox because a swimming pool is deeper at one end than the other. The boys dug a hole at the other end of the sandbox. It too was 17 inches deep. The boys concluded that the depth of the sand was the same throughout the sandbox.

section of the thermometer. The 40s might have blue tape, the 50s green, the 60s yellow, the 70s orange, and the 80s red. Young children can read the thermometer by noting to which color the needle points. They can use a calendar or other chart format to record the temperature at different times of the day. The measurement of temperature can be combined with measuring time by recording the temperatures at different times of the day. As the children progress in their skills, the tape can be removed, and children can be taught about the increments between each of the sections on the thermometer. Couple this math activity with a science investigation on melting or evaporation so children can discover the correlation between the temperature and its effect on these two science concepts.

Measuring volume.   Children use measuring cups and spoons of a variety of sizes when they take part in food preparation (see recipes in Chapter 15) or in making various doughs. Children can use these measuring implements during play as they work with materials such as birdseed, sand, or water in the water table.

Working with Money
Purposes:

- strengthen ability to count money
- experience real-life applications of the planning for the use of money
- increase vocabulary and understanding of concepts related to money

Creating snack menus.   Provide children with the USDA guidelines for nutrition (see Chapter 15). Give them paper to chart their daily food intake so they can match it with the guidelines. With adult guidance, children can take on the responsibility of developing snack menus along with the shopping lists, an approximate budget, and cost per child.

Work with money in dramatic play.   Children will often create their own grocery stores, pet stores, or restaurants. These play scenarios are a perfect setting for children to work with concepts of money. They can price items, purchase items, use cash registers, count money, and give change. Children can make menus and coupons. Use grocery ads to incorporate literacy.

Geometry
Purposes:

- increase awareness of geometric shapes in the environment
- strengthen ability to examine, describe, and create two- and three-dimensional shapes in geometrical terms
- increase geometry-related vocabulary

Observational drawings.   Bring in a variety of interesting objects for children to examine. Discuss the shapes the children see and talk about straight and curved lines. Have children draw the objects by paying attention to these details. This observation technique is a component of the project approach (see Chapter 8.)

Origami. Provide copy paper or any paper that can easily hold a crease. Scaffold children's experience in folding the paper to create sculptures. Children can search the Internet to find origami patterns. Have conversations about the shapes and angles that are created as a result of folding the paper.

Paper airplanes. Fold copy paper to make a variety of styles of paper airplanes. Test the airplanes and measure their flying distances. Use the Internet to help find new paper airplane designs. Use paper clips and tape to change the weight and balance of the airplanes. Solicit the help of parents who may have a fond childhood memory of making airplanes.

Block labeling. Adults and children can work together to discover the geometric names of blocks. Children can make labels for the blocks. Notice the shapes of the faces (sides) of the blocks. For example, a triangular prism has two faces that are triangles and three faces that are rectangles.

More Math Activities

Snack Patterns

To help children practice the skill of re-creating a pattern, have them prepare kabobs. Older children can use serrated knives to cut fruits and cheese into equal-sized chunks. (Younger children may require help from an adult, or an adult can do this part.) Supply one bamboo skewer per child. The adult makes a pattern using alternating pieces of different fruits interspersed with cheese. Ask the children to form similar kabobs for themselves.

Pizza Fractions

Provide several large pizza shells. (These can be found in the frozen-food section of the market.) Supply the necessary toppings: mozzarella cheese, parmesan cheese, pepperoni, sliced mushrooms, and so on. After baking the pizzas, ask the children to count the number of children in the group and decide into how many pieces to cut each pizza.

How Many Are There? Estimating

Estimate numbers by guessing how many objects are in a jar. Obtain a large (16 ounce) clear glass or plastic jar. Fill the jar with pretzels, crackers, or other small snack items. Place the jar in front of a chart labeled "Weekly Food Estimates." Provide small cards or slips of paper near the jar and a marking pen. Ask children to write down their name and an estimate of how many objects there are in the jar. At the end of the week, ask a "Math Team" of several children to open the jar and count the items. (Remember to use health practices of washing hands and using food-handling gloves.) The math team must decide how to divide the snack among the entire group of children.

Double the Recipe

Use measuring cups to measure ingredients and learn about fractions of a cup such as one-fourth, one-third, and two-thirds. Discover what quantities are needed when a recipe is doubled. Children can practice measuring by using measuring cups and containers with materials such as water, corn meal, or bird seed. Children can draw pictures in their science journals or create a poster of the equivalencies they discover. Adults can scaffold individual children's learning in these activities by listening to and observing each child's mathematical thinking.

Math Equipment to Have Available

- measuring cups and spoons
- rulers, meter sticks, tape measures, calculators
- scales: balance, spring, electronic
- thermometers
- pretend money
- stopwatches, timers, traditional and digital clocks

Guidelines for Child Care Staff Members

There are some guidelines to help child care leaders plan activities that allow children the maximum opportunity for learning. They are:

- Set up enticing learning centers or have materials easily available for children to explore and experiment on their own. Observe and scaffold the children's experiences while letting children take the lead in their process.
- Listen to the children to find out what they are interested in, and then supply them with the means to pursue those interests. In addition, stimulate them to explore new interests.
- Do not give answers too readily. Ask divergent questions that stimulate children to hypothesize, predict, or think of other possibilities. Listen to the children to find out what they already know or what they are thinking. Help them correct any misinformation or add to the knowledge they already have. Design appropriate activities that will lead them to a higher level of understanding.
- Make a special effort to encourage girls to enjoy science. Many young women believed at an early age that science was not for them. Girls need to hear about successful female scientists such as Madame Curie, Rachel Carson, Lt. Col. Eileen Collins (the first woman space shuttle commander), Dian Fossey, and Dr. Myra Logan (the first woman to perform open-heart surgery).
- Document children's work and learning. By making learning visible, administrators, parents, and the children themselves can readily see that the activities children engage in cause them to think critically and develop cognitively.

SUMMARY

- School-age child care is an arena for children's development of scientific literacy skills and a place to practice math skills with the goal of becoming more comfortable and competent with math.

- A before- and after-school program provides children with many opportunities to use and reinforce the math concepts they are learning in school and to experience the use of math in everyday life.

- School-age children are natural scientists and mathematicians as they observe investigate, predict, draw conclusions, and develop theories about things in the world around them.

- Science and math are integrated in activities that allow children to experience the scientific process while learning the content of science.

- The school-age child care environment includes space for science and math activities. The intentional caregivers thoughtfully plan the activities and scaffold children's experiences.

- Children receive sufficient time to explore freely with enticing materials that maximize learning opportunities.

- Caregivers listen to children to ascertain what children know, help them correct any misconceptions, and encourage them to find answers to their questions.

- The adult leader provides additional information and materials as needed and asks divergent questions to encourage children's critical thinking.

- Caregivers are intentional in their planning and interactions with children to enhance children's skill development.

- Science activities focus on the children's natural inclinations as they ask, "How can I make it move? How can I make it change? How do I fit in, and what is my role?"

- Math activities arise out of daily events such as preparing for snack or keeping score for a board game.

KEY TERMS

constructing
  knowledge
divergent questions

logicomathematical
  knowledge
physical knowledge

scientific literacy
social knowledge

REVIEW QUESTIONS

1. Children are natural scientists and mathematicians. Explain this statement and how it relates to the development of scientific literacy.

2. Explain what it means to construct one's own knowledge.

3. Explain the difference between the *process of science* and the *content of science*.

4. Explain why the child care leader is considered the most important component of the science environment.

5. Briefly describe two physical science activities with integrated math.

6. Describe an activity that engages children in answering the question, "How can I make it change?"

7. Explain how you can structure life science activities to actively involve children.

8. Name three unplanned or spontaneous situations in which children must use math.

9. The text presents guidelines for staff members when planning and implementing science and math activities. What are they?

10. Describe how children can document their science and math discoveries.

Olivia and Juanita, both age eight, have been watching two slightly older boys work with a combination of rain gutters and blocks to create a raceway for their cars. The boys abandoned their work to play a game with some other friends. Nicole, the child care leader, noticed that the girls appeared interested in the boys' exploration.

1. What questions could Nicole ask that would help the girls think about the inclined plane exploration and ultimately entice the girls to explore the gutters?

2. What science and math concepts could the girls learn from working with gutters and cars?

3. How could the girls document the scientific concepts they learned? How could Nicole document their work?

STUDENT ACTIVITIES

1. Plan one of the activities described in this chapter and implement it with a group of school-age children. Record your observations of the children as they participate in the activity. What did they do and say? Bring the materials and observations to class and share them with your fellow students.

2. Plan a field trip for a group of school children to a local site of scientific interest. The power generating station, the beach, an observatory, a nature reserve, a museum, and a radio or television station all provide insights into how fundamental science is to civilization. Follow up the trip with discussions about what the children learned. Describe the trip to your classmates. Were there things you would do differently next time?

3. Visit your local library to find some background information about an aspect of science. (Hint: Books written for juveniles are easily understood by the science novice, and you can also bring them to the child care facility as a resource for the children.) Find at least two books on a subject and develop an age-appropriate, exploratory activity for school-age children. Bring the books and an activity plan that you can share in class.

4. Plan a snack menu for a week for a group of 35 school-age children. Develop a grocery list and cost of the food per child. Design a plan to implement involving the children in this process and share your project with the class.

5. Visit at least three websites that provide curriculum ideas. Briefly describe the idea and analyze its appropriateness for school-age child care. Be prepared to share one activity and your evaluation of it with the class.

6. Consider the scenario in which you are required to bring all the materials each day into an elementary classroom or a school gymnasium. Evaluate the science activities in the text and determine what ones you could use, or modify to use, in this setting.

SUGGESTED READINGS

Blaw, L. (1994). *Super Science*. Bellevue, WA: One from the Heart Educational Research.

Chaille, C. (2008). *Constructivism Across the Curriculum in Early Childhood Classrooms, Big Ideas as Inspiration*. Boston, MA: Pearson.

Clements, D. H. & Sarama, J., eds. (2004). *Engaging Young Children in Mathematics, Standards for Early Childhood Mathematics Education*. Mahway, NJ: Lawrence Erlbaum Associates.

DeVries, R., Zan, B., Hilderbrandt, C, Edmiaston, R., & Sales, C. (2001). *Developing Constructivist Early Childhood Curriculum: Practices and Principles*. New York, NY: Teachers College.

Hauser, J. F., & Kline, M. (1999). *Gizmos & Gadgets: Creating Science Contraptions That Work (& Knowing Why)*. Charlotte, VT: Williamson.

Johnstone, L., & Levine, S. (2003). *Kitchen Science*. New York: Sterling.

Kamii, C, & Housman, L. B. (2000). *Young Children Reinvent Arithmetic: Implications of Piaget's Theory*, 2nd ed. New York: Teacher's College Press.

Lind, K. K. (2000). *Exploring Science in Early Childhood Education*. Clifton Park, NY: Thomson Delmar Learning.

Moomaw, S., & Hieronymus, G. (1997). *More Than Magnets*. Beltsville, MD: Gryphon House.

Tolman, M. N. (2002). *Hands-On Science Activities for Grades K-2*. Indianapolis, IN: Jossey-Bass.

Tolman, M. N., & Morton, J. O. (2002). *Hands-On Life Science for Grades K-8*. Indianapolis, IN: Jossey-Bass.

Unwin, E., & Edom, H. (1993). *Science with Plants*. Danbury CT: Scholastic Library.

Zike, D. (1993). *The Earth Science Book, Activities for Kids*. New York: John Wiley & Sons.

WEB RESOURCES

http://www.smithsonianeducation.org
Source of information on science and nature

http://www.spaceplace.nasa.gov
Children's activites from the National Aeronautics & Space Administration (NASA)

http://www.jpl.nasa.gov/kids
Link to NASA information about earth, solar system, stars and galaxies

http://www.aimsedu.org
Sample activities from AIMS (Activities Integrating Mathematics and Science)

http://www.lawrencehallofscience.org
Activities for children from the Lawrence Hall of Science

http://www.ScienceU.com
Science U includes interactive exhibits, animated explanations, science graphics, and activities using geometric formulas and facts and a library of reference materials.

http://mathforum.org/dr.math
Ask Dr. Math provides a forum for answering children's math questions. It also includes searchable archives for additional information. Click on "Ask Dr. Math." Activities for students and teachers using math.

http://www.eduref.org
Science and math lesson plans from the *Educator's Reference Desk*

REFERENCES

Cross, T. C., Woods, T. A., & Schweingruber, H., eds. (2009). *Mathematics Learning in Early Childhood: Pathways Toward Excellence and Equity.* Washington, DC: National Academies.

Harms, T., Jacobs, E. V., & White, D. R. (1996). *School-Age Environment Rating Scale.* New York: Teacher's College Press.

National Research Council. (1996). *National Science Education Standards: An Overview.* Washington, DC: National Academy Press.

National Science Board. (2006). *A National Action Plan for Addressing the Critical Needs of the U.S. Science, Technology, Engineering, and Mathematics Education System.* Arlington, VA: National Science Foundation.

National Science Foundation (2006). *National Science Investing in America's Future: Strategic Plan FY 2006-2011.* Arlington, VA: National Science Foundation.

13

Helping Children Develop Literacy Competency

LITERACY IN SCHOOL-AGE CHILD CARE

It is widely recognized that **literacy**—being able to read and write—is necessary for success in school and later in life. Today's society demands more advanced levels of reading proficiency as more jobs require employees to communicate through e-mail and instant messaging, fax, and the Internet. Historically, these communications were performed verbally over the telephone or in person. By third grade, literacy skills are necessary for children to fully engage in reading various subjects such as science, history, and mathematics; and these skills are necessary for continued learning throughout life.

Literacy plays a part in out-of-school programs whether they have a philosophy of enrichment or a philosophy of care. It can have a role if children are housed in a center where there is dedicated time and space for reading- and writing-related activities. If the program is in a gymnasium, the caregiver can read to a group of children in a corner. Children can sit on bleachers while playing reading-related games. If child care takes place in a regular elementary classroom and children are unable to use any of the materials of the classroom, caregivers can bring in a chapter book to read to the entire group and materials for fun, meaningful activities that involve literacy. An outdoor program can offer a bucket of materials such as paper, markers, and clipboards for children to use in a grassy area under a tree. A blanket and a board game or a basket of books can create an inviting outdoor area that promotes the literacy interests of children. Literacy can be a part of any kind of school-age program such as summer camp, a recreational program, a program with limited hours, or even one with sporadic attendance by children.

In some states, children come to their school-age child care setting as young as four years, nine months, and may

LEARNING OUTCOMES

After reading this chapter, you should be able to:

✔ Discuss the importance of literacy in a school-age child care program.

✔ Articulate the skills that lead to reading comprehension and writing.

✔ Create an environment that supports children's literacy development.

✔ Explain how child care leaders can enhance children's development in complex language, reading, and writing.

✔ Discuss how caregivers can support language acquisition for English language learners.

✔ Plan and implement developmentally appropriate activities with intentionality that include complex language, reading, and writing components.

have a wide range of early exposure to reading and writing in their daily lives. They also come to their school-age program with reading and writing experiences and homework requirements from their regular school day. Many children are exposed to literacy from birth. Their parents and caregivers read to them and encourage children to have conversations. These adults also model purposeful reading and writing in their everyday life. Other children, due to life circumstances, have little or no exposure to the written word and have possibly never seen their own name in printed form. Some have never been read to or held a book; never had a pencil, crayon, marker, or paint brush in their hand to make a squiggle that represents writing. Some children have not been exposed to the value of literacy because they have never had an adult model reading and writing for them.

Additionally, some children have limited knowledge and understanding of the English language. According to the U.S. Department of Education, more than ten percent of all K-12 students are **English language learners** (ELL), that is, children who primarily speak a language other than English in the home and are not fully fluent in English (National Clearinghouse for English Language Acquisition, 2006). These school-age children encompass a wide range of knowledge of the English language—from understanding and speaking no English to being fluent in English.

All of these children come to an elementary school experience where there are uniform academic expectations for speaking, reading, and writing in English. The children who are chronologically young, lack an early foundation in literacy, or are not fluent in English soon fall behind their same age peers and feel unsuccessful. As a result, reading becomes a difficult task and a negative experience for these children.

These same children of such varied experiences are also in school-age child care settings, and they all need support from caregivers in their academic development. In most school-age child care programs, this support happens when caregivers help children with homework. Caregivers can provide additional support by intentionally incorporating meaningful literacy components into the daily activities. Child care leaders can also plan specific literacy activities that are enjoyable, encouraging, and empowering to children while enhancing their literacy skills.

There is significant evidence that school-age caregivers should embrace literacy-related activities as a part of their curriculum. The importance of literacy in the field of child care was highlighted when the International Reading Association (IRA) partnered with the National Association for the Education of Young Children (NAEYC) and developed a joint position statement entitled, *Learning to Read and Write: Developmentally Appropriate Practices for Young Children* (NAEYC & IRA, 1998). The statement's premise is that all teachers of young children—from birth through age eight, including those in child-care programs—have a responsibility to promote children's literacy development and to use the most current knowledge of how children learn to read and write.

In January of 2002, the No Child Left Behind Act was passed and signed into law by the President of the United States. This legislation, referred to as NCLB, was intended to ensure that every child has the fundamental knowledge and skills to read by the end of third grade. NCLB also

literacy
being able to read and write

English language learners (ELL)
children who primarily speak a language other than English in the home and are not fully fluent in English

states that reading instruction should occur in high-quality and literacy-rich environments with strategies that are research-based. NCLB cites the importance of programs to include language development in conjunction with the other developmental domains. While this task falls on the shoulders of elementary school systems, it has implications for school-age child care programs. Caregivers nurture the development of the whole child (physically, cognitively, linguistically, socially, and emotionally) and support the child's school experiences.

Keep in mind that children want to feel empowered, competent, and successful. They also want to feel that the caregiver is committed to promoting these feelings, which build positive self-esteem and emotional development. However, statistics indicate that only 33 percent of fourth-grade children performed at or above the proficient level, and 33 percent performed below the basic level in reading in 2010 (National Center for Education Statistics). These statistics indicate that many children need support in reading. These children may not feel competent or successful, and perhaps not empowered. A lack of motivation to read is cited as one of the barriers to children becoming skilled readers (Snow et al., 1998). This lack of motivation may, in turn, result from their being unsuccessful in reading. The lack of success is evident specifically in children who lack sufficient **emerging literacy skills**—that is, reading-related skills that children obtain prior to actually reading and writing.

emerging literacy skills
reading-related skills that children obtain prior to actually reading and writing

THE DEVELOPMENT OF LITERACY

Learning to read and write is a developmental milestone in our society. It was once believed that the language and literacy skills of reading and writing would simply develop when the child was ready. Children typically learn to walk and talk on their own when they have matured enough to be physically ready, but literacy skills do not come that easily. Children need direct instruction and practice. They need encouragement to practice complex language skills and experience how those skills translate to the written word. School-age children need meaningful experiences that help them relate literacy skills to events in their everyday lives. School-age child care should support the educational experiences of children by providing opportunities for them to practice what they are learning in school, enhancing what they are experiencing in their daily life, and giving children additional opportunities to understand the relevance of reading and writing as lifelong skills.

Children have daily opportunities to experience reading and writing within their communities. Stores have names and signs and are filled with products with printed labels. Magazines are available in many of these stores. There are street signs, flyers, and advertisements providing various types of information, and sometimes in languages other than English. Restaurants provide menus. The mail carrier delivers readable items, and adults write notes and letters to communicate with one another. Some families have newspapers delivered to their house every day, while libraries

Motivation is very important in children developing strong literacy skills.

emergent literacy
reading-related behaviors and skills that precede formal reading and writing

conventional literacy
formal reading and writing

print knowledge
knowledge about the alphabet, letter sounds, and concepts of print

print
concepts of the difference between a word, a syllable, and a letter; recognizing that print moves from top to bottom and left to right on a page, and there are forms of punctuation to end a thought

phonological awareness
the ability to hear phonemes, beginning, middle, and ending sounds in words, syllables, and rhyming sounds

phonemes
the smallest sounds of our speech stream

and bookstores are filled with books for personal reading pleasure and for gaining knowledge. Many homes have computers that are used for communication with others, writing, or gathering information.

Children move from **emergent literacy** to **conventional literacy**. Emergent literacy refers to reading-related behaviors and skills that precede formal reading and writing—which is conventional literacy. Typically, this emergent level of literacy is evident in many children through first grade. Beginning reading and writing includes several phases and usually occurs between the ages of five and eight.

- Emergent readers and writers: prekindergarten through first grade
- Early readers and early writers: first through second grade
- Early fluent/fluent readers and writers: second through third grade.

The grade levels associated with each phase are only approximate. Within each grade level there will likely be children in all phases. There isn't a clear distinction between skills learned during the preschool years and those learned during school-age years. Development appears to be a result of exposure to literacy, brain development, and maturation rather than a result of chronological age.

A review of the research (Lonigan, 2006) indicates that the three most significant emergent literacy skills are print knowledge, phonological awareness, and complex oral language skills (see Figure 13–1). Ideally, these skills are developing before the child enters the elementary school system and they continue to develop in the early grades. **Print knowledge** means having knowledge about the alphabet, letter sounds, and concepts of print. Concepts of **print** include knowing the difference between a word, a syllable, and a letter; recognizing that print moves from top to bottom and left to right on a page; and that there are forms of punctuation to end a thought. **Phonological awareness** is the ability to hear phonemes, beginning, middle, and ending sounds in words, syllables, and rhyming sounds. **Phonemes** are the smallest sounds of our speech stream. **Complex oral language**, also known as **language comprehension**, refers to the child's vocabulary, as well as his or her ability to understand and use those words to convey thoughts.

The development of these three literacy skills is key to preparing the child for conventional reading. Evidence suggests that the two primary components necessary for successful reading are **decoding** and language

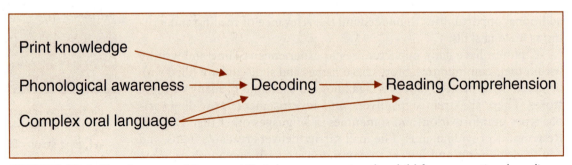

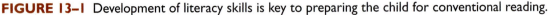

FIGURE 13–1 Development of literacy skills is key to preparing the child for conventional reading.

comprehension skills. (Torgesen, 2002) Decoding is sounding out words by breaking them apart into their letter sounds. Understanding the printed word is **reading comprehension**. Successful reading requires that readers can decode and have sufficient oral language skills to know the meaning of the words and the thoughts they convey.

Children initially demonstrate emergent skills when they recognize familiar logos and connect a logo with a store or restaurant name. If they have had frequent opportunities to see their own name in print, they may say, "There is an R like in my name!" These children are beginning to make the connection between symbols and what they represent. Not all children enter elementary school with these emergent skills. A caregiver can use scaffolding to help these children to develop the emergent literacy skills of relating alphabet letters to sounds, acquire more complex language skills, and develop phonemic awareness.

The development of children's writing skills correlates with their understanding of reading and depends on their fine-motor-skill development. They must have the physical abilities to hold and control a pencil. The precision of this skill comes with practice and time. Most kindergarten children have adequate fine-motor skills for writing; however their finger coordination and muscles are not developed sufficiently for them to write perfectly. When children have been exposed to literacy they imitate the writing of the older children and adults in their life. Initially they start with scribbles. Soon these emergent writers learn that the scribbles represent some form of communication and they engage in pretend writing. This pretend writing varies from child to child and may include various letter forms, strings of letters, and a combination of zigzag writing that follows the directionality of conventional writing. For example, the conventional direction used

complex oral language
the child's vocabulary as well as his or her ability to understand and use those words to convey thoughts; also known as language comprehension

language comprehension
the child's vocabulary as well as to his or her ability to understand and use those words to convey thoughts; also known as complex oral language

decoding
sounding out words by breaking them apart into their letter sounds

reading comprehension
understanding the printed word

Children begin writing with invented spelling.

> ***Mark*** resisted writing. He just wasn't interested. He could easily write his name, and he knew the alphabet and many of the letter sounds, yet he would put minimal effort into his homework assignments. He said that he didn't like writing. One day near the end of October, teacher Kevin brought a stack of advertisements for toys from the newspaper to add to the writing center. Mark spent time that day looking through the ads. The next day he came in, went straight to the writing center, grabbed a piece of paper and announced, "I am going to make my Christmas list." He spent time every day for a week writing his list. (Demonstrates: motivation, concepts of print)

when writing in English is from left to right across the page and from the top of the page to the bottom of the page. The next developmental writing step is for children to begin writing words or letters that represent words. Often they write someone else's name or "Mom" or "Dad." Children who have had sufficient literacy exposure during preschool years usually write their first name and several other letters when they enter kindergarten. Children who enter kindergarten without these emerging writing skills begin their formal schooling developmentally behind their peers.

invented spelling
writing with some letter-sound relationships, but not generally representing accurately spelled words

For children to develop the motivation to write, they must understand that the purpose of writing is for communication. Emergent writers use pretend writing to represent their names or ideas, and often ask, "How do you spell?" These children have some alphabetic knowledge. As they begin to understand that writing has meaning and is intended for communication, they begin to communicate through **invented spelling**. This is writing with some letter-sound relationships, but it does not generally represent accurately spelled words. "Iwntuthprk" could be a child's writing of "I went to the park." They have learned that writing is speech written down. They may not understand that there are spaces between words. By first grade, children use more conventional writing and will still use invented spelling. It isn't until the later grades when children are fluent writers that they can refine their writing by proofreading, editing, and revising. In these early writing stages, the process of writing is more important than the product or the end result. The goal is to motivate children to want to write and to make their own decisions about what to write. The following example demonstrates how Mark's knowledge of the concepts of print was connected to his motivation to write, making him feel successful.

THE LITERACY ENVIRONMENT

There are many ways that the school-age child care environment can support children's literacy development. The intent is to expand children's experiences and extend their learning. For programs that are already housed in their own space or center, this may require only some minor adjustments and the intentional addition of designated centers for reading and writing. For other programs, it will require more creative thinking. Programs that are outside because of a lack of classroom space, are in a school cafeteria, or share space with a regular classroom typically have very little storage space. (The available storage space may be dedicated currently to crafts, projects, games and outdoor equipment.) The challenge will be to decide how to integrate reading and writing activities into the course of the day. As already described, some activities, such as playing with sound, don't necessarily require additional space; they require awareness of literacy development, intentionality, and planning on the part of the caregiver. Maybe there isn't space to store a lot of books, so consider how you could have a few books in a basket or small container that can be rotated frequently with other books. The caregiver can carefully evaluate the games used to determine if they include a literacy component, such as including items that need to be read. Perhaps other games should be made available. Consider the craft materials, and how they can serve a dual purpose for writing activities. Writing implements, paper, staplers, and hole punches are versatile materials that easily serve both purposes.

One of the subscales of the *School-Age Care Environment Rating Scale* (Harms, Jacobs, & White, 1996) is language/reading activities. (This assessment tool is further discussed in Chapter 17.) For this subscale, the authors of the *SACERS* recommend the following practices for quality care of school-age children:

- At a minimum, children should be read age-appropriate stories by a fluent reader or told stories on a weekly basis.
- An environment that supports developmentally appropriate care includes many books and age-appropriate language games.
- The staff engages in language games with children and encourages children to use reading and writing in practical situations.
- In a high-quality setting, the child care staff takes the children to the library to borrow books on a weekly basis.
- Children are encouraged to bring books from home to share with others.
- The staff engages in helping children write stories, poems, and the class newspaper.

When school-age child care is housed in a center or dedicated school-age child care classroom, it can more easily promote literacy through centers that are specifically designed to promote and encourage reading and writing. A reading center should have a variety of books for various reading competency levels. There should be fictional books with engaging,

Six-year-old Elizabeth approached the computer telling her child care leader, "I went to the art museum with my mother and saw paintings by Picasso. Can you help me find him on the Internet?" (Demonstrates: alphabetic knowledge, reading comprehension, motivation)

Five-year-old Ethan, a kindergartner, approached me one day. "Teacher Jennifer, how do you make an H?" My response was, "Ethan, can you think of a place in our room where we could find the letters of the alphabet?" He looked around the room, spotting the chart on the wall. As he approached it he sang, "A, B, C, D, E, F, G, H." and pointed to the letters as he sang each one. When he reached the H, he shouted with delight, "H! H! H! There is the H!" (alphabet knowledge)

nonviolent stories. Informational books would include books about specific subjects that appeal to boys and girls, as well as a picture dictionary, a typical elementary school dictionary, and a set of encyclopedias. Adult level print materials can be included for caregivers to assist children in gaining information about topics of interest. Other print materials include children's magazines, which often are filled with interesting feature stories and age-appropriate factual literature that would be interesting to school-age children. The use of computers and the Internet can provide additional reading opportunities for children.

Provide a cozy space for reading that is well-lit, quiet, and removed from noisy activity areas. Set it up in a place that protects individuals from intrusion by others. Place the writing center near the reading center. The writing center should include a variety of writing implements, adequate amounts of paper, and items for binding child-made books—such as a hole punch and yarn, tape, blank homemade books, and a stapler. The alphabet chart can be displayed somewhere close to the writing center.

The reading and writing centers often complement each other. A child involved in writing a book may decide to retrieve a book to see how the title page is set up. A child reading about snakes may decide to make a snake-shaped bookmark for his book or create his own book about his adventure of seeing a snake in his backyard.

Other centers in the environment lend themselves to books and printed materials. The block or construction area may have books, posters, and magazines of architecture such as bridges and buildings or woodworking. Print and make instructions for how to play games available for children when they choose to play table games. Add science-related books, encyclopedias, journals, and magazines to the science center to pique children's curiosity. Many of the drama activities suggested in Chapter 11 also lend themselves to books and printed materials. The environment should also be rich with functional print—print that encourages both reading and writing. **Functional print** is print that has a purpose. Labeling the various items around the classroom—such as door, clock, and table—has no purpose. On the other hand, a sign that says, "Needed: 4 children to help prepare snack. Sign up here" has a purpose. Have individual mailboxes in the room to encourage children to communicate with one another in writing. Provide clipboards with paper and pencils in the other areas such as blocks and dramatic play. You never know when children will want to make a list or write a note.

functional print
print that has a purpose

ROLE OF THE CAREGIVER IN LITERACY ACTIVITIES

It is important for school-age caregivers to recognize that their role is not to be the reading and writing teacher, but rather to support each child in developing mastery in her level of literacy developmental through developmentally appropriate practices in a quality setting. The discussion thus far is merely an introduction to the intricacies of the process of how children learn to read and write, and provides caregivers with some basic knowledge of some of the factors that influence this process.

It is imperative that caregivers themselves have sufficient reading and writing skills in English. Caregivers cannot model, guide, and support children in the development of skills that they do not themselves possess. Caregivers have daily opportunities to provide meaningful experiences with reading and writing. They should be intentional about guiding children in literacy skill development. As a rule of thumb, children should have daily opportunities to:

- have reading modeled for them.
- have writing modeled for them.
- explore literature or read something of personal interest.
- express themselves through writing.

When caregivers plan with intentionality, they know what they are doing, why they are doing it, and can articulate their purpose to other caregivers, administrators, and most importantly to parents.

Caregivers should enthusiastically and daily model reading for pleasure, information, and communication. Adults who take time to read to children model their love of reading, and the value of seeking information through printed materials, as well as providing opportunities for meaningful conversations with children. You will be surprised at the number of children who seek out books about things such as spiders, termites, volcanoes, or dinosaurs. Other children are drawn to books about famous people, like Benjamin Franklin, Abraham Lincoln, or Picasso. Your local librarian can be very helpful in finding great read-aloud books that are meaningful and engaging. *The Read-aloud-Handbook*, by Jim Trelease (2006) provides a current and comprehensive list of books for a variety of ages, as well as reading strategies and techniques to consider. If your program is closely tied to the local elementary school program, you can learn about and perhaps borrow books that relate to what the children are doing in school.

In addition to picture books, caregivers should carefully select engaging chapter books to read to children. This form of reading takes several sittings and requires children to remember what has been read previously. Chapter books expose children to a broader vocabulary and a richer sentence structure, and they may be written at a more advanced reading level than that of the child. They do not have pictures in them, so children are challenged to listen attentively and create mental pictures about the story and the characters. Select books that are not familiar to children or books that follow the story line of television programs or movies. Unfamiliar books will help maximize children's imagination and interest level. In addition to the literary benefits, reading chapter books to children creates predictability in your program, something for children to look forward to. In a before- and after-school program, reading to children is a great technique to settle them down in the morning before sending them off to class.

Reading to children is an opportunity to build complex language skills. Research has identified dialogic reading as the most effective method of reading to children so they can increase their complex oral language skills (Lonigan, 2007). **Dialogic reading** first teaches children the vocabulary of the book, and then expands on the story itself. Ideally, you will read to a small group of children, no more than eight, and all the children will sit so everyone can see the book at the same time. Each child needs to be able to talk during the reading session in order to practice language skills. Start by looking at the cover of the book. Ask, "What do you think this story is about?" Give children time to study the cover and respond. This strategy, known as the five-second wait time, is useful whenever you ask children a question. They need time to process the question and to formulate their response. You could do a "book walk" by thumbing through some of the pages and talking about the pictures. It is important to point out to children that the pictures give us ideas about the story, but the words actually tell us the story. The first time you read a story, you don't want any significant interruption while you read so you should do most of the talking yourself. Point out the names of things children may not know and briefly define new vocabulary. A child may ask what a word means and it is important to answer that kind of question to help the child understand the story. Take time for follow-up questions that encourage children's recall of the story, engage their memories, and encourage them to speak with complex language. "What happened

dialogic reading
first teaches children the vocabulary of the book and then expands on the story itself

Reading to children is an opportunity to build complex language skills.

to the boy in this story?" "Wh" questions (What? Why? When? Where?) engage children's thinking and encourage them to give more than a simple "yes" or "no" response. Respond to children's answers in a way that encourages further conversation. This dialogue, as a part of the reading process, helps children understand concepts of print, increases their vocabulary, and increases their complex oral language skills.

Caregivers should model writing every day so children can see it as an important means of communication. Children need to witness a purpose to writing and see the conventional forms of writing letters, words, sentence structure, and punctuation. They should be involved in purposeful writing themselves. Initially, this might entail putting their name on their paper. This helps to establish ownership of the paper. You will find that many children come to school knowing how to write their names. In time, children will want to communicate by writing notes to their friends or letters to their parents. Caregivers scaffold this by actually writing as the child dictates a message or perhaps helping the child sound out words to write the message herself. The child or the caregiver can read it back to the child, and the child can make the correlation between writing and reading. In time the child will write messages independently. At the kindergarten level, a child might write a sign that says, "Dont nok dwn blks." This invented spelling means, "Don't knock down my blocks." Connect reading and writing whenever possible by empowering children to make lists, notes, etc. More early and fluent writers may come to you wanting to read what they have written. Take time to listen and encourage them. This is not a time to correct children's writing and insist on perfection. Remember, you are also building self-esteem and empowering children to see themselves as writers.

Caregivers should keep in mind that the goal is to motivate and encourage children to engage in purposeful writing. They should be aware of the various developmental stages of writing, how to identify each child's developmental level, and how to help the child develop mastery at that level. Adults should also scaffold learning for the child who is emerging to a new skill level. Do not insist that children practice writing. The drill of practicing letter formation or accurate spelling in an attempt to develop skills will surely kill the child's intrinsic motivation. Avoid drill, skill, and kill.

Reading and writing can be incorporated into many aspects of your day with children and in a variety of settings. It is necessary for the caregiver to develop an awareness of the opportunities for infusing literacy to be more intentional. Consider the following examples of empowering children and providing meaningful literacy experiences:

- You are getting ready to put a CD in the CD player and you are looking for a certain song. Give the CD to a child and ask for help in locating the song on the album. The child with emerging skills may use the first letter sound to locate the song (alphabetic knowledge, phonemic awareness, decoding, reading comprehension).
- You are planning snack for next week and need to make a grocery list. Encourage a group of children to be the snack team and work with you to create the snack schedule. You can provide them with

a list of acceptable snacks. Older children can be given nutritious guidelines to follow. Children can write the shopping list and the snack schedule for the week (vocabulary, decoding, writing).

- Your class is forming teams for a volleyball game. The youngest of the children can help make team lists by sorting preprinted names into piles to represent the teams (decoding, alphabetic knowledge).
- Your class needs additional art supplies and you must place an order. Dictate your supply order to a group of children. Be prepared to help scaffold the spelling of some of the words (vocabulary, decoding, phonemic awareness, writing).
- Your class has developed a new class rule about name-calling. This calls for a new sign in the room. Develop a rotating "sign-maker" job in the classroom. As the caregiver you will provide the appropriate amount of support to encourage the child to write the sign as independently as possible and to be successful (vocabulary, reading comprehension, decoding, phonemic awareness, writing).
- You know that the custodian who cleans your child care center consistently does a wonderful job. Create a "Thank You" book for the custodian from you and the children. You and each child should include a personal "thank you" note in the book (vocabulary, phonemic awareness, decoding, reading comprehension, writing).

background knowledge
knowledge that is learned through experiences, reading, movies, and television

The caregiver sets the stage for children to gain **background knowledge**. This is knowledge learned through experiences, reading, movies, and television. Think of this as placing hooks in the child's brain so that when the child later reads about this topic, he has a hook to hang the new knowledge on. He can connect with the reading. The larger the child's experience base (background knowledge), the more mental hooks the child possesses to help him understand what he reads. Consider the child who has helped plant and harvest a garden. She learns about root vegetables by planting radishes and onions and vegetables that grow on bushlike plants such as beans and tomatoes. Later, when the child hears the story *Tops and Bottoms* by Janet Stevens, she has an experience to draw upon so she can relate to the story. Reading comprehension is much easier if you have some knowledge of

One of the children at group time said, "Eskimos live in igloos." My immediate response was, "Yes, they do." Fortunately, teacher Michele quickly thought about it and realized that this was a stereotype, and she actually had limited knowledge of Eskimos. She asked the children how they could find out about Eskimos and igloos. They responded, "In books! On the Internet!" That afternoon, Michele facilitated an Internet search about igloos with some of the children. Michele realized that as a caregiver, she didn't have to know all the knowledge, but she had to know how to find information and guide the children to answers to their questions in books and on the Internet (motivation, reading comprehension).

the subject about which you are reading. Caregivers have more flexibility in the curriculum they provide for children than do elementary school teachers. The caregiver can listen to and expand upon the interests of children. The curriculum chapters in this textbook are filled with ideas to help children build background knowledge about the world in which they live.

Caregivers must be intentional about guiding children in the development of complex language skills. Developmentally appropriate practices indicate that caregivers should engage in sustained conversations with individual children as well as small groups of children. Sustained conversations allow caregivers to talk with children about their experiences outside of school, what they are reading, what they are studying in school, and about what they are interested in learning. Both adults and children express their complex ideas with rich vocabulary (Bredekamp & Copple, 2009). The intentional caregiver must develop a conversation style that encourages children to develop their complex language skills. Try these discussion starters with children (and remember the five-second rule: wait five seconds for children to think about your question and respond):

- What's happening?
- How can you find out. . . ?
- What would happen if. . . ?
- What do you think the problem is?
- Tell me how you did that.
- How would you feel if. . . ?
- What do you notice about. . . ?
- What else can you use?
- Can you think of another way?
- What do you need to do next?

Caregivers should help children develop and enhance their phonemic awareness by playing with sound themselves and encouraging children to play with sound. Children love to make up silly words and languages that they think adults don't understand. You might remember some of these games from your own childhood. Share them with the children. Activities such as tongue twisters, rhyming games, and "knock, knock who's there" jokes invite children to focus on sounds. Encourage children to play with sound through songs, raps, chants, and bebop.

Caregivers Supporting English Language Learners

There is a plethora of research and literature on language acquisition and teaching English language learners that extends far beyond the scope of this text. The intent of this discussion is to briefly examine the role of the caregiver and provide strategies that support the literacy development of children who are English language learners. A primary goal is to provide high-quality experiences for English language learners. Caregivers must be intentional in planning activities that integrate language development with other curriculum areas, such as science and math, visual and performing arts, games, and outdoor play. These experiences will give children the opportunity to work in tandem with children who are more skilled in English language and literacy, and will provide time to explore activities and practice speaking English (Zarate, 2008). Additionally, caregivers are particularly conscientious about having conversations with children who are English language learners. Often these children are behind in vocabulary and other aspects of language learning (Bredekamp & Copple, 2009). Use the following strategies to further support English language learners:

- Visual aids: Whenever possible, provide pictures along with written words in English and the child's home language to give ELL children visual cues.
- Sufficient wait time: Give ELL children additional time to formulate thoughts and answers in English. Some children may be translating their home language into English. Others may need time to find the appropriate words.
- Model spoken language: Do not correct children's spoken language. Instead, expand on and model English. For example, if you ask the child about the picture he is drawing, and he says, "Soccer," you might respond with, "You are drawing a picture about playing soccer."
- Respect the home language: Use a translator or language dictionary to assist you with understanding words in the child's home language.
- Recognize the silent phase: ELL children go through a silent phase. Do not force the child to speak as this may cause embarrassment, and the child may feel overly self-conscious, developing a sense of inferiority. This can also create a scenario in which other children will laugh at the child. Plan language-rich activities: Think of the individual ELL children in your program and intentionally develop activities to enhance language and other literacy skills.

FUN EXPERIENCES TO BUILD LITERACY

Activities that give children the opportunity to learn more about literacy and to practice their skills should always be enjoyable to children. This requires the caregiver to be intentional about activity planning with literacy in mind. The intentional caregiver will provide activities that: increase children's vocabulary and understanding of language, increase their motivation to read and write, and give reading and writing a purposeful function within the school-age program.

Activities

The following activity ideas can be implemented in varying degrees depending on the level of fluency of the children in your care. Some children will be able to do these tasks independently while others will only be able to do part of the activity and will need your help through scaffolding. Provide a variety of activity options so children can engage in the things that are of most interest to them.

Reading for a Purpose

Purposes:

- increase understanding of reading as an important life skill
- develop motivation to read
- practice decoding and reading comprehension skills

As you set up activities, think of how you can provide written instructions for children to read. Fluent readers can help less skilled readers and English language learners.

How to garden.   Your science activity involves children planting seeds and bulbs. Write the step-by-step instructions on a large piece of paper and post them on a wall or easel next to the science table. Early readers will need you to read the directions prior to planting. Encourage fluent readers to read the instructions themselves. Add pictures for each instruction to provide additional support to early readers and ELLs.

Cooking from a recipe.   You are planning a cooking activity in which children are making bean burritos. Create step-by-step recipe cards to place on the table. Each step requires the child to read and complete a specific task. Each step can include a picture of the task.

Step 1: Wash hands.
Step 2: Take a paper plate and put your name on it.
Step 3: Put one tortilla on your plate and put one large spoonful of beans on the tortilla.
Step 4: Sprinkle cheese on top of the beans.
Step 5: Fold the tortilla over the beans and cheese. Bring the bottom up first, then fold in each side, then fold down the top.
Step 6: Place plate in microwave and heat for one-and-a-half minutes.
Step 7: Eat your burrito.

Provide written instructions for children to read.

Washing hands routine.   You have noticed that the children aren't following the steps for proper hand washing and you frequently have to give them verbal reminders. Take photographs of a child in the various steps of hand washing. Mount the pictures on a long strip of paper or poster board. Invite the children to help write the captions for each photograph and hang the instructions near the sink. You will find that children will refer to the pictures and read the words to themselves and to each other.

You've got mail!   Write notes to the children and put them in a place designated for mail. This might be cardboard boxes with compartments that sit on a counter, individual cubbies, or perhaps a hanging shoe bag. Each child should have a place with his or her name on it to receive mail.

These notes can be brief. "We missed you yesterday when you were sick." "I see that you have been working hard at jumping rope!" "Thank you for your ideas for next week's cooking project." Also, encourage children to write notes to each other.

Extra! Extra! Read all about it! The older, more fluent writers in your care may want to form a writers club. Encourage them to write a weekly newsletter announcing the events of the week. It could include a calendar, short articles about activities going on in the child care center, and any announcements you want to make. Post a new activity schedule and snack schedule in the room for children to read.

Writing for a Purpose
Purposes:

- practice writing skills of concepts of print
- increase awareness of the purposes of writing
- develop motivation to write

Sign up list. Children frequently want a turn at such activities as working on the computers, doing an art activity, or playing handball. Provide a whiteboard, clipboard, or some other regular place for children to sign up for a turn. Younger children can write their first name. As children become more skilled, alter this writing task by encouraging them to write their first and last names and include their middle name, or write just initials. For fun, children can create nicknames. This will give them an opportunity to figure out how to spell a different name.

Children should be encouraged to express strong feelings.

Write those feelings.   Every day presents itself with opportunities for children to express strong feelings. Children can be encouraged to tell their story to a caregiver. Often just stating what has happened and having it be acknowledged by an adult helps a child feel they have been heard. Encourage skilled writers to write the story themselves. Less skilled writers or English language learners can create a pictorial representation of what happened, and the caregiver can write down the child's dictation and read it back to him.

Say it with a sign.   The environment is filled with many types of signs. There are signs that give directions, others that advertise products, and signs that give the names of businesses. Often these are written in languages other than English. Show children pictures of signs and discuss the purpose of signs, the languages used, and how signs help communicate information. Provide materials on an ongoing basis for children to make signs of their own. As children come to you with thoughts they want to convey to others, lead them into making a sign.

It is special! Remember it with words!   Children do many things that you as a caregiver think are special. These are times when you can validate children by encouraging them to document their ideas and work. Help children document things they do by writing down their thoughts, inventions, and creations.

Play Production.   Help the children in your program plan and present a play. This can be as simple as role-playing a few finger plays, acting out a favorite story, or as involved as actually scripting a play. Children's authors such as Jan Brett have websites that provide supplemental materials you can download and print. For example, the website provides masks you can print and use to play the characters in *The Mitten* (Brett, 1987). You can guide children in writing scripts or cue cards, creating advertisements, and developing a program for their production. Encourage them to interview

Elizabeth was sad that her big brother was going away to college and that she wouldn't see him for four months. Caregiver Kevin asked her if she would like to write a letter to her brother. She seemed excited about the idea, and told Kevin that she didn't know how to write all those words. Kevin gave her a choice of writing the letter with his help or telling him the words to write. Elizabeth chose to tell him the words. Kevin wrote Elizabeth's thoughts exactly as she said them. When she was finished, Kevin read it to her. Elizabeth then took the paper and said, "Now, I am going to write my letter myself!" She sat down and copied the letter. When she was finished, she asked Kevin to read it to her again. Then she put it an envelope, sealed it and put it in her backpack to take home.

Caregiver Raul overheard Chris singing to himself as he was building with blocks. "Chris, it sounds like you have a new song." "I made it on the piano," Chris replied. Raul encouraged him to sing it again. Chris sang, "Kick, kick, kick. Kick, kick, kick the ball. Kick, kick, kick the ball. Kick, kick, kick, the ball very fast." "Would you like to write that down?" asked Raul. "I can't write it. I'm just in kindergarten. I can only play it on the piano." Raul continued to tell Chris about composers and wrote Chris's song on paper as Chris sang it again. Chris watched as Raul wrote. "I want to make a song book!"

the main characters and write an article for your center's newsletter. Engage the children in writing announcements to be sent home to parents, inviting them to attend the production of the play. Create materials in the various home languages of the children in the program. Sometimes parents may be enlisted to help with the writing of these languages.

Personal Writing
Purposes:

- practice writing skills for the purpose of preserving personal ideas
- increase phonemic awareness in writing
- encourage application of print knowledge to personal writing
- engage in reflective thinking

Calendar journaling.   This activity encourages children to reflect on their day and write about events that are important to them. Provide children with a calendar for a week or a month. Establish a routine for children to think about their favorite part of the day or week, something they want to remember. Encourage each child to write it on his calendar. Give children materials to create covers for their personal calendars and a place for them to be stored. Model this activity for the children. Brainstorm with the children the events of the day or the week, writing on the whiteboard or a large piece of paper. You may need to model this by thinking out loud about the joys of your day and what you would want to remember. Model writing on your own calendar. Be aware that some children will want to copy what you have written. They may believe that what you think is important to you should be important to them. If this happens, try to empower children to write what is important to them.

Play plans.   Children often come to their child care setting with ideas about the things they want to do. Some children need help getting settled and making play decisions. Writing play plans is a strategy that guides children to think about their goals as well as helping them with literacy skills. This is also an opportunity for you to let children know that their ideas are important. As an added bonus, play plans serve as documentation of children's progress and a tool to help you stay tuned into children's interests. You can plan more meaningful and enjoyable activities for children when you know about their interests and capabilities.

When children arrive, give them a half sheet of paper. If your program is small and you have enough adult help you can have children write daily play plans, or you may choose to have children write them only once or twice a week. Children draw a picture on the top half of the paper to illustrate what they want to do in child care. The bottom of the page is the space to write a sentence about what they want to do. Kindergarten children who are not yet writing can draw lines to symbolize each word. They simply draw a horizontal line for each word across the page. For example, "I want to play with blocks" would be symbolized by a line for the word "I," another line for the word "want," and so forth. You will have to model this technique. You may have to draw the lines while the child dictates her thoughts. Next, write the child's words on the lines. As the children gain more alphabetic knowledge, they will begin writing the first sounds of some of the words, use invented spelling, and write familiar words such as "the" or "play." More skilled writers will write independently and should be encouraged to discuss their play plan with you. Let each child date their work with a date stamp. Be sure to find time during the day to talk with children about their plans and their progress. Your desire to hear children's ideas is validating and gives them a sense of self-worth. Help children organize their play plans in an individual notebook or folder.

Diary journaling.   Introduce children to the concept of journaling as part of one's profession or for personal reasons. Have a discussion about people who must write journals to document their work. Scientists keep track of various aspects of their experiments. Pilots keep flight logs; doctors make notes about their patients. Children may know about journaling that their parents do. You might tell them about keeping a diary of your own when you were their age. Do you journal now as an adult? If so, what are the ideas you choose to write about? Is it to remember the events of the day or for writing down your feelings? Perhaps you like to write poems or stories. Share your writing passion with children. Help them generate thoughts about their own interests and what they might want to write about. Older children can do this independently. Younger, less skilled writers and English language learners can use the play plan strategy as previously described or dictate their words to you while you do the actual writing. Keep in mind

Six-Year-old Allison discovered the joy of writing. Every day after school she would go to a desk in the corner of the room and write. She would say, "When I get big, I am going to be a writer!" Allison was also interested in science and said she wanted to be a scientist; and she struggled with her dilemma of also wanting to be a writer. One day Allison came bouncing into the room, "Teacher Jennifer! I got it. I am going to write about science!"

that this should be one of several activities that children can choose from. Some children simply will not be interested in this activity.

Enhanced Dramatic Play
Purposes:

- enhance awareness of reading and writing in daily lives
- provide opportunities to role play meaningful reading and writing

Dramatic play easily can be augmented to include reading and writing. School-age children enjoy pretending to be adults in various occupations. Consider how you can add reading- and writing-related materials in multiple languages to dramatic play areas. Whenever possible, involve the children in making the literacy-related play props.

Doctor's office. Provide manila folders, clipboards, and paper for children to write prescriptions and notes about a patient's condition. Hang posters on the wall and include health-related pamphlets in the environment. Include an area for a pretend waiting room with books and magazines.

Restaurant. Provide menus for patrons to use when ordering their food. Many take-out restaurants have paper menus available. You can easily make your own menus by cutting pictures out of newspaper ads, mounting them on paper, and adding captions. Include language that encourages the development of new vocabulary such as "entrees," or words for foods of other cultures. Waiters and waitresses will need order pads, and cooks will have to read the orders. Patrons will need their bill so they can pay for their food.

Pet store. Literacy items in a pet store would include a variety of signs, books about pets, packages of pet food, and other pet-related items. The store could have a sign (made by the children, of course) stating the store's hours of operation. Include pretend order forms on clipboards. Post advertisements from newspapers for local pet stores.

Office. Old computer keyboards, telephones, telephone books, paper, envelopes, and pencils are key literacy-related items for a pretend office.

Play with sound
Purposes:

- enhance children's phonemic awareness
- empower children to play with language

Silly songs. One way to present sounds to children is through songs. Many familiar tunes can be used to create songs that allow children to play with sounds.

Example 1: To the tune "The Farmer in the Dell." Use a child's name, the first letter of the name, and the sound the letters makes to create this song.

Sammy starts with *S*
Sammy starts with *S*

Si, so, si, serio
Sammy starts with *S.*
Barbara starts with *B*
Barbara starts with *B*
Bi, bo, bi, berio
Barbara starts with *B.*

Example 2: To the tune "B-I-N-G-O." Use the children's names to focus on syllables. Clap the syllables as you sing. In this example, you clap once for "Char" and once for "vin."

There was a class that had a friend
And Charvin was his name-o
Char-vin
Char-vin
And Charvin was his name-o.

Example 3: To the tune "The More We Get Together." Choose any letter for this song and use the names of the children in your program or other words that start with that sound. Produce the sound of the letter when you see it underlined in the song. When making the sound of the letter, ensure that you don't inadvertently add an extra vowel sound to it, such as "da."

Did you ever hear a *"d"* sound, a *"d"* sound, a *"d"* sound?
Did you ever hear a *"d"* sound go *"d. d. d. d, d"?*
There's *"d"* as in David, and *"d"* as in Daniel
There's *"d"* as in Mallard and *"d"* as in Merced.
Did you ever hear a *"d"* sound go *"d, d, d, d"?*

Play languages.   Some of you may remember speaking pig latin when you were elementary school age. You take the first letter of every word and place it at the end of the word with a long "a" vowel sound. Yes, would be es-ya. Tomorrow would be omorrow-ta. "Esya, omorrowta, ewa oga ota etha arkpa" is "Yes, tomorrow we go to the park."

Egg language is an even more challenging way of speaking. Insert the word "egg" before every vowel in the words. Yes, would be "Yeggs, Teggomeggoreggow wegge geggo teggo thegge peggark."

A word of caution: Only engage in play languages when all of the children you care for are fluent English speakers. Play languages are fun, however they will feel defeating for your English language learners. These children already struggle to learn the meaning and pronunciation of words in English. They do not have the ability to distinguish between a play word such as "yeggs" or "esya" and the actual word "yes." Learning English is difficult enough without your making it more difficult by introducing nonsense words.

Bookmaking
Purposes:

- enhance motivation to read and write
- provide creative expression of writing

Bookmaking enhances motivation to read and write.

- increase application of print knowledge
- explore the use of technology as a tool for writing

Recipe book.   Develop recipe books made from the recipes the children use in their cooking projects. Children can search the Internet for "kid friendly" recipes.

Block structures.   Take photographs of children's block structures and their architects (the children who built the structure). Invite the children to write a brief description and story about their structure. If computers are available, use a PowerPoint program to create pages for a class book.

Text message dictionary.   Some children are discovering the use of cell phones for text messages. Guide children in creating a dictionary of text message abbreviations and their proper spelling.

A book of my own.   Provide materials for children to make their own books. Once they begin to understand the parts of books, children often enjoy becoming authors and writing about their own ideas. Use staples, tape, or yarn for binding the pages of the book together. Writers can use a word processing program to write and edit their stories.

Predictable class books.   There are many predictable books that help children to read. A predictable book is one in which the text repeats itself. Children in your care can write a predictable book. Each child receives a paper with a written phrase such as "I played on the playground and I played with ___." The child is asked to fill in the blank with an idea.

She can illustrate her page with a picture. An alternative would be to take pictures of the children as they play and use them as the illustrations for the book. Put the pages in a notebook in plastic sleeves for protection. Read the book to the class and then keep it in your library; it is a book the children will read again and again.

Equipment to Have Available

- dramatic play props such as writing pads, clipboards, magazines, posters, pamphlets
- paper, markers, and clipboards in all centers of the classroom
- wipe-off white boards with dry-erase markers
- chalkboards and chalk
- writing materials outside for score keeping or note taking
- overhead projector, blank transparencies, and transparency markers
- tape recorder and blank cassette tapes for recording children's songs and stories
- large variety of books including both fiction and nonfiction
- CD Player and music that encourages playing with sound
- materials for binding books such as yarn, hole punches, tape
- computer, printer, and paper

GUIDELINES FOR CHILD CARE STAFF MEMBERS

Keep in mind that the more children understand the purposes of reading and writing, the greater their motivation and the more likely they will be to want to be readers and writers. The more they read, the better readers they will become. Your role is not to be the teacher of reading and writing, but to enhance and support the work that children do. You will scaffold learning when appropriate and provide purposeful activities. You are the role model for the children as you model your own love of reading and writing. There are several key guidelines for caregivers of school-age children to keep in mind as they are enhancing children's development of their literacy skills.

- Be intentional. As you plan each part of your program, think about how you can intentionally add literacy and support English language learners. Planning with literacy in mind will ensure that you integrate print knowledge, phonemic awareness, oral language skills, and writing into your daily curriculum.
- Plan enriching activities that will increase children's knowledge of their world and build background knowledge.
- Listen to and talk with children to increase their complex language skills.
- Model reading and writing.
- Create meaningful, purposeful opportunities for children to practice their reading and writing skills.

- Read to all children of all ages, using dialogic reading techniques.
- Provide opportunities for children to read and write every day.
- Rotate the books in the library so there are new and interesting books and magazines for children to read and explore.
- Design a cozy, inviting reading area that is prominent in the room.
- Create scenarios for children to write something every day.
- Show interest in the things children write and read.
- Incorporate reading and writing materials in as many centers and activities as possible.

SUMMARY

- Children enter their school years with a wide range of emerging literacy skills and experiences.

- School-age child care is a place for children to be supported in their development of reading and writing—specifically print knowledge, phonological awareness, and complex oral language skills—through developmentally appropriate activities.

- Caregivers do not replace classroom teachers as reading and writing teachers, but they can create an environment with adequate time, space, and materials that motivates and supports children to engage in purposeful reading and writing.

- Caregivers are intentional about literacy components as they design the environment, the activities they plan and implement, and the support they provide to children.

- Children practice literacy within the context of other curriculum areas and in daily routines.

- Caregivers model reading and writing every day so children can come to understand that these are important life skills.

- Caregivers support English language learners by intentionally planning language rich activities and incorporating a variety of strategies specifically to help the ELL child with language acquisition. Plan activities and engage in sustained conversations with children about their experiences in and out of school to find out what their interests are and to help children develop background knowledge and complex language skills.

- Caregivers ask open-ended questions, encouraging children to think and give a complex response within the context of rich activities that provide children opportunities to learn about their world around them.

KEY TERMS

background knowledge	decoding	English language learner
complex oral language	dialogic reading	functional print
conventional literacy	emergent literacy	invented spelling
	emerging literacy skills	

language comprehension	phonological awareness	print knowledge
literacy	print	reading comprehension
phonemes		

REVIEW QUESTIONS

1. Define emergent literacy skills. Why are they important to the reading success of children?

2. Describe the role of the school-age caregiver in supporting children's literacy development for children fluent in English and for English language learners.

3. Identify at least 10 literacy-related materials that could be included in a child care program.

4. Explain why the process of writing is more important than writing letters perfectly with accurate spelling.

5. What are five phrases that can be used as discussion starters?

6. Why are complex language skills important to the development of reading and writing skills?

7. Give at least three examples of how caregivers can model writing daily.

8. Explain dialogic reading.

9. Give at least three examples of how literacy can be incorporated in a child care program held in a cafeteria after school.

Case Study

Ethan is a kindergartner with little knowledge of print. He has just started writing his name, and the only other word he knows how to write is "Mom." He loves dinosaurs and is interested in the science activities you have been presenting in class. Cassandra, a first-grader, is already reading chapter books. She carries a book with her wherever she goes. She is often very quiet, choosing quiet activities such as art and the computers. Juanita is in second grade, and you know that she is in the lowest reading group in her class. She speaks Spanish at home. She struggles with decoding words and has already told you that she hates to look at books. She particularly enjoys spending time outside with her friends jumping rope or playing handball.

1. How would you plan activities that support each of these three children's reading abilities?

2. What writing activities could you plan that would be motivating and meaningful for each of these children?

3. What activity could you plan that might be interesting to these three children and give them background knowledge?

STUDENT ACTIVITIES

1. Plan and implement one literacy writing activity with a group of school-age children. Record your observations of the children. Evaluate your observations of at least two of the children and determine the child's developmental level of writing.

2. Create a file of songs and chants appropriate for school-age children that encourage children's phonemic awareness.

3. Write a letter to parents explaining how you are supporting children's literacy development in your child care program.

4. Plan and implement a story time with a group of four to eight children. Decide how you will read the story, what new vocabulary you will discuss, and the follow-up questions you will ask to encourage complex language skills. Write a report of your experience and share it with the class.

5. Engage in a conversation with children using at least one of the discussion starters presented in this chapter. Remember to use the five-second wait time rule. Analyze your experience, determine its effectiveness, and share it with the class.

6. Plan and implement one activity to help children build background knowledge. Identify strategies you would use to support an English language learner, as well as the key concepts to which children will be exposed, and state how you will present them in a developmentally appropriate way.

SUGGESTED READINGS

Edwards, S., & Martinez, K. (2004). *Fun Literacy Activities for After-School Programs: Books and Beyond*. Nashville, TN: School-Age Notes.

Neuman, S. B., Copple C., & Bredekamp, S. (2000). *Developmentally Appropriate Practices: Learning to Read and Write*. Washington, DC: National Association for the Education of Young Children.

WEB RESOURCES

http://www.janbrett.com
Children's author Jan Brett shares many downloadable materials to accompany her books.

http://www.dancrow.com
Music resource for songs that play with sound from Dan Crow, former speech therapist turned children's musician.

http://www.rif.org
Reading Is Fundamental: reading activities, parent guides, literacy games, interactive Spanish link.

www.readinglady.com
Teacher support for various literacy skills from a reading coach.

REFERENCES

Bredekamp, S., & Copple, C. (2009). *Developmentally Appropriate Practice in Early Childhood Programs.* (3rd. ed.) Washington, DC: National Association for the Education of Young Children.

Brett, J. (1987). *The Mitten.* New York: G. P. Putnam Sons.

Harms, T., Jacobs, E. V., & White, D. R. (1996). *School-Age Care Environment Rating Scale.* New York: Teachers College.

Lonigan, C. J. (2006). Development, assessment, and promotion of preliteracy skills. *Early Education and Development,* 17(1), 91–114.

Lonigan, C. J. (2007). *Development and promotions of early language and literacy skills in young children.* Research Series Presentation at California Preschool Instructional Network, January 25, 2007, Sacramento, CA.

NAEYC & IRA (1998). Learning to read and write: Developmentally appropriate practices for young children. *Young Children,* 53(4), 30–46.

National Center for Education Statistics. (2010). The nation's report card. Trial urban district assessment. Reading 2009 NCES 2010-459. Washington, DC: U.S. Department of Education.

National Clearinghouse for English Language Acquisition (2006). *The Growing Numbers of Limited English Proficient Students:1993/94–2003/04.* Washington, DC: U.S. Department of Education.

Snow, C. E., Burns, M. S., & Griffin, P. (Eds.). (1998). *Preventing Reading Difficulties In Young Children.* Washington, DC: National Academy Press.

Stevens, J. (1995). *Tops and Bottoms.* New York: Harcourt Brace.

Torgesen, J. K. (2002). The prevention of reading disabilities. *Journal of School Psychology,* 40, 7–26.

Trelease, J. (2006). *The Read-Aloud Handbook.* (6th ed.) New York, NY: Penguin

Zarate, C. V. (2008). *Maximizing After School Opportunities for English learners.* Los Angeles, CA: Alliance for a Better Community.

Preparing Children for Adult Roles

IMPORTANCE OF PREPARING CHILDREN FOR THE FUTURE

There is a revolution taking place in the workplace, said Alvin Toffler (1990) in his book *Powershift: Knowledge, Wealth, and Violence on the Edge of the 21st Century*. In his latest book *Revolutionary Wealth (2009)*, Toffler discusses the importance of the latest technologies (e.g., YouTube, social networking, the Internet, cyber-economics) and looks at how these are changing wealth systems. These technologies make it possible for unlimited global markets and wide-reaching changes in monetary transactions. Workers will need to be fluent in English, as well as minimally literate in other languages, and must be willing to work with colleagues in a global society. Toffler predicts there will be few places for the uneducated or people without the required characteristics and skills.

High school or college is too late to begin preparing young people for their future employment. The process begins in early childhood and continues throughout the school years. While it is impossible to know what kinds of jobs will be developed in the future, we do know that many future career opportunities will involve literate, educated workers. In order to help them be prepared, children must be encouraged to be motivated learners who retain and use what they have studied. They must have **meaning-based experiences** that emphasize thinking, cooperative problem solving, decision making, and an opportunity to challenge preconceived ideas. Many of the activities throughout this book stress just those skills.

In addition to acquiring skills for the future, children should have an opportunity to experience the real world of work. At each stage of development, children differ in their ability to think about the future and their own role as adults.

LEARNING OUTCOMES

After reading this chapter, you should be able to:

✔ Explain the importance of preparing children for future adult roles.

✔ Plan and implement experiences that help children explore a variety of jobs and workplaces.

✔ Understand how child care staff can help children practice the skills they may need as future workers.

meaning-based experiences
learning experiences that emphasize thinking, cooperative problem solving, decision making, and an opportunity to challenge preconceived ideas

As they grow and experience more, their ideas change. Tai, whose drawing is shown in Figure 14–1, wants to be a babysitter. At age seven, being grown up may mean being a teenager who can take care of younger children as her sister does. Ten-year-old Elizabeth, whose drawing appears in Figure 14–2, already knows she is going to be a zoologist. She has developed an engrossing interest in animals and has a large collection of pets. She may very well continue this focus, but she could also branch out into other areas as she learns more about the adult world.

The school-age period is a good time to introduce children to adult jobs and workplaces. Although you may not have the equipment or resources to introduce children to advanced technology, you can help them experience a variety of jobs. Start with their interests. Listen to their conversations, watch their play, and observe what they draw. Implement their ideas through the use of theme units or special-interest clubs. Plan visits to local workplaces.

HELPING CHILDREN EXPLORE THE OPTIONS

The following activities represent only a small sample of the careers or job opportunities that might interest children. Use them as a starting point from which to develop experiences that will spark the enthusiasm of your particular group of youngsters. Have children work in small groups and share their results.

FIGURE 14–1 "When I grow up I want to be a babysitter." Tai, age 7.

FIGURE 14–2 "Feeding my bird." Elizabeth, age 10.

Activities

Map Maker (Cartographer)
Purposes:

- provide practice in portraying concrete objects as symbols on a map
- encourage cooperative problem solving
- increase awareness of spatial relationships
- reinforce math concepts of area, distance

Set up an interest center with a globe, an atlas, and maps of the area surrounding your school. Prepare activity cards asking the children to find specific places on the globe or map. Sample directions might include:

- Find the country we live in.
- Outline the state in which our city is situated.
- Find our school on the map.
- Find your street on the map.
- Mark a route from your home to school.
- How many blocks is it from your house to school? How many miles?
- How long does it take to drive from home to school? How long would it take if you were to walk?
- Where do your grandparents live? How many miles away?
- How long would it take to get to your grandparents' house in a car? By airplane?

Map your neighborhood. Provide children with notepads and pencils. Take them on a walk around the school neighborhood. Instruct them to write down distances in blocks. Tell them to note where buildings are located. When you return to school, have the children draw a map of your neighborhood on a large piece of paper.

Construct models of the buildings in your neighborhood to place on the map.

Equipment to Have Available for Map Making

- atlas, maps
- cardboard
- compass
- glue
- map maker
- marking pens
- paper, variety of sizes
- pencils
- rulers, measuring tape
- scissors
- T-square
- tape

Place the neighborhood map in the block area. Encourage children to use blocks to construct the buildings.

Call the planning office at your city hall and obtain a plot plan of the area around your center. Discuss the types of information shown on the print and how it is used.

Provide map puzzles. There are wooden and jigsaw puzzles of the United States available in toy stores, or you can contact your local history museum.

Construction Worker

Purposes:

- increase vocabulary to include words related to construction projects
- practice ability to translate an idea into a concrete object
- strengthen decision-making skills
- provide opportunities to work together cooperatively
- learn to use a variety of tools safely

Children enjoy using real tools related to carpentry or construction.

Let children plan and organize a workshop area.   Discuss the common tools needed to construct objects from wood. Supply the suggested tools, and demonstrate how each is used. Stress the safety precautions that must be observed. Ask the children to draft a set of rules for the care and use of tools.

Build an object from wood.   Provide different kinds of wood: soft pine, balsa, plywood, doweling. Encourage the children to develop their own ideas about what to construct. Show them how to plan a project by making a drawing of the finished product. Provide rulers to make exact measurements, emphasizing the importance of understanding mathematical concepts to have a good finished product. Have the children list the materials they will need, and then let them implement their project. Some possibilities are boxes for storing small items, a puppet theater, or games. They might also build boats, trucks, cars, airplanes, and a diorama setting for their models. Coordinate a woodworking project with map making by building a model of your neighborhood with wooden stores and houses.

Make a replica of a construction project.   Discuss different kinds of construction projects: home building, office complexes, freeway construction. Collect and display pictures of construction projects in progress and finished buildings. Provide toy replicas of equipment needed (earth movers, trucks, cement mixers) to construct the areas of a city. Encourage children to create a city in progress in the sandbox using houses from their woodworking projects.

Invite a carpenter to visit your class.   Ask him or her to bring special tools used on construction projects. Discuss the use of each of the tools, and allow the children to ask questions. They might ask: What are the qualifications for the job? What do you have to know to be able to do the job? What do you like about your job? What do you do each day?

Equipment to Have Available for Construction Working

- assorted nails and screws
- awl
- C-clamps
- hammers (11 to 13 ounces)
- level
- miter box, miter saw
- planes
- pliers
- rasp
- rulers, measuring tape, T-square
- safety glasses
- sandpaper, assorted grades
- sawhorses
- saws (coping, crosscut, rip)
- screwdrivers (slot and Phillips)
- vise
- wood pieces, assorted sizes and shapes
- wood glue
- workbench

Chefs Club

Purposes:

- provide opportunities to explore career options
- work cooperatively to prepare and serve a snack for the group
- strengthen group decision-making skills
- practice measuring using fractions and whole numbers

Develop a bulletin board of people cooking at home and in restaurants.   Ask children to contribute pictures of their family cooking together or pictures they have found in magazines. Encourage them to discuss what is needed to prepare a meal for a family or the patrons of a restaurant.

Visit a restaurant.   Talk to the chefs. Tell children to observe the processes for preparing meals. What do the chefs prepare ahead of time? What kinds of things have to be done just before serving a meal? Ask the chefs how or where they learned to cook. What do they have to know to be a chef? What are the qualifications for the job? What is the hardest part of their work? What do they like best?

Visit a bakery or factory that produces large quantities of a food product. Tell children to notice the kinds of equipment needed to automate food

Chef's Club members can work cooperatively to prepare a snack for the group.

production. Find out if computers are used to program the machinery. Interview a worker or supervisor. What are the qualifications for the job?

Prepare pizza for a snack. Set up an assembly line to prepare the pizzas. Use frozen bread dough, canned biscuits, English muffins, or bagels for the crust. At station one, have the children roll the bread dough or canned biscuits into rounds and placed on a cookie sheet. At station two, seasoned tomato sauce is spread on the rounds. (There are several kinds of pizza sauce available at any supermarket.) At station three, grate the cheese and sprinkle it over the tomato sauce. At station four, you can add additional toppings such as olives, mushrooms, pepperoni, or cooked sausage. Children at station five are responsible for putting the pizzas in the oven and watching them until they are done.

If large rounds of bread dough were used as the crust, the final station, six, must decide into what number of pieces to cut each pizza to serve the group.

Prepare a snack from a recipe that requires measuring. In Chapter 15, Figure 15–2 is a recipe for Navajo fry bread. Also, look for cookbooks with simple recipes. The NAEYC book *More Than Graham Crackers* listed at the end of Chapter 15 has many recipes that are designed for children.

Set up a restaurant and kitchen. Have children arrange an area of the room with a table and chairs plus a kitchen area where food can be prepared. They can create signs for the restaurant, decorate the table with flowers, and write a menu. Supply them with aprons and chefs' hats. Add tableware and some cookware. Some children can role play being the chef while others can be the waitstaff and patrons.

Equipment to Have Available for Chefs Club

- aprons, chefs' hats
- baking pans
- blender
- chopping boards
- electric frying pan
- ice cream maker
- knives
- measuring cups and spoons
- mixer, food processor
- mixing bowls
- oven
- pictures of food and food products
- popcorn popper
- pot holders
- recipe books
- rolling pins
- sponges, buckets for cleanup

- spoons
- spatulas
- tableware
- trays
- vegetable scrapers

Space Travel and Communication
Purposes:

- foster curiosity about the solar system
- increase knowledge about the U.S. space program
- challenge preconceived ideas about outer space
- strengthen the ability to think creatively

Design a space alien.   Research which planets have conditions that might support life. As an example: Venus has an atmosphere that is brownish yellow and is made up primarily of carbon dioxide gas with clouds of sulfuric acid. The temperature is around 880° Fahrenheit (470° Celsius). Design a space alien who could live in those conditions. Either draw a picture of the alien or construct one from papier-mâché or other materials.

Explore communication between astronauts and the ground.   Have children research the technology used to make Earth-to-space communication possible. Sources where children can write for information are cited in Chapter 12. Obtain pictures of a communication room at Cape Canaveral. Provide used circuit boards, computer equipment, and telephones. Encourage children to set up a communication center where they can role-play interactions between earth and a spaceship.

Build a space shuttle or spaceship.   Provide children with large pieces of cardboard or large packing boxes. Encourage them to design and build a spaceship. They can paint the outside and equip the inside with places for the astronauts to work. Place the spaceship near the communication center so the children can talk back and forth.

Brainstorm space travel in the future.   Ask children to imagine what space travel will be like in the future. Will people go into space as easily as they fly across the country? Will spaceships land and stay for a period of time on other planets? What part would they like to play in the space travel of the future? Ask them to write down their thoughts or draw a picture. Display the various responses.

Equipment to Have Available for Space Exploration

- aluminum foil
- balloons
- books, posters, photos from NASA

- cardboard pieces
- colored marking pens, crayons, art paper
- duct tape
- glue
- old computers, keyboards
- packing boxes
- paint and brushes (black, silver, white)
- papier-mâché
- plastic tubing
- ruler, yard stick, tape measure
- telephone, microphones
- wires

Environmental Conservationists
Purposes:

- develop awareness of environmental issues
- strengthen ability to plan and carry through a long-term project
- practice cooperative problem solving
- increase ability to communicate ideas

Create a bulletin board showing environmental issues.   Examples are images of burning rain forests, soil erosion because of logging, and polluted streams or lakes. In conjunction with a study of weather, investigate how these practices affect not only the immediate environment but also the global environment. Ask children to brainstorm alternatives to these harmful practices. Write down their responses, and include that information on the bulletin board.

Increase pollution awareness.   Have children write to companies that have the potential for polluting their communities. What are they currently doing to eliminate pollution? Are there additional plans as information becomes available and technology advances? What would the children do when they are adults to prevent environmental pollution?

Start an ecology club.   Let the children choose interest areas concerning the environment: ozone layer, smog, greenhouse effect, nuclear waste, solar energy, lasers, and sound waves. Have them research what these elements might be doing to the environment and what is being done to prevent further damage.

Compile a scrapbook.   Have children collect newspaper or magazine articles on the destruction or preservation of natural resources: rivers, forests, lakes, wilderness areas, animal habitats. Classify the information according to the kind of resource. Compile a large scrapbook of the articles, and leave it in the reading corner for children to browse at leisure.

Analyze food packaging for potential harm to the environment.   Examples are candy wrappings that contain a plastic wrap inside a cardboard

It is important to develop awareness of environmental issues in children.

box. All sorts of foods are sold or packaged in Styrofoam, which does not biodegrade. When the Styrofoam breaks up, wildlife can eat it. Plastic rings that hold six packs of drinks can strangle birds and fish. Have children write to companies that make these products or publish an article about the issue in the child care center newspaper.

Concerned Consumers
Purposes:

- increase ability to infer results based on previous information
- think creatively when finding new uses for household objects
- communicate information and ideas to others

Survey packaging materials that are biodegradable or nonbiodegradable.   Explain to the children the meaning of the words biodegradable and nonbiodegradable. **Biodegradable** refers to those objects that will disintegrate over time such as paper, food scraps, and garden clippings. **Nonbiodegradable** refers to objects that will not disintegrate such as plastic, metal, and Styrofoam. Ask the children to think of things they have at home that fit into the two categories. Group the children in twos or threes and tell them that each group will survey an aisle in the grocery store. Take a trip to a nearby store. (Get permission from the store manager before planning this trip.) Provide children with paper, pencils, and clipboards or other firm surfaces to write on. Assign each group an aisle of the store. Tell them to go slowly through the items on the shelves, noting things that are packaged in biodegradable and nonbiodegradable packaging. After the grocery store trip, discuss the information they have gathered back at the

biodegradable
objects that disintegrate over time

nonbiodegradable
objects that will not disintegrate over time

center. Can they think of better ways to avoid filling the environment with trash that will still be around many years into the future?

Sort items into biodegradable and nonbiodegradable. Collect items and ask children to bring in empty boxes, bags, or other materials that were used to package goods. Have the children sort these materials into piles according to their degradability.

Survey the trash at the child care center. Have children collect the contents of the classroom wastebaskets in plastic bags. Sort the contents according to those that could be reused and those that can be sent to a recycling center. Ask the children for their suggestions on how to decrease the amount of trash. Have them prepare a list of suggestions to distribute to the school.

Test the biodegradability of several items. Have children dig one hole for each item in an unused part of the playground. Pour some water in the hole and let it soak into the ground. Place one object in each hole and cover it with dirt. Mark the places with small signs to show what is buried there. Some suggestions for items to bury are: newspaper, egg carton, tin can, plastic food carton, paper bag. Have the children predict which items will deteriorate. Dig up the objects at the end of 30 days. How accurate were their predictions? Would some of the items degrade if they were left longer?

Recycle household objects. Ask children to bring one object from home that would have been thrown away. Place all the objects on a table, and ask children to think of things that could be done with each. Provide any additional materials they need to make useful items from the objects. Some things children might make are sand shovels from plastic bottles; a paint applicator from roll-on deodorant bottles; a rocket from an oatmeal box; or towers from painted cans of all sizes to add interest to block buildings. A large variety of objects can also be used to create sculptures or other art projects.

Equipment to Have Available for Consumer Awareness

- bulletin board
- computer
- cups, bowls
- glue
- newspapers, magazines
- paper, pencils
- scale, balance or digital
- scissors
- scrapbooks
- shovels, buckets

- tape: masking, duct, cellophane
- tape recorder

Advertising
Purposes:

- develop critical thinking skills
- evaluate and challenge preconceived ideas
- increase ability to observe objectively
- communicate information to others

Develop children's awareness of how television shapes our buying habits.   Ask children to think about the commercials they remember from watching television. Talk about the claims made by the ads. Discuss the purpose of the ads. Did the ads make them want to buy the product?

To further children's awareness, record a half-hour children's television show and view it with the children. Have them keep track of the number of commercials and the amount of time devoted to them. Discuss their reactions to the commercials. Do they want to buy the product? Why or why not? Do they believe the claims in the ads? Are there distortions in the way the product is shown? Discuss how television creates illusions when showing products.

Ask children to bring from home something they bought or had their parents buy after seeing a television ad. Ask them to write an ad that is honest but would make people want to buy the product. Have them read their ads aloud and post them on a bulletin board.

Set up a product testing lab.   Bring in several products that would be found in most households. Allow children to test and compare the different brands. For example, test two brands of paper towels, each claiming to be strong and absorb more water. Ask children to decide how they can test those claims. Pour the same amount of water on each and pull the edges. Which paper towel held up without tearing? Another example: Certain cereals claim to contain more raisins per serving. Select two brands and pour out the contents into two large bowls. Have children count the number of raisins in each. Yet another example: Two brands of chocolate chip cookies claim to have more chips per cookie. Ask the children how they can test that claim. (Dissolve the cookie in water, then extract the chips for counting.) Ask the children for other possibilities for testing, then implement those ideas.

Taste-test products children are familiar with through advertising.   Select one product to compare, such as crackers, cola, or canned fruit. Choose several brands of the product. Cover the outside of each of the items so they cannot be identified, and label each with a number or letter. Provide children with a cup, a bowl, and a spoon. You will also need a serving spoon for fruit or other products that need to be spooned. Ask the children to take small portions of each item, then rate each product. Use a numerical scale or the labels Best, OK, Not Good to show their assessment of each. Did they all agree which one was best, or were there differences?

Solicit ads for newspaper publication.   Ask children to survey other adults at the center or their parents to see if they want to place an ad in the center's newspaper. Have the children write the ad copy and include any appropriate artwork. If a computer is available, they can find clip art for this purpose. They can also cut and paste pictures on their ads for photocopying later.

Equipment to Have Available for Advertising

- computer, word-processing program, clip art
- bowls, spoons
- paper
- pens, pencils
- videotape player, television

Newspaper Publication
Purposes:

- work cooperatively on a common task
- increase decision-making skills
- plan and organize a series of tasks
- increase writing and communication skills

Write, edit, and publish a newspaper.   Have the children plan the various tasks: reporter, editor, photographer, illustrator, cartoonists, and production staff. Discuss the length of the paper and when it will be published. Have them set a schedule for completing tasks. They can interview adults in the center, obtain interesting stories from other children, gather information from their parents, or write an editorial on a topic pertinent to the center. Produce the paper and distribute it to other classrooms and parents.

Plan a trip to a local newspaper office.   Arrange to visit a newspaper office, and schedule interviews with several employees. Prepare children by asking them to think of questions they would like to ask. They might want to know how someone becomes a reporter or what are the most exciting parts of the job. How are other jobs they see being performed important to the final product? What are the best and most difficult parts of any of the job categories? Follow up the visit with a discussion of the complex process of producing a newspaper and what kinds of jobs they might like to prepare for.

Equipment to Have Available for Newspaper Work

- camera
- colored marking pens

- computer, word-processing program, printer, scanner
- newspapers
- paper (printer and drawing)
- tape recorder

Scientist
Purposes:

- increase awareness of the different fields of scientific study
- develop familiarity with research devices
- provide experience in using a variety of scientific tools
- stimulate curiosity about the sciences

Scientist for a day.   Provide a variety of tools that scientists use, such as a microscope and prepared slides, telescope, metal detector, compass, barometer, or rain gauge. Teach the children how to use these devices, then allow them to experiment freely. Ask them to imagine the kinds of scientists who would use the devices and what types of information they may be able to find.

Visit a site where scientific devices are used.   For example, you can visit a weather station, a university research lab, a water-treatment plant, a company with a research component, or any other appropriate site in your community. Arrange to have an employee at the site explain how the devices fit into the overall purposes of the facility and what are the qualifications for workers.

Encourage children to develop familiarity with research devices.

Equipment to Have Available for Scientists

- barometer
- compass
- metal detector
- microscope, prepared and blank slides
- telescope

GUIDELINES FOR CHILD CARE STAFF MEMBERS

As children participate in curriculum activities, encourage them to practice the skills suggested by Toffler. He said workers of the future will need to take an active role in decision making, resolve problems, and challenge preconceived assumptions. The following list includes Toffler's suggestions as well as some additional ones.

Future workers will probably need to be able to:

- solve problems
- work cooperatively

- make decisions
- understand spatial relationships
- think creatively
- read and speak fluently
- practice safety procedures
- plan for use of time and materials
- operate complex and technological equipment
- use a variety of tools
- be accurate and precise
- be able to be retrained for a new career
- evaluate and challenge preconceived ideas
- have a college degree or advanced specialty training

When you invite speakers to visit your center, prepare the speaker by suggesting topics of special interest to the children. Set a time limit. Ask the presenter to bring visual materials whenever possible: pictures, videos, tools, or instruments are some examples. Ask the children to think of questions they might want answered.

Plan just as carefully for visits to community workplaces. Visit the site yourself, and determine what will be of interest to your group. Talk to the person in charge to plan exactly what the children will see. Prepare the children by describing what will happen on the visit, and follow up with a discussion at your center.

One of the exciting aspects of working with school-age children is that they are such avid learners. They want to explore the world outside of their own families, schools, or neighborhoods. They are eager to be competent and will work diligently to accomplish difficult tasks. You can capitalize on these characteristics when you plan your curriculum. In addition, you are helping to prepare these young people for their future as adult workers in a complex global society.

SUMMARY

- Future workers will have to manage complex technology and will need skills that allow them to take an active role in a changing global society.

- Practice in work-related skills can be built into the activities at a child care center.

- The theoretical concepts of industrial technology can best be presented to the school-age child through relatively simple activities.

- Invite speakers to visit your center to talk about their jobs.

- Arrange field trips to community workplaces. Follow up the visit with a discussion.

KEY TERMS

biodegradable   meaning-based experiences   nonbiodegradable

REVIEW QUESTIONS

1. Why is it important to expose children to a variety of adult work roles?

2. When do children begin developing ideas about what they will be when they grow up?

3. List several activities related to map making.

4. Describe how to set up a production line for the preparation of pizza for a snack.

5. Name two activities to help children become aware of how to decrease the amount of trash they accumulate.

6. List five characteristics future workers will need.

7. Do you agree with Toffler's premise that future workers will have to take a more active role? Write several sentences supporting your answer.

8. List guidelines for planning and implementing a field trip to a community workplace.

During group time, the children in Vera and John's room were discussing what they wanted to be when they grew up. Amy declared she wanted to be a nurse. Seth said he wanted to be a gardener and take care of people's yards like his dad did. Evan loudly declared that those were "dumb" jobs, and that he was going to be a doctor so he could make a lot of money.

1. Would you respond in any way to Evan's choice of a job based on the amount of money he could make? If so, what would you say?

2. What could you say to Amy and Seth?

3. How could you help each of these children broaden their thinking about their future?

STUDENT ACTIVITIES

1. Survey your child care group concerning what they want to be when they grow up. Are their interests similar to or different from those discussed in this chapter?

2. Visit your community library. List available resources you could use in planning this curriculum area. Besides books, does the library have videos, films, or recordings?

3. Plan a field trip to a work site in your community. Choose a company that uses computers to automate production.

4. Discuss with your parents and grandparents any changes they have seen during their lifetime in regard to modes of travel and communication or advances in science or medicine. Find out what their lives were like without these technological advances. Share this information with a group of children.

SUGGESTED READINGS

D'Amico, J., & Drummond, K. (1996). *The Science Chef Travels Around the World—Fun Food Experiments and Recipes for Kids.* New York: John Wiley & Sons.

Gardner, R. (1994). *Science Projects About Chemistry.* Springfield, NJ: Enslow.

Kenda, M., & Williams, P., 2nd ed. (2009). *Science Wizardry for Kids.* Hauppauge, NY: Barron's Educational Series.

Petty, K., & J. Maizels (2002). *The Super Science Book.* Cornwall, UK: Bodley Head Children's Books.

Robinson, T. (2001). *The Everything Kids' Science Experiments Book.* Cincinnati, OH: F+W Publications, Inc.

Roth, J. A. (advisor) (2007). *Just Add Water: Science Projects You Can Sink.* New York: Scholastic Childrens Press.

WEB RESOURCES

action.sierraclub.org/site/PageServer?pagename=bookshome
Books for children and adults on environmental issues.

careerplanning.about.com
Helping children make career choices.

REFERENCES

Toffler, A. (1990). *Powershift: Knowledge, Wealth, and Violence on the Edge of the 21st Century.* New York: Bantam.

Toffler, A. (2009) *Revolutionary Wealth.* Knopf Doubleday: New York, NY.

15

Getting Fit, Staying Fit

HOW HEALTHY ARE OUR CHILDREN?

Health-care providers, teachers, and child care workers frequently see children who are obviously in poor health or who do not get needed medical treatment. Approximately 19 percent of children live in families with incomes below the poverty level, and these families have no health insurance coverage. Consequently, the children suffer from a variety of **chronic health conditions** (Children's Defense Fund, 2008) including obesity, asthma, oral problems, and food allergies. Child care professionals know that good health and overall fitness are essential to children's development and achievement. Caregivers are committed to helping children overcome these circumstances.

Children's Health Conditions

Caregivers and the children themselves need to understand the impact of chronic conditions on the ability of children to function and thrive, as well as how to prevent or ameliorate these problems.

Obesity

In Chapter 4 you read that between 16 and 33 percent of American children between the ages of 12 and 19 are obese. Overweight children are at higher risk for a variety of health problems, including increased blood pressure and blood cholesterol levels. These children may also have orthopedic or respiratory problems. In addition, they cannot keep up with their peers during active play, and frequently suffer from poor self-esteem.

LEARNING OUTCOMES

After reading this chapter, you should be able to:

✔ Discuss the physical health and common chronic health conditions of children in the United States.

✔ Plan and implement age-appropriate nutritional activities.

✔ Plan and implement age-appropriate fitness experiences.

✔ State suggestions for caregivers when implementing a fitness program.

Asthma

Asthma is a chronic health condition that affects almost 5 million children (Children's Defense Fund, 2004). This illness can be minor or life-threatening, ranging from mild shortness of breath to chest pain and an inability to breathe that necessitates a visit to an emergency department. Many things can trigger attacks, such as irritants (smoke or strong odors), dust (dust mites, molds), exercise, upper respiratory infections, and even the weather. It helps to keep a record of asthma attacks to determine what seemed to trigger them and avoid them in the future.

Oral Health

The Children's Defense Fund has published some shocking statistics about children's oral health. Their information indicates that more than half of all children ages six to eight and 78 percent of all 17-year-olds have untreated dental problems. Dental problems should be taken seriously because they can progress into infections and abscesses. Some children fail to consume adequate diets because their teeth hurt.

Food Allergies

Food allergies affect about 5 to 8 percent of young children. Some will outgrow these allergies, but others will continue to be affected (KeepKidsHealthy. com). Symptoms include wheezing, breathing difficulty, itchy skin rashes, nausea, abdominal pain, and swelling of the mouth and throat. Symptoms may be mild or severe depending upon how much of the allergen the child ingests. The most common foods that cause allergies include: peanuts, tree nuts, fish, shellfish, eggs, milk, soy, and wheat. As with asthma, it helps to keep a record of the foods that seem to have caused a reaction to avoid a recurrence.

Helping Children with Chronic Health Problems

It is important to provide children with experiences that foster attitudes and practices that will improve their well-being. You can also give them knowledge that will enable them to continue these practices throughout their lifetimes.

- Because snack time is already a part of every session in after-school child care, it is a good place to start. Teach children what their bodies need to stay healthy and what foods may cause allergic reactions.
- Help children plan to make changes in their food habits. Ask them to decide on one change, making it as specific as possible. They may decide to change the kinds of snacks they consume rather than eliminating all snacks.
- Take responsibility for providing nutritious snacks each day that are not high in fat or sugar. This may involve being creative at times to avoid the foods that cause allergies in some children, but it will be worth the effort. Fruits, vegetables, whole-grain breads, cottage

chronic health condition
conditions that last 12 months or more and create some limitations in activity

cheese or yogurt, whole-grain cereals, and nuts or nut butters all can make flavorful and nutritious snacks. (Note: some of the foods on this list do cause allergies, so choose carefully.)

PLANNING NUTRITIOUS COOKING ACTIVITIES

An effective way to help children change their food habits is to involve them in food-related activities.

Activities

Good Food, Good Health

Purposes:

- increase ability to make informed decisions about food choices
- expand knowledge of nutritional requirements
- encourage participation in planning food for snacks

Teach children what their bodies need to stay healthy. Prepare a bulletin board that shows the **food guide pyramid** with its new name **MyPyramid**. This latest version highlights the inclusion of personalized food plans for adults, children, and the elderly. MyPyramid for Kids has information and games specifically geared to school-aged children (My Pyramid.gov.) Encourage the children to consider their own diet. How many food groups did they have for breakfast? How many are in today's snack? What are some things they could have for a snack that would be nutritious? The food guide pyramid is shown in Figure 15–1.

food guide pyramid
U.S. Department of Agriculture guide to healthy food choices and number of servings per day

MyPyramid
new name for food guide pyramid

Health and overall fitness are essential to children's growth and development.

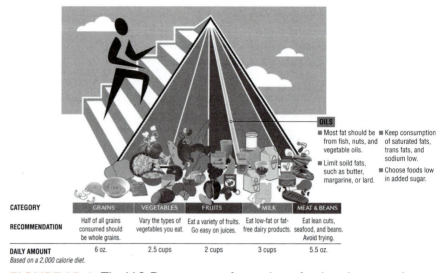

CATEGORY	GRAINS	VEGETABLES	FRUITS	MILK	MEAT & BEANS
RECOMMENDATION	Half of all grains consumed should be whole grains.	Vary the types of vegetables you eat.	Eat a variety of fruits. Go easy on juices.	Eat low-fat or fat-free dairy products.	Eat lean cuts, seafood, and beans. Avoid frying.
DAILY AMOUNT	6 oz.	2.5 cups	2 cups	3 cups	5.5 oz.

Based on a 2,000 calorie diet.

FIGURE 15–1 The U.S. Department of agriculture food guide pyramid.

Navajo Fry Bread

Purposes:

- increase cultural awareness
- practice math concepts by measuring ingredients
- foster cooperation

Prepare a snack of Navajo fry bread. This is a snack that represents a culture and can be prepared fairly quickly by hungry children. Assign two or three children to do the initial measuring and mixing. Divide the dough in half, allowing two more children to roll it out and cut it. Two more children can be assigned to fry the finished squares.

CAUTION: Be sure to set up the preparation area to allow maximum safety. Place the electric frying pan on a table. Extend the cord from the pan to a convenient wall outlet, then push the table against the wall. The cord will be out of the way so children will not trip on it. Caution the children not to touch the hot pan and to use long-handled tongs to turn the bread. Supervise carefully when the frying is taking place. See Figure 15–2 for the recipe.

Fancy Five Sandwiches

Purposes:

- reinforce knowledge of foods from the food guide pyramid
- expand experiences with different foods
- communicate information about choices to others

Provide the following foods from the MyPyramid:

- Bread: whole wheat bread, wheat pita bread, whole wheat tortillas
- Fruits and vegetables: cucumbers, tomatoes, bananas, raisins, apples, sprouts
- Meats and meat substitutes: peanut butter, hard-cooked eggs, sliced turkey

---

Navajo Fry Bread Recipe

1 cup whole wheat flour
1 teaspoon baking powder
1/2 teaspoon salt
1/2 cup lukewarm water
8 to 10 tablespoons salad oil for frying

Sift the flour, baking powder, and salt together into a bowl. Stir in the water, then use your fingers to finish the mixing. Knead the dough with the heel of your hand, dusting it with flour if it gets sticky.

Roll out the dough to 1/4 inch thickness. Cut it into squares.

Pour the oil into an electric skillet. (Use just enough to coat the bottom of the pan.)

When it is hot, but not smoking, quickly fry the squares of dough a few at a time.

Using a long-handled slotted spoon, brown one side, then turn them over and brown the other. When browned and puffed up, remove from the pan and place them on a paper towel. Serve them with honey or jam.

The recipe makes about 24 fry bread squares.

FIGURE 15–2 Navajo fry bread recipe.

- Milk: low-fat Swiss cheese, low-fat cheddar cheese, low-fat cottage cheese
- Fats: low-fat mayonnaise or margarine.

Group the foods on trays labeled with their group name. Allow each child to make a sandwich using as many of the food groups as possible. During snack time have each child describe his or her sandwich and name the food groups.

Taste Trip
Purposes:

- increase cultural awareness and appreciation
- expand food preferences

Select foods from several different countries. Set them out on trays with labels indicating where they are from. Encourage children to taste several items and write their reactions. The following are some suggested foods, but you can visit your local supermarket to find others.

- From Haiti: mango; peel, slice, and add to fruit cups
- From Central and South America: burro banana; add to salads or fruit cups
- From Hawaii: papaya; cut in half, seed, peel, and slice
- From Japan: Asian pear; eat raw or bake
- From Mexico: cactus pears; peel and eat or add to salads
- From New Zealand: feijoa (also called pineapple guava); peel and slice
- From New Zealand: kiwi fruit; serve in thin slices peeled or unpeeled
- From New Zealand: passion fruit; scoop out pulp and serve over yogurt
- From China: lichee fruit; buy in cans at most supermarkets

- From Mexico: jicama; peel and slice, serve with a seasoned cottage cheese dip
- From East Indies, Haiti, or Mexico: mango; peel and slice
- From South America or Hawaii: pineapple; peel, core, and cut into chunks

Menu Planning
Purposes:

- expand ability to make cooperative decisions
- practice mathematical calculations when determining how much to buy
- use food pyramid to make food choices

Plan snacks for a week. Appoint a committee of children to plan nutritious snacks for a week. Instruct them to include items from at least two food groups. When they have completed their menu, ask them to make a shopping list of the required ingredients. They may have to consult cookbooks or ask someone to help them determine quantities. If you have a cook at your center, he would be a good resource person. Schedule a trip to the supermarket to purchase the food. See the reading list at the end of this chapter for books that contain recipes, and find a list of scrumptious snacks in Figure 15–3.

Apple slices, peanut butter, raisins
Assorted raw vegetables with seasoned cottage-cheese dip
Banana slices—dip in honey, roll in nuts
Celery stuffed with peanut butter or cheese spread
Cheese balls—form balls with softened cheese, roll in chopped nuts
Cottage cheese with fruit
Deviled eggs—add yogurt, mustard, salt, and pepper to the yolk
Fresh fruit gelatin—any fruit in season; do not use kiwi or fresh pineapple
Fruit kabobs—banana wheels, pineapple chunks, cherries, strawberries, orange wedges
Fruit shakes—blend fruit and nonfat dry milk in blender with a few ice cubes
Graham crackers, peanut butter, and applesauce
Granola or Grape-nuts® sprinkled on yogurt
Ice cream with fruit—in milk shakes or in make-your-own sundaes
Nachos—tortilla wedges, refried beans, cheddar cheese. Heat in microwave oven until cheese melts.
Nut bread with cheese spread
Peanut butter on whole wheat bread with raisins, dates, apples, banana, applesauce, chopped celery, shredded carrots
Pizza—use pizza dough or English muffins, add pizza sauce, cooked ground meat, cheese, tomatoes, mushrooms, chopped bell peppers, olives
Tacos or burritos—fill with cheese, leftover meat, sliced tomatoes
Tiny meatballs made with ground meat, rice, and seasoning
Wheat toast with tuna salad or cheese, broiled to melt
Yogurt with fruit

FIGURE 15–3 Scrumptious snacks.

Plan nutritious snacks that include items from at least two food groups.

Ice Cream in a Bucket

Purposes:

- observe the physical changes that take place when the mixture freezes
- participate in a group effort to achieve a goal

Make ice cream in a bucket. Most children have never had the opportunity to make homemade ice cream, and this is a unique experience. The recipe shown in Figure 15–4 gives the directions.

As a variation to this method, use one of the ice-cream makers that are on the market. Several types are electric, and one operates with a handle that must be turned. The hand-operated freezer is ideal for making frozen yogurt. Just mix crushed fresh fruit with plain yogurt, add a small amount of sugar or honey, and pour it into the container. Freeze according to the machine's directions.

Parent Demonstration

Purposes:

- increase awareness of the cultural meanings of food preferences
- expand food experiences to include those from other countries

Invite a parent to cook a favorite recipe that is representative of her culture. Demonstrate how the food is prepared and cooked. Let children taste the final product. Note: Discuss the food with the parent before the presentation. Remind her that it has to be something simple that can be prepared quickly. Hungry children will not want to wait too long before tasting. Consider also the constraints of your facility. Where will the food be prepared? Will it be safe? Do you have an oven, a frying pan, or whatever else will be required? Ask the parent to choose a food that children enjoy. Have the parent

You need:
a large plastic bucket
a one-pound coffee can with a plastic lid
2 cups of rock salt
Beat together in the coffee can:
1 egg
1/4 cup honey
Add 1 cup milk
1/2 cup cream
1 teaspoon vanilla
dash of salt
Be sure the coffee can is only half-full or the ice cream will spill over the sides as you freeze it.
Put a layer of ice in the bottom of the pail. Crushed ice freezes faster, but cubes will work also. Sprinkle the ice with part of the salt. Put the lid on the coffee can and set the can on top of the ice. Pack more salt and ice in the pail around the sides of the can. Sprinkle layers of ice with salt as you fill the bucket. When the ice is almost to the top of the can, take off the plastic lid. Stir the ice-cream mixture around and around with a big wooden spoon, letting the can turn too. Keep on stirring and watching. Let the children take turns with stirring because it will take from 15 to 30 minutes for the ice cream to freeze to mush. You will probably want to eat it right away while it is soft. If you want to wait until it hardens, put more ice and salt around the can and let it sit for an hour or two.
This recipe will serve four to five children. You will probably want to make more than one batch. Also if you are concerned about possible salmonella bacteria in the raw egg, you can coddle it. Heat water to 140 degrees. Pour enough water into a cup to completely cover the egg. Let it stand for one minute. Any bacteria will be killed and the egg will not cook.

FIGURE 15–4 Ice cream in a bucket.

explain whether this is a dish the family might eat frequently or if it is served only on special occasions. Some possibilities are:

- An Asian stir-fry dish—provide chopsticks and ask the parent to demonstrate how to use them
- Mexican burritos with homemade salsa
- Japanese noodles and vegetables
- Jewish potato latkes or cheese blintzes
- Indian puri
- Spanish sopapillas

Cookbook
Purposes:

- cooperative effort to achieve a goal
- increase reading and writing skills
- plan and carry out a long-term project

Compile a book of the children's favorite recipes–either those they have prepared at school or the ones they eat at home. The children may have to consult a cookbook or ask their parents for help with this. Use a computer to type the recipes and make copies for each child in your group. Use a loose-leaf binder to collect and preserve the recipes. Let each child decorate a cover for their book or add drawings of the food. You can also use a digital camera to take pictures of dishes ready to be served.

Cook, Cook, Cook
Purposes:

- reinforce knowledge of nutritional requirements for health and fitness
- practice in decision-making skills
- experience foods from different cultures

Involve children in cooking projects often. Each experience is an opportunity to reinforce good nutrition and the importance of making appropriate food choices. These experiences also offer an opportunity for children to broaden their tastes and try foods from different cultures.

Japanese Rice Balls

1 cup short-grain white rice
1½ cups water
salt
pickled Japanese plum
seaweed (optional)

Put rice in a saucepan and add water. Soak for 30 minutes, then cook until all the water is absorbed. Let the rice cool with the pan covered for about five minutes or until it is cool enough to handle. (You can use pre-cooked, cold rice if no stove is available.) Tell children to wet their hands and take a scoop of rice. Form the rice into a ball and make a hole in the middle. Place a pickled Japanese plum in the hole. If you wish, wrap the ball with a piece of nori (seaweed).

Flour Tortillas

4 cups whole wheat flour
1 teaspoon salt
⅓ cup vegetable oil
approximately 1 cup warm water

Mix the flour and salt: add oil, mix together with fingers. Stir in enough water to make a firm ball. Knead the dough until it is smooth, then let it rest for 20 minutes. Pinch off a golf-ball size piece of the dough. Roll it out on a floured board until it is 4 inches in diameter. Cook on an unoiled griddle for about 2 minutes on each side.

Equipment to Have Available

You will need some equipment for food preparation or cooking. If your center has a kitchen, most items will be available there. If not, accumulate the basics and add to them as your children become more involved in their culinary projects. The number of each item that you require will depend on the size of your group of children.

- bottle and can opener
- bowls, several sizes for mixing ingredients
- cake pans, both sheet and layer pans, muffin tins
- colander, strainer, flour sifter
- cookie cutter, cookie sheets
- cutting boards, plastic or wooden, large boards and individual size
- eggbeaters, scrapers
- fork, tongs, both long-handled
- gelatin molds, both single and individual
- grater, four-sided is best for children to hold
- hot plate
- knives, serrated for greater safety (if ends are pointed, round them with a tool grinder)
- measuring spoons, liquid and dry measuring cups
- pancake turner, spatula, wooden and slotted spoons
- pastry brushes
- potato masher
- saucepans
- rolling pin (you can also use pieces of dowel)
- skillet (electric)
- timer
- vegetable peeler, apple corer
- computer for copying recipes
- printer
- digital camera

When you can, add the following:

- corn popper
- electric blender and mixer
- electric food processor
- ice-cream freezer
- portable bake oven

Schedule exercise sessions before snack time.

GETTING FIT, STAYING FIT

The kinds of outdoor play experiences available to children today are vastly different from those of the past. Many children live in apartments in urban areas where there is little or no space to play. Even in residential areas where there are yards, many children do not go outdoors because of fear for their safety—or because they would rather sit indoors watching television. Even when children are outdoors, studies show they are not active enough to raise their heart rates for very long periods of time. The Centers for Disease Control and Prevention (CDC) conducted a longitudinal study and launched the Youth Media Campaign that was reported in the Morbidity and Mortality Weekly Report (2003). The study found that 61.5 percent of children ages 9 to 13 do not participate in any physical activity during school hours. During after-school time, only 22.6 percent do any physical activity. The high rate of obesity among young children and teenagers certainly indicates a lack of fitness. Obesity is discussed at length in Chapter 4.

Although an after-school child care program provides a safe place where children can play outdoors, there is still a need to institute an exercise regimen. The fitness statistics described at the beginning of this chapter indicate that children are far from fit. Many children do not conform to the standard of fitness described by the American Alliance for Health, Physical Education, Recreation, and Dance **(AAHPERD)** (1995). The alliance describes fitness as a physical state of well-being that allows people to:

- perform daily activities with vigor
- reduce their risk of health problems related to lack of exercise
- establish a fitness base for participation in a variety of physical activities

Their standards address several components: aerobic endurance, body composition (proportion of fat and lean), muscular strength, and flexibility. A good fitness program will address all of these. In addition, exercise can also relieve some of the tensions children feel because of the pressures of school or family problems.

AAHPERD
American Alliance for Health, Physical Education, Recreation, and Dance: develops standards for aerobic endurance, muscular strength, and flexibility that indicate fitness

Planning Fitness Experiences and Activities

Exercise does not have to be an organized activity, but includes encouraging children to be active during outdoor time or in the classroom. Have equipment that stimulates active play readily available in the outdoor play area. Include several jump ropes, short ones and longer ones. Individual children can jump or they can organize a game with several participants. Large balls, small balls, and Nerf balls can be used by an individual child or children playing together. Design an obstacle course using the balance beam, a rope ladder on the ground, a small hill to traverse, a tunnel to crawl into (use a section of large concrete pipe), and a line of boulders on which to walk. The course can be changed as children develop their skills in traversing it. There are several websites that offer DVDs or activities to get children moving.

At **http://fitnessbeginnings.com** you can find DVDS that children will enjoy. A sample of the offerings at this site are:

- Mark Rothstein's World of Rope Jumping
- Denise Austen's Fit Kid
- Bayou–That Hot New Dance Workout

Another website that has exercise activities for children is **http://www .heart.org/HEARTORG.** Among other resources, this site offers:

- Jumping Rope for Heart
- Hoops for Heart
- Information on nutrition for healthy kids
- Suggestions for parents to help their children be active
- Activities for children with cardiovascular disease

Allow children to choose an activity according to their developmental capabilities or fitness level.

Equipment to Have Available

In addition to exercises, there are some simple pieces of equipment that will encourage children to participate in physical activities. They are not expensive, and in fact may already be in your center.

- Jump ropes. Have several so more than one child can jump at a time. Have at least one that is long enough for two children to hold while others jump.
- Beach balls, gigantic balls. Children can throw or roll on the balls.
- Nerf balls. Use with paddles described in Chapter 10 (PomPom Paddle Ball). Imagine a volleyball game played with a Nerf ball and nylon paddles!
- Hoops. Children can jump in and out. Lay hoops in patterns on the floor so children have to hop or jump from one to the other.
- Frisbees®. Can be played by two or more children.
- Balance beam. You can find a low beam in many school equipment catalogs, and they are simple to make. Children can walk across the beams with eyes open or closed. Have them try to walk across holding a plastic or wooden egg in a spoon.
- Use natural elements such as a line of boulders that children can walk across.
- DVD player and exercise DVDs available from above websites.

GUIDELINES FOR CHILD CARE STAFF MEMBERS

Remember that cooking and eating food should be fun. Do not pressure children to taste unfamiliar foods. If you keep offering interesting varieties, their curiosity will probably get the better of them. Also, they will see that others try out those strange things you bring to class, and they may want to get involved.

Set up a cooking environment with the maximum safety in mind. Position the cooking table against a wall, with the electrical cord behind the table and out of the way. Teach children the rules and how to accomplish the tasks safely. Children are quite capable of cutting up vegetables without getting hurt and using an electric frying pan without getting burned. (We, the authors, have used both knives and frying pans with preschoolers without mishap.) Supervise them closely, and never leave an area where children are cooking.

Try not to impose your own food likes and dislikes on children. If you really hate a particular food, do not include it. You may think you can hide your dislike from the children, but they will sense it.

Be a good role model. Do everything you can to be healthy yourself. Demonstrate good eating habits by bringing only healthful foods to the center for yourself.

Provide a variety of activities and materials that encourage active play. Tag games, ball games, jump rope, follow-the-leader, and obstacle courses are all possible physical activities that can be incorporated into the daily program.

Equipment can encourage children to participate in physical activities.

Allow children to choose an activity according to their developmental capabilities or fitness level. A vertical ladder leading to a high piece of climbing equipment may be too difficult or intimidating to the youngest children. They might be able to master a short ladder leading to a low platform. Young children can hit a ball on a support, while older children may be ready to try hitting a ball when it is pitched to them.

Set up active play stations indoors and outdoors. Chapter 10 includes suggestions for active games to be played indoors. Begin with those and add others of your own design. Install basketball hoops outdoors at different heights, and provide places to toss balls at a target, a place from which to jump, or cement areas for skating.

Allow ample opportunities for children to practice skills. This means having more than one ball or organizing activities for a small number of children. Only-one-ball or large-team games entail children waiting idly for a turn with little chance to participate and practice.

Enjoy exercising yourself and children will enjoy it. Avoid any comparisons or competition.

This is not a time to see who can do the most sit-ups or jump the highest. Be careful not to use phrases such as "Let's see who can keep the ball in the air the longest." Simply say "Keep the ball in the air as long as possible."

Encourage parents to use health-care resources for themselves and their children. Find out what is available in your community and share this information with parents.

Be an advocate for good health programs and policies for children. Join professional organizations that will lobby for health programs. Speak or write to local government officials about the need to protect children.

Volunteer for health-related events in your community. Include your child care group when you can. Health fairs, running, or bicycling events are some examples.

The health of children is too important to be overlooked.

SUMMARY

- Health-care providers, teachers, and child care workers all see children who are overweight and have chronic health conditions such as asthma, allergies, and ear infections.

- As a child care worker, you can provide children with experiences that foster attitudes and practices that improve their health.

- One way to develop health consciousness is to introduce children to the MyPyramid for Kids and help them plan and prepare nutritious snacks.

- Although children who are in child care spend time each day playing outdoors, there is still a need to focus on fitness.

- There are some simple pieces of equipment that encourage children to engage in physical activity: balls, hula hoops, jump ropes, balance beams and frisbees.

- Suggestions for caregivers who are instituting a good food program include making it fun, insuring safety, and being a good role model.

- Be an advocate for good health programs in your community by participating in health-related community events.

KEY TERMS

AAHPERD   food guide pyramid   MyPyramid
chronic health condition

REVIEW QUESTIONS

1. Name two agencies that have done studies on the fitness of American children. What were their conclusions?

2. Name the food groups in the MyPyramid for Kids. State the recommended daily servings of each.

3. Describe an activity a parent might conduct in a child care center.

4. Describe two activities that encourage children to try new foods.

5. Name 10 pieces of equipment that you need for food preparation.

6. Define fitness.

7. List four pieces of equipment that will encourage children to be active.

8. What can caregivers do to foster children's health and fitness?

Case Study

Heather and Monica are 11 years old and beginning to look and act like teenagers. They sit together for long periods of time looking at teen magazines that Heather brings in her school backpack. They talk about the clothes, the models, and the film stars featured in the magazines. At snack time, they often refuse the food, saying it will make them fat. An assistant caregiver in their group thinks the magazines should be banned from the program.

1. Do you agree or disagree with the position of the assistant? Explain your reasoning.

2. What would you say to the girls?

3. Can you think of some activities to include in your program that might help the girls to have a more realistic image of young girls and women than what is portrayed in teen magazines?

STUDENT ACTIVITIES

1. Make either Navajo fry bread or ice cream in a bucket at home. Invite your family or friends to taste-test the results. Did they like the food? If not, why not? Were there any difficulties you encountered that were

not provided for in the recipe? How can you change the procedure to eliminate the problem?

2. Make a list of your own favorite foods. How many are healthful and how many are unhealthful?

3. Buy or borrow one of the pieces of equipment listed in this chapter. Try it out. How many activities can you think of to do with this equipment?

SUGGESTED READINGS

Dietz, W. H. & Gortmaker, S. L. (2001). Preventing obesity in children and adolescents. *Annual Review of Public Health*, 22: 337–353.

Gianciolo, S., with R. Trueblood-Noll & P. Allingham (2004). Health consultations in early childhood setting. *Young Children*, 59(2): 56–61.

Cook, D. (1995). *Kids' multicultural cookbook*. Charlotte, VT: Williamson.

Hedges, S. (1995). *Multicultural snacks*. Everest, WA: Warren Publishing House.

Heyhoe, Kate, (2009). *Cooking with kids*. Online at www.cookingwithkids.com.

Newacheck, P., & Taylor, W. (1992). Childhood chronic illness: Prevention, severity, and impact. *American Journal of Public Health*, 82(3), 364–371.

Perrin, J. M., Bloom S. R., Gortmaker, S. L. (2007). The increase of childhood chronic conditions in the United States. *JAMA*, 297 (24): 2755–2759.

Wanamaker, N., Hearn, K., & Richarz, S. (1979). *More than graham crackers*. Washington, DC: National Association for the Education of Young Children.

WEB RESOURCES

http://www.mypyramid.gov
MyPyramid for Kids. Click on "Food and Nutrition"

http://www.cspinet.org
Center for Science in the Public Interest

http://www.eatright.org
American Dietetic Association

http://www.kidshealth.org
Children's Health Information

http://www.KeepKidsHealthy.com
Parents' guide to children's health.

REFERENCES

AAHPERD (1995). *Moving into the future, national physical education standards*. Reston, VA: The American Alliance for Health, Physical Education, Recreation, and Dance.

Children's Defense Fund (2004). *The state of America's children*. Washington, DC: Author.

Children's Defense Fund (2008). *The state of America's children*. Washington, DC: Author.

Centers for Disease Control and Prevention, (Aug. 22, 2003). *Morbidity and Mortality Weekly Report*, 52(33).

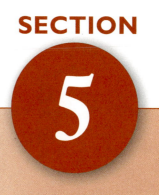
Resources and Regulations

Using Community Resources

HOW COMMUNITY RESOURCES CAN SUPPORT SCHOOL-AGE PROGRAMS

School-age children are ready and eager to learn about the world outside their immediate environment. When they go to kindergarten, they take that first step away from their home and out into the community. Most find it a fascinating place and are eager to find their own place out in the world. Developmentally they are ready. They have good muscular control and want to try out their skills in new ways. Cognitively, they have a good memory and a much longer interest span than at earlier ages. Coupled with this, they can postpone rewards, allowing them to work on projects that take a long time to complete. They are ready to consider different ways of thinking or doing things. They find that not everyone lives or thinks as they do. When presented with alternatives, they like to consider the options. In addition to all these characteristics, school-age children have a high energy level. They need to have lots to do and challenges to meet.

One way to involve children in the community is to invite residents or representatives from agencies and organizations to participate in activities at your center. This method has a distinct advantage because it eliminates transportation problems and does not entail travel time. Another advantage is that the school gains exposure, and this may be helpful when fund-raising is necessary. Most important, however, is that both children and outside adults benefit from this relationship.

LEARNING OUTCOMES

After reading this chapter, you should be able to:

✔ Discuss how community resources can support school-age programs.

✔ Describe ways to use intergenerational resources outside the child care center.

✔ State ways to make a volunteer program effective by removing barriers to community participation.

Service Learning

service learning
combining meaningful service with curriculum-based learning

intergenerational programs
child care programs that utilize older people and young adults or teenagers as volunteers

The opportunity for involvement in service-learning projects helps young people to become engaged in their communities, and offers them a new awareness of how they can make a difference in their own lives and the lives of others. Many private and public programs use service learning projects to involve children in their community. The Children for Children organization website (www.childrenforchildren.org) describes **service learning** as "…a teaching method that combines meaningful service to the community with curriculum-based learning." The organization also points to the importance of helping children reflect on their experiences and meet curriculum objectives. Children achieve this through writing about the experience.

INTERGENERATIONAL PROGRAMS

Intergenerational programs are one way to bring the community into the child care center. These programs use older people and young adults or teenagers as volunteers. Older people especially are often looking for meaningful ways to share their energies. At the same time, some children either do not know or do not live close to their grandparents. Both young and old can benefit from a relationship. The adults will feel they can still make a difference in someone else's life. The children will enjoy increased self-esteem from meeting someone who listens to and cares about them. Both can learn to appreciate the similarities and differences that exist between the generations.

Partnering with Seniors

Child care centers can benefit from the talents of older adults who come from a variety of jobs and professions. Artists, teachers, musicians, scientists, gardeners, veterinarians, and cooks are just a few who have knowledge and skills they can share with children. These people can do what grandparents do: plan special activities, demonstrate how to do things, go on outings with the children, and celebrate holidays and special occasions. Recruit older people from the following:

- active living centers
- community centers
- groups for active seniors
- parks and recreation departments
- senior centers
- retirement communities
- churches
- special-interest groups: hobby clubs or computer users
- subsidized housing complexes for people over 55
- senior citizens service agencies (county or city)
- notices in volunteer information columns of newspapers

You can also write to organizations for seniors to find groups in your community. Try:

American Association of Retired Persons
601 E Street NW
Washington, DC 20049
1 888-687-2277

Gray Panthers
1612 E Street NW Suite 300
Washington, DC 2006
800-280-5362

Activities for Seniors and Children

The following is a list of just a few things older adults can do with children. You can develop other ideas based on the needs of your particular center or the talents of the adults available to you.

Tutoring: Assist Individual Children with Math, English, or Homework.

Many retired teachers want to maintain contact with children outside the structure of a classroom setting. They might enjoy helping in a child care center. Children will appreciate the help with school work or someone who will listen while they practice conversing in English.

Science Experiences

Demonstrate scientific phenomena: electricity, chemistry, weather.

> Plan and conduct hands-on science activities for the children. Schedule hands-on activities to follow a demonstration. Any of the activities described in Chapter 12 or those contained in the books on the reading list for that chapter would be suitable.
>
> Share an interest in exotic plants (orchids, cacti, tropical plants, etc.).
>
> Work with children to make exhibits for a school science fair. Invite other school groups and parents to see the results.

Cultural Awareness

Demonstrate musical instruments specific to a culture. Let children play them.

> Cook and taste ethnic foods. Use traditional cooking pots and implements.
>
> Teach the dances of native peoples. Make costumes and plan a performance of dances.
>
> Prepare a list of greetings in different languages from around the world. Encourage the children to use them when greeting friends or family.

Children and senior citizens can both benefit from intergenerational relationships.

Display toys and games used by children in different cultures. Tell how they are used and let the children try them out.

Read children's books from different countries in the native language, then translate it into English. Discuss how the stories reflect life in that country.

Show children folk arts or crafts. Teach them how to create some typical folk art.

Share with children how holidays and special occasions are celebrated in other countries.

Develop a network of pen pals from different countries. Help children write letters to a pen pal.

Encourage children to use the Internet to find pen pals in other countries. Here is one site to try: http://www.epals.com.

Collections

Share special collections: rocks, shells, fossils, insects, stamps. Work with children to classify and organize their own collection. Act as an adviser to a collections club and set up displays of the collections.

Chess, Checkers

Teach children how to play and organize chess or checkers tournaments. Take the role of adviser for a club. Plan and conduct a tournament. Consider a tournament between adults and children.

Cooking

Prepare a variety of foods with children: bread, ice cream, muffins.

Share favorite recipes or recipes passed down from family members. Prepare holiday specialties.

Help the children put together a book of recipes for foods they and their families especially enjoy.

Share recipes specific to a particular culture or ethnic group.

Reading

Read stories to the children. Children love hearing stories read to them in groups or one on one.

Listen while children read aloud. Discuss the story or ask questions about the story. "What happened when... ?" or "What if... ?"

Take individual children on a trip to the library. Browse together and choose books to take back to the center.

Puppet Making

Help children make puppets and put on a puppet show. This can be a long-range project beginning with writing a script, making the puppets, planning the production, and then performing.

Life Stories

Older adults can tell children about their own childhoods. Many children cannot conceive of a world without the modern conveniences they take for granted. A good storyteller can paint a picture of life in "the old days."

Adults can share photo albums of their own childhood with the children. Show themselves as babies, as "school-agers," and as teens.

Help children compile their own life story using a computer. Show them how to insert photos they bring from home. Younger children can portray their life story through photographs and drawings or collages. Add the narration for those who cannot do it themselves.

Art Projects

Work on special art projects. Teach children new techniques for creating art: airbrush painting, mold making, charcoal drawing. Accompany children on a tour of the studio of an artist who uses one of these techniques. Help children plan and paint a mural. This can either be a child-only project or a joint project between adults and children. Each can contribute something to the finished product.

Field Trips

Accompany children on trips to museums, plays, or factories. Extra adults provide better supervision and can share their knowledge with children as well.

Woodworking

Teach children the proper use of power and hand tools. Supervise woodworking projects.

Accompany children to a furniture manufacturing site.

Computer Assistance

Help children use the computer in new ways. Work with them to set up an e-mail newsletter to their family. Discuss the topics they think their family would want to know about. Help them set up a format that can be used each month as they update the information. Guide them in writing articles and inputting them into the computer. They will also have to obtain e-mail addresses from their family members to set up an address list. Print copies can also be distributed through parent mail boxes at the child-care center.

Play computer games with the children. Be sure to check the content before introducing them to a new game since so many have content that is inappropriate for children.

Help children develop a pen pal network with children in other child care settings or even in other countries. You can use the website mentioned above (http //www.epals.com) or type "pen pals" in the search engine of the computer to choose other pen pals options.

Gardening

Teach children the basic needs of plants. Help them to prepare, plant, and maintain a garden. Plant a vegetable garden and harvest the vegetables.

Prepare vegetables for a snack: raw vegetables and a dip, or zucchini bread.

Bicycle Maintenance

Teach children how to repair and maintain their own bikes. Teach safety rules to observe when riding a bike.

Photography

Teach children the basics of using a camera. If possible, help the children develop or print out their own pictures.

Help children put together an exhibit of their photographs for a family bulletin board.

Needlework

Teach children how to knit or crochet. Help them create simple garments: scarves, hats, small blankets.

Teach children embroidery stitches. Help them create pillow covers, placemats, or wall hangings.

Help children make a simple hand loom. Teach them how to weave placemats, wall hangings, pot holders.

Accompany children to needlework shops to see the variety of materials available. Purchase the materials needed for a project.

Partnering with High School and College Students

Although many young people can do the things suggested for older people, they may have a different approach. They may also be better suited for some activities. The following are some activities at which young people may be especially proficient.

Sports

Teach children the proper techniques for playing popular sports: tennis, basketball, baseball, soccer, golf, swimming, or gymnastics. Practice with individual children who need help in perfecting their skills.

Organize a game with another child care center, possibly at a nearby park.

Drama

Work with children to write, produce, and perform a play. Children can make their own costumes, design and construct scenery, or set up proper lighting.

Dance

Teach children how to dance ballet, tap, clogging, or current popular dances.

Help children choreograph a dance and perform for other children or family members.

Conversation

Talk with and listen to children. Teens may be able to help children express their worries or fears or to discuss their problems.

Field Trips

Accompany children on active field trips: to the park, zoo, beach, or on a nature walk.

Exercise

Organize a jump rope game or start a ball game. Lay out hoops in a pattern so children can jump or hop from one to the other. Set up a balance beam for children to walk across.

Cultural Awareness

High school exchange students from other countries can explain about life in their homeland: their play activities, school, and their family.

High-school- and college-age students often have a different approach to activities than older people.

Games

Play table or language games with children. Children and teens enjoy Monopoly®, Clue®, Trivial Pursuit®, Scrabble®, Life®, or card games. Teens will contribute their own enthusiasms for language games such as telephone, taking a trip, 20 questions, or charades.

Partnering with Community Facilities and Businesses

You may decide you do not want volunteers coming to your center, but would rather schedule periodic activities for the children using facilities in your community. Nearly every area will have some resources that will interest children. Check your neighborhood, call government offices, and talk to other caregivers. If you have lived in the area for a long time, where did your parents take you when you were a child?

Museums

Natural history museums are an excellent source of people to do presentations or conduct tours of the museum. Consider presentations on local history, plants, or animals indigenous to the area.

Children's discovery museums are marvelous places for a field trip. In these places children can touch and manipulate displays, and participate in a variety of activities.

Museums are an excellent place for children to learn from seeing demonstrations and participating in a variety of activities.

Art museums may conduct tours especially designed for children. Most large museums have a docents program; docents are volunteers who know a great deal about the artwork in the galleries. Sometimes a tour may be followed by a session in which the children can create their own art.

Library

Many libraries have a children's librarian who will help children choose books. They may also have reading incentive programs which reward children who read a specified number of books.

Libraries often have film series or other activities that are suitable for young children.

Ask whether the library can supply or recommended storytellers. Ask the storyteller to visit the child care program to tell about the art of storytelling, and then tell a story.

Businesses

Some businesspeople may be willing to conduct a tour of their facility and then answer questions or tell children how to prepare themselves for that line of work. A newspaper office, dairy, radio station, or a computerized office might interest the children. Check with the children's parents for other possibilities.

Fire Station

Take a tour of the facility. Discuss the requirements for becoming a firefighter.

Some departments have fire-prevention programs featuring Smokey the Bear and might offer a presentation.

Police Station

Take a tour of the facility. Discuss the requirements for qualifying to be a member of law enforcement.

Some departments have drug prevention programs and could provide a presentation geared toward children.

Wildlife Refuge

A few communities have areas set aside for endangered animal species or plants. Some conduct nature walks. Others may have plant propagation workshops where children help plant seeds or transplant native plants or trees.

Parks or Other Amenities

Find out whether your children can use a local riding stable, swimming pool, or public tennis courts.

Some fire departments have fire-prevention programs and will do presentations for children.

Partnering with Organizations and Agencies

Many national and global organizations as well as governmental agencies provide websites with information about service-learning projects and activities that are ideal for school-age children. Here are just a few possibilities:

- **Children for Children Organization**

  http://www.childrenforchildren.org

  Provides a clear definition of the meaning of service learning along with some examples of projects. The site cautions teachers to revise their curriculum so that learning is experiential and partnered with community-based organizations.

- **Environmental Protection Agency**

  http://www.epa.gov

  Provides questions about the environment and the work of the agency. EPA's Explorer's Club website for children features information about recycling, pollution, and endangered plants and animals. The website includes interactive games and information to captivate young audiences.

- **Environmental Protection Agency (site for Kids)**

  http://www.epa.gov/water/kids.html

  Provides websites written for children suggesting activities to preserve wetlands, reduce waste by recycling, conserve water in the home, and prevent pollution of water resources.

- **Earth 911**

  http://www.earth911.org

  Earth 911 is a Public and Private Sector Partnership that is guided by information from the U.S. Environmental Protection Agency and other federal, state, and local agencies to empower communities to improve their quality of life. Their website includes links to information about recycling centers, energy conservation, safe disposal of household waste, composting, and environmental education for children.

- **Service Learning, Inc.**

  http://servicelearning.childreninc.org

  This website describes a wide variety of projects suitable for children in K-12 grade levels. Each activity lists goals and adds core content areas for curriculum enrichment. The site also provides information for related websites.

- **USA Freedom Corps**

  www.volunteerkids.org

  A volunteer service started by President George W. Bush in 2002 is an effort to expand the ways that young people can give back to their communities. Key components of the USA Freedom Corps

has been continued under President Obama. The website has links to projects and games that teach citizenship concepts.

Start a Recycling Center

Explore the immediate environment of the child care center, collecting any materials that can be recycled. Collect the items in separate bins, and contact the center's trash service to obtain a schedule for pickup.

Survey the neighborhood immediately adjacent to the center, picking up items that can be recycled. Add these to the center's bins.

Many schools and communities are already encouraging recycling by setting up bins or convenient places to leave recyclable materials. Some communities have recycling days when residents can bring their items.

Adopt a Wetland Area

Visit a wetland area in your community. Pick up any trash that may endanger indigenous wildlife: plastic pieces, discarded tires, bottles, plastic bags, etc.

Provide a Habitat for Butterflies or Birds

Plant a part of the center's outdoor area with plants that attract butterflies or hummingbirds. Consult a garden book for specifics to your geography. Some plants that attract butterflies are: agapanthus, armeria, cosmos, echinacea, buddleia, lantana, and honeysuckle. Hummingbirds will seek out: columbine, lupine, azalea, bottle brush, buddleia, cape honeysuckle, dahlia, and lavender.

GUIDELINES FOR USING VOLUNTEERS

It is important to have an organized method of managing the people from your community who participate in your program—your **volunteer corps**. They should see themselves as an integral part of what you are trying to achieve. To begin with, they will be more valuable if they know what they are expected to do, if they are trained and supported while working with you, and if they perceive that they are appreciated. Time and effort spent in setting up this type of program will pay off in the long run, and your volunteers will be more likely to stay with you longer. They will contribute to your curriculum rather than becoming an added burden.

Prepare a booklet of information that clearly states the expectations for volunteers. Spell out what their job is and what their hours will be. Let them know who will be supervising them and to whom they can go when problems arise.

Check your local licensing requirement regarding fingerprinting volunteers. If it is necessary, tell volunteers where it can be done.

Assign volunteers to simple, specific tasks at first. Start by having them work with one child alone at an activity. As you learn more about each person's abilities and strengths, you can gradually allow greater responsibility.

volunteer corps
group of older adults and young people or teenagers who volunteer in a child care center

Plan and conduct an orientation for each volunteer. Develop a program that gives a general overview of your center and its goals and philosophy. Suggest ways for the volunteers to interact with the children. State rules that apply to the children and to the volunteers.

Ask for a specific time commitment from each volunteer. Because a lot of effort goes into making a volunteer program successful, it is important to avoid constant change in its members. Have each volunteer tell you how much time and for how long a period they can commit to your program. Can they participate on a daily basis or only once a week? Is their participation limited to a month, a year?

Provide ongoing supervision and training. As volunteers become more familiar with your program, additional training will enhance their self-esteem and strengthen their commitment.

Evaluate and provide feedback periodically. Remember that volunteers are not getting paid for their time. To make it worthwhile, they must feel that they are appreciated and that they are learning.

Set realistic expectations for your volunteers. Remember that they may not always be available when you need them. Older people sometimes have health problems, and young people have many other demands on their time.

You may have to make some adaptations to your environment to foster an effective intergenerational program. Consider the following changes to accommodate both older adults and teenagers in your setting.

- Place small sofas or wide armchairs in a quiet corner. This will invite an adult or teen and one or two children to sit together and read or talk.

Volunteers who are trained and supported as they work with you will contribute to your curriculum.

- Install an extra-wide swing in the playground. The favorite place for many children of past generations was in the porch swing with grandpa or grandma. Not many enjoy that experience today, but a wide swing can bring a little of that atmosphere to your playground.
- Provide at least one table high enough for an adult or a teenager. Let children sit on stools so they can work with the adult at this table on art projects, science experiments, writing, or whatever they wish.
- Provide a place where children can leave a message for the adult or teenager. Most volunteers are not on site on a daily basis, but children may want to write them a note about something that happened or just leave them a special drawing. This can be an important avenue for developing a relationship.
- Provide a place where the adults or teens can keep their own belongings.
- Plan a means for thanking volunteers. Write a letter at the end of a specified period of time, or give an award. You can also have a special meeting or dinner to recognize the contributions that volunteers have made to your program.

REMOVING BARRIERS TO COMMUNITY PARTICIPATION

At the beginning of this chapter, we indicated that many caregivers have mixed reactions to the use of community resources. They cite a variety of reasons. Here are some solutions that other programs have found successful:

- Walk to places that are close to the child care center.
- Rent or use donated buses and vans from churches (these are usually not used by the church during the week).
- Take small groups at a time, using public transportation or private cars.
- Divide groups according to the children's age levels and take trips to different sites.
- Use senior volunteers to take small groups or individual children for a walk into the community.
- Have parents pick up their children at the place being visited—park, swimming pool, or library.

REMINDER: Before you take any children on trips outside your child care facility, you must obtain written permission from their parents. You should also check with your insurance agent to ensure that the form of transportation you use is covered by your policy.

Intergenerational contact is not a new concept. In past generations young children were often cared for by older brothers and sisters, aunts, uncles, and grandparents. Each age level contributed to the child's knowledge of what growing up means. Each age level was a model children could imitate. Today's children, who live in nuclear and mobile families, may miss that experience. Using volunteers can recreate that kind of environment. It is well worth the effort in terms of benefits to the children and to the volunteers themselves.

SUMMARY

- Teachers and caregivers are sometimes reluctant to use community resources because of the difficulty of recruiting and training volunteers, problems transporting children, the short time children spend at the center, and the fact that children are at such different age levels.

- One way to involve children in the community is to invite seniors or teens or representatives of agencies to visit the center.

- Community agencies, organizations, and businesses may have resources for activities that will interest children.

- An organized method of managing volunteers will make the program more effective. Prepare a manual, conduct an orientation, provide supervision, and give volunteers feedback.

- You may have to alter your physical environment to provide places for adults to be comfortable, for children to leave messages for volunteers, and where adults can keep their belongings.

- Remove barriers to community participation by using public transportation, walking to nearby sites or renting church-owned vehicles.

KEY TERMS

intergenerational programs   service learning   volunteer corps

REVIEW QUESTIONS

1. Caregivers are often reluctant to use community resources. List the reasons discussed in this chapter.

2. State five places from which to recruit senior volunteers.

3. Describe five activities in which seniors can share their cultural heritage with children.

4. Name two activities that are especially suited for teens and school-age children.

5. State the resources that are often available through museums.

6. This chapter listed seven things you can do to make a volunteer program more effective. What are they?

7. In what ways can you change the environment of a child care center to make it easier for volunteers to interact with the children?

8. This chapter stated seven ways to remove barriers to community participation. What are they?

Case Study

Ed Fuller is 67 and retired two years ago from a computer software company. He has seven grandchildren with whom he loves to spend time, and he decided he wanted to volunteer to work with young children. He found that the director and caregivers at a local business-sponsored program welcomed him with open arms. He came twice a week to the center, taught the children woodworking techniques, and spent a lot of time showing them how to use the computer. Most of the children looked forward to his days at the center, but three boys never participated in the activities he organized. When he was not there, they sometimes imitated the way he walked and made fun of the fact that he was almost bald.

1. What should the child care leaders do about the attitude of the three boys toward Ed?

2. Is there something Ed could do to help the boys feel more comfortable with him?

3. Can you think of an activity that will enable children to be more accepting of older people?

STUDENT ACTIVITIES

1. Talk to an older person in your family about his or her childhood. How different was it from your own growing years? In what ways might this information help you understand that older person better?

2. Visit a senior center in your community. Find out whether they have any volunteer programs. If they do, ask what seniors hope to get out of participating in their community. If the center does not have a volunteer program, ask why.

3. Plan one activity either a teenager or older person could do with a group of nine-year-olds. List the materials that they would need and describe any special procedures.

SUGGESTED READINGS

Berman, S. (2006). *Service learning: A guide to planning, implementing and assessing student projects.* Thousand Oaks, CA: Corwin Press.

Horsfall, J. (1999). Welcoming volunteers to your child care center. *Young Children,* 54(6), 35–36.

Kaplan, M., Duerr, L., Whitesell, W., Merchant, L., Davis, D., & Larkin, E. (2003). *Developing an intergenerational program in your early childhood care and education center.* Penn State University: Penn State University.

Kazemek, F., & Logas, B. (2000). Spiders, kid curlers, and white shoes. Telling and writing stories across generations. *The Reading Teacher,* 53(6), 446–451.

Lierman, H.W., & Mosher-Ashley, P. M. (2002). Strategies to expand a pen pal program from simple letters into a full intergenerational experience. *Educational Gerontology*, 28, 337–345.

Seefeldt, C, Warman, B., Jantz, B., & Galper, A. (1990). *Young and old together*. Washington, DC: National Association for the Education of Young Children.

Smith, B. J., & Yeager, A. (1999) Intergenerational communities: Where learning and interaction go hand-in-hand. *Child & Youth Services*, 20(1/2), 25–32.

17

Quality and Standards

CHANGES IN THE GOALS FOR CHILD CARE

Only a few years ago, school-age child care was seldom included as a topic for workshops and presentations at many conferences organized by the professionals in early childhood education. Now it is frequently discussed at professional gatherings. According to the website www.childstats.gov, in 2007, 77 percent of families with children under age 18, both parents worked outside the home. 46.9 percent of those children are cared for by someone other than the parents.

The need has brought about rapid proliferation of programs. However, the increase in numbers must be accompanied by attention to quality.

Research studies show that children who attend quality programs benefit in other aspects of their life. The National Association of Child Care Resource and Referral Agencies (NACCRRA) (1999) found that children in quality programs score higher on reading and math tests, and are more likely to complete high school. These children are also less likely to be retained in a grade or placed in a special education program.

Public perception of school-age child care has also changed. Early generations of after-school programs were located in settlement houses, with the purpose of caring for the children of poor or indigent families. Some were set up to offer a safe haven for children who lived in high-crime neighborhoods, to foster self-esteem, or to overcome academic deficits (Halpern, 1992). The adults were seen as supervisors or babysitters, and little training was required or encouraged.

Early models for the curriculum were the traditional day camp or recreational prototype. During World War II, centers were set up to provide care for the children of families

LEARNING OUTCOMES

After reading this chapter, you should be able to:

✔ Discuss changes in the goals for school-age child care.

✔ State the current laws and associations that relate to the quality of today's child care programs.

✔ Relate the progress that has been made toward developing a credential.

✔ Discuss evaluation of programs.

✔ Describe how to assess children's progress as part of the overall quality of a program.

working in the war industries. The centers were seen as a safe, exciting place led by activity directors and supervisors of play. Questions were being asked about what constituted quality in child care, and some workshops and technical school classes were available. Often, space had to be shared with other facilities for children. At present, school-age care is recognized as an important part of services for children. It is now seen as a place for growth, nurturing, and learning life skills. The role of the adult is that of a facilitator of positive development through healthy interactions. Questions about quality focus on the kinds of adult-child interactions that promote growth. Degree and credential programs are available for training, and child care staff members are working collaboratively with school personnel.

A critical need—to promote and maintain quality—is the involvement of all those who are concerned with the education and care of children in a community. Involving such a wide range of people means there must be communication between parents and programs and between programs and community agencies. There should also be some coordination between the various types of programs. To address the coordination issue, some communities have developed **child care councils** made up of representatives from the various factions of the child care community. Their meetings and discussions focus on the needs of the community, policies regarding quality, ways to facilitate communications, and ways to affect legislative actions. More recently, state and federal departments of education are seeing the need to become involved.

child care councils
groups of representatives from the various factions of the child care community

CHILD CARE IN THE 21ST CENTURY

Former Secretary of U.S. Department of Health and Human Services Donna Shalala gave the keynote address at the Annual State Child Care Administrators Meeting in Washington, DC, on July 29, 1998. She opened her address with a discussion of quality. She expressed her admiration for caregivers, calling them "heroes," but said that even heroes need a helping hand sometimes. She challenged state and county administrators across the country to provide support as well as financial incentives. She pointed to the challenge made by President Clinton's Child Care Initiative and his commitment to providing quality care for all children. To that end, the Child Care Bureau was created, and in turn the bureau set up a National Child Care Information Center that shares trends and ideas with states and communities. Money has been added to the new welfare law to promote quality care.

Secretary Shalala listed what she believes constitutes quality care:

- good interaction between the provider and parents
- a continuous improvement strategy based on current child development research
- strong and meaningful relationships with families, based on trust and sharing information about children

- teaming up with health experts and building a system where children's health is monitored
- supportive directors who respond to staff needs but also demand accountability
- good working conditions for all providers—meaning decent pay, leave, and family friendly policies as well as a good working space

Shalala further urged her audience to involve the community. She pointed to the wisdom and experience of teachers, parents, clergy, businesses, and law enforcement. She said they should all be a part of decisions about funding, safety, training, eligibility, and access.

On January 8, 2002, President George W. Bush signed legislation putting into effect his education policy, "No Child Left Behind (**NCLB**)." The NCLB Act expands the federal government's role as outlined in the Elementary and Secondary Education Act (ESEA) of 1965. No Child Left Behind is still the standard for care of young children. NCLB focuses on disadvantaged students and sets strict requirements and deadlines for participation. The law requires states to set high standards for student achievement and a means for assessing progress to receive federal funding.

Although at times President Barack Obama had criticized NCLB because it stresses the student test-taking rather than learning, his 2011 budget proposal for the Department of Education indicated his desire to overhaul the No Child Left Behind Act. He cited new evidence that the single most important factor in determining children's achievement is their teacher. He included additional funding for education spending, and appointed U.S. Secretary of Education Arne Duncan to dole out the money to schools that increased their testing standards and teacher accountability guidelines. Obama said the goals of NCLB were the right ones, but that President Bush failed to provide money for upgrades. Obama said he intends to see that schools get adequate funding.

There are four main points to NCLB:

- education accountability measured by frequent testing
- more flexibility in how states, school districts, and schools use the federal funds
- more options for parents of children from disadvantaged backgrounds
- more use of teaching methods based on scientifically proven research studies selected by government agencies

In addition, the act guarantees that every classroom is staffed by qualified teachers and that the gap between advantaged and disadvantaged children, as reflected in test scores, narrows. Although this law does not directly affect what happens in after-school programs, it is important that child care personnel be aware of what is happening in schools. Some aspects of NCLB are controversial and are being questioned by teachers and professional organizations. More information about the No Child Left Behind law can be found at the following website:

http://www.ed.gov/nclb.

No Child Left Behind Act
federal legislation that enacts the theories of standards-based education reform

Accreditation and Standards: National AfterSchool Association (NAA)

Several years have gone into developing the standards that **NAA** uses. The pilot statement was drafted in 1995 after several years of research and field testing, but revised in 1997. The Council on Accreditation Standards upgraded the core concepts of the original standards. The entire document is available on the website http://www.COAafterschool.org. The standards reflect the best practices for children between the ages of five and 14. These standards are intended for use in group settings where children attend on a regular basis. Programs can use the guidelines for a self-study leading to accreditation.

The professionals who developed NAA standards believe there is a need for an accreditation and improvement process that specifically addresses school-age care. Some of the unique characteristics of programs that serve this population are the following:

- They usually serve a wide range of ages, from age five to 14.
- They often share facilities with other programs, preschools, recreational buildings, and elementary schools.
- Staff members may work at other jobs as well as caregiving.
- They often must organize their calendar around school schedules.
- A unique combination of skills is necessary to do the work well.

NAA also states that there is a need for a system that raises public awareness of the importance of out-of-school care and its impact on the future development of children. It was the NAA's intent to develop a process whereby centers could use the guidelines to improve quality whether they eventually apply for accreditation or not. Experience has shown that most programs continue to work toward improving quality even after completing the accreditation process.

NAA Standards

The standards are divided into six sections. The following paragraphs present a brief summary of each of those sections.

Human Relationships

Interactions between staff and children should be positive and appropriate to the needs of the children. This guideline includes sensitivity to each child's interests and abilities, as well as to her culture and home language. Interactions should help children make choices, become more responsible, and learn the skills they need to be successful. Staff members should use positive guidance techniques that encourage children to resolve their own conflicts and to interact with one another in positive ways. This section also contains statements about including families and ways that staff should work well together to meet the needs of children.

Indoor Environment

Indoor space should meet the needs of the children a program serves, including space for all activities. The space should be arranged so that a variety of activities can take place and allow children to participate without disruption. Indoor space encourages children to explore their own interests by providing convenient places to store and retrieve materials. Work space should reflect the children's interests.

Outdoor Environment

The outdoor environment should meet the needs of school-age children and allow them to be independent and creative. For every three-hour block of time, there should be at least 30 minutes of outdoor play during which children can use a variety of equipment or participate in a variety of activities.

Activities

The daily schedule should be flexible, allowing transitions to be smooth and children to go at their own pace. There should be enough time for children to choose from a variety of activities that reflect the mission of the program. There should be enough materials to support those activities.

Safety, Health, and Nutrition

The safety and security of children in the center should be of the utmost importance. All observable hazards should be secured, and systems in

Indoor space should meet the needs of the children served and be arranged so that a variety of activities can take place.

place to protect children from harm. The environment should enhance the health of children, and staff members must be responsive to individual health needs. Children should be supervised in such a way as to maintain safety at all times and in accordance with their ages, abilities, and needs. All foods served at the facility should be healthy and appropriate for the ages and sizes of the children.

Administration

The number of staff members should vary according to group size, the ages of the children, and the complexity of the activity. There should be a staff plan for maintaining adequate supervision of children at all times. There should be policies in place to keep parents informed and support their involvement in the program. Administrative policies should foster cooperation with schools and the community. Administration guidelines also should include statements regarding the qualifications of staff and the establishment of policies that encourage ongoing training and adequate working conditions.

With the current increase in the need for care for young children when the school day ends, this seems an optimum time for looking at ways to increase the quality of that time. The NAA standards are certainly one way to achieve that.

The full text of the standards can be obtained from:

National AfterSchool Association
P.O. Box 34447
Washington, DC 20043-4447
703-610-9028
http://naaweb.site-ym.com

Self-study by a committee of staff members and parents is the first step in the accreditation process.

National Association for the Education of Young Children (NAEYC)

NAEYC is a large national professional association that provides a service for accrediting programs that serve children from birth through the elementary years. The system is voluntary and involves a three-step process: self-study by the director, staff members, and parents; validation visits by trained professionals; and an accreditation decision by a team of early childhood experts. Schools can pace the length of time involved in completing the process, but it usually takes from four to 18 months.

The critical step in the process is the self-study. The program administrator pays a fee and receives an accreditation manual. The director, staff, and parents use the manual to rate the quality of the program in 10 different categories. When the study is completed, the program administrator prepares a final report and sends it to the academy. Academy personnel review the materials to determine whether the information is complete or if further information is needed.

Accreditation covers the following categories of center operations:

- interactions among staff and children
- curriculum
- staff/parent interactions
- staff qualifications and development
- administration
- staffing patterns
- physical environment
- health and safety
- nutrition and food service
- evaluation process

When all the materials are ready, the academy appoints one or more validators who schedule a visit. The purpose of the visit is to observe the day-to-day operations to verify the accuracy of the report. The final step involves an accreditation commission consisting of three professionals. The commission reviews the information provided by the validators and decides to grant accreditation or defer it until further improvements are made. Deferred centers may appeal the decision. Accreditation is valid for three years, during which time centers must submit annual reports. Before expiration, the accreditation process must be repeated. You can find further information about accreditation from:

National Association for the Education of Young Children
1313L Street NW Suite 500
Washington, DC 20005
800-424-2460/202-232-2777
E-mail: NAEYC@naey.org
http://www.naeyc.org/accreditation

NAEYC
National Association for the Education of Young Children, a large professional organization that accredits programs for children from birth through the elementary years

National Association for Family Child Care (NAFCC)

According to **NAFCC**, 1 million family child care providers care for 4 million children, some of whom are elementary school ages. Along with the move to professionalize all child care settings, NAFCC held that it was important to develop a process for accrediting home-based child care. The quality standards for NAFCC accreditation were developed in conjunction with the Family Child Care Project at Wheelock College in Boston, Massachusetts.

The provider reviews the accreditation workbook and identifies areas that need improvement. The next step is to design a professional development plan followed by improvements. When the provider is ready, she notifies NAFCC to schedule a visit. The provider receives an observer visit packet, including a self-observation form to complete before the observer visit. The visit is scheduled, and the observer scores the visit. If the provider has met the standards, she is awarded accreditation for three years. If the score is not high enough, accreditation can be deferred until conditions can be corrected. If a provider moves, the new site must be reaccredited. The categories used to score a setting for accreditation follow:

- relationships that convey a sense of belonging to children, parents, provider's family, and community
- a welcoming environment with enough materials to engage children and support their interests
- activities that are both child-directed and adult-directed
- developmental learning goals that are appropriate for the ages of the children
- policies and procedures that ensure children's safety and health
- professional and business practices that reflect concern for ethics and legality, as well as time for professional activities

You can obtain the NAFCC Quality Standards for Accreditation, 1999 edition, from:

The National Association for Family Child Care
1743 W, Alexander Street
Salt Lake City, UT 84119
800-359-3817
FAX: 801-886-2325
E-mail: nafcc@nafcc.org
http://www.nafcc.org

CREDENTIALS

Credentials are a means for documenting training of early childhood teachers. They show the goals of a training program and the curriculum of graduated experiences the teacher has completed. Most importantly credentials show a commitment to professionalism.

Child Development Associate

Upgrading the quality of programs can also be accomplished through training and credentialing of teachers. The Child Development Associate (**CDA**) credential is a nationally recognized credential for early childhood teachers and has been used in preschools, child care, and Head Start programs. The curriculum for attaining the credential was designed by the Council for Early Childhood Professional Recognition and contains a set of goals and a series of graduated experiences. The goals are

- to establish and maintain a safe, healthy learning environment
- to advance physical and intellectual competence
- to support social and emotional development and provide guidance
- to establish positive and productive relationships with families
- to ensure a well-run, purposeful program responsive to participant needs
- to maintain a commitment to professionalism

These graduated experiences are divided into three phases. Phase I is fieldwork with students participating in the daily activities of a program. The students also must prepare written work, complete exercises, and read. During Phase II, students attend courses or seminars offered by local colleges, universities, or postsecondary institutions. The final phase, Phase III, is designed to integrate and evaluate the student's experiences. During this period, the student returns to working with children while also completing a series of exercises. The last step in the process involves interviews with a council representative and a review of all the documents. If the representative's review is positive, the candidate receives a Child Development Associate credential that is valid for life.

For information about the CDA credential, contact:

Council for Early Childhood Professional Recognition
2460 16th St. NW
Washington, DC 20009-3575
202-265-9090
800-424-4310
FAX: 202-265-9161
http://www.cdacouncil.org

CDA
Child Development Associate; nationally recognized credential for early childhood teachers and caregivers

NIOST
National Institute on Out-of-School Time; focuses on education and training, community development, consultation, research, and public awareness

National Institute on Out-of-School Time (NIOST)

Formerly called the School-Age Care Project, **NIOST** has been working to improve the quality of out-of-school time since its inception 20 years ago. The organization's focus has been on five areas: education and training, community development, consultation, research, and public awareness. The target population has been parents, program staff members, community leaders, and government officials.

NIOST began a project to evaluate innovative approaches for both the care of children and the preparation and training of staff. The institute named the project MOST (Making the Most of Out-of-School Time). Three cities (Boston, Chicago, and Seattle) spent three years implementing and evaluating the project. A consulting firm, Nilsen Associates, was commissioned to write a report on one of the most important questions raised by the MOST initiative (Nilsen, 1999): staff preparation and credentialing. The report uses the definition of a credential proposed by G. Morgan (1998) that a credential is a formal certificate, permit or document that certifies that an individual has mastered a set of skills and has demonstrated competence in caring for children." Colleges and universities issue credentials, as do some professional associations. Community organizations and even employers sometimes award a credential or certificate to those who complete specified requirements. School-age care professionals are questioning who is best suited to establish the criteria for a credential relevant to their occupation.

A national survey conducted by Nilsen found that half of the states already provide a credential for school-age child care professionals, are doing a pilot study, or are planning one. About one-third do not have a credential and are not planning one. There were 21 credentialing programs from 17 states with the following common characteristics:

- Almost half were offered by a college.
- Entry requirements were minimal.
- About 75 percent offered college credit.
- Most required the candidate to pay a fee.
- The program took an average of two years to plan.
- Many community entities participated in the development.
- Most had some paid staff.

The Nilsen survey found that some credentials require little investment in time—as little as a day—while others take up to two years. Many states are using the CDA credential even though it is specifically designed for the caregivers of children under five years of age. Therefore, child care professionals across the United States are discussing the question of what components should comprise a credential.

Report Recommendations

The report made recommendations to both local and national leaders about ways to expedite credentialing efforts for school-age care. The following list is a brief summary of those recommendations.

Locally

- Planning efforts should include as many community individuals and organizations as possible.
- If at all possible, there should be a source of funding for the planning process.
- Planners should think creatively about the relationship with a state licensing agency.

Nationally

- Information should be gathered about who will receive credentials and the impact on quality outcomes.
- Some in the school-age child care (SAC) community advocate that National School Age Care Alliance (**NSACA**) take on credentialing in the same way that the Council for Early Childhood Professional Recognition has done. That would require tremendous resources and would conflict with some of the innovative programs already in place.
- There is an expressed need to set guidelines or standards for what a credential should include, such as the following:

  - core competencies or bodies of knowledge
  - number of hours to spend on training
  - qualifications of instructors
  - evaluation methods
  - alternative methods to demonstrate knowledge or competence
  - provisions for ensuring access to a diverse population in the workforce

The report also recommended tying standards to the Advancing and Recognizing Quality (ARQ, Assessing School-Age Quality self-study) and the accreditation process NSACA uses (described in a previous section).

You can obtain the full Nilsen Associates report and the ASQ from:

National Institute on Out-of-School Time (NIOST)
Center for Research on Women
Wellesley College
106 Central Street
Wellesley, MA 02481-8203
781-283-2547
FAX: 781-283-3657
E-mail: niost@wellesley.edu
http://www.wellesley.edu

NSACA
National School Age Care Alliance

SACERS
School-Age Care Environmental Rating Scale, a method of rating programs that serve children five to 12

EVALUATION

The quality of a child care program is affected not only by the background and training of the staff members but also by how the environment meets the needs of the children being served. Thelma Harms and her colleagues developed a rating scale to determine how well that is being achieved.

School-Age Care Environmental Rating Scale (SACERS)

Developed by Thelma Harms and her two Canadian colleagues Ellen Jacobs and Donna White, the **SACERS** evolved out of a need to have a method of rating programs that serve the five- to 12-year age range. Harms, Jacobs, and White drew from a number of sources, starting with the criteria for developmentally appropriate practice. They also used research studies done in Canada and the United States (Galambos & Garbarino, 1983; Vandell & Corasanti, 1988; Vandell, Henderson, & Wilson, 1988). The SACERS is also an adaptation of an earlier rating scale, the Early Childhood Environment Rating Scale, that Harms created.

Specially trained observers use a numerical scale to perform the assessment. They rate each of the seven categories on a scale of one to seven based on written criteria for each item. The following is a brief description of the items listed in each category.

Space and Furnishings, Indoor Space

The scale assesses whether there is sufficient space for gross-motor activities, as well as space for privacy. The room arrangement should have adequate space for all activities: homework, routine care, and learning and recreation. Furnishings should allow for children's relaxation and comfort as well as gross-motor activities. There should be easy access to the host facility and space for staff.

Health and Safety

This section examines health policies and practices. Emergency and safety procedures must be in place. Attendance should be monitored and departures managed to provide maximum safety for the children. Meal times should be planned as a learning experience, and personal hygiene must be part of the educational program.

Activities

Eight types of activities are described in this section: arts and crafts, music and movement, blocks and construction, drama/theater, language/reading, math/reasoning, science/nature, and cultural awareness. Assessment is made on the basis of frequency, variety of materials and equipment available, and age-level appropriateness. The cultural-awareness category includes ways that the staff encourage acceptance of differences.

Interactions

This section refers to staff interactions with children, parents, and one another. Interactions with children should support autonomous behavior and convey feelings of respect and interest. Staff should also talk to children about ideas related to play activities, helping children extend their ideas. Parents should be informed about policies concerning discipline and receive information on parenting, health care, sports, and cultural activities for families. Parents should be included in decision making as well. The program should promote positive interactions among staff members and classroom teachers.

Program Structure

The day's schedule should allow for smooth transitions and time for children choose activities. The center should use community resources to plan

Trained observers use the School-Age Care Environmental Rating Scale (SACERS) to provide a method for rating programs that serve the five to 12 year age range.

field trips or special occasion activities. The director and a key staff member should meet on a regular basis with the host of the program to discuss and resolve any problems that arise.

Staff Development

Staff should have opportunities and support to attend professional conferences or workshops. Staff meetings should include planned opportunities for participants to share new ideas and materials. Self-evaluation by staff should be an ongoing process.

Special Needs Supplementary Items

This section is used in conjunction with the preceding items when children with special needs are included in the program. Items address the objectives to bring about individualization, appropriate learning opportunities, efforts to promote peer interactions, and how the staff promotes communication.

The full text of this rating scale can be obtained from:

Teachers College Press
Columbia University
1234 Amsterdam Avenue
New York, NY 10027
212-678-3929
FAX: 212-678-44149
E-mail: tcpress@tccolumbia.edu
http://www.tcpress.com

ASSESSING CHILDREN'S PROGRESS

An important part of evaluating the overall quality of a program should also include an assessment of individual children. According to Lilian Katz (1997), "Assessment should serve one of the following purposes: to determine progress on significant developmental achievements; to make placement or promotion decisions; to diagnose learning and teaching problems; to help in instruction and curriculum decisions; to serve as a basis for reporting to parents; and to assist a child with assessing his or her own progress." Child care leaders do not need to make decisions concerning children's promotions from one grade level to the next, but all of the other purposes Katz stated pertain to the child care setting.

Observation

There are several ways to assess children's progress by observing and recording behaviors. One of these is the **anecdotal record**. The child is observed in a variety of situations while the adult writes down what he does and what he says. This may not be the most accurate picture of a child's behavior because the adult can only record a small portion of what

anecdotal record
written observations
of a child in a variety
of situations

event recording
observer chooses a specific situation in which to observe a child

time or duration sampling
observation of a child's behavior at intervals of time and for a specified period of time

video camera or tape recording
most accurate methods of observation

checklist
a list of predetermined behaviors to be observed

self-assessment
a list of goals that children can use to assess their own progress

is happening. What is there is what the adult decides is important, and this may present an incomplete picture. It is also true that two people looking at the same situation may see entirely different actions (Click, 2008). Another form of observation is **event recording**. The observer chooses a specific situation in which to observe and record behavior. For instance, if the adult wants to determine how a child reacts during group times, the observer must see the child in that situation several times.

The **time or duration sampling** looks at behavior at intervals of time and for a specified period of time, such as every half hour for five minutes. This kind of observation may reveal the presence or absence of certain behaviors. This method can be especially helpful in detecting the frequency of aggressive outbursts, determining whether a child spends more time alone or with other children, or observing a child's attention span.

The most accurate observation occurs when the adult uses a **video camera or tape recording**. This method is especially useful because more than one person can observe behavior and make the assessment. Further discussion among the observers can yield more pertinent information. (Please note that before photographing children you must have written permission from their parents.)

Observers can also use a **checklist** to assess a child's behavior. This is a list of predetermined behaviors to be observed. The observer checks off one of several choices indicating whether the behavior occurred. The following is a sample of a checklist regarding a child's interactions with other children (see Figure 17–1).

Self-Assessment

Children should be encouraged to assess their own progress using a **self-assessment**. A conference between the adult and child can result in a list of goals. What does the child want to improve or what does he need to concentrate more on? Is it his ability to hit more balls during baseball games, or his ability to curb aggressive behaviors and make friends? These goals should come from the child with adult support to clearly define them. Most children, once they reach the school-age years, are fairly realistic about what they can and cannot expect to do. Katz (1995) also says "In principle, unless children are consulted about their own views of their own progress, they cannot learn to assume some responsibility for it."

	Usually	Sometimes	Never
Approaches others			
Uses appropriate language to enter a play situation			
Disrupts the play			
Is cooperative			

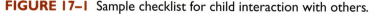

FIGURE 17–1 Sample checklist for child interaction with others.

Additional information about assessment is available at the following websites:

- **Center for the Study of Testing, Evaluation, and Educational Policy** Position papers and policy statements.
- http://www.bc.edu/research/csteep
- **Project Spectrum**
- Articles on assessment.
- http://pzweb.harvard.edu/Research/Spectrum.htm

SUMMARY

- The perception of school-age care has changed from just providing a safe place for children to providing one that offers growth, nurturing, and life skills.

- There is a critical need for ways to ensure quality.

- Child Care Information Center: Secretary Donna Shalala of the U.S. Department of Health and Human Services established a set of quality guidelines.

- The National School Age Care Alliance (NSACA) developed a set of eight standards that it uses for accreditation or to upgrade programs.

- The National Association for the Education of Young Children (NAEYC) also developed a set of standards that can lead to accreditation.

- Family child care providers can also be accredited by the National Association for Family Child Care (NAFCC) if they follow the organization's guidelines.

- To upgrade quality, the Council for Early Childhood Professional Recognition designed the Child Development Associate (CDA) credential that is used in preschools, child care, and Head Start programs.

- National interest in improving quality has prompted the National Institute on Out-of-School Time (NIOST) to focus on advocating for credentialing or certification.

- Thelma Harms and two colleagues developed the School-Age Care Environmental Scale (SACERS). Evaluators use seven categories with which to rate programs: space, indoor space and furnishings, health and safety, activities, interactions, program structure, and staff development.

- Assessment of individual children should be part of evaluating the overall quality of a program. Observation is frequently the method of choice, and includes anecdotal records, event recording, time or duration sampling, and a checklist.

- Children should be encouraged to assess their own progress.

KEY TERMS

anecdotal record
CDA
checklist
child care councils
event recording
NAA

NAEYC
NAFCC
NCLB
NIOST
NSACA

SACERS
self-assessment
time or duration
  sampling
video camera or tape
  recording

REVIEW QUESTIONS

1. Discuss how the public perception of after-school care has changed.

2. What has NSACA done to upgrade standards for out-of-school time?

3. Describe the accreditation process NAEYC uses.

4. Can family child care providers be accredited? If so, by whom?

5. List the goals on which the Child Development Associate credential is based.

6. How has NIOST worked toward increasing quality in child care?

7. What is the name of the rating instrument that Thelma Harms and her colleagues developed?

8. List the seven categories Harms used to assess the child care environment.

Case Study

Susan Weir, the director/owner of the Little Oaks Child Care Center, has already achieved accreditation for her preschool program. She is very proud of this fact and believes it helped to fill her enrollment and even to generate a waiting list. Susan has just returned from a conference where she heard about the National School-Age Care Alliance. She learned that the alliance has developed a set of standards for school-age programs that can lead to accreditation, and she obtained a copy of their material. She is eager for her after-school staff members to review the standards and start the process leading to accreditation. Most of the caregivers are eager to start, but several are resistant, saying they don't think they need a stamp of approval on their program.

1. Why do you think some staff members resist the idea of accreditation?

2. What would you do about the attitude of the resisters?

3. How can Susan help them be more positive toward the process?

STUDENT ACTIVITIES

1. Log on to the National Afterschool Association website (http://www .naaweb.org) and print out the standards for accreditation. Work with other students in small groups to discuss one of the sections. Would

the center where they work or practice teach be different if it were applying for accreditation by this organization?

   a. Describe the center's environment, both indoors and outdoors.
   b Delineate ways that interactions would be fostered.
   c. Describe what is being done to foster good health and nutrition.
   d. What administrative procedures are in place?

2. Ask students to determine which centers in their community are accredited and by whom. Assign small groups to interview selected center directors. Have them ask the following:

   a. How difficult was it to go through the process?
   b. Which people were the most helpful in achieving your goal?
   c. How long did it take?
   d. What has the result been?
   e. Was the effort worth it?

3. Have each group report to the class on their findings.

SUGGESTED READINGS

Leach, P. (2009). *Child care today*. NY: Random House.

Marion, M., & Mindes, G. (2004). Resources on assessment. *Young Children*, 59(1), 54–55.

NAEYC (2004). Where we stand on curriculum, assessment, and program evaluation. *Young Children*, 59(1), 51–53.

WEB RESOURCES

http://www.naaweb.org
   National After-School Association

http://www.naccrra.org
   National Association of Child Care Resource and Referral

http://www.naeyc.org
   National Association for the Education of Young Children

http://www.nafcc.org
   National Association for Family child Care

http://www.cdacouncil.org
   Council for Early Childhood Professional Recognition

http://www.wellesley.edu/WCW/CRW/SAC
   National Institute on Out-of-School Time

REFERENCES

Click, P. (2008). *Administration of programs for young children* (7th ed.). Clifton Park, NY: Cengage Learning.

Galambos, N., & Garbarino, J. (1983). Identifying the missing links in the study of latchkey children. *Children Today*, 13, 2–4.

Halpern, R. (1992). The role of after-school programs in the lives of inner city children. *Child Welfare*, 71, 215–230.

Katz, L. G. (1995). *Talks with teachers of young children: A collection* Norwood, NJ: Ablex.

Katz, L. G. (1997). A developmental approach to assessment of young children. *ERIC Digest ED407172.*

Morgan, G. (1998). *Credentialing in out-of-school time programs.* Wellesley, MA: National Institute on Out-of-School time, Center for Research on Women.

National Association of Child Care Resource and Referral Agencies. (1999). *High quality child care matters.* Arlington, VA: Author. http://www.naccrra.org/policy/background_issues/high-quality-chilld-care matters.

National School-Age Care Alliance. (1998). *The NSACA standards for quality school-age care.* Boston: Author.

Nilsen, E. A. (1999). *On the road to SAC professionalism, emerging models, trends, and issues in credentialing: A working paper.* Wellesley College, Wellesley, MA: National Institute on Out-of-School Time.

Vandell, D. L., & Corasanti, M. A. (1988). The relations between third-graders' afterschool care and social, academic, and emotional functioning. *Child Development*, 59(4), 868–875.

Vandell, D. L., Henderson, V. K., & Wilson, K. S. (1988). A longitudinal study of children with day-care experiences of varying quality. *Child Development*, 59(5), 1286–1292.

APPENDIX A

Internet Links for Further Information

INTERNET DISCLAIMER:

The authors and Cengage Learning affirm that the website URLs referenced below were accurate at the time of printing. However, due to the fluid nature of the Internet, we cannot guarantee their accuracy for the life of the edition.

- ADA and Disability Information: [http://www.ada.gov]
- Administration for Children and Families: [http://www.acf.hhs.gov]
- Afterschool.gov: [http://www.afterschool.gov]
- The American Academy of Pediatrics: [http://www.aap.org]
- Association for Childhood Education International: [http://acei.org]
- Bureau of Labor Statistics: [http://www.bls.gov]
- Center for the Child Care Workforce: [http://www.ccw.org]
- Centers for Disease Control and Prevention: [http://cdc.gov]
- Child Care Bureau: [http://www.acf.dhhs.gov/programs/ccb]
- Children's Defense Fund: [http://www.childrensdefense.org]
- The Council for Exceptional Children: [http://www.cec.sped.org]
- Day Care Provider's Home Page: [http://www.daycareproviders.ca]
- ERIC Education Resources Information Center: [http://www.eric.ed.gov]
- Food and Nutrition Information Center: [http://www.nal.usda.gov/fnic]
- Frank Porter Graham Child Development Center: [http://www.fpg.unc.edu]
- General Accounting Office (GAO) Reports: [http://www.access.gpo.gov]
- Harvard Family Research Project, Harvard University: [http://www.gse.harvard.edu/hfrp/projects/afterschool/resouces/index.html]
- Office of Head Start: [http://www.acf.dhhs.gov]
- U.S. Department of Health & Human Services: [http://www.hhs.gov]
- I Am Your Child Public Engagement Campaign: [http://www.iamyourchild.org]

- Military Child Development Program: [http://military-childrenandyouth.calib.com/index.html]
- National Association for the Education of Young Children (NAEYC): [http://naeyc.org]
- National Association for Family Child Care: [http://www.nafcc.org]
- National Association of Child Care Professionals: [http://www.naccp.org]
- National Center for Health Statistics: [http://www.cdc.gov/nchs]
- National Child Care Information Center: [http://nccic.org]
- National Dissemination Center for Children and Youth with Disabilities: [http://www.nichcy.org]
- National Institute on Out-of-School-Time: [http://www.niost.org]
- National Network for Child Care: [http://www.nncc.org]
- National Parent Information Network: [http://npin.org]
- National Program for Playground Safety: [http://www.uni.edu/playground]
- National Resource Center for Health and Safety in Child Care: [http://nrc.uchsc.edu]
- National SAFEKIDS Campaign: [http://www.safekids.org]
- National Afterschool Association: [http://www.naaweb.org]
- Quality Care for Children: [http://www.qualitycareforchildren.org]
- School-Age Notes: [http://www.schoolagenotes.com]
- The Food Allergy & Anaphylaxis Network: [http://www.foodallergy.org]
- The Future of Children: [http://www.futureofchildren.org]
- The Urban Institute: [http://www.urban.org]
- U.S. Census Bureau: [http://www.census.gov]
- U.S. Department of Education: [http://www.ed.gov]
- U.S. Department of Health and Human Services: [http://www.dhhs.gov]
- U.S. Government Printing Office (GPO): [http://gpoaccess.gov/index.html]
- Work/Family Directions: [http://workfamilydirections.com]

APPENDIX B

Lesson Plans

Newspaper Sculptures

Brief description: Firmly rolled newspapers are taped together randomly to create a three-dimensional structure.

Materials:

- ½" dowels, 3' long (at least 4)
- newspaper
- masking tape
- large piece of cardboard for the base of the structure

Procedure: Lay newspaper flat. Place dowel on one corner of the paper at an angle. Roll paper tightly around dowel, rolling from one corner to the opposite corner. Secure with a small piece of tape. Slide dowel out from paper. Continue making paper rolls (50 or more will be needed).

Begin constructing the sculpture by taping one end of each newspaper roll to the cardboard base. The other end will be taped to other rolls in whatever manner the children decide.

Role of the Leader: Gather materials. Most of these can be brought in by children or donated by parents. Purchase dowels at your local hardware store. Dedicate ample space for the ongoing sculptures, and encourage children to work in teams.

Extension: Paint the sculpture when completed.

Craft Dough Sculptures

Brief description: Children will make free-form sculptures that can be dried and painted.

Materials:

- 1 cup cornstarch
- 2 cups baking soda (1 lb. box)

- 1¼ cups water
- tempera paint
- small paintbrushes
- wax paper

Procedure: Combine cornstarch, baking soda, and water and cook until thickened to a dough-like consistency. Turn mixture out onto a pastry board and knead. Cover with damp cloth or keep in plastic bag. Children will mold pieces of dough to desired results. Place sculptures on wax paper. Let air-dry. (It may take several days.) Children can paint sculptures when dried.

Role of the Leader: Dough must be prepared and cooled prior to use by children. Be available to scaffold for children who struggle with implementing their ideas. They may need techniques to use. Encourage children to share their techniques with one another.

Extensions: Experiment with other types of dough. Advance to modeling clay. Introduce tools used for working with clay. Use tools such as toothpicks, the ends of straws, combs, scissors, etc., to create details in dough.

Tissue Paper Art

Brief Description: Children will explore books by Eric Carle to see how he uses tissue paper in his illustrations. Children will make their own creations by cutting and layering tissue paper pieces.

Materials:

- Several colors of tissue paper (cut into pieces about 4" square)
- 12" × 18" white drawing paper
- scissors
- thinned white glue
- containers to hold thinned glue
- ½- to 1"-wide paintbrushes
- books by Eric Carle

Procedure: Children will examine pictures in Eric Carle books, notice the colors used, and make predictions about how the tissue papers are layered. Children will cut tissue paper into desired shapes. Thinned white glue will be painted onto paper in areas where tissue paper will be placed. Children will lay tissue paper shapes onto the glue to create designs or pictures.

Role of the Leader: Prepare materials. Search websites for information about Eric Carle's illustrations made from tissue paper. Experiment with making tissue paper art to determine how much to thin the glue.

Extensions: Learn about other illustrator techniques used in children's books. Try some of them and determine if any are appropriate for children's use.

Salt Painting

Brief description: Children will paint a picture or design and sprinkle salt onto the wet paint. The salt gives a unique sheen to the finished painting.

Materials:

- variety of brightly colored tempera paint
- variety of sizes of easel paintbrushes
- 12" × 18" black construction paper
- salt in saltshakers

Procedure: Children will paint desired picture or design on paper. When finished they will sprinkle salt onto paint. Finished paper will be placed on a flat surface in the sun for drying.

Role of the Leader: Provide ample materials and drying space for painting. Involve children in setup and cleanup of materials, including washing the paintbrushes.

Extensions: Paint on different colors of construction paper. Sprinkle glitter, sand, or soap flakes onto wet paint.

Printing

Brief description: Children will make their own stencil, paint it, and make a print of their stencil.

Materials:

- clean Styrofoam™ meat trays (run them through the dishwasher for disinfecting prior to use)
- blunt pencils
- small paint rollers
- two to three colors of tempera paint placed in Styrofoam trays
- plain newsprint cut into pieces slightly larger than the meat trays

Procedure: Children will use blunt pencil to press into the bottom of the meat tray making a design or picture. Press only hard enough to indent into the Styrofoam creating an imprinted design. Use the paint roller to apply a thin layer of paint to the entire bottom of the tray. Place a piece of paper on top of the paint, press, then lift off; it should be a print of the design. Children will have to work at the technique of getting the right amount of paint to produce a clear stencil.

Role of Leader: Leaders will collect materials. Ask parents to donate Styrofoam meat trays. Pour a small amount of paint into a Styrofoam tray and spread with a paint roller to get the roller ready for painting. Involve children in cleanup of activity.

Extension: Place paper over stencils and rub with the sides of crayons to make crayon rubbings.

MUSIC LESSON PLANS

Foot Conducting

Brief description: Children will use instruments to make music by following the directions of a conductor who conducts with his feet.

Materials:

- at least four kinds of instruments
- hoops approximately 2' in diameter (These can be made from yarn or tape on the floor; need one hoop for each kind of instrument, that is, five kinds of instruments requires five hoops.)
- instrumental music and CD or record player

Procedure: Children sit in a circle (or semicircle) with the conductor in the middle. Distribute instruments to children so that children with the same kind of instrument are sitting next to each other. Place the hoops on the floor, one in front of each group of musicians. The conductor will step in and out of the circles to direct the musicians. Children will accompany the instrumental music by playing their instruments when the conductor has his or her foot in the hoop in front of them.

Role of the Leader: Gather instruments and select a variety of instrumental music. The leader will need to model the process of conducting. Select children to take turns conducting the musicians. The leader should continue to facilitate the activity even though children are conducting.

Extensions: Children can learn how to conduct using their hands. Visit a local school band practice or performance to watch the conductor.

Who Stole the Cookie Jar Chant

Brief description: Children will work together to clap in rhythm and accompany clapping with a chant.

Materials:

None

Procedure: Children will sit in a circle. Leader will begin clapping rhythm (clap, then slap hands on thighs, clap, slap, etc.). Everyone claps and chants throughout the entire chant. Once class is in rhythm, the leader begins the chant.

"Who stole the cook-ie from the cook-ie jar?" (Clap and slap on the underlined words and syllables.)

"(Child's name) stole the cookie from the cookie jar!"

Child responds: "Who me?"

Leader: "Yes, you!"

Child: "Couldn't be!"

Leader: "Then who?"

That child continues with the chant naming another child. The same rhythm continues throughout the chant. Chant continues until all children have been called on to play. The last child responds, "Leader's name stole the cookie from the cookie jar."

Leader: "I stole the cookie from the cookie jar."

Role of the Leader: Organize children into a circle. Model the chant and explain the rules. Begin and end the chant.

Extensions: Change the rhythm of the chant. Change the body movements to stomping and finger snapping. Let children chose the body movements or make up new words for the chant.

Stories of Music

Brief description: Children use their imaginations to draw pictures that tell a story based on the music they hear.

Materials:

- colored markers, one set per child
- drawing paper, one piece per child
- instrumental music of varying tempos and instruments
- CD or record player for playing music

Procedure: Children will close their eyes and listen to segments of the music. Leader will ask children what the music makes them think of. Leader will play another segment and again ask what it makes the children think of. The children then receive paper and markers to draw what they are thinking as they listen to the entire piece of music. Children will share their stories with the group.

Role of the Leader: Choose music and facilitate children's thinking as they listen. The leader will also facilitate children's storytelling to the entire group, in small groups, or with one other person.

Extensions: Listen and draw to different kinds of music, especially music from other cultures. Children can move according to how they feel instead of drawing what they think.

Composing to the Beat

Brief description: Children will work in groups of three or four and create rhythm patterns. They will write their rhythms pictorially on paper and play them on instruments. Rhythms can be recorded on a tape player.

Materials:

- instruments, one per child
- paper and pencils or markers
- tape recorder

Procedure: Leader will introduce the idea of a four-beat rhythm in music and model a few rhythms with an instrument. Children will repeat the rhythms with their instruments. The leader then should elicit ideas from the children about how to represent the rhythm pictorially. The leader can write one of these ideas as an example. Children will be divided into teams to create their own rhythms. The leader will encourage them to write their rhythm in whatever manner makes sense to them. The team will practice their rhythm following their written plan. Lastly they will play their rhythm and record it on a tape player.

Role of the Leader: Gather enough instruments so everyone has an instrument. Facilitate this activity by modeling and playing rhythms, encouraging children to repeat the rhythms. The leader further facilitates the activity by managing groups as they work on rhythms. Some groups may need additional scaffolding.

Extensions: Children can be exposed to the formal method of recording rhythms by use of whole notes, half notes, etc. Make rhythms with different numbers of beats. Children can listen to patterns in music and try to repeat them.

Bottles of Music

Brief description: Children will experiment with various levels of water in glass containers to make music.

Materials:

- glass bottles or large water glasses (five or more)
- pitcher of colored water (use small amount of food coloring)
- spoon
- measuring cup
- funnel (to assist in filling the bottles if necessary)

Procedure: Children, working in teams of two, will fill containers with different amounts of water. One may have ¼ cup, ½ cup in the next, ¾ cup in the next, and so on. Children should note the different levels of water in the glasses and put them in sequential order. Children tap on the side of the containers with a spoon to make musical tones. Children can use the glasses to tap out various familiar tunes such as "Happy Birthday" or make up their own tunes.

Role of the Leader: Leader will gather materials. It may be possible for parents to donate the bottles. The leader can scaffold the measuring of the liquid for children not yet familiar with measuring liquid. Leader will facilitate the activity by asking divergent questions to guide children's observations and discovery. "Which container gives the highest tone? Why? What would change the tone?"

Extensions: Find other items to use for making music, such as pan lids, metal bowls, etc. Children can sequence these other items from high to low sounds and again try to make music.

MATH LESSON PLANS

Bubble Math

Brief description: Children will make bubbles to explore counting, addition, and measurement.

Materials:

- liquid dish soap (½ cup to each gallon of water)
- water
- container to hold bubble mixture

- small containers for individual children's bubbles (such as empty yogurt containers)
- bubble wands
- paper and pencil
- measuring tape (as used in construction)

Procedure: Make bubble mixture the day before it is to be used. Pour bubble mixture into individual containers for each child. Children will use bubble wand to blow bubbles. They will work in teams of two to complete the following math tasks:

- One team member will blow bubbles while his partner counts the number of bubbles and records the information on paper. Each person will blow bubbles five times. The bubble scores will be added to get a total number of bubbles for each person.
- Each team member will blow bubbles and the team will watch and follow the bubbles to see which one travels the farthest. The team will measure the distance from where the bubble was initiated to where it was when it disappeared. The distance will be recorded. Each person will blow and measure distances at least two times.

Role of the Leader: Some children may not have had any distance-measuring experience and will need the task scaffolded for them.

Extensions: Other instruments can be used to blow bubbles. Children can determine if there is a relationship between the size of the bubble maker and the number of bubbles that can be blown. Other bubble makers might include the plastic rings that hold soda cans together, small hoops, or some other item with a hole in it.

Build a School

Brief description: Children will work together using blocks and cardboard to replicate the length, height, and perimeter of their classroom and the school.

Materials:

- unit blocks of various sizes
- random sizes of cardboard
- cardboard scissors
- clipboards, paper, and pencils

Procedure: Children will work in teams to examine their classroom and draw it on paper. They will then build it with blocks and cardboard. This process will involve discussion about where doors and windows are placed in relationship to the size of walls. Once children understand the process of examining and replicating the classroom, they can move on to larger spaces, such as building a model of the entire school or even the city block.

Role of the Leader: The facilitation of this activity will require the leader to be available to listen to children as they brainstorm ideas and to provide needed materials. The leader will introduce new vocabulary such as length, width, and perimeter. This activity will take several days, so space will need to be dedicated to this work.

Extensions: Create a model on a smaller scale using Popsicle™ sticks and wood glue with cardboard as a base. Bring in blueprints of a building for children to examine. Visit a construction site.

Catapults

Brief description: Homemade catapults will be used to launch objects and measure distances of trajectory.

Materials:

- wooden rulers
- rubber bands
- plastic spoons
- pom-poms or small paper balls (crumpled newspaper densely squashed into a spherical shape)
- crayons
- yard sticks or measuring tapes
- masking tape or sidewalk chalk

Procedure: Children will construct the catapults and paper balls. To construct the catapult, lay a plastic spoon onto a wooden ruler with the bowl of the spoon with about 1" of the handle beyond the end of the ruler. Face the bowl of the spoon toward the ruler. Secure with a rubber band tightly wrapped around the spoon handle and ruler. Cut newspaper into pieces about 8" square. These will become the paper balls. Color the newspaper with the crayon with large scribble-like lines. (Each child will need his or her own crayon color.) Crumple the newspaper as compactly as possible. To play the game, children will place a paper ball in the bowl of their spoon on the catapult. Holding the spoon and the ball, pull back on the spoon slightly and then let go. The paper ball will be launched onto the playing field. The playing field consists of an area that is marked off with parallel lines of masking tape every foot. Children can launch five paper balls and then measure the distance of their flights. Use additional rulers to measure exact distance between the lines. Children can record their scores on their clipboards.

Role of the Leader: The leader will construct the playing field by placing rows of masking tape on the floor one foot apart. Use sidewalk chalk to make the lines on concrete or blacktop. The leader should experiment with the catapults to determine the depth of the playing field. The leader will also need to determine the rules, where children will stand, and when there is a no-launch time so children are safe while measuring distances.

Extensions: Experiment with other safe objects such as cotton balls for launching. Read about catapults.

Pattern Prints

Brief description: Children will design their own pattern and print it on paper.

Materials:

- variety of rubber stamps
- ink for stamps (preferably more than one color)
- drawing paper

Procedure: Children will review the concept of patterns. Each child will create a pattern on the border of his paper. They can use paper as invitations or placemats. It can serve as the background paper for displaying another piece of artwork in the classroom. Encourage children to print patterns in other ways on their paper. Children will verbalize their patterns (such as frog, frog, snake, frog, frog, snake).

Role of the Leader: The leader will facilitate a discussion about patterns. Scaffolding may be necessary for some children who aren't familiar with patterns.

Extensions: Examine patterns in wallpaper and have children make their own wallpaper pattern. Examine patterns in wrapping paper. Then encourage children to make patterns on easel paper to be used later as wrapping paper. Use paint or markers to make the patterns.

Sink the Ships

Brief description: Children will play this game in teams of two while they learn about using coordinates. The goal of the game is to find and sink each other's ships.

Materials:

- graph paper
- pencils (one per child)
- marker (one per child)

Procedure: Each child will make his game card in the following manner. (Younger children may need the playing card made for them.) Each player has his own playing graph. To begin, each player places his ships on the graph by letters in the spaces. The letter *B* is for battleship, *C* for cruiser, *D* for destroyer, and *S* for submarine. Each player will place four battleships (*B*), three cruisers (*C*), two destroyers (*D*), and one submarine (*S*). Each kind of ship must be in a line vertically, horizontally, or diagonally as displayed in the example. Children play in teams of two. For example, Susie will begin play by calling out coordinates, such as G4. Lena looks to see if that coordinate corresponds to the placement of one of her ships. If it is a hit, the Lena tells what has been hit. "You hit one of my cruisers." Lena will put a large *X* on the cruiser that was hit. Susie will write "*C*" in the G4 space on her paper. Children take turns calling out coordinates until all of one person's ships have been sunk.

Role of the Leader: The leader may want to make the game cards ahead of time. These can be easily made on a computer and printed.

Extensions: The coordinate system can be changed to more closely match that used in geometry. Instead of a column of letters, the column could be numbers. The submarine in the above example is at point (3,2). More advance children can use an X-Y axis system that incorporates negative numbers.

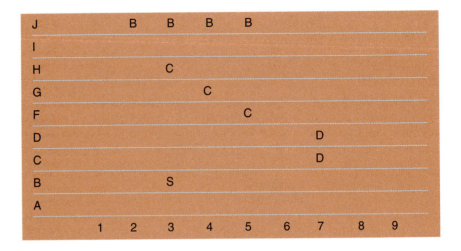

CRACKER DIVISION

Brief description: Children will use math strategies and math communication abilities to figure out how to divide up a plate of food at the snack table. Children should work in groups of three of four.

Materials:

- *The Doorbell Rang* by Pat Hutchins
- counters (small objects such as beans or buttons that can represent crackers; a minimum of the same number of crackers)
- crackers (enough for the group of children to count and divide)
- tongs (for moving crackers)
- napkins (one for each child)

Procedure: Read *The Doorbell Rang*. Give children an opportunity to discuss the problem in the story and ideas about how the problem was solved. Pose the problem of having a plate of crackers and not knowing how to divide it so every child has an equal amount. "What ideas do you have about how we could divide these crackers?" Give children counters to simulate crackers to count and move around as they explore the division process. Once children have figured out a solution to the problem, they can use their strategy to divide up the plate of crackers. How many will each one receive? As children become proficient at this, provide an unequal amount of food requiring them to have remainders. Let them solve what to do with the remainders.

Role of the leader: This teacher-directed activity requires the leader to introduce the problem and facilitate children's conversations and implementation of the strategies.

Extensions: Once children have had experience working with this type of problem, they can move toward more independence in this type of problem solving. Children can think about how to divide up art materials or resources for other projects. Working in teams of two rather than three or four will be more manageable for independent problem solving.

CONSTRUCT A HOPSCOTCH

Brief description: Children will use measuring tools to make hopscotch board on playground. They will explore the concepts of length and width and the attributes of squares, and develop skills in linear measurement.

Materials:

- rulers, meter sticks, tape measure (as used in construction)
- protractor (to measure 90-degree angles)
- pencils and paper for recording information
- clipboards for holding papers
- sidewalk chalk

Procedure: Show children a drawing of the hopscotch game board. Put the children into teams of two to four to decide how they can make one. Children will need to practice jumping and measuring the distance of their jumps. They can use that information to determine what size squares they need to draw. Children can record their measurements on paper, then use those measurements to make a drawing of their hopscotch.

Role of the Leader: Scaffold drawing squares by using a protractor to make 90-degree angles. Model how to use measuring tools. Support the children with scaffolding the process, but allow children make discoveries and mistakes independently.

Extensions: Children can use these materials to create various regular and irregular polygons. Leaders can provide support to children in learning the names of the polygons.

SCIENCE LESSON PLANS

Interactive Inventions

Brief description: Children will work in teams to explore objects and their properties to determine how they interact to move objects through the air.

Materials:

- dishpans (one for each team of three to four children)
- objects to interact: cotton balls, clay or dough, clothespins, straws, rubber bands, wooden craft sticks, paper clips, corks, pipe cleaners, plastic gears, string, plastic spoons, scissors, berry baskets, any other materials available ("found materials")
- easel paper and markers or science journals

Procedure: The leader will introduce the idea of inventions by highlighting that inventions happen as a result of inventor's ideas and that everyone has ideas. Children will work in teams to explore the materials in their tub. The focus of this free exploration is to see how objects can work together to move objects through the air. After a predetermined length of time, teams will work together to report their ideas and discoveries either on a piece of easel paper or in their science journals.

Role of the Leader: The leader will gather materials and elicit donations from parents. The leader sets the stage for exploration by talking about inventors and how inventions start. The leader further guides the scope of exploration by clearly stating the goal of determining how materials work together (interact). The leader will monitor children's progress and, if needed, guide their explorations with questions or thoughts such as "I wonder what would happen if . . ."

Extensions: Children implement their invention ideas and test them by propelling an object such as a cotton ball or dough through the air. Children can read about various inventors.

Solutions and Emulsions

Brief description: Children will experiment with a variety of materials to experience what combinations of matter and water become solutions and what combinations are emulsions.

Materials:

- small clear plastic cups
- teaspoon
- stirring sticks
- pitcher of water
- things to mix with water: vegetable oil, vinegar, sand, salt, sugar, baking soda, flour, cornstarch
- science journals

Procedure: The child will pour a plastic cup half full of water. The child will put one teaspoon of one of the other materials in the cup and gently stir to the count of 15. Let the mixture settle and observe what happens to the added matter. If it disappears, the mixture has become a solution. If it is cloudy or separates, the mixture is an emulsion. The mixture is then dumped into a large container and the experimenter again pours the cup half full of water and tests another material. Each child can record her findings in her science journal after completing the project.

Role of the Leader: The leader must have a basic understanding of solutions and emulsions. The leader will explain these two new vocabulary words to children and model the process by pouring a cup half full of water and measuring out a teaspoon of salt. The leader will then ask the children to predict what they think will happen. The leader will elicit a few responses, then put the salt back into the salt container encouraging children to be scientists and make those discoveries themselves.

Extensions: Children can continue their exploration of solutions by adding another teaspoon of matter and stirring. If the water is again clear, another teaspoon can be added. Keep adding until no more will dissolve. This means that the solution has reached the saturation point.

Melt the Crayons

Brief description: Children will devise experiments to see what helps crayons melt when placed in the sun.

Materials:

- crayon pieces
- items to place under the crayons: small disposable pie pans, black construction paper, white construction paper, foil, and wax paper.

Procedure: Children will make predictions about what material will help crayons melt the fastest. They will put a crayon piece each on five different substances and place them in the sun outside. (Be sure they are placed on a surface that will not be harmed if the crayon melts.) Children will observe their science project every 15 minutes for the next two hours and record their observations in their science journals.

Role of the Leader: The leader should be prepared by having completed the activity herself to determine which brand of crayons melts the easiest. This will help set up the children for success. Monitor the weather and do this activity on a sunny, warm day.

Extensions: Melt ice cubes in a similar fashion using items that may absorb or reflect the heat. Discuss heat reflection and absorption as it pertains to clothing.

Shadows in Time

Brief description: Children will work in teams to explore how their shadow changes throughout the day.

Materials:

- sidewalk chalk
- measuring tapes
- clipboards, paper, and pencils

Procedure: Children will work in teams of two tracing each other's shadows. Begin this activity on the morning of a sunny day. Children must work in a place with adequate blacktop or concrete to outline the shadows. Trace around the person's shoes and shadow. Measure the distance from the heels of the shoes to the farthest point on the shadow. Record the measurement and the time of day. Children will return to the shadow tracings every one to two hours and stand in their traced footprints. Each time, the children will trace the shadows, measure their lengths, and record the new measurements. Near the end of the class day (before the sun goes down) children will trace and measure one last time. Children will examine their tracings of the day and draw conclusions.

Role of the Leader: The leader should anticipate the changes in the shadows and ensure that children have enough space between their individual shadows to allow for the changes in size. The leader should facilitate the activity by asking children divergent questions to encourage critical thinking. "Why does the shadow change size? Where do you think the shadow will be this afternoon?"

Extensions: Children can do this activity at different times of the year and notice how their shadows change. Further study can help them understand the tilt of the earth on its axis and how it changes the placement of the sun in the sky.

Feed the Ants

Brief description: Children will create an experiment to try to determine what attracts ants.

Materials:

- ant trail (found outside)
- paper plate divided into eight pie-shaped sections (one per team)
- very small portions of food (sugar, vegetable oil, bread, candy, meat, cheese, fruit, vegetables, etc.)

Procedure: On the first day, lead children in a discussion about ants. Who has had them in their house? Why do they come in? What food do they go after? Divide children into teams of four to discuss what foods they think ants would like. Each team will make a list of the foods. Encourage children to bring in very small portions of food from home for the experiment. Each team will decide what eight foods they want to offer the ants and place a different type of food on each section of the paper plate. Teams will then search for an ant trail outside and place their paper plate near the trail. Children will observe the plates throughout the day and record any ant activity in their science journals.

Role of the Leader: Leaders should gather some background knowledge of ants. They will have to work with each team to ensure that team members have access to needed food items.

Extensions: Children can be encouraged to do Internet searches to learn about different kinds of ants. Other outdoor insects can be explored in a similar fashion.

Are You Ready to Absorb?

Brief description: Children will experiment with absorption and color mixing.

Materials

- tray with wax paper lining the bottom
- eye droppers
- containers of water colored with food coloring or liquid water colors (red, blue, yellow)

Procedure: Provide the children with a tray lined with a piece of wax paper. Using eyedroppers, drip droplets of colored water onto the wax paper. Encourage children to count the number of droplets of each color. Older children can measure the diameter of the droplet. When the children have finished experimenting with dropping the colors, ask, "Are you ready to absorb?" Have the children lay an absorbent paper towel onto the droplets. Children can measure the diameter of the absorbed liquid and note changes.

Role of the leader: Listen to what the children say, observe their explorations, and identify the scientific processes of their investigations. Scaffold learning by asking questions such as "Do you remember how many drops of liquid you used to get that color of green? I notice that this area of absorbed liquid is larger than the other one. Why do you think that happened?" Encourage children to document their work.

Extensions: Provide different types of absorbent materials such as coffee filters, a variety of paper towels, or fabrics.

Marble Rollways

Brief description: Children explore the direction, distance, and speed of a rolled object as they work in teams to create a structure to roll marbles through.

Materials:

- thin cardboard in pieces of various sizes
- paper cups
- paper towel and/or toilet-tissue cardboard tubes
- paper
- masking tape
- yarn or string
- berry baskets, juice cans, small plastic containers
- marbles
- other recycled materials as available
- scissors, rulers, pencils, markers

Procedure: Display materials on a table. Entice the children by asking a divergent question: "How could you use these materials to create a structure that will let the marbles flow through it?" Divide children into teams to create their structure. (Hint: Create teams with a variety of ages. An older child can be a leader for younger ones.)

Role of the leader: Set up environment and give children time and space for their project. Observe children; ask divergent questions to scaffold learning or encourage further exploration. Encourage children to document their work.

Extensions: Create larger rollways for larger balls with recycled materials.

Oil and Water

Brief description: Children try to combine oil and colored water in an attempt to make them mix.

Materials:

- small container of vegetable or corn oil
- small container of water colored with a small amount of tempera paint (preferably a color that contrasts with the yellow of the oil, such as blue)
- spoons (one for each container)
- construction paper, wax paper, foil
- tray to hold construction paper
- spoons for mixing

Procedure: Children should first predict what they think is going to happen when they put the two liquids together. Place the paper, foil, or wax paper on a tray. Drop a spoonful of oil and one of colored water onto the paper. Notice how each liquid stands out on the paper. Tip the tray, causing the liquids to run toward each other on the paper, and try to get them to mix. After exploration, encourage children to think of something they can use to mix the liquids. Allow the children to mix. Encourage them to wait and see what happens.

Role of the leader: Observe and scaffold children's experiences. Encourage children to document their work.

Create a Worm Environment

Brief description: Children will create a temporary worm environment to learn about worms' tunneling behaviors, bodies, habitat, and diet.

Materials:

- tall, thin jar (preferably no more than 5 inches in diameter)
- sand, soil, and water
- ruler
- magnifying glasses
- worms (from a bait shop)
- ½ apple
- ½ onion
- knife and cutting board
- two containers for mixing
- nonfiction books or resource information about worms

Procedure: Place soil in container and mix with enough water to make damp. In another container, mix sand with water, making the sand damp enough to clump together. Layer the soil and sand in the tall thin jar in 1-inch layers. Place the worms on top of the top layer. Handle them with care and respect them as living things. Watch what the worms do. Cut onion and apple into ½-inch pieces. Put these on top of the soil. Place the container in a box, making sure no light can enter the box. Leave for four days. During that time, read about worms and predict what they will do while they are in the box. After four days, take the container out of the box and examine the tunnels. Use magnifying glasses before or after the activity to examine the structure of the worms. Be sure to keep the workspace moist. Worms don't like to be in the light, so examinations must be brief. Return worms to a safe place in a garden when finished.

Role of the Leader: Read about worms to acquire some background knowledge. Ask divergent questions. Investigate with the children. Supervise to ensure the respect of nature.

Extensions: Children can use the internet to learn about how to create habitats for other creatures such as snails, polliwogs, or ants.

GLOSSARY

A

AAHPERD—American Alliance for Health, Physical Education, Recreation, and Dance: develops standards for aerobic endurance, muscular strength, and flexibility that indicate fitness

academic approach—an approach to programming that involves determining outcomes related to school performance that can be measured and then planning a program to help children achieve those goals

accommodations—changes that are necessary when planning activities to include special-needs children

ADA—Americans with Disabilities Act

adjunct learning tools—additional ways to learn that are not part of traditional curriculum activities. Computers can be a vital element of learning if they are integrated into the total curriculum.

adolescence—Freud's fifth stage, in which there are changes to sexual organs and in appearance, accompanied by strong sexual urges

age appropriateness—programs are planned according to universal, predictable growth and changes that occur in children

anal period—Freud's second stage, in which children increase body awareness and focus of attention is on the anus as a source of pleasure

anecdotal record—written observations of a child in a variety of situations

anti-bias curriculum—a curriculum that addresses cultural diversity by including gender and differences in physical differences; is based on children's developmental tasks as they construct identity and attitudes; directly addresses the impact of stereotyping, bias, and discriminatory behavior in young children's development and interactions

anti-bias education—An educational approach that supports children's full development in our multiracial, multilingual, multicultural world and gives them the tools to stand up to prejudice, stereotyping, bias, and eventually to institutional "isms"

authentic feedback—a description of a child's real accomplishments

autonomy vs. shame and doubt—Erikson's second stage, in which the focus is to become independent by gaining control over bodily functions

B

background knowledge—knowledge that is learned through experiences, reading, movies, and television

biodegradable—objects that disintegrate over time

BMI—body mass index; a measure of the ratio of weight to height

bullying—unprovoked aggression that is intended to inflict injury or discomfort on the victim

C

caregiver—name for an adult in child care when the emphasis is on the caring role

CDA—Child Development Associate, nationally recognized credential for early childhood teachers and caregivers

centering—Piaget's observation that young children focus on only one dimension of a form at a time

checklist—a list of predetermined behaviors to be observed

child care councils—group of representatives from the various factions of the child care community

chronic health condition—conditions that last 12 months or more and create some limitations in activity

classical conditioning—conditioning brought about by proximity of stimulus and response

clique—groups of children who have similar characteristics and interests

code-switching—a complete change of language form when addressing adults and when talking to other children

complex oral language—the child's vocabulary as well as his or her ability to understand and use those words to convey thoughts; also known as language comprehension

concrete operations—ability to think symbolically and to reverse processes when information is presented concretely

constructing knowledge—children develop their own theories about how the world works

conventional—Kohlberg's second stage of moral development, in which there is an emphasis on the social rules of the individual's family, group, or nation

conventional literacy—formal reading and writing

convergent thinking—a process of thought that narrows down many ideas into a single focused point

curriculum—a plan of activities that accomplishes the goals of a program

Cyber-bullying—use of electronic means to bully others

D

decoding—sounding out words by breaking them apart into their letter sounds

developmentalist—name for an adult in child care who is versed in the developmental aspects of the child

dialogic reading—first teaches children the vocabulary of the book and then expands on the story itself

divergent questions—questions that have no specific answer and require a child to think critically

divergent thinking—a process of thought or perception that involves considering alternatives, taking a line of thought that is different from the usual

E

educare—a name for an adult in child care reflecting the multifaceted aspect of working with school-age children

ego—in psychoanalytic theory, the rational aspect of personality

elaborated code—a communication that uses a more extensive vocabulary, is correct grammatically, and is longer

emergent curriculum—activities that are planned as a result of caregivers noting the current interests of children or that develop as children play

emergent literacy—reading-related behaviors and skills that precede formal reading and writing

emerging literacy skills—reading-related skills that children obtain prior to actually reading and writing

English language learners (ELL)—children who primarily speak a language other than English in the home and are not fully fluent in English

ethics—a study of right, wrong, duty, and obligation

event recording—observer chooses a specific situation in which to observe a child

extended family—members of nuclear family plus grandparents, aunts, uncles, and cousins

F

food guide pyramid—U.S. Department of Agriculture guide to healthy food choices and number of servings per day

formal operations—ability to consider hypothetical problems without concrete examples

functional print—print that has a purpose

G

gangs—groups of children who gather together to be out of the realm of adults but also to be antisocial

H

holistic approach—a curriculum that focuses on the development of the whole child and evolves from children's individual and group abilities and interests

I

id—in psychoanalytic theory, the part of the personality that is the source of pleasure-seeking drives

identity vs. role confusion—Erikson's fifth stage, in which adolescents search for their identity as individuals in a society

inclusion—placing children with disabilities in settings with same-age peers

individual appropriateness—refers to each child's unique pattern and timing of growth

Individualized Education Plan (IEP)—set of goals determined by a team of professionals and parents to reflect what the child should accomplish within a year's time

industry vs. inferiority—Erikson's fourth stage, in which children expend all their energies on mastering new skills at home, in school, on the playground, and in their neighborhoods

initiative vs. guilt—Erikson's third stage, in which children attempt new activities that can result in either pride (initiative) or guilt when unsuccessful

integrated curriculum—the linking of two or more subject areas such as literacy and math, or linking an academic subject to the community or vocations

integrated learning—interrelated disciplines such as language, math, or science to achieve a goal

intergenerational programs—child care programs that utilize older people and young adults or teenagers as volunteers

invented spelling—writing with some letter-sound relationships, but not generally representing accurately spelled words

L

language comprehension—the child's vocabulary as well as his or her ability to understand and use those words to convey thoughts; also known as complex oral language

latency period—Freud's fourth stage, in which children's sexual urges are unobtrusive and energies are directed toward school activities and sports

lateralization—specialization in function of the two hemispheres of the brain

learning—processes by which environmental influences and experiences bring about permanent changes in thinking, feeling, and behavior

literacy—being able to read and write

logical consequence—a tool for changing behavior in which the result of a child's misbehavior is related to the behavior

logicomathematical knowledge—how objects compare to one another

M

maturation—progression of changes that takes place as people age

meaning-based experiences—learning experiences that emphasize thinking, cooperative problem solving, decision making, and an opportunity to challenge preconceived ideas

modeling—adults exhibit the behaviors that are expected of children

moral realism—a stage of moral development in which children believe that rules are determined by an authority figure and they are not to be changed

moral relativism—a stage of moral development in which children view punishments as fair or unfair, are more flexible in their thinking, and can discuss moral issues

morality—our perception of what is good or right

morality of caring—Gilligan's theory that girls are socialized to be caring and nurturing and reluctant to judge right and wrong in absolutes

morality of justice—Gilligan's theory that boys will determine what is right or wrong and then follow it with a clear solution when faced with making choices

multipurpose equipment—equipment that has many possibilities for play activities

multiracial family—marriage between two adults of different races

MyPyramid—new name for the food guide pyramid

N

NAA—National AfterSchool Association has developed standards for the best practices for children ages five to 14

NAEYC—National Association for the Education of Young Children, a large professional organization that accredits programs for children from birth through the elementary years

NAFCC—National Association for Family Child Care; has developed quality standards for accreditation

nature—a variety of characteristics that are inherited from parents

NCLB—No Child Left Behind Act; federal legislation that enacts the theories of standards-based education reform

negotiable rules—rules that are based on choices

NIOST—National Institute on Out-of-School Time; focuses on education and training, community development, consultation, research, and public awareness

nonbiodegradable—objects that will not disintegrate over time

non-negotiable rules—rules that are used for actions that can be harmful to others or destructive to property and that are not open for discussion

NSACA—National School Age Care Alliance

nuclear (intact) family—mother, father, and children

nurture—all the experiences and influences people are exposed to from the moment of conception on throughout a lifetime

O

obesity—a measure of the ratio of weight to height or the BMI

operant conditioning—the process by which children act upon their environment and are reinforced for their behaviors

optional rules—things that children can reasonably control themselves

oral period—Freud's term for the first stage, in which the infant gains pleasure through sucking

P

phallic period—Freud's third stage, in which the genital areas are the focus of pleasure and children become aware of physical differences

phonemes—the smallest sounds of our speech stream

phonological awareness—the ability to hear phonemes, beginning, middle, and ending sounds in words, syllables, and rhyming sounds

physical knowledge—how objects behave as a result of their characteristics

postconventional—Kohlberg's third stage of moral development, in which there is an emphasis on moral values and principles

preconventional—Kohlberg's first stage of moral development, in which there is an emphasis on punishment and rewards

preoperational period—ability to begin to think symbolically and to remember experiences and objects independently of the immediate encounter

print—concepts of the difference between a word, a syllable, and a letter; recognizing that print moves from top to bottom and left to right on a page, and that there are forms of punctuation to end a thought

print knowledge—knowledge about the alphabet, letter sounds, and concepts of print

project approach—an in-depth investigation of a topic worth learning more about

R

reading comprehension—understanding the printed word

reconstituted or blended family—families that include children from previous marriages plus those from the present union

recreational supervisor—name for an adult in child care when the emphasis is on the recreational aspects

restricted code—communications that are more limited and may rely on gestures and voice intonation to convey meaning

rough and tumble play—aggressive behavior, but the children usually have positive facial expressions or may be laughing

S

SACERS—School-Age Care Environmental Scale, a method of rating programs that serve children five to 12

safety audit—survey of all playground structures in comparison to standards, guidelines, and laws set by federal and state agencies

scaffold—support system that supports children as they move from one intellectual level to the next

scientific literacy—knowledge and understanding of science concepts and process

self-assessment—a list of goals that children can use to assess their own progress

self-image—our perception of ourselves plus the perceptions conveyed by others

sensorimotor period—Piaget's first period, in which infants use all their senses to explore and learn about the world around them

service learning—combining meaningful service with curriculum-based learning

single-gender family—two adults of the same gender plus children

single-parent family—father or mother and children

single purpose equipment—play equipment that can be used for only one kind of play

social knowledge—information children cannot construct for themselves

storage strategies—methods children use to increase their memory

superego—in psychoanalytic theory, the part of the personality that controls behavior through the development of conscience

T

time or duration sampling—observation of a child's behavior at intervals of time and for a specified period of time

trust vs. mistrust—Erikson's first stage, in which babies learn to trust that others will take care of their basic needs and that others can be depended upon

typically developing—children without disabilities

V

values—the qualities we believe to be intrinsically desirable and that we strive to achieve in ourselves

video camera or tape recording—most accurate methods of observation

volunteer corps—group of older adults and young people or teenagers who volunteer in a child care center

zone of proximal development—the hypothetical environment in which learning and development take place

INDEX

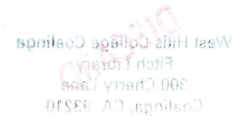